JOURNALISTS FOR EMPIRE

Recent Titles in
Contributions in Comparative Colonial Studies

The Selling of the Empire: British and French Imperialist Propaganda, 1890-1945
Thomas G. August

The Transition to Responsible Government: British Policy in British North America, 1815-1850
Phillip A. Bruckner

The India Office, 1880-1910
Arnold P. Kaminsky

Moral Imperium: Afro-Caribbeans and the Transformation of British Rule, 1776-1838
Ronald Kent Richardson

Black and White in Southern Zambia: The Tonga Plateau Economy and British Imperialism, 1890-1939
Kenneth P. Vickery

The Carrier Corps: Military Labor in the East African Campaign, 1914-1918
Geoffrey Hodges

Germans in the Tropics: Essays in German Colonial History
Arthur J. Knoll and Lewis H. Gann

War, Cooperation, and Conflict: The European Possessions in the Caribbean, 1939-1945
Fitzroy André Baptiste

No Country for a Gentleman: British Rule in Egypt, 1883-1907
William M. Welch, Jr.

Railway Imperialism
Clarence B. Davis and Kenneth E. Wilburn, editors, with Ronald E. Robinson

Countdown to Rebellion: British Policy in Cyprus, 1939-1955
George Horton Kelling

Science and Social Science Research in British India, 1780-1880: The Role of Anglo-Indian Associations and Government
Edward W. Ellsworth

JOURNALISTS FOR EMPIRE

The Imperial Debate in the Edwardian Stately Press, 1903–1913

JAMES D. STARTT

Contributions in Comparative Colonial Studies,
Number 29

GREENWOOD PRESS
New York • Westport, Connecticut • London

Library of Congress Cataloging-in-Publication Data

Startt, James D., 1932-
Journalists for empire : the imperial debate in the Edwardian Stately Press, 1903-1913 / James D. Startt.
p. cm.—(Contributions in comparative colonial studies, ISSN 0163-3813 ; no. 29)
Includes bibliographical references and index.
ISBN 0-313-27714-1 (alk. paper)
1. Commonwealth of Nations. 2. Tariff—Great Britain—History—20th century. 3. Alien labor, Chinese—South Africa—History—20th century. 4. South Africa—Politics and government—20th century. 5. Great Britain—Politics and government—1901-1936. 6. Great Britain—Colonies—History—20th century. 7. Journalists—Great Britain—Attitudes—History—20th century. I. Title. II. Series.
JN248.S73 1991
909′.0971′241—dc20 90-22394

British Library Cataloguing in Publication Data is available.

Library of Congress Catalog Card Number: 90-22394
ISBN: 0-313-27714-1
ISSN: 0163-3813

First published in 1991

Greenwood Press, 88 Post Road West, Westport, CT 06881
An imprint of Greenwood Publishing Group, Inc.

Printed in the United States of America

The paper used in this book complies with the Permanent Paper Standard issued by the National Information Standards Organization (Z39.48-1984).

10 9 8 7 6 5 4 3 2 1

Copyright Acknowledgments

Earl Grey Papers courtesy of the University of Durham.

Lord Crewe Papers Courtesy; Lord Harding Papers of The Syndics of Cambridge University Library.

J.L. Garvin Papers courtesy of Harry Ransom Humanities Research Center, University of Texas at Austin.

Geoffrey Dawson Papers courtesy of *The Times* and Mrs. William Bell.

J.H. Asquith Papers; James Bryce Papers; J.S. Sandars Papers courtesy of The Bodlein Library, Oxford.

Lord Milner Papers. By permission of the Warden and Fellows of New College, Oxford.

A.J. Balfour Papers; John Burns Papers; Lord Northcliffe Papers; J.A. Spender Papers courtesy of The British Library.

The Honourable Sir Michael Herbert Papers. Property of the Earl of Pembroke at Wilton House.

Leopold Maxse Papers courtesy of A.J. Maxse and the Maxse family.

Joseph Chamberlain Papers by permission of the University of Birmingham.

Alfred Lyttelton Papers, The Chandos Collection. Courtesy of Churchill College, Cambridge.

Andrew Bonar Law Papers; J. St. Joe Strachey Papers in the House of Lords Records Office, reproduced by permission of the Clerk of the Records and of the Trustees of the Beaverbrook Foundation. Strachey Papers also by permission of the *Spectator*.

To Catherine, my wife

Contents

Preface

Between 1903 and 1913 an extensive public debate involving the self-governing dominions of the Empire occurred in the British press. It centered on three large topics: Tariff Reform, South African reconstruction, and imperial unity. This study inquires into the involvement of a number of renowned journalists of the quality press in this debate. It is an examination of Edwardian imperial thought as reflected by their work. Since the era was not only an anxious one for supporters of imperial interests but also a precarious one for the quality or stately press, it also provides an opportunity to examine their political journalism and to see if it merits the attention of later generations of journalists and historians. The book begins with several chapters of an introductory nature and then proceeds to examine the three central imperial issues. It concludes by placing the entire subject in its broader twentieth-century setting.

A few explanations are in order about the terminology used in the book. "The quality press" refers to those serious publications that aimed to influence well-informed readers as well as the politically active. Since the great issues of state commanded so much of its attention, it can also be called "the stately press." It should be distinguished from the mass circulating popular press. "The Empire" is used (in the capitalized form the Edwardians often gave it) to designate Britain in its relationship to the self-governing dominions and in order to distinguish it from other imperial entities (i.e., the Indian Empire and the vast assortment of British dependencies scattered across the globe). "Political journalism" is used to distinguish the heart of journalism involving the discovering, reporting, processing, and interpreting of news and opinion from the press in all of its modern complexity. The men featured in this study were involved in the making of public opinion. They were political journalists who believed that the interpretation of events and issues was the highest priority of journalism, the one that legitimatized its claim to professional status.

These men (J. L. Garvin, St. Loe Strachey, J. A. Spender, and the leaders at *The Times*) were all respected figures in Edwardian journalism. The papers they edited (the *Observer*, the *Spectator*, the *Westminster Gazette*, and *The Times*) were among the best and most influential publications in the land. They were all men of strong political conviction and represent a cross-section of Edwardian political preferences found among those publicists who held a firm commitment to the cause of the Empire. These featured journalists, indeed, not only believed in the Empire but even thought that Britain's twentieth-century world position depended upon it. To distinguish them from other journalists of imperial persuasion and for purposes of collective reference, they will be called "the imperial journalists."

Acknowledgments

No one can write without the aid of many people who provide encouragement and professional assistance, and I wish to thank those who helped to make this book possible. I am indebted to Mrs. Ursula Slaghek who graciously talked and corresponded with me about her father, J. L. Garvin, and granted me permission to publish excerpts from his private papers. Lady Brittain also met with me to discuss the work of her late husband, Sir Harry Brittain, and kindly shared with me his private correspondence and various personal materials kept in her possession. Mr. and Mrs. William Bell were especially hospitable and helpful. I thank them for allowing me to use the private papers of Geoffrey (Robinson) Dawson at their home in Northamptonshire and for granting me permission to publish excerpts from his papers there and elsewhere. Many years ago Mrs. Alice Bell Prindiville helped to stimulate my interest in the British friends of her father, the American correspondent Edward Price Bell. I remain in her debt, for many of his friends appear as featured journalists in this study.

It is never possible to thank all the librarians and archivists who helped at various stages of research although they all deserve one's gratitude. I would be remiss, however, if I failed to acknowledge B. S. Benedikz at the University of Birmingham, J. M. Fewster at the University of Durham, Patricia Gill at the West Sussex Record Office, and Gordon Phillips at the Archives of *The Times*.

I also wish to acknowledge a number of repositories and other custodians for permission to publish excerpts from collections in their charge. They include the Archives of *The Times* (for the C. F. Moberly Bell, G. E. Buckle, and Sir Valentine Chirol papers), the Bodleian Library (for the H. H. Asquith, James Bryce, and J. S. Sandars papers), the British Library (for the A. J. Balfour, John Burns, Lord Northcliffe, and J. A. Spender papers), Churchill College Library, Cambridge (for the Chandos papers), the Clerk of the Records at the House of Lords Record Office and the Trustees of the Beaverbrook Foundation (for the Andrew Bonar Law and John St. Loe Strachey papers), the Harry Ransom

Humanities Research Center, The University of Texas at Austin (for the J. L Garvin papers), the Property of the Earl of Pembroke at Wilton House (for the Honorable Sir Michael Herbert Papers), the Syndics of Cambridge University Library (for the Lord Crew and Lord Hardinge Papers), the University of Durham (for the papers of the 4th Earl Grey), and the West Sussex Record Office, A. J. Maxse, and the Maxse family (for the Leopold Maxse papers). I also want to thank the *Spectator* for permission to publish excerpts from John St. Loe Strachey's correspondence in various repositories and the Warden and Fellows of New College, Oxford for permission to use excerpts from Lord Milner's correspondence at the Bodleian Library and the Churchill College Library. Excerpts from the Joseph Chamberlain papers are used by permission of the University of Birmingham.

My colleagues at Valparaiso University have supported this study in many ways. I gratefully acknowledge the support I received from the university's Creative Work and Research Committee and also from the Alumni Association. Their grants made it possible for me to pursue research for this volume both in England and at various repositories in the United States. I wish to thank the staff of the university's Moellering Library, which has always been helpful and cheerful in responding to my many requests. Our department secretary, Beth Schoppa, has made my work easier in numerous ways, and I thank her especially for typing the manuscript and helping to prepare it for publication.

Impossible as it is to recognize fully the sustaining contributions made by those nearest to you, I offer my wife Catherine my deepest thanks. She has been an unfailing source of understanding and encouragement to me both in the research and writing of this book, and it is to her that I dedicate it.

1

The Edwardian Public Debate and the Press

Seldom has the press been a more engaging part of society than in Edwardian Britain. This early twentieth-century institution had tremendous diversity and reach. In terms of political journalism, it covered all of the many domestic, foreign, and imperial problems of the day. Its talented editors, part of "a golden age of editors," were men of unusual ability and intellectual scope whose steadfast defense of the canons of journalism is hard to fault. W. T. Stead, a journalist whose experience and reputation justified his writing with authority about his peers, described these editors as "public councillors."[1] Those featured in this study were leaders among their professional contemporaries of the stately press. They mastered the art of developing formidable and continuing commentary throughout years of sharp public debate and during years when their own craft faced serious problems.

THE PUBLIC DEBATE

The years following the Anglo-Boer War (1899-1902) were full of uncertainty for the British. Although it might appear as a time of security and spacious debate before the deluge of world war and revolution struck, or as the twilight flickering of the last vestiges of a supposed Victorian stability, it was an era of lively political battles and protests. Young Winston Churchill said a new time of "strange methods, huge forces, larger combinations—a Titanic world" had arrived.[2] Mounting domestic problems and shifts in the balance of world powers combined to infuse national politics with a feeling of urgency. Great issues captured and held the attention of both the political parties and the press. The era's public debate manifested a prolonged controversy about these issues, and since it was a time when loyalty to political leaders had such high priority, references to them punctuated that controversy. Some of these men had popular appeal while that of others was more restricted, but together they represent an interesting array of political figures.

Consider the most prominent leaders in the country's two major political parties. Arthur Balfour, who succeeded his uncle Lord Salisbury as prime minister in 1902, was an unusual figure for such an elevated position. His Conservative, or Unionist, party claimed credit as the great defender of the empire, yet while prime minister, he failed to articulate a convincing imperial policy. He was an adroit politician whose parliamentary dexterity even his opponents admitted, yet he remained out of touch with public opinion and was hardly a popular or inspiring leader for a nation in which democracy experienced steady growth. His tentativeness—his opponents called it dilatoriness or ineptitude—sometimes rendered his leadership less than decisive; but even after his resignation as prime minister in 1905, he served until 1911 as party leader and held together a party divided over the issue of Tariff Reform. Then the more practical, if also more pedestrian, Andrew Bonar Law became party leader. Lacking Balfour's sophisticated demeanor and intellectual range, he guided the party away from broader imperial concerns and into confrontation with the Liberals over Irish Home Rule. Balfour and Law faced worthy opponents in their Liberal counterparts. When Sir Henry Campbell-Bannerman, an old Gladstonian who had served as Liberal leader in Commons since 1899, became prime minister in 1905, the party's Radical and Liberal Imperialist wings were still uneasy with one another. But as his courageous and celebrated "Methods of Barbarism" speech, in which he denounced wartime concentration camps in South Africa, had helped to keep the party together during the Anglo-Boer War, so his skill at balancing factional interests helped to continue party reconciliation during his premiership. So, too, did his bold policy for South African reconstruction, for which he deserves a place of distinction in Imperial-Commonwealth history. Herbert Henry Asquith, who succeeded him upon his retirement and subsequent death in 1908, served as prime minister longer than any other Edwardian. Although a Liberal Imperialist, Asquith was sympathetic to many of the Radicals' demands for social reform, and he was a calm, even deliberate, leader as well as an effective public speaker and cabinet manager. Liberal supporters praised his imperturbability; opponents labeled him a cunning opportunist. Regardless, inescapable political forces limited his field of action in matters of policy, as they had that of Balfour.

Some of these forces came from within the traditional party framework while others lay beyond it. Both parties had to respond to serious pressure from advanced and demanding forces in their own ranks. Joseph Chamberlain and David Lloyd George personified these forces for the Unionist and Liberal parties respectively. Both men added an edge of excitement, and sometimes disruption, to contemporary party affairs. The politics of the age, of course, went far beyond that of the two major parties—a fact underscored by the unrest, and sometimes the violence, caused by suffragettes, workers, and the Irish at the time. As in all modern eras, political life during this period was full of movement and demands for change.

Certain anxieties also marked the politics of the age. No serious-minded person interested in the public debate could dismiss them. For instance, to what degree should the state become an agency for the common good? If it assumed the responsibility for greater social justice, how should that activity be financed? How could the nation's defense, politics, and industry be made more efficient? "Efficiency" was a shibboleth of Edwardian society, but it was a term easier mentioned than agreed upon or defined. "Muddle" was no longer to be tolerated, at least by those who made efficiency or National Efficiency a virtue. But how could that enthusiasm be translated into a political program? Political democracy was spreading, but was it causing the death of British Liberalism? If it were, Conservatives failed to profit from the problems their Liberal opponents faced; they lost three consecutive general elections during the era and seemed unable to reach the greater voting public needed to reverse their political fortunes. Or, consider the House of Lords. Would it be able to continue in its traditional, constitutional role in the nation's politics? Perhaps there would be no place for it at all in the greater democratized nation.

Indeed, an unease appeared throughout Britain's social and economic order as disparities between capital and labor and fears about workers' security led to strikes and riots. Concern about the need for social reform permeated political dialogue and policy at many junctures. Both parties responded to this need, the Conservatives with their Tariff Reform movement that would provide for social reform at home, and the Liberals by introducing the "social service state" after 1906, and each denounced the response of the other. Major problems in the realm of foreign affairs only increased national anxieties and expanded debate about them. The sequence of crises between the European powers and the expansion of German naval power forced Britain to reconsider her commitment to Europe and her role among the powers. That reconsideration also rested on the relative decline of Britain's position in world manufacturing and trade, especially when measured against the surging industrial strength of Germany and the United States. Problems such as these held the attention of the Edwardians in all of their public forums (i.e., press, platform, Parliament), and there were imperial ramifications for them all, whether they dealt with domestic reform or foreign policy strategies. It is against this backdrop of issues that the imperial debate must be placed.

By the beginning of the century, the British had acquired the largest empire known to man. The Indian Empire, a collection of greater and lesser dependencies, and a group of self-governing colonies composed this vast and varied enterprise. At times the public debate focused on problems and events associated with the Indian Empire, particularly on an outbreak of violence or on a great imperial occasion such as the royal durbar of 1911. The Indian Empire, however, never became a continuing controversial subject in the public debate.

Even the important India Councils Act of 1909, the product of the heralded Morley-Minto reforms, received only modest notice in Parliament and in the press. India was a special case and it remained largely in the domain of the experts. The same can be said about affairs in the dependencies and discussions about their colonial administration. On the other hand, the self-governing colonies, the subject of the present study, received attention throughout the era as politicians and publicists made problems about Britain's relationship to them into public issues. At a time when anti-colonial feeling was growing across the world and national movements were mounting to challenge the British empire at many points, and at a time when her world position appeared to be slipping, the Empire acquired unique significance. The Indian Empire was perpetually in a state of unrest, and the dependent empire was, in many respects, a burden, but as Nicholas Mansergh says, "There was a difference in kind between the states that were self-governing and even the greatest of imperial dependencies."[3] In their relationship to these colonies or dominions, the British were part of a particular international community that involved economic, defense, and cultural ties. Amid the shifting balance of the great powers that implied a reduction in Britain's world power status, her special relationship to these states became all the more valuable. The question was how to preserve and nurture that relationship. It was controversy about that question in its changing forms that provided such a strong imperial content for the era's public debate.

Although foreign observers perceived the Empire as a source of British strength, problems about it abounded. Just as the rise of democracy at home lessened steady resolve for the imperial idea, so the rise of colonial nationalism made imperial ties and all hopes of greater imperial cohesiveness more tenuous. Beyond this basic divergence of imperial aspirations and dominion nationalism, a number of troublesome incongruities existed to fetter the formation of imperial policy. At the very least, it was difficult to reconcile the tradition of British liberty with any form of infringement on dominion autonomy. Any effort to strengthen imperial unity by means of preferential tariffs would run counter to the free trade tradition, a belief of uncommon force that had represented conventional economic wisdom in Britain since the mid-nineteenth century. Britain, moreover, had vast and increasing defense obligations at home and across the empire. The imperial navy had to be enlarged, but who would pay for it? If taxes were raised at home, the nation's traditional low public expenditure would be threatened. If the dominions contributed money, men, or ships to the imperial navy, there were problems of control to resolve, and any contribution would always have to be measured against the dominions' own needs and responsibilities. In the nineteenth and early twentieth centuries, Britain granted self-government to its major settlement colonies. This policy of allowing them a free hand in domestic affairs worked well. Liberals even claimed it represented "the magic of freedom at work."[4] Nevertheless, would colonial self-government lead to imperial demise? Such perplexities were part of all the great problems regarding the Edwardian Empire (i.e., Tariff Reform, South African reconstruction, and imperial unity). The imperial journalists worked amid these uncertainties, and as they did a fundamental implicit question became manifest in their commentaries: did the Empire have a future?

In the opinion of the imperial journalists, the fate of the Empire depended on the resolution of a number of problems at home and abroad. Not the least of these was the problem of Irish Home Rule. Since the Act of Union of 1800 that united Ireland and Great Britain, various forms of conflict disturbed Anglo-Irish relations. It was both a domestic and an imperial problem, but it had a number of implications for British relations with the Empire. Conservatives linked together the development of the Empire and that of the Anglo-Irish union. If Irish Home Rule were enacted, they believed, in the words of *The Times*, that it would constitute "a peril to the Empire."[5] Such a grant would start a disintegration of imperial ties, for the Empire would no longer be solid at the center. Many Liberals, whose belief in the virtue of self-government was uncontested, claimed just the opposite. They thought it absurd that self-government should be denied to Ireland when it proved such a success throughout the Empire. That feeling grew among them after the grant of self-government to the Transvaal in 1906, and became pronounced when, as a result of the general election of January 1910, the party became dependent on Irish support. More important, the Irish issue entered into the political passions of the time. It stirred all of the deepest political feelings of the imperial journalists. They never entirely divorced their thought from it and were fond of drawing numerous analogies between the Irish question and imperial problems. The Irish Home Rule controversy not only charged the public debate with emotional content, but it also demonstrated the wide range of issues to which imperial questions could relate.

There can be no question that the ramifications of imperial problems reached into numerous aspects of national politics. Nor can there be any doubt that problems about the Empire were part of a core of issues that permeated the entire era. No effort to understand the public debate of the time can be complete without knowledge of the role the press performed in ongoing argumentation about these problems.

THE PRESS

Unfortunately, perceptions about the role the Edwardian journalists played in the imperial debates can be blurred. The distortion stems in part from the popular but faulty view held of the pre–World War I empire, particularly by many Americans. They tend to oversimplify the subject and to allow preconceptions about the nineteenth-century imperial experience in India and sub-Saharan Africa to shape their idea of the Edwardian empire. In part, the trouble lies also in the failure to understand the nature of the early twentieth-century British press. Too often it is portrayed in terms of the developing popular press of the day. The common image of the press in imperial discussion and controversy is frequently stereotyped as a chauvinistic and jingoistic enterprise. That image reflects the rise and growth of the late Victorian popular press and how it performed before and during the Anglo-Boer War more than it does the Edwardian press or even the popular press of the post–Boer War years. At any rate, the popular press was only one medium in a crowded and diverse institution.

The Edwardian press reflected the variety that characterized its Victorian predecessor. As a result, any effort to describe the mosaic of publications that composed it can be frustrated by the abundance of numbers as well as by the range of types. Nevertheless, some sense of its composition at the national level can be gained by classifying it in the following six categories.[6] Morning newspapers compose the first of these groupings. Included in this group were the great dailies such as the *Daily Chronicle* (founded 1872), the *Daily News* (f. 1846), the *Daily Telegraph* (f. 1855), the *Morning Post* (f. 1771), the *Standard* (1857 as a morning paper), and *The Times* (f. 1785). Two popular papers of more recent origin, the *Daily Mail* (f. 1896) and the *Daily Express* (f. 1900), also were morning dailies. Evening newspapers formed a second category. Its most important publications were a number of small but influential papers such as the *Echo* (f. 1868), the *Globe* (f. 1803), the *Pall Mall Gazette* (f. 1865), the *St. James Gazette* (f. 1880), and the *Westminster Gazette* (f. 1893). These were distinguished papers, bolder and brighter in format and typography than the quality morning dailies, but they remained within the bounds of serious newspapers and were significant political publications. There were also some popular evening newspapers published such as the *Evening News* (f. 1881) and the *Star* (f. 1888).

The four remaining classifications contained mainly, but not exclusively, weekly and periodical publications. The third category can be labeled the weekly press. Crowded into this grouping were a variety of commercial, financial, industrial, dramatic, literary, religious, and sporting publications. Of special importance to the present study, it also included a number of weekly "political publications," journals that contained articles and commentary on much more than politics but were known and followed for their political views. Among these "political publications" were the *Economist* (f. 1843), the *Nation* (f. 1907), the *Outlook* (f. 1896), and the *Spectator* (f. 1828). Review literature composed a fourth category and contained journals such as the *Edinburgh Review* (f. 1802), the *Fortnightly Review* (f. 1865), the *National Review* (f. 1883), and the *Nineteenth Century* (f. 1877). Along with literary articles and ones of general intellectual interest many political essays could be found in these journals. Sunday newspapers represented a fifth category. Although the period of the great expansion of the Sunday newspapers dates from World War I, the British tradition of popular and sensational Sunday papers was kept quite alive in the

Edwardian era by publications such as *News of the World* (f. 1843) and *Reynolds News* (f. 1850). There were also several old Sunday papers, especially the *Observer* (f. 1791) and the *Sunday Times* (f. 1821), that catered to readers of intellectual tastes, and in the years before 1914, the *Observer* gained recognition as one of Britain's most influential newspapers. In a sixth and final category of specialized popular publications can be placed a large number of miscellaneous ones, such as popular, mostly periodical, prints including ones for children and young people, illustrated papers, and sundry other specialized and cheap productions. The Edwardians, consequently, could never complain that the press failed to satisfy their various preferences for news, commentary, and journalistic entertainment. Nor could they complain that the great issues of the day failed to receive full coverage, particularly in the quality press that served the informed public.

It was this quality press, not the popular press, that was so central to Edwardian national politics. A popular paper like the *Daily Mail* might have mass circulation, but it had little influence in the Whitehall-Westminster-Fleet Street triangle that was at the heart of the era's politics. Politicians valued it as an instrument of publicity. But papers like the *Daily Mail* rarely led, and only seldom did other newspapers, at home or abroad, quote their opinion. For deep and sustained argumentation on public issues, the political elite turned to newspapers such as *The Times* and the *Westminster Gazette*. These and other papers and journals of the quality press, they trusted, quoted, and even read for their opposing views. The imperial journalists worked in the quality press, but there is no reason to suppose that they performed their work in lofty seclusion. They were students of politics and in close touch with national leaders as well as with their own journalistic sources. They were also competitive journalists engaged in combat to influence some significant position of public opinion. As they pursued the great issues of their time, they also had a battle to wage within their own craft. There were major forces at work challenging the quality journalism they represented. They all had to face and respond to three major problems confronting the stately press: the increasing commercialization of the press, the forceful development in the press known as the New Journalism, and the perceived lessening of journalistic influence. An understanding of these problems can provide insight into the journalistic environment in which the imperial journalists worked.

The growing commercialization of the press is bound up with its development as a modern institution. Reasons for it are many. The new technology of the nineteenth century brought far-reaching changes in the press due to its application to printing, communication, and transportation. By 1900 cable networks snaked their way across the earth's oceans and soon would become yet more extensive. Wireless telegraphy had become a reality. The new reading and voting public referred to so often in the history of this era was already exemplifying the twentieth-century trend of mass readership to be more interested in news than in political commentary. It also preferred that the definition of news be broadened to include many things that the quality press previously excluded. The new technology provided the means for the procurement and for the rapid transmission of news from near and far, and the expansion of staff made possible additional features that would please and attract readers in large number. The idea was to push down the cost of newspapers and to increase their circulation and attractiveness as an advertisement medium. It all was expensive and traditional newspapers that so valued political journalism found their finances strained by the effort to remain competitive as the commercial side of journalism grew.

Many of the Edwardian journalists who inquired into the nature of the press in their time commented at length about the growing commercialization of their craft. It was "the greatest change of all," wrote William Maxwell.[7] There was little exaggeration in his claim. The shifting nature of newspaper proprietorship helps explain why. Family firms controlled newspaper industries in the nineteenth century, and until the end of the century newspaper proprietors were known as journalists, whether or not they were practicing journalists. They desired, of course, to preside over profitable properties, but they were usually content to combine the desire for profits with journalistic principle.[8] Around the turn of the century, however, the trend in press properties grew away from family firms and toward cooperative ownership, and the modern shareholders who invested in these properties were not journalists. They were mainly concerned with dividends. In 1893 there was not a single newspaper corporation listed on the London Stock Exchange. Twenty years later, 90 percent of leading daily and evening papers belonged to corporations.[9]

This growing commercialization of the press had a number of ramifications on Edwardian journalism. It made an editor's position much more precarious. The drive to increase circulation was great and the loss of circulation, even for a worthy cause, was a matter for serious concern. Newspapers became more expensive properties. Operation cost increased; competition became keener. Some papers failed to survive. In 1901 London could boast of twenty-one metropolitan dailies. One was gone by 1905 and two more had merged with other newspapers by 1912.[10] Accordingly, the trend of newspaper consolidation that has characterized the twentieth-century British press had begun in the decade before World War I. Moreover, as that trend began to unfold and as press empires with their proliferating properties began to grow, it became more difficult to start new papers. W. T. Stead, who was a journalistic genius in many respects, tried to launch a new daily, called simply the *Daily Paper*, in 1904. His effort failed in a matter of a few weeks. In 1906 a new Liberal daily, the *Tribune*, appeared "with the backing of a deep purse and a staff of brilliant journalists."[11] It managed to last less than two years. Were quality papers "played out," as H. W. Massingham, one of Fleet Street's most prominent editors, commented to Herbert Gladstone, the Liberal Chief Whip, in 1905?[12]

The age became an increasingly competitive one for the press. At one time in the previous century, as the journalism historian Francis Williams has observed, *The Times* dominated British political journalism with a circulation of 50,000.[13] Few papers would now consider that circulation adequate unless they had other resources upon which to rely. Some papers, unable to survive on their own, had to depend on subsidies—by no means a new practice in political journalism. Subsidies had existed before in a number of forms, but evidence of their widespread use at this time indicates the precarious financial base of even important papers. It was not unusual for politicians and political parties to provide some financial assistance for papers whose support they valued. The *Westminster Gazette*, the most influential Liberal paper of these years, received regular subsidies from the Liberal party, and it appears that the *Observer*, the *Standard*, the *Globe*, and the *Pall Mall Gazette* all received from Unionist party funds, sometimes as much as £10,000 a year.[14] Additional revenues, in fact, were needed by newspapers of various types. When Lord Northcliffe became the chief proprietor of *The Times* in 1908, he was able to do so partly because it was believed he would be able to save Britain's most prestigious paper with his own vast resources. Even the organs of the popular press were susceptible to the possibility of financial ruin. In 1911 R. D. Blumenfeld, the editor of the mass circulating *Daily Express*, had to appeal directly to the wealthy Canadian Max Aitken (later Lord Beaverbrook) to save the paper. Aitken responded with a loan of £25,000. That marked the beginning of Aitken's influence on the *Daily Express*, but it was insufficient to solve the paper's problems. The following year, faced with continuing financial needs, Blumenfeld had to accept Unionist party subsidies managed by Aitken and several other men of financial means.[15] Aitken went on in subsequent years to become the paper's controlling shareholder.

More than anything else, the New Journalism, which Edwardian publicists so often discussed, epitomized the commercialization of the press. It involved, of course, much more than journalism as a business, but commercial considerations were central to it at this time. In all of its forms, the New Journalism made a formidable impact on the Edwardian press. No grasp of the Edwardian press can be had without understanding what this new force was and why it posed such a challenge to the established political journalism found in the quality press.

The New Journalism appeared in London in the 1880s. Its antecedents were numerous and could be found on both sides of the Atlantic.[16] In fact, some of its features were as old as English journalism itself. Full of entertaining and sensational content, it had a light, brash, and energetic style. Innovative printing techniques such as short paragraphs, crossheads, and bold headlines characterized its heavily illustrated pages. Such newspapers had a broader definition of news than the quality and more expensive dailies and were full of interviews, sprightly human interest stories, and picturesque language. Compared to those of stately newspapers, their editorials were shorter, more alarmist, and more focused on personalities. Yet these popular and cheaper (priced at a halfpenny) journals did champion some causes in the public interest. Critics contended that the newspapers of the New Journalism were overcommercialized, too anxious to cater to popular whim, too hesitant to champion a good if unpopular cause, and too much like American metropolitan newspapers, which was another way of saying they were disreputable. Such criticism could be overstated, but there was enough truth in it to make it a serious concern for the upholders of the traditions associated with the stately press. Moreover, a succession of journalists who would be accorded a distinctive place in journalism history were leaders of the New Journalism. During the Edwardian period Alfred Harmsworth (later Lord Northcliffe) personified this type of journalism. He became the country's most powerful press baron and, despite his many eccentric ways, a figure of commanding force in the British press. The Edwardians considered his *Daily Mail* with its circulation of over 700,000 per day the vanguard of the New Journalism that was transforming—some would say destroying—the best traditions of the press.[17]

It is, however, only fair to the quality papers to mention that they were not as unchanging as is frequently claimed. During their Victorian heyday, there was little in them to alleviate the weight of their appearance. Heavy, long, and dreary columns of small print, unpunctuated by paragraphs and crossheads, and unrelieved by pictures, characterized their format. Dominated by political matters, there contained little that was entertaining or lively. These ponderous dailies appealed little to the new reading public that emerged late in the century.

Yet changes in the stately press slowly did appear. The *Daily Telegraph*, for instance, led the quality press throughout the late Victorian decades in modernization of format and content. Starting in the early 1870s the *Daily News* began to offer "picturesque descriptions" of public events in its pages. It even introduced lighter touches in its reporting of Parliament news. "With trembling hand a dash of color was splashed upon the parliamentary summary of the *Daily News*." As one of its writers of that time later recalled: "Attempt was made to invest the columns with some of the light that nightly blazed in the House of Commons. The editor was not shocked. The public seemed to like it."[18] Moreover, that vitalized type of parliamentary summary remained a prominent feature of the paper. Or, take the case of sporting news. Once held in disdain by the quality press though never completely ignored, it grew, particularly in the 1890s, to occupy a larger position in those respectable papers.[19] Impressed by the transition under way, one journalist associated with the metropolitan press of the time reflected, "They [the older papers] all denounce its [the New Journalism's] ways, and timidly imitate some of them."[20] Modernizing changes continued to appear in the quality newspapers throughout the Edwardian years, and they contributed to the gains in circulation that papers such as *The Times* and the *Observer* were able to make. Still, the New Journalism remained a threat to the quality morning press.

Why was this so? The answer rests upon the fear that popularization would penetrate into the bastion of the quality political press. Indeed, the development of the *Daily Telegraph*, with its blend of serious yet humanized treatment of news and its brilliant cultural features, into a mass circulating one-penny morning paper proved that the penetration was already under way in pre-Edwardian years.[21] But the *Daily Telegraph* had its established place among the great morning dailies. The *Daily Mail* was the threat, and the fact that Harmsworth, with all of his power and genius, commanded its fortunes made it a formidable challenger to the older journalistic tradition. The success of the *Daily Mail* was certain to attract imitators, and C. Arthur Pearson proved the point in 1900 when he founded a second popular morning paper, the *Daily Express*. The presence of the *Daily Mail* and the *Daily Express* represented an expanding element that could damage, perhaps even destroy, older more traditional quality papers like *The Times* or the *Morning Post*.

How far would the intrusion of popular journalism go into the domain of the quality morning papers in the new century? To what degree would it force changes in the quality papers to make them competitive? Would those changes in language, content, space allotment, and format reduce the serious tone of the quality papers and force a lowering of journalistic standards? More than anything else, critics of the popularizing trend in journalism were apprehensive about the commercialization of the press that they believed to be a by-product of the trend. Harmsworth proved that his type of journalism could be financially rewarding and could attract a mass circulation, which in turn became a magnet that drew advertisements to the paper. Profits thus accumulated could be used to improve the production of the paper even more or to expand Harmsworth's empire of publishing properties. That point bothered the critics, for they tended to view him as a man of shallow political views and as a destabilizing force in political journalism. They did not wish to see his network of publications expand. But in a general sense, their apprehension went beyond Harmsworth himself and focused on the commercially successful style of journalism he represented. That explains why the comment on the subject by Kennedy Jones, one of the founders of the *Daily Mail*, has become such an often repeated one in journalism history. "You, Lord Morley, left journalism a profession," he said. "We [he and Harmsworth] have made it a branch of commerce."[22] When the Edwardian journalist R. A. Scott-James addressed the subject of commercialization in his perceptive study of the press, he concluded that it was bringing the press "under the thumb of the advertiser." Papers were made more popular to push up circulations, he said, "to increase the value of the advertisement columns."[23] What did it all mean? If the emphasis were placed on journalism as commerce, what would become of journalism as a part of the public debate? The increased space devoted to advertising or to the lighter articles and features needed to attract advertisements might force a reduction of the space allotted to serious commentary. That alone might make it appear less serious and thus disregard the old Roman virtue of treating important things in an important manner. Or, would advertisers or corporate proprietors tolerate falling circulations or ones impaired by a paper's taking an unpopular stand on a popular issue?

Political journalism, then, confronted a serious challenge from the combined assault of commercialization and the New Journalism. Is it any wonder that its practitioners in the quality press feared that their influence was waning? John St. Loe Strachey, one of the featured journalists in the present study and a student of the press in his time, expressed this anxiety when he wrote in the middle of the Edwardian years, "Journalism is unquestionably at this moment on its trial and grave men throughout the world are beginning to doubt whether the tremendous claims which we at one time put forward on behalf of the Press as the beacon light, or, to change the metaphor, the watch dogs of the world, do not in truth rest upon mere rhetoric or even imposture."[24] Reasons existed for his concern.

The problem of influence was a particularly troublesome one. When applied to social trends and traits, styles and fashions, and to many other facets of broader culture, the fact of press influence is a reasonable one to accept. It becomes a problem only when the discussion turns to political influence and the dissemination of ideas intended to shape public opinion. Part of the problem lay in the inability of the press to deliver expected results. The Election of 1906 was a striking case in point. At that time the Unionist press was far stronger than that supporting the Liberals in terms of number of dailies and circulation, but the Liberals won a sweeping victory in the election. Moreover, the Labour party, which did not have a single daily newspaper on whose editorial support it could rely, returned twenty-nine candidates to the House of Commons. A few years later when the great political battles of 1909 raged in the country, the Unionist press, still superior to the Liberal press in size, again failed to provide the desired results. As one observer reflected, such evidence warranted "the inference that the partisan newspaper has sustained an enormous loss of power."[25] While it was true that editorial independence was growing, particularly among the popular newspapers, there were other variables to take into account. Consider the case of the Unionist press in the Election of 1906. The main issue of Tariff Reform was a divisive one for all Unionists including editors, and the prospect of defending the Unionist policy of using Chinese labor in the Transvaal was about as unattractive an issue as a press could be asked to champion. Regardless, press influence appeared to be waning, and its failure to deliver voters was symptomatic of that fact. The reasons can be traced to changes in the newspaper-reading and voting public. Their interests in news and opinion might well diverge from those of the elite political press with its close identity with the two-party system. To make matters worse, there was a tendency to confuse influence and power (the press possessed the former, not the latter) and to perceive the institution as losing its stature as the Fourth Estate of government.

Since the idea of the press as the Fourth Estate has enjoyed such longevity in the Anglo-American political and journalistic lexicon, it deserves brief examination at this point. It remained an attractive idea for the Edwardians, but it was popularized in the previous century. Even *The Times* overstated its own unique position in the Victorian era when it described itself as a "perpetual committee of the legislature."[26] Early twentieth-century commentators on the press were no less assertive. "Our Parliamentary institutions seem to have been in the process of weakening . . .," wrote one contributor to *Sell's Dictionary of the World's Press*, "and the chief force that has modified their influence and checked their authority has been the Press, which is now . . . rising . . . to the position of the First not the Fourth, of the Realm's Estates."[27] When proponents of the press as Fourth Estate explained that idea, they usually had a number of things in mind. Accordingly, the political press so described was free and powerful, professional in conduct, anchored in public opinion, and capable of having its views be of weight in the chambers of political power. The press as Fourth Estate spoke with authority and force. There was some truth in the idea, but the claims made for it and rhetoric spoken in its behalf were excessive.[28] Yet the idea still had pulling power in the Edwardian era and lingered as a standard against which to measure current press performance. That was unfortunate because the idea itself was an outgrowth of the class and political party system of the Victorian era and of the sober, middle-class political press that gave them expression. As the greater democratization of British life changed both its class and political systems, so it changed the role of the press in politics. Fourth Estate rhetoric only confused the issue of influence by making it appear more dramatic. Edwardian journalists all assumed that the press was influential. The problem was how to make that influence more effective. That was problem enough.

The Edwardian quality press had to adapt to a number of new circumstances forced by these problems. Its editors worked in a perilous environment. More and more their survival depended on profits, on the public appeal of their work, and even on their political preferences. The age was one in which the position of proprietors in the press was growing, many times at the expense of editors. Proprietors, as well as editors, had strong political views and party preferences, and a change in proprietorship could spell disaster even for an esteemed editor. Disagreement between an editor and proprietor over journalistic principle or over the political stance a paper should take could be enough to force an editor from his position. As H. A. Gwynne, the editor of the *Standard*, told A. J. Balfour in 1911, "I have struggled hard to sink my personal likes and dislikes in order to retain control of a paper in which I might do useful work for the party and the Empire but there are differences in journalistic principles so wide between my present proprietor and myself that I am afraid they are quite insuperable."[29] The list of Edwardian editors who lost their positions because of a clash with a new or old proprietor is long enough to prove how insecure editorial posts could be. Editors like the imperial journalists, who were leading publicists of the stately political press, worked in troubled times for their brand of journalism. Beneath all of the institutional problems they faced lay two large questions. First, would it be possible for them to retain their editorial independence amid the burgeoning proprietary, commercial, and even political pressures of the day? Second, would it be possible for them to forge their quality publications into effective political instruments in an increasingly democratic age?

2

The Imperial Journalists

The editors of the quality press were relentless in their engagement of the great issues of the time. Although disturbed by the fear that the press was losing strength as a political force, they all, in the words of Stephen Koss, accepted the widespread belief that press commentary "materially affected developments within, between, and beyond parliamentary groups."[1] The imperial journalists—J. L. Garvin, John St. Loe Strachey, J. A. Spender and the leading figures associated with *The Times*—shared this belief as they did a commitment to the cause of the Empire.

JAMES LOUIS GARVIN

Edwardian Britain knew no greater supporter of Empire than James Louis Garvin. Yet there was much in his youth and early career that could have produced an enthusiasm for political ideals far removed from those associated with Empire. He was born on Easter Sunday 1868, of Irish parents living in England. After his father died at sea when James was only two years old, his widowed mother, who struggled to provide for her children, raised him in an Irish, working-class district of Birkenhead. There he attended St. Laurence's Roman Catholic school until he was thirteen. Although Garvin came to reject the stern and narrow type of Catholicism fostered by that school, he found other things there to value. Before leaving the school he acquired a lifelong passion for history and literature that would surface years later in his famous leading articles.[2]

He began working for newspapers while still in his teens, first in Hull and later in Newcastle. Of his earliest writing for the Hull *Eastern Morning News*, his most recent biographer writes, "Nearly all of it was Irish propaganda, vehemently expressed but often prudently argued."[3] In Newcastle he worked for

Joseph Cowen's *Newcastle Daily Courant* and was the regular correspondent in the north of England for *United Ireland*, a weekly Dublin paper. Cowen, Garvin's senior by many years but a man whom he considered a friend and mentor, was a Liberal politician. He had been an M.P. for twelve years, a supporter of Home Rule for Ireland, and a man who had many connections with European radicals and socialists. The two men had similar political views, and Cowen even said there was a "community of feeling" between them.[4] In terms of his perception of the dynamics of politics, it was while he was still a young journalist in Newcastle that Garvin revealed a fascination for the dramatis personae of public life. He was drawn to those figures who might be called movers of politics, if not of history, and it was the great Irish nationalist leader Charles Stewart Parnell who captivated him at this point. After hearing him speak in Newcastle, Garvin wrote of Parnell as "the first man of our race" who spoke with such "fire and force, restrained yet hinting at volcanic depth" that he awoke in all who heard him a feeling that would be "slow to die."[5] The young journalist's admiration for Parnell was profound, and as his daughter remembered many years later, he had an abiding love for the Irish people.[6] Such was the ironic background of a man who became a great champion of the British Empire. It would more fit that of a committed Irish Home Ruler and perhaps even that of an anti-imperial, Irish nationalist.

How can his evolution into a devotee of Empire be explained? Perhaps the full explanation will never be known, but there are a number of clues that provide a degree of understanding. Even in his early journalism, for instance, there were traces of what his biographer calls "the tug of a wider patriotism in which Irish and English would share alike."[7] Evidence exists to support that statement and the nature of his admiration for Parnell. The great Parnell, Protestant landlord that he was, might appear as an unlikely leader of the Irish Home Rule cause, but he was a man who saw things in large perspective. In 1898 Garvin wrote a spirited article on him in which he stressed the theme that "Parnell was more important than Home Rule." Garvin described him as a man with a "spacious" mind who had united all nationalist Ireland and who, had he lived to govern an Ireland with Home Rule, would have brought into that union the remaining elements (i.e., the Ulster Unionists and Protestant gentry). He compared Parnell to Napoleon, Bismarck, and Cecil Rhodes. His reference to Cecil Rhodes, the great South African imperialist, in his list of historic figures is significant. Parnell died in 1891 leaving his followers divided as a result of being named co-respondent in the notorious O'Shea divorce case, but Garvin mused that if only he had lived "he would have become at once an Imperial force as strong as Mr. Rhodes."[8] No one, of course, would doubt that Cecil Rhodes was an imperial force, but it should also be remembered that he believed in a proper Irish Home Rule bill capable of creating a closer imperial union, even imperial federation.[9] Garvin, indeed, stated some years later: "There was a time when I shared Cecil Rhodes' opinions upon Home Rule. I had in my youth dreams of an Imperial Federalism."[10] Then there is Garvin's association with Joseph Cowen, the owner of the Newcastle *Daily Courant* with whom he shared affinities of thought on political matters. Cowen was, as we have seen, not an ordinary Liberal. He supported Irish Home Rule but disliked Gladstone. He questioned the Liberal gospel of Free Trade, opposed Little Englandism, and valued Britain's connections with the self-governing colonies, and he was one of the founders of the Imperial Federation League.[11] Cowen, then, had definite imperial sympathies, and Garvin apparently shared them. "At Newcastle on Tyne," he wrote some years later, "I was always an extreme Imperialist like my friend & chief the late Joseph Cowen."[12]

Eleven years after Garvin entered London journalism, he offered Austen Chamberlain a revealing explanation of his commitment to the Empire. Writing at a time when the Irish question was again surfacing in British politics, Garvin said:

> I feel it is better to write to you about the new phase of the Irish question. I have been reluctant to do it because I only came into the Unionist party a dozen years ago and nothing but the question of Imperial and foreign policy brought me into it at all. However, as the power & union of the Empire have been the steady objects of my thought all my life, and *means* must necessarily alter if men through long periods of time keep *ends* in view, I think after all that you may care to have my opinion even on this matter.[13]

Garvin's explanation seems reasonable and provides a framework for his emphatic imperial views during the Edwardian years. Rather than accept the taunt that he was a Parnellite turned Imperialist, in which Garvin admitted later there was partial if misleading truth, it would be better to describe him as a one-time Parnellite and always an imperialist.[14]

Political views alone fail to convey the way in which someone like Garvin vitalized Edwardian public debate. The style and passion of his journalism must also be taken into account, for they were distinctive traits of his work. His writing conveyed life, excitement, and a sense of importance. His rhetoric was bold and insightful and contained memorable turns of phrase. Indeed, it was the uncommon element detectable in his writing that won him a place in 1895 as a contributor to the prestigious journal *Fortnightly Review*. After he joined the staff of the *Daily Telegraph* in 1899, his place in national journalism rose steadily. In 1905 he became editor of the *Outlook*, a weekly journal attempting to counter the influence of St. Loe Strachey's *Spectator*, a leading Free Trade advocate. Three years later, praising him as "the greatest journalist in England," Northcliffe offered him, and Garvin accepted, the editorship of the *Observer*, Britain's oldest Sunday newspaper.[15] Garvin reversed the fortunes of that paper, which had become a mere relic in 1908, and made it a journalistic success and a power in Unionist politics. In the process, he gained a reputation as one of the great cause-oriented publicists of the era. Professional contemporaries recognized a special, even an extraordinary, talent in Garvin. "I always learn more from listening to you either talking, or speaking, or from reading your writing," said Leo Maxse, the fiery editor of the *National Review* for which Garvin also wrote, "than from any other authority on public affairs. This is not flattery but the exact truth."[16] Garvin was always thorough, studied, and courageous in what he wrote, and he disdained the idea prevalent in so much of popular journalism of giving the public what it wanted. To the contrary, he set out "to give the public what they don't want."[17] By that statement he meant he intended to improve public taste, to broaden its vision, and by force of argument to enlighten and persuade it on the great issues of the day. To him, the Empire was the issue that mattered most. "Imperial Consolidation," he told Northcliffe, "is the passion of my life, and I want to mould national opinion and address large masses and move them . . . . Until the newspapers command and cease to follow opinion of conventional parliamentary people, always years behind their age, nothing will be well in this nation."[18]

JOHN ST. LOE STRACHEY

Although the opposite of Garvin in terms of background and temperament, St. Loe Strachey could match Garvin as a champion of the Empire. Born in 1860 into a prominent family, Strachey became an esteemed figure among his contemporaries as an editor in the field of weekly political publications. He edited the *Spectator* from 1898 to 1925, and his background prepared him well for that post.

His family had a long tradition of connection with the empire. Strachey's father, Sir Edward Strachey, was trained for East India Company service at Haileyburg, but never served in India because of a sudden infection in his knee that occurred as he was about to leave for the subcontinent. It left him with a physical disability for the next twenty years. He was, however, a man of letters, a public servant active in local affairs, and someone who had a keen interest in politics. St. Loe Strachey recalled in later life the "many old talks" about political history that he had with his father when he was young. He said his father "always inculcated in us the Whig view of the Colonies. He, however, never looked forward to a break up of the Empire but rather insisted that the Whig policy would keep the Empire together."[19] St. Loe Strachey was also fond of pointing out the significant role his family had played in empire building. One of his ancestors, William Strachey, was the first secretary to the colony of Virginia. Another, Sir Henry Strachey, was private secretary to the famous Robert Clive in India, whom the Stracheys considered their "patron saint." It was through his financial generosity that Sutton Court, the family estate, had been saved for the Stracheys.[20] In the nineteenth century two of Strachey's uncles, Sir

Richard Strachey and Sir John Strachey, had served on the India Council and one of his cousins, Charles Buller, was secretary to Lord Durham on his famous mission to Canada in 1838 and had a hand in writing his historic report on Canada.[21]

There is no question about the family's political inclination. As Strachey said late in life, "I may class myself as thrice-blessed in being brought up in Whig ideas, in a Whig family, with Whig traditions."[22] But as the Whigs evolved into Liberals, what did it mean to identify with the Whig tradition? Strachey addressed himself to that question many times. On one occasion, for instance, he reflected: "After all why should not one hold the Whig spirit with enthusiasm as our forefathers did. Moderation and the happy mean have been justly applauded in all ages and though they are far more difficult to attain than extremes they ought to call for the maximum of devotion. After all liberty can and does only reside in moderation and the avoidance of violence and fanaticism."[23] To Strachey, Whiggism originated in the party of Cromwell and of the Independents, embodied the principles of the Glorious Revolution of 1688 and the Bill of Rights, and found its representative figures on both sides of the Atlantic, in John Locke, Chatham, and William Pitt as well as in George Washington and John Adams. It was a broad-minded political philosophy stressing "liberty in all matters of opinion," moderation, and the belief "that the will of the majority of the nation as a whole must prevail, and not the will of any section, even if it is a large section and does manual work."[24] All signs indicate that he would be a stalwart member of the Liberal party. That was not the case. When Gladstone introduced his first Irish Home Rule bill in 1886, Strachey broke with the party and joined the Liberal-Unionist party. Then he became an "unhyphenated" Unionist.

During the Edwardian years, he identified with the Unionist Free Trade wing of that party. He defended the Unionist principle of union with Ireland but opposed any form of the protectionism that then attracted the majority of the party. Throughout this period he referred to himself as a defender of the "Left Center" in politics, and often expressed his willingness to do "everything in the way of encouraging a closer connection between the Colonies [the self-governing Colonies] and the Empire."[25] In his memoirs, he explained: "Throughout my life I have been a strong democratic Imperialist. To me the alliance of the free self-governing Dominions, which constitute the British Empire, has a sacred character. . . . But though I was always so ardent a supporter of the British Empire and of the Imperial spirit, I was not one of those people who thought that the mere word 'Imperialism' would cover a multitude of misdeeds."[26] Armed with such views, he settled in London after completing his education at Oxford.

During his first several years there, he wrote for a variety of London newspapers and reviews. From 1887 to 1892 he served as coeditor of the *Liberal Unionist* for the party by the same name and began writing for the *Spectator*. When he became editor and proprietor of that weekly journal in 1898, it became in his own words "the pivot of my life."[27] His reputation as a journalist rests on his association with the *Spectator*. Although the journal was a literary as well as a political weekly, reflecting Strachey's own wide knowledge of literature and language, it is his weekly leading article on public affairs that attracts our attention, for Strachey claimed his life was "altogether given over to politics."[28] His journalism, as he often explained, was of a "watchdog" variety. It was the "journalism of advocacy."[29] Those qualities clearly characterize his political writing in the *Spectator*, but they fail to capture the spirit of the journalism he admired and practiced. His journalism was as broad-minded and tactful as it was definite, thorough, and steady. Although he was deep into political party journalism, he took pride in his editorial independence and often referred to his belief in that principle. He recommended it to others. When Geoffrey Robinson became editor of *The Times* in 1912, Strachey wrote to Lord Northcliffe, then chief proprietor of the paper:

> I feel sure you have got a good man in Geoffrey Robinson . . . . When I wrote to congratulate him I told him I hoped he would soon get an opportunity to stand up to his public over some matter, as in the end nothing helped a newspaper more than the sense that its editor was independent and quite prepared to say unsmooth things to his readers if necessary.[30]

No matter what Northcliffe, with his eye ever fixed on a paper's circulation, thought of that advice, it did exemplify the journalistic philosophy of the *Spectator*'s editor.

JOHN ALFRED SPENDER

Like Garvin and Strachey, J. A. Spender was a writing editor. Born in Bath, he was raised by parents who were no strangers to writing. His father was a physician and medical writer. "Medicine apart," Spender later recollected of his father, "he was eminently a bookish man."[31] His mother, Lily Spender, was a novelist, who, though not among the greats, received some acclaim in her time. She wrote twenty-one novels and published a number of essays. Her literary earnings provided for the education of her eight children, including a university education for her four sons. John attended Bath College when T. W. Dunn, a demanding but inspiring teacher, was headmaster. Of him Spender commented in his memoirs: "What I owe him is more than I can tell . . . . He was, in some ways, the most remarkable man I have ever known, and for my school years and many years later, by far the strongest influence in my life."[32] Young Spender had a natural curiosity and a wandering mind. When he became a student at Balliol College, Oxford, those qualities earned him a rebuke from the renowned master, Benjamin Jowett, who thought they impaired the young man's powers of concentration. It was also Jowett who warned him when he left Oxford, "Journalism is not a profession, not a profession, Mr. Spender."[33] How ironic it must have seemed for him to have the proprietor of the first newspaper for which he worked say to him not long afterwards, "You have had an Oxford education, and it will take some time to get over that."[34]

His long career as a journalist and writer began soon after he left Oxford in 1885. After a year of working on various newspapers first in Hull and then in London, he returned to Hull to edit the *Eastern Morning News* for five years. Then he went again to London, wrote *The State and Pensions in Old Age*, and continued his journalism as a free lance writer. Positions in London journalism in those years were hard to find, but Spender was among the fortunate. E. T. Cook, the Liberal editor of the *Pall Mall Gazette* appointed him his assistant editor in 1892. Events shaping Spender's career then proceeded in quick succession. The *Pall Mall Gazette* 's proprietor sold the paper to a Conservative, the first Lord Astor. That change in proprietorship also changed the political stance of the *Gazette*, which had been one of London's influential Liberal papers, and Cook and Spender and most of the rest of the staff resigned. They were, however, rescued by George (later Sir George) Newnes, who had made a fortune in popular journalism and who now decided to launch a new Liberal evening paper. He appointed the men who had left the *Pall Mall* to staff the new paper, and he made Cook and Spender editor and assistant editor respectively. Named the *Westminster Gazette* and published on light sea-green paper, the new paper appeared on 31 January 1893. Spender served the next three years as assistant editor, and became editor early in 1896 when Cook left to assume the editorship of the *Daily News*. Spender remained the *Westminster*'s editor for twenty-six years, until it became a morning paper in 1921.

His editorship of the *Westminster Gazette* won him an esteemed position in British journalism history. Under his guidance the *Westminster* came to be the highest reputed publication in the class of evening papers that were small in circulation but large in political influence. In 1904 W. T. Stead, who was in a position to know all aspects of London journalism, named the *Westminster Gazette* along with *The Times* as one of the country's two most influential papers. "No Minister, no diplomatist, no public man can afford to miss reading *The Times* in the morning and the *Westminster Gazette* in the evening," he said. "Both are party papers, but both are read by men of both parties; and, as they are on opposite sides, whoever reads both may feel secure that he misses nothing."[35] People read the *Westminster* mainly for Spender's leading articles that appeared regularly on the front page. Exemplifying as they did his fair and broad-minded writing and his liberal persuasion, his leaders still impress one today, nearly a century later, for their lucidity of prose and argument. Spender advocated moderate liberalism with its emphasis on gradualism as a guiding principle for social and political change. Since his earliest days in journalism he was a social reformer and, as Max Beloff has claimed, he was the "principal journalistic exponent of liberal journalism."[36] Those were the views that permeated his leaders with a consistency rarely found in modern journalism. During the Edwardian era, politically astute people throughout Britain and abroad considered the *Westminster Gazette* the most authoritative voice of the Liberal opposition before 1905 and of the Liberals in power after that date.

Spender's views on the Empire were those of a man who wished to apply the creed of moderate liberalism to imperial affairs. During the Anglo-Boer War, when so many Edwardian imperial opinions were shaped, he tried to defend a precarious middle position between the opposite views on the war held by the two wings of his party. He agreed neither with the Liberal supporters of the war nor with those Radicals in the party, known as the pro-Boers, who opposed the war policy of the government. As Spender later explained, he had no enthusiasm for the war, the responsibility for which lay on both the British and the Boer sides. "So I . . . looked beyond the war to the policy which should follow upon it, and begged the readers of the *Westminster* to bear in mind that the Boers were not a common enemy, but men who would somehow have to be reconciled to the British Empire, if South Africa was to prosper." Liberal supporters of the war found that line "unpatriotic." Once the war began, Spender was for vigorous military measures to bring it to a speedy end. He saw "no solution of the South African trouble but the ultimate union of British and Dutch [the Boers] under the British flag."[37] Such logic won him the condemnation of the pro-Boers. Clearly, Spender was not opposed to the Empire so long as it was grounded in reasonable liberal principles. That position on Empire he defended during the Edwardian era, and during that time his contemporaries thought of him as sympathetic, in particular, to the Liberal Imperialist element in the Liberal party. He was, in fact, a moderate in the party who wished to see the party unified and who much preferred the imperialism of a Liberal leader, such as the former minister Lord Rosebery, to that of a Conservative imperial advocate such as Joseph Chamberlain.[38] Throughout the Edwardian years, Spender's *Westminster Gazette* was the steadiest and strongest supporter of a Liberal imperial policy to be found in the press.

It was Spender himself who gave the paper its reputation. His scrupulous fairness, the consistency of his commentary, and the sincerity with which he presented his Liberal opinion, impressed his readers. They assumed that he wrote the paper's leading articles, and that they reflected the opinion of Liberal leaders. No one in the British press was better connected within his party than Spender. He was close to every Liberal leader since the time of Lord Rosebery and was on intimate terms with all the Liberal Imperialists. He saw the prime minister and foreign secretary on a regular basis and was close to most of the other members of the Liberal cabinet after 1905. Indeed, some members of that cabinet thought of him as a colleague. His ties with Liberal leaders disturbed some of his professional contemporaries. Radical journalists like A. G. Gardiner and H. W. Massingham contended that Spender's association with members of the government compromised his liberalism. Massingham, for instance, believing it his duty to question the Government, considered Spender a ministerial and orthodox Liberal editor, and he intended neither term to convey approval.[39] In fact, the charge of Spender's being "ministerial" or a "ministerial apologist" has found its way into journalism history.[40]

It is necessary to contemplate that charge in order to understand Spender's journalism for the years covered in this study. During that time, while he offered solid support of Liberal policies, the *Westminster Gazette* ran an annual deficit of £14,000. It survived by subsidies provided by its proprietors, Newnes until 1908 and then a group of prominent Liberals. The paper was never a commercial success, yet the Liberals valued it for its influence. Did the financial backing provided by various Liberals and Spender's intimate association with Liberal leaders impair his journalistic integrity? Sir Edward Grey, the Foreign Secretary from 1905 to 1916, provided a clue that helps to answer that question. In the process of inquiring about the paper's finances to make sure it was "satisfactorily provided for," he told Spender, "You manage to combine independent thought with unswerving support of the party in a way which is very rare. I think that is what Mr. G. [Gladstone] meant by the power of putting one's mind into common stock & it makes your articles like the opinion of a valued colleague. I know nothing else in journalism like it, & I should think many of us feel the same about it."[41] Although the purpose of Grey's communication was to relieve Spender of any anxiety he had about the intention of the *Westminster's* new proprietors to support the paper and its editor adequately, the statement quoted above touches on several basic elements in Spender's journalism. He believed that the imperative condition of political journalism was that it be free of commercialization and the race for vast circulation.[42] The proprietors' subsidies for the paper gave it that freedom, and as we have seen, it was a common practice at the time for the political press to be subsidized by private or party funds in some way.

Did his association with Liberal leaders affect journalistic independence? In answering that question, it is important to remember that a broad agreement existed between men like Spender, Asquith and Grey on all of the great political issues of the day. They respected one another and one another's views. The Liberal leaders wanted Spender to be informed but did not expect the *Westminster Gazette* to be an organ for government publicity. They respected Spender's advice and his journalistic independence. Clearly, he was free to write what he wished, and what he wrote usually, but not always, pleased the various Liberal leaders, who after all were not always of one mind. Spender was particularly close to Asquith and Grey, and several times in later life he provided retrospective comments that illuminate the fact that he was able to maintain both those friendships and his journalistic independence. For instance, toward the end of 1926, five years after his editorship of the *Westminster* ended and at a time when Asquith was retiring from his "responsibilities of leadership,"

Spender wrote to the former prime minister to say that his association with him had been a "rare privilege." He told Asquith of how he valued the fact that he was the type of leader with whom an editor could have "self-respecting relations." Asquith, he said, was a chief who neither resented criticism nor asked for "favor or flattery." Spender concluded, "Many more important tributes will be paid to you, but it may be worth a little niche in your memory that you helped to smooth the paths and lighten the work of a Liberal editor."[43] Or, take the case of Spender's relations with Sir Edward Grey. In the years before World War I, the *Westminster Gazette* was sometimes called "the organ of Sir Edward Grey." Spender later refuted that charge when he wrote that the "literal truth" was "that never once in the ten years that he was Foreign Minister had Sir Edward Grey ever suggested to me to write an article in the *Westminster Gazette* or ever proposed to take one line rather than another in foreign affairs."[44] Spender's concept of journalistic independence may not have been that of Lord Northcliffe, who practiced a different type of independence in the popular press, but it was a valid one in which a number of political journalists of the quality press believed.

LEADERS AT *THE TIMES*

The senior staff at *The Times* was particularly proud of that paper's independence. Although *The Times* no longer exerted the independent temper it did under its great nineteenth-century editors Thomas Barnes (1817-1841) and John Thadeus Delane (1841-1877), when people spoke of it as "The Thunderer" and critics complained of its "atrocious articles" and its "dangerous eminence," they were emphatic in proclaiming its current independence.[45] To them the principle meant freedom from government control and interference and freedom from proprietary and commercial intrusion into editorial policy. It meant the freedom to resist popular pressure in the name of defending the national good and the freedom to support the political party of their choice without being subservient to a party machine. Within the parameters of that support, they claimed the right to disagree with party policy when it ran against the traditions of the paper or the settled opinion of the editors. While it is true that *The Times*, in many respects, tried to hold the balance between parties and to articulate a consensus opinion on public issues in its impressive news columns and in its capacious and well-substantiated editorials, it is also true that the paper had a definite party preference. The editors recognized the fact in their private correspondence.[46] Since the formation of the Unionist party in 1886, *The Times* staked its reputation on preventing Irish Home Rule. Consequently, it supported the Unionist party and opposed Liberals as long as they were Home Rulers. On the other hand, the paper tried to be generous to the party in power and extended that principle to the Liberal governments after 1905 when it thought it proper to do so. The Edwardian understanding of journalistic independence in the quality press did not imply impartiality. In this sense, *The Times* enjoyed an enviable reputation as a fair-minded and thorough paper that appealed to men's thoughts in a rational and intellectual manner. Even the *Nation*, the leading Radical journal of the era, spoke of its "tradition of independence" and its "authority."[47]

The Times did speak with authority. It had a vast news-gathering network and an unmatched number of contacts with public figures, including many at high levels of government. Its extensive news articles and reports, its wide-ranging foreign correspondence, and its exhaustive editorials, gave it the reputation of a national resource of trustworthy news and sound opinion. Nevertheless, its authority had declined since its time of greatest influence in the middle of the previous century. At its peak of preeminence, as Francis Williams described it in his history of the British press, the paper was an "Everest of a newspaper with sales ten times those of any other daily combining leadership in circulation, in news services . . . in advertisement revenue, commercial profit and political influence to an extent no other paper in the world has ever done before or since."[48] That position could not and did not last. Following the repeal of advertisement duty in 1853 and the stamp duty in 1855, the number of newspapers published in the United Kingdom more than doubled.[49] The political press, particularly penny newspapers, now came to rival *The Times* with its greater bulk and higher costs. After the 1860s, its circulation began a long downward turn. From over 60,000 in the 1860s and 1870s it fell to 38,000 in 1908. At that time, its most successful rival, the *Daily Telegraph*, circulated over 200,000. To make matters worse, the paper suffered for many years from its disclosure about Charles Stewart Parnell in 1887. Based on documents received by the paper, it charged that Parnell condoned the assassinations of two British officials in Ireland some years before, in 1882. A long official inquiry into the matter proved the documents were forgeries and *The Times'* accusation incorrect.[50] The paper's reputation for inerrancy suffered as a result. So did its finances, for it had to pay the 200,000-pound cost of the inquiry. On into the twentieth century, when old and new publications intensified competition, the paper continued to suffer the consequences of the Parnell case. It is a credit to the senior staff's belief in *The Times* that it continued to possess the great prestige it did throughout Britain and the world. Its editor in 1909 even boasted that "it was the greatest, the most renowned, the most powerful paper in the world."[51] Those were the words of G. E. Buckle.

The Times never had a more loyal servant than George Earle Buckle, though he remains somewhat unheralded in the distinguished line of its editors. After achieving a brilliant record at Oxford, he joined the staff of *The Times* in 1880 as assistant to the editor. Four years later at the age of twenty-nine, he became editor and held that position for an unprecedented twenty-eight years. During that time, he made the paper his sole and absorbing professional interest and succeeded in maintaining its great features. When he retired in 1912, he took pride in handing over the paper to his successor "the same Times as ever, only more so!"[52] While its editor, he considered the verdict of the paper in the public debate as "being generally regarded as a corporate not a personal pronouncement—not the opinion of an individual." He felt in editing the paper that "it was not so much important to emphasize what you as an individual thought but what ought to be the view of that great impersonal organ, *The Times*."[53] Buckle was not a writing editor, but he did control the paper's broad policy. He was a strikingly old-fashioned editor in his work habits, with a keen interest in politics, and in the words of one of his colleagues, he was "tenacious in his hold of large underlying principles."[54]

Buckle was a man of moderate conservative persuasion whose policy as editor can be described as "watchful independence." He believed the paper should give "critical support" to the party in power. On occasion, however, that "critical support" could take the form of "definite opposition."[55] It would be a mistake to call *The Times* under his direction a strictly Conservative paper, and more erroneous yet to call it, as people abroad frequently did, the official voice of the British government. But its contents reflected Buckle's many connections with political, particularly Unionist, leaders. Few journalists were better connected than he. His colleague, Moberly Bell, was one.

Charles Frederic Moberly Bell was one of the most formidable journalists of his time. A tireless worker until his death at his desk in 1911, Bell had been born in Egypt where, after a few years of school in England, he worked for twenty years in business. In time, when he became a correspondent for *The Times*, he so impressed the paper's chief proprietor Arthur Walter that he brought him to London to be associated with the paper there. Between 1891 and 1911, Bell was in succession assistant manager, manager, and manager director of *The Times*. Over the years he "became known to more people of prominence in political and other circles than any of his colleagues, not excepting the Editor."[56] Like Buckle, Bell made *The Times* his life; like Buckle, his political preference was Unionist; and like Buckle he remained old-fashioned in his habits of work (he abhored the telephone as well as secretarial help and conducted a prolific correspondence by his own hand). Bell and Buckle actually shared in directing the editorial policy of the paper. When he became chief proprietor of *The Times* in 1908, Lord Northcliffe observed that Bell "engaged the staff, sent out foreign correspondents, altered leading articles, and . . . was in command."[57] In the conduct of the paper's imperial and foreign policy, Bell played the "paramount" role.[58]

Both Buckle and Bell supported the imperial cause. If during the Victorian age *The Times* "took little pleasure in 'painting the map red,'" it did recognize the Empire as a "guarantor of peace." Therefore, as the paper's official historian observes, "The twentieth-century goal was a consolidation of the colonies and dependencies."[59] Buckle had believed in maintaining the Empire since the early days of his editorship. As for Bell, his daughter later described his imperial commitment in this manner: "As he grew older the Imperialism [his imperialistic sympathies] whilst it remained broad-minded, became more and more marked, and the principal part of his political creed came to be a belief in Empire; while his views on Ireland, South Africa and Tariff Reform, and every other question that agitated his generation, were determined by their Imperial aspects."[60]

Several other figures at Printing House Square were connected with the paper's imperial policies. They were all men of strong commitment to the Empire. Chief among these were Valentine Chirol and Lord Northcliffe. Chirol's credentials as an expert on foreign and imperial affairs were impeccable. His reputation as premier foreign correspondent and world traveler preceded him when he became *The Times'* foreign editor in 1899, a position he held with distinction until 1912. Though he was a sensitive, nervous, and introspective man, Chirol's industrious labors on behalf of the paper gained him a unique reputation among British journalists of foreign affairs. Any of the world's great newspapers would have welcomed, valued, and paid dearly to have had his services. He had intimate professional associations with many diplomats and few if any of his journalistic contemporaries could match his knowledge of world affairs. He was a particular authority on India, and his efforts to further Anglo-Indian understanding and to promote the Morley-Minto Indian reforms of 1909 led to his knighthood three years later. Lord Northcliffe (Alfred Harmsworth), whose imperial credentials were also beyond question, was a man of different stripe. He became the paper's chief proprietor in 1908 and a major irritant to its senior staff. The impetuous Northcliffe was a driver who wished the paper to become a more effective champion of Empire, and in pushing the senior staff toward that goal he was not above intervening in editorial matters. Consequently, during their final years at *The Times,* the old senior staff at Printing House Square, the home of *The Times,* had to fight against his proprietary interference in order to maintain the paper's independence which was, as Buckle said, "the basis of its authority."[61]

Leopold Amery and Geoffrey Robinson, the last two *Times'* figures who have a place in this study, were younger men. Amery joined the staff in 1899 and served the paper until 1910, first as its principal South African correspondent and then as colonial editor and in various other capacities. Robinson (he changed his name to Dawson in 1917) had the distinction of serving twice as *The Times'* editor (1912-1919 and 1923-1941). Both Amery and Robinson were ardent imperial advocates, and both had been associated with Sir Alfred Milner (later Lord Milner) in South Africa. Robinson was part of the "kindergarten," that group of energetic and able young men who worked with Milner in reconstructing South Africa in the years following the Anglo-Boer War. Amery, whose connection with *The Times* took him back to London, enjoyed the status, according to his son, of honorary membership in that group.[62] After Milner left South Africa in 1905, Robinson continued his involvement in politics there, and he served as editor of the *Johannesburg Star* from 1905 to 1910. For most of those years, he was also a correspondent for *The Times*. He championed the imperial cause in all of these endeavors, and Amery championed that cause in London. There he founded an imperial discussion group known as the Compatriots, which tried to advance the idea of imperial unity. It is difficult to overestimate the influence Milner had on Amery and Robinson. His ideas about South African unity, imperial consolidation, and the mission of the Empire in world affairs affected their thought throughout this era and far into the future.

. . .

These journalists—Garvin, Strachey, Spender, and the leading figures at Printing House Square—who will be featured in this study, formed no group, club, or association. They were men of different political persuasions, backgrounds, and ages. Bell, who was fifty-six in 1903, was the oldest among them. At that time Garvin was only thirty-six and Amery and Robinson were yet younger men. They were also men of different temperaments who were exponents of various journalistic styles. It is possible, however, to detect certain common attitudes among them. As practitioners of political journalism in the stately press, they all believed their work was instrumental in the political life of the nation. Notwithstanding their concern with current conditions of British society, they shared a common pride in the nation's achievements and in its great traditions and institutions. British civilization was the standard against which others should be measured, and sometimes that led to statements of racial pride in their dialogue about the Empire. References to the "British race," "men of British blood," and "the instinct of race" as well as those many explanations of South Africa as a "white man's country" provide indication enough of this element in the thought of the imperial journalists. It might even be reasoned that a racial element was part of the desire for greater imperial unity. Yet the racial factor in their commentary was far from aggressive or jingoistic. Even in the case of South Africa, they were more interested in racial relations than in racial differences and tried to protect the political rights of the Africans where they could. Racial perceptions of a cultural rather than a scientific variety influenced their views about the Empire, but they did not determine them.

Most of all, the imperial journalists shared a general perception of the Empire as a unique international entity. It was a free Empire based on British institutions and ideals. They all believed it was their duty to help preserve and nourish it, for Britain's world position depended on it and because it was a force for good in the emerging global order of powers. Could it be preserved? There was no guarantee that it could. Indeed, Joseph Chamberlain touched on the common anxiety among them when he stated, "The future is with the great Empires, and it rests with us to say whether our own shall be counted for many ages to come as one of the greatest or whether we shall split up into minor and comparatively unimportant nationalities."[63] How could it be nourished? On that question turned the great issues of the Edwardian imperial debate.

3

The Crucible of Tariff Reform

The future of the Empire remained a fixed element in the public debate in the decade following the Anglo-Boer War—and for good reason. That war raised doubts about Britain's imperial authority and tarnished the nation's international prestige. During the war, Britain fielded an army of a half-million men only to find that it took thirty-one months to defeat the Boer republics. A jingoistic spirit emerged in Britain during the early phases of the war, but as the conflict progressed, a mood of disillusionment grew.

Whatever else can be said about the South African war, it clearly failed to manifest imperial greatness. Too much went wrong for the British during the war for that to be the case. The trouble involved more than military operations. Critics of the government's policy at home questioned the legitimacy of the war. A number of individuals, including some prominent politicians and journalists, condemned the war. Called the "pro-Boers" by their opponents, they denounced the conflict with a vehemence that countered the intemperate advocacy of the war voiced by the most outspoken ministerial supporters. Nowhere was the divided opinion about the war more apparent than in the ranks of the Liberal party, which was split on the proposition of supporting the war. Most discouraging of all, since the time of the Jameson Raid in 1895, rumors spread that mining magnates in the Transvaal and other capitalists were promoting their interests at the expense of the Boers and in league with imperial authorities. Eventually, critics who chanted this line charged that this "capitalist conspiracy" dragged the British to war. Even if many historians have come to doubt the truth of that accusation, the fact remains that Chamberlain and Milner pushed for war if necessary against the Transvaal, and numerous critics at home thought the government's policy was precipitous and expressed sympathy for the republic. Therefore, after the conflict began, anti-war organizations emerged, and they "joined in the anti-capitalist chorus."[1] At the end of the war John Hobson published his *Imperialism, A Study*, a book that would become one of the major anti-imperialist statements of this century. Pure anti-imperialism was only a minority persuasion at the turn of the century, but it was an indication of the dissatisfaction that existed about the Empire.

Far more than dissatisfaction, however, was an uneasiness that permeated the mainstream of opinion about the Empire. For a variety of reasons, the Anglo-Boer War forced a reappraisal of Britain's world position and led to an abandonment of its so-called "splendid isolation" as well as to military and naval reforms. Britain's alliance with Japan of 1902 and her entente with France two years later were consequences of the reassessment of the country's policies and international relations that occurred.

Yet, the fact of the recent war in South Africa and its ramifications for the British fails to explain the degree of anxiety that imperial advocates felt. That explanation lies in a wider cluster of circumstances. Japan's defeat of Russia in 1905, for instance, had far-reaching implications for the relations between the powers and in the British-imperial perception of the world. It signified the rising, or reemergence, of Asian power, a fact that could have only the most serious meaning for the British in India and elsewhere in the East. Britain, moreover, had been the world's first industrial power, and in that capacity, she acquired global interests. But the industrialization that spread across western Europe and the United States later in the nineteenth century, with its new industrial technologies and new patterns of regional and world trade, diminished Britain's earlier advantageous position. New industrial states, Germany and the United States, and new or revived empires, the German, French, Japanese and Russian, in particular, emerged that challenged and changed Britain's nineteenth-century position as the great global power. Their commercial competition threatened Britain's claim as the "workshop of the world." By the end of the century there were a number of world workshops, and it was impossible to deny their impact upon British trade, international interests, and national well-being.

Finally, there was the belief, widespread enough among imperial thinkers to be taken seriously, that the future would be dominated by great land-based powers—Russia, the United States, and perhaps China. What then would be the fate of Britain, an insular power with interests in and involvements on all the world's continents. "The problem, therefore," as Ronald Hyam has written, "of perpetuating British world power into the twentieth century, where it might co-exist equally with the great land-based powers, seemed to depend on making it more of an integrated empire."[2]

THE NEW IMPERIAL PROGRAM

Only circumstances and personality made the much-heralded program of Tariff Reform and imperial preferences new. A number of imperial enthusiasts had been interested in some type of inter-imperial organization since the early decades of the nineteenth century. In the late Victorian era, it was a commonly discussed idea in those numerous imperial societies that sprouted into existence after the 1860s. The most important of these societies was the Imperial Federation League. Established in 1884 it lasted only nine years, and like most of the imperial societies, it was composed of specialists. But its influence should not be underestimated. It espoused the idea of imperial unity in its own journal and its members published numerous articles in other respected publications such as the *Fortnightly Review* and the *Nineteenth Century.* It addressed itself to the political elite both in Britain and in the colonies. The League also inspired many other imperial groups that appeared at the end of the century and on through the Edwardian era. Later in this study we shall see how the idea of imperial unity remained alive long after the demise of the League.

One of the things that hampered the League's promotion of constitutional designs for imperial organization was the prominence it gave to the idea of imperial preferences. Britain, of course, had been the world's greatest Free Trade nation since the repeal of the Corn Laws in 1846. That principle was the cornerstone of its trading policies. The other powers, however, had tariff policies, and they increased them to protectionist levels toward the end of the century. Even the British colonies introduced tariffs as they received self-government. In 1881 the National Fair Trade League was formed to urge the cause of Tariff Reform in Britain; it urged "fair play" for British industry against foreign competition. The League failed to persuade the government to abandon its economic orthodoxy of Free Trade, but it did have some noticeable support among workingmen. About this same time, in 1885, the government appointed a royal commission to investigate the "depression of trade and industry." The commission concluded that there was a depression, that prices were low, investment opportunities poor, and that unemployment and surplus production were at serious levels. It could not, however, agree on a remedy. It offered a majority report supporting continuation of the Free Trade policy and a minority report considering a system of Imperial Preference. As opposed to tariffs for protection, revenue, or retaliation, an imperial preferential tariff policy could also serve as a tie conducive to unity. However, if elevated to the level of a self-contained imperial economic union between the mother country and the colonies fenced off by tariffs from the outside world, the scheme would be restrictive to the colonies as well as to Britain. Nevertheless, some form of simple imperial preference involving differential duties favorable to the mother country could be acceptable to the self-governing colonies. The idea that the mother country and its self-governing colonies were economically compatible and might play complementary roles in one another's economies was not new, but it did begin to attract increased speculation in the 1880s and thereafter.

The idea continued to surface on into the new century. In 1887 the Cape Colony's J. H. Hofmeyr proposed a 2 percent tax on imports with the revenue designated for imperial defense. That plan came to naught. Then in 1894 and

1897 the Canadian government decided to give British goods preference—25 percent at first and later 33 1/3 percent.[3] Other colonies began to follow the Canadian example. Imperial Preference became a subject discussed at the various Colonial Conferences beginning in 1887. The scheme most promoted by British advocates of the idea at these conferences, one involving an Empire-wide customs union, ran against colonial opinion. The colonials felt that an imperial customs union might impede their own trade beyond the Empire as well as their industrial development. That scheme failed to win their support when it was put forth by the powerful colonial secretary, Joseph Chamberlain, at the Colonial Conference of 1902. Afterwards he turned away from the idea of an imperial customs union and to the idea of simple imperial preference. To that the colonies were receptive. They found preferences, as Nicholas Mansergh has observed, "at once compatible with policies of protection at home and with special trading relations with the Empire overseas."[4] The only problem was that Britain, which still adhered to Free Trade as the guiding principle for its own commercial policy, was in no position to participate in a reciprocal way in any type of imperial preferential system. Chamberlain spent the remainder of his political life trying to change that salient fact.

Chamberlain was the greatest imperial statesman of his day—and one of the most provocative. A successful manufacturer before he entered politics, in the 1870s he became a reformist Liberal mayor of Birmingham. Although a Radical within the Liberal party, he seemed destined for high office. But he was a man of independent mind and capable of bucking party leadership. In 1885, true to his social reformist convictions, he pressed for his own radical program of reforms in the election of that year. One year later he broke with Prime Minister Gladstone and the Liberals by opposing the Irish Home Rule Bill and joined a third force known as the Liberal Unionists. Increasingly he supported the Conservatives, and appreciation of him among that party's leadership grew. He was a force in British politics. When Lord Salisbury formed his third cabinet in 1895, there was a place for Chamberlain in it.

Actually he was a Radical Liberal Unionist in Salisbury's Unionist coalition. The Conservatives were the largest single block in the Unionist party, and that presented a problem for Chamberlain. Many of them would never accept him as a party leader, dynamic personality though he was and despite the fact that his credentials seemed to qualify him for leadership. To them he remained "pushful Joe" who had disdained Conservative peers with his Radical rhetoric in the 1880s. Having broken with the Liberals and now held suspect by a number of Conservatives, Chamberlain knew he would never become prime minister. Consequently, in 1895, rather than accept the chancellorship of the exchequer, which had been offered to him, he chose the Colonial Office. That position had rarely been one of high status, but Chamberlain elevated, even magnified, the office. By this time he was not only "Radical Joe" but also a devotee of the imperial cause and a consummate politician as well. Salisbury recognized the popularity and forcefulness of his new colleague and usually allowed him the power of a "co-premier."

No one with any knowledge of men and politics in our century can deny Chamberlain his rightful place among the great personalities of the pre-World War I era. R. C. K. Ensor wrote of him: "In sheer parliamentary and platform strength, the country had not seen his equal since Disraeli and Gladstone. Yet an air of frustration clings around his record. As a leader he had high qualities but he . . . lacked what Napoleon thought a leader's first requisite—'luck': which may or may not be a synonym for a certain final felicity of judgement."[5] But if he lacked "luck" he had an abundance of drive, ability, and vision. In short, Chamberlain was a man whose presence was felt—a leader who in order to achieve his great imperial goal was willing to challenge and attempt to revolutionize the imperial thought and policy of the British. After 1902 it was he, rather than the more detached new prime minister, Arthur Balfour, who represented the center of the Unionists on imperial affairs.

Chamberlain believed that the twentieth-century world would be one of great powers, of great empires.[6] Accordingly, the securing of a viable future for the British Empire became the overwhelming passion of his life. To accomplish that end, he advanced a program of Tariff Reform and Imperial Preference. The basic elements of the plan had been growing in his mind since before the South African War.[7] At the Colonial Conference of 1897 he had tried but failed to establish firmer ties of imperial unity. The fact, however, that the self-governing colonies sent troops to assist the British in South Africa during the Anglo-Boer War heartened the colonial secretary and led him to believe that an opportune time had arrived for the strengthening of imperial connections.

The Colonial Conference of 1902 appeared to frustrate that hope, but one possibility remained open. When the colonial premiers gathered in London for that meeting, as we have seen, they gave no indication of interest in forming an imperial customs union. They approved of little to better the organization of the defense of Empire, and they refuted Chamberlain's proposal for closer imperial organization in a "Council of Empire." They did, however, once more express interest in establishing an Imperial Preference system that would allow them to retain control over their own fiscal policies. Chamberlain acted on that proposition.

At this point an interesting confluence of programs occurred. The budget introduced by chancellor of the exchequer Sir Michael Hicks-Beach in 1902 contained a small duty on imported corn to finance debts resulting from the recent war. Shortly after that, Canadian prime minister Sir Wilfrid Laurier was asked to comment on the possibility of Canadian goods receiving a preference in British markets. He replied, "We are in a position to make offers to the imperial government which we could not make in 1897."[8] Laurier, consequently, linked the newly introduced British duty to the idea of preference, and Chamberlain exploited that "offer." He won the provisional consent of the cabinet to retain the duty on grain imported from foreign countries but to remit it for grain imported from the colonies. Believing the cabinet willing to make this experiment, at least for one year, he departed for a tour of South Africa. While the colonial secretary was away, however, the new chancellor of the exchequer, C. T. Ritchie, an old supporter of the Fair Trade movement but now one of Chamberlain's unforgiving foes, persuaded the Cabinet against granting preference. Returning home, Chamberlain found that preference was not to be given, and in order not to offend the colonies, he urged that the duty be repealed altogether. The 1903 budget abandoned the corn duty.

Chamberlain, however, had not abandoned his plan to alter imperial economic relations. On 15 May 1903, he made a rousing speech in Birmingham in which he challenged the prevailing fiscal orthodoxy and called upon his countrymen to recognize that consolidation of the Empire could only come from bonds of interest as well as from those of sentiment. "You have an opportunity; you will never have it again," he announced as he explained that the Canadians had offered additional tariff preference if it could be matched by British preference in their favor.[9] Tariff Reform thus became a paramount item for public debate. How would Prime Minister Balfour react to this attack on Free Trade by the most powerful of his colleagues? In an effort to keep his cabinet together, he chose a middle course and announced that he was, at this time, in favor of tariff retaliation against foreign countries as a means of fiscal reform. On September 14, Chamberlain resigned his position—not to go into opposition but to take his case to the people.

Conversion of the country to a new fiscal program would be difficult. Chamberlain knew that. Many Englishmen were attached to Free Trade as a fundamental principle of national life. Free Traders not only dominated the Liberal party but also could be found in Unionist ranks. They were bound to offer stalwart resistance. Nevertheless, despite the fact that most Liberals, whom he had defied by his departure from their party over Irish Home Rule in 1886, disliked him and some Conservatives at least distrusted him, Chamberlain was the person to spearhead the new program if anyone could. His ability at political organization, his parliamentary skill, his superb fighting qualities, and his reputation as a statesman both at home and abroad, all combined to make him a formidable proponent of any cause. As Winston Churchill, who opposed Tariff Reform, said, "We are fighting a giant."[10]

Once introduced, the issue of Tariff Reform remained an intractable part of British political life during the entire Edwardian era. It challenged so much. The national fiscal orthodoxy of Free Trade was held almost sacrosanct by British Liberals, and by many Conservatives too. In terms of general perception, Free Trade was a fundamental principle associated with, and impossible to separate from, Britain's world position and prosperity and all that those achievements represented. Tariff Reform, consequently, became a passionate political issue that compelled the attention of both the major political parties. It was a frequent subject of discussion for a number of those small, elitist groups, such as the Co-efficients Club and the Compatriots Club, that punctuated Edwardian political culture. Organizations such as the Tariff Reform League, the Free Trade League, and the Unionist Free Trade Club were formed to publicize one side or the other of the issue, and they too became a feature of Edwardian politics. The issue united the Liberal party and divided the Unionist party. It became a common subject in the popular press, and, of course, it was one that the imperial journalists followed with acute and persistent interest.

THE VOICE OF PRINTING HOUSE SQUARE

The senior staff of *The Times* took pride in the great traditions of the paper, in its collective rather than personal stature and its independence. Buckle believed the latter was the real source of its authority.[11] As we have seen, independence meant freedom from political and commercial interference, not neutrality. It meant having the leeway to editorialize based on the question, as put by Buckle, "What ought *The Times*, with its history and traditions, to say about this?"[12] With its combination of emotional public appeal and substantive depth, Tariff Reform was the type of issue that all major newspapers had to address. From the beginning to the end of the public debate surrounding it, *The Times* never failed that test.

In his autobiography, L. S. Amery, who became a fervent disciple of Chamberlain, recollected being at his office at *The Times* on the morning of May 16, the day after Chamberlain's Birmingham speech, when in rushed Leopold Maxse, the impetuous editor of the *National Review*. "Seizing both my hands in his he poured forth a paean of jubilation at the thought that, at last, there was a cause to work for in politics."[13] Such enthusiasm, however, hardly would describe the reaction of the chief figures at Printing House Square. Theirs was a careful and deliberate response.

That is not to say that they had no opinions of their own on the issue. Moberly Bell, the paper's manager, understandably wished to support Tariff Reform. He may have been, as his daughter claimed, one of the "staunchest supporters" of Chamberlain and his program from the start.[14] As an admirer of Chamberlain, he sympathized with the colonial secretary's desire for a closer union between Great Britain and the colonies.[15] Moreover, he appreciated the difficulties that existed with the country's Free Trade policy since both foreign nations and the colonies were protectionist. "If we can help to cement the Empire even by some financial sacrifice," he admitted, "we have to do it."[16] Nevertheless, he knew that the paper's approach to such a controversial issue would have to be cautious. Buckle was cautious by nature. Unfortunately, less is known about his political views than about those of any other past editors of *The Times*. He wrote his letters himself and kept no record of them. He shared his ideas and his information with few of his colleagues. After retiring as editor, however, he did provide some retrospective clues to his views at this time. On one occasion, for example, he explained himself to Jack Sandars, Balfour's private secretary, in this way: "I do not know what your opinion may be in looking back on the years 1902-5; but my feeling has always been that an incompetent . . . Chancellor of the Exchequer [C. T. Ritchie] was the true villain of the piece; and I have always regretted that his objection, & threat of resignation should have been allowed to prevent the experiment of Imperial Preference as an existing duty on corn."[17] Moreover, in reference to Chamberlain and his program Buckle later reflected that he was then on "decidedly friendly" terms with him (quite a switch from earlier years when the Radical Chamberlain was the "principal antagonist" of the paper) and "strongly supported his Colonial and Imperial policy; and followed him—with moderation—in his tariff reform policy."[18] Buckle and Bell, however, were too tied to *The Times'* tradition of impartiality to abandon it in this instance. They decided to give the issue a thorough and fair consideration and not to determine the paper's policy on it at the outset. Buckle even admitted to one devout tariff reformer that *The Times* was "wobbling" on the issue.[19]

Several distinct tendencies appeared in *The Times'* presentation of the debate surrounding Chamberlain's program. First of all, it underscored time and again that the inquiry into policy that Chamberlain sought was both necessary and timely. In advancing the question, Chamberlain performed an "unquestionable service," *The Times* claimed.[20] For too long, it contended, the people had been "too ready to accept dogma" and they should now consider setting aside "cherished preconceptions" if the results of inquiry justified doing so.[21] "Our columns bear ample witness every day to the crying need for inquiry and discussion," it editorialized.[22] And, it explained in an even more explicit statement: "We are trying to get away from the abstract, to escape from the tyranny of phrases, to set aside stereotyped deductions from 'principles' which are dead and buried in every sphere except that of tariffs, to look at things as they are, and to fit our policy to the conditions in which we live."[23]

In welcoming inquiry and in attempting to place practicality before time-honored principle, *The Times* accepted many of the premises upon which Chamberlain based his argument. It contended, for instance, that Free Trade was the preferred policy to pursue but questioned if it were possible to have it in a world where protectionist countries abounded and grew in prosperity. The paper doubted if the policy that won markets under a particular set of conditions that no longer existed should be kept at a time when those markets not only were being invaded but even were "being wrested from us by peoples who practise protection."[24] How should Britain respond to such "universal commercial hostility?"[25] As the international doors of commerce were being "shut and barricaded" against the nation, the British were helpless to do anything other than "make impotent protest in the name of fair play."[26] Where would such circumstances lead?

Throughout the debate *The Times* was emphatic in its defense of Chamberlain the man. Far from being a visionary or a reckless intruder into economic and colonial policy, Chamberlain was, in the paper's portrayal of him, a realistic, indeed inspiring, statesman who had responded to conditions that already were damaging British trade and to "the appeal of the Colonial Premiers in 1902 when they asked if something could not be done to strengthen the bonds of Empire by preferential trade arrangements."[27] When Chamberlain's critics suggested that he was acting in a manner disloyal to Balfour, the paper responded that his relationship with Balfour was one "of mutual friendship, admiration and confidence of very uncommon strength."[28] It insisted that Chamberlain was a practical and loyal public servant who, believing he detected "weak places in the Cobdenite doctrine," was responding to conditions that Richard Cobden, the patron saint of Free Trade, never had to tackle, and was pleading for "frank and open" discussion.[29] In short, Chamberlain had the honesty and strength to tackle what *The Times* believed was the necessary task of questioning the country's fiscal and imperial policies.

No theme permeated the paper's editorial articles on Tariff Reform more than the imperial one. Max Beloff has commented that this argument was the strongest one that emerged against the opposition to Tariff Reform.[30] The record of *The Times'* handling of the subject substantiates that claim. The imperial argument appeared time and again in the editorials. Beyond all question the paper believed that imperial consolidation was a vital concern for both Britain and the colonies. It reasoned along these lines:

> The British Empire makes up so large a portion of the world that its constituent parts, if brought into due union and cohesion, would for all practical purposes be independent of the remainder. How best to effect such union and cohesion is the problem which now presents itself alike to our statesmen and to our people; and upon the soundness of the conclusions at which they arrive the future greatness of the Empire must depend.[31]

The day of expansion had passed and now, the argument ran, the British had to contemplate how to keep "the Empire for the Empire." If the nation failed in that undertaking there was "nothing before us but collapse."[32] As for its own position, *The Times,* while friendly toward Chamberlain's program, hesitated to endorse it.

In the course of its commentary, the paper advanced a definition of "imperialism." To be an imperialist one did not have to agree with Chamberlain. Only agreement with the reasons that led him to propose the program was necessary. What were those reasons?

> They are that this is a critical period in the history of the Empire; that the foundations of unity are being economically sapped; that, while we are talking of sentimental bonds, other people are forging the more enduring bonds of common interest and settled business relations with our colonies; that unless we can reverse this process, the Empire must disintegrate instead of consolidating; and that it is well worth while, from the most 'squalid' as well as from the most exalted point of view, to make a serious effort, should it even involve some immediate sacrifice, in order to bind the Empire together by commerce as well as by sentiment.[33]

If one could agree with such reasons, he was an "Imperialist" even though he might disapprove of Chamberlain's particular program. If one did not agree he was a "non-Imperialist" and if one opposed such reasons he was an "anti-Imperialist."

Indeed, *The Times* acknowledged the fact that Free Traders could be genuine imperialists. Differences between imperialists were only of degree. Urging Free Trade imperialists to be flexible it argued, "You will surely not refuse to budge upon a question of a little more or a little less, when by showing flexibility you render possible a scheme for strengthening the Empire which at least offers some prospect of success, and to which there is no alternative but inaction." Imperialists, it stated, cared more for the Empire than for "blind adhesion" to the outdated gospel of Free Trade.[34]

If from the beginning *The Times* stopped short of endorsing Chamberlain's program, it offered little opposition to it. The paper insisted that Tariff Reform receive the prominence it deserved. Buckle was correct in saying the paper was "wobbling" in its handling of the subject, for he himself did not wish to go the whole way with Chamberlain. Bell, on the other hand, sympathized with Chamberlain's program but had some doubts about its success.[35] Nevertheless, no one could say that they failed to provide Tariff Reform a compatible forum with which to reach an important audience. There are not only the paper's own editorials, supportive of the cause if not the program itself, to consider. In June 1903, when discussion of Chamberlain's proposal was flourishing, the paper engaged W. A. S. Hewins, the organizer and first director of the London School of Economics, whose reputation as a reformer and as a critic of the Free Trade orthodoxy went back to the late 1880s, to contribute a series of articles on the subject.[36] Hewins, who incidentally agreed that Buckle was rather "wobbly" on the issue, strongly advocated Tariff Reform.[37] He responded with a long, authoritative exposition of sixteen articles extolling the virtues of fiscal reform and preference. Those articles received not only prominent display in the paper but also its frequent and friendly editorial references. In response to Hewins's articles, which *The Times* published anonymously, by signing them "An Economist," fourteen economists signed a manifesto condemning his views but not his motives. The paper also published that statement, and it tried to persuade Alfred Marshall, the foremost academic economist of the day, to engage in a public correspondence with Hewins over the issue. Marshall, however, refused that offer.

It was then that Leopold Amery provided his own response to the manifesto. This young man, who would spend a lifetime arguing the case for the Empire, had considerable intellectual range and depth. He was now in London serving as a leader writer for the paper and as its military correspondent, and he supported Chamberlain from the start.[38] Early in August 1903, Buckle allowed Amery to publish three of his own statements in answer to the eminent professors. Written as letters to the editor under the pseudonym "Tariff Reformer," they defended Chamberlain and attempted to counter the manifesto. Years later Amery wrote in his memoirs, "If my long political life has had any meaning it has lain in my constant struggle to keep the Tory Party true to a policy of Imperial greatness and social progress."[39] He was championing that idea already in 1903.

Amery's son, however, was only partially correct some years later when he wrote that "*The Times* was . . . a main exponent of the new policy."[40] As we have seen, such a statement fails to describe the paper's position at this time when its support for the proposal was contextual rather than explicit. But his father was an enthusiastic Tariff Reformer. He wrote a number of *The Times'* editorials on the subject as well as his own "Tariff Reformer" articles, and it was Amery who persuaded Hewins to write his series of articles for the paper.[41]

Nevertheless, *The Times'* official position on the proposal was non-committal. The harsh treatment it dealt to Chamberlain's critics as well as the emphasis it placed on colonial news and responses to the program were indications of where its sympathies lay. Still, the paper did not endorse the program as such. Most of all, it wished to take the lead in the imperial education of the British, believing that it was a prerequisite to the realization of imperial unity.[42]

In attempting to achieve that goal, Buckle and Bell believed they had treated the issue of Tariff Reform impartially. Whether others perceived it as impartial, however, is open to question. Bell claimed the paper received about the same number of letters each week "lauding our impartiality as we receive others deploring our partiality" and reflected that "the writers never seem to realize that what they regard as impartiality is only coincidence in views and what they call partiality is difference in views."[43] Regardless, when St. Loe Strachey of the *Spectator* suggested *The Times* had been partial in handling the subject of Tariff Reform, he received a pointed response from the paper's manager. "You have no right to say . . . that *The Times* has 'dropped its better tradition of impartiality,' because that is a statement which is untrue and therefore unjust and offensive," Bell declared. He also told Strachey that J. A. Spender of the *Westminster Gazette* had made a similar charge against *The Times* for which he already had received an apology. As he told Strachey: "He [Spender] excused its appearance by his own absence from the office, expressed his regret that it should have appeared and acknowledged that our impartiality could not be called into question. You have possibly the same excuse—I feel sure you will act as honourably."[44]

In fact, *The Times* questioned some aspects of Chamberlain's program. Would it cause foreign powers to retaliate economically against the colonies?[45] What was the position of India going to be in the scheme? Would the program impair harmony within the Unionist party? The last of these concerns no doubt explains the paper's profuse efforts to reconcile the opinions of Chamberlain and Balfour. Regardless, Chamberlain had raised a necessary question and as Moberly Bell said, he did not regret it. "I believe the probable result will be something that avoids the two extremes and that will in the long run benefit the Empire if properly thrashed out."[46]

J. L. GARVIN

The vigorous advocacy of fiscal reform that Garvin provided made the "impartiality" of *The Times*, however construed, appear sedate in comparison. He championed that cause as well as that of the Empire with a verve and power given to few journalists in his or any other time. Before he gained the editorship of the *Observer* in 1908, Garvin already had a reputation for being a power in the British press; but not until 1905, when he began a two-year association with the *Outlook*, did he hold an editorial chair. He made his name as a contributor to journals, particularly the *Fortnightly Review*, and as a leader and special writer for the *Daily Telegraph*. A study of his writing on the Tariff Reform issue in 1903 helps to explain why his reputation grew, and it introduces us to the thinking of one of Chamberlain's most enthusiastic supporters. His lengthy expositions contained a combativeness and an analytical quality sufficient to make them one of the most distinct series to appear in Edwardian journalism.

Though his articles on the subject were exhaustive and can by no means be recapitulated here in full, it is possible to detect in them the broader categories of argument that Garvin employed. He began by attempting to define the problem and place it in the fullest possible setting as he perceived it. Then he addressed himself to emerging apprehensions and criticisms of Chamberlain's scheme. Finally, he offered an assessment of what Britain had to do in order to engage the future with confidence.

In terms of his own persuasion, Garvin believed that Chamberlain had raised the "issue of an epoch." It represented the first real attempt by any British statesman to construct a policy for the Empire, and upon the outcome of the effort hinged the whole industrial future of Britain as well as the continuance of the Empire. In Garvin's words this was "not a matter, as the doctrinaires would have us believe, for economic logic-chopping or for repeating pious phrases as Tibetans turn praying-wheels."[47] He detected in the coming struggle over Tariff Reform "the revolt of a whole generation" that rejected "the dead hand of traditional Radicalism" and wished to adapt to the condition of its time.[48] "Darwin's law of the struggle for existence has taught us," Garvin reflected, "that survival depends upon adaptation to environment, upon the power of a living type to change as all around it changes. That is the iron law for nations as for nature."[49] Examination of available statistics on a wide range of economic topics led Garvin to conclude that, as a result of the last thirty years of trading, Britain's commercial supremacy had been destroyed. Trade with the colonies was an exception to the rule.[50] Therefore, the need to change the country's economic and imperial policy had become a national imperative. Either she would change, or despite whatever temporary economic successes remained for her, continue to decline.

By word and figure, Garvin produced a dismal picture of the state of British economic life. He portrayed the increase in production, exports, and population that Germany and the United States had experienced in recent decades. Germany's iron and steel output now exceeded Britain's; that of the United States was twice as great. During the last twenty years, Britain had slipped from first place to third in terms of iron and steel production. Garvin even feared that unless she recovered her position in iron and steel production vis à vis Germany, Britain could not hope to retain its "shipbuilding and carrying supremacy nor could . . . [she] permanently keep the sea."[51] His analysis of economic realities called into question Britain's existing trading policy. Between 1899 and 1902 German importation of British goods decreased (from £31,000,000 to £27,800,000) while during the same time German exports to the United Kingdom increased (from £40,000,000 to £48,000,000).[52] A similar pattern was found in the case of the United States. British exports to the United States had dropped from £40,700,000 in 1872 to £32,100,000 in 1890 to £23,800,000 in 1902.[53] Meanwhile, since 1890, the year of the McKinley tariff, America had increased her sales to Britain from £97,280,000 to £141,000,000.[54]

In general, British exports appeared to be losing their competitive edge and Garvin offered his readers the following proof.[55]

Comparative Exports, 1872-1902

	1872 Million £	1890 Million £	1900 Million £	1902 Million £
British Exports:				
To British possessions	61	87	94	109
To Foreign Countries	196	176	197	174
Total	257	263	291	283
German Exports	116	166	238	241
French Exports	150	150	164	170
U. S. Exports	89	176	304	282

As can be seen from the preceding figures, Britain *was* progressing economically. Nevertheless, Garvin warned that the country was progressing at a "feeble rate . . . , not enough to prevent us from being driven down by the two great protected countries to the third place in the world commerce, long before the twentieth century . . . entered upon its second quarter."[56]

Such figures led Garvin to conclude that the Free Trade policy, which he preferred to call only a free import policy, had failed the British. Other countries legislated tariffs and prospered. By Free Trade, however, Britain opened its markets to foreign competitors while allowing those same competitors to tax British goods. Since tariffs would continue to restrict British trade, the only way to increase output would be to secure the home market and expand the colonial. Only preference could achieve that end.

In 1846 England had been the chief workshop of the world. Why had its economic position changed? Was the prosperity of workers secured? Beyond obvious reasons associated with the arrival on the world scene of new industrial competitors, Garvin believed that the failure of Free Trade explained the change. "After sixty years of Free Trade," he observed, "we are told by Sir Henry Campbell-Bannerman that we must no longer speak of the submerged tenth, but of the submerged third."[57] He believed that Richard Cobden had been wrong in his calculations in 1846 when he led the fight to repeal the Corn Laws just as Free Traders were now mistaken in adhering to their philosophy. Cobden had imagined that the world would follow the British example of Free Trade.[58] It had not. The prosperity Britain enjoyed in the thirty years following the repeal of the Corn Laws appeared to justify Cobdenism, but, in fact, Garvin claimed that the source of that prosperity was not Free Trade but rather the need for British products and investment occasioned by the discovery of gold in California and Australia, the development of steam and rail transportation, and the mid-nineteenth-century wars. Moreover, during those years of prosperity, the cost of bread and meat rose as did the cost of living in general. "But the nation had higher profits and higher wages, and preferred them though food was dearer than before the repeal of the Corn Laws," Garvin said. "In other words, it is successful production that creates prosperity, not cheap consumption." Finally, he claimed that Free Trade failed utterly in the second generation after the repeal of the Corn Laws as a new economic epoch sprang to life with "the industrial awakening of the Continent and America . . . , and with it the end of the manufacturing monopoly we had held for a century."[59]

The problem, however, had a brighter side. Britain possessed a great asset in its colonial trade, which had increased from £61,000,000 in 1872 to £109,000,000 in 1903. In the process, Garvin contended that particular trade had saved Britain's "commercial supremacy."[60] Aside from the colonies there were the country's fine geographical position, its port facilities, its rich coal resources, its command of the sea, and its immense accumulated wealth to consider. He acknowledged advantages such as these and claimed Chamberlain's proposed program would develop them as Free Trade never could hope to do. Yet Garvin recognized that many of his countrymen opposed Chamberlain's scheme and others were uneasy about it.

As a true conservative, Garvin believed that England was "always more and greater than her people." He thought in terms of generations, of national continuity, and of historical responsibility. All generations pass, and the present one must learn to look "before and after" and to apply the results of such vision to the realities of the present. Why did Englishmen hesitate to act in this manner regarding economic policy? The answer brings us to the second broad category of Garvin's argumentation, British apprehensions about abandoning Free Trade.

Essentially, he believed, there were two reasons for the British reluctance to support Chamberlain's program. They were attached to the principle of Free Trade, and they feared that the introduction of colonial preference would damage the economy in other areas. Garvin had little patience with the way in which much of the British mind remained fixed on the idea of Free Trade. "Unreasoning tradition," he protested, obscured "rational discussion." Specifically, he argued: "The policy of the Corn Laws has been more perversely misread than any other chapter in our history. . . . Upon this subject alone the opinions of a violent fanaticism have been accepted as a substitute for research and fostered by an outworn party endeavoring to establish a claim upon the confidence of the future by writing a certificate of its own services in the past." Believers in Free Trade simply ignored historical facts, and according to Garvin, misinformed the public. When Lord Rosebery referred to the thirty years before the repeal of the Corn Laws as a time of "terror, horror, [and] famine," Garvin charged that the former prime minister spoke the language of mythology. During the thirty years before the repeal, he reasoned, there had actually been a decided decline in wheat prices, but no parallel reduction had occurred during the thirty years after repeal.[61]

Another apprehension about Chamberlain's program rested on the fear that Germany and the United States would retaliate if the British introduced tariffs. Garvin believed that the retaliation argument also was a myth and thought the proper reply to "industrious partisans who threaten us with the anger of Protectionist countries—with retaliation and reprisals—if we dare to call our economic soul our own, . . . [was] the reply of Dr. Johnson to the disappointed lady who asked why the wicked words were not in the dictionary. 'You have been looking for them, madam!'"[62] Specifically, he reasoned that the recent German exclusion of Canada from "most favored nation treatment" simply was a case of Germany's effort to prevent greater imperial unity in the British Empire. The fact was that Germany exported more to the United Kingdom, India, Australia, Canada, and South Africa than she imported from them, and she would not place that valuable export trade in jeopardy.[63] Fears about American retaliation were equally groundless, he argued. They reflected only "the catchwords of reactionary Radicals" who insisted on, to use the words of Lord Beaconsfield, "making themselves miserable in anticipation of evils that never occur."[64] The reaction of the United States to imperial reciprocity, in fact, was crucial, but Garvin claimed that no economic retaliation would come from that quarter. Chamberlain proposed only a mild form of the very principles that guided the Americans in their tariff policy, and the United States, with its expanding economy, needed the British market. It was her best one. Moreover, the United States had just negotiated a reciprocity treaty with Cuba and "therefore admits our right to arrange a preferential tariff with any British possession."[65] So Garvin announced that "the nightmare of a tariff struggle with the world . . . [was] the merest figment of unpractical imaginations."[66]

Opponents of Chamberlain claimed he stood for "dear food" while they defended "free food." Garvin countered that claim with a number of arguments. Many imports into Britain (e.g., tea, sugar, coffee, cocoa) were already taxed. Chamberlain, he pointed out, proposed to readjust these existing "Free Trade taxes" and on the balance to reduce the overall taxation on food by introducing Imperial Preference. It was not, he observed, a matter of taxing food but whether those taxes contributed to "economic *waste*" or were "*productive*" by intent. Besides, the price of bread already varied from place to place in the United Kingdom by as much as three halfpence per four-pound loaf. Chamberlain only suggested a tax of a halfpenny for that loaf and would use it for the purpose of extending trade. Preference, moreover, would encourage production both in Canada and in England and place "supply ahead of demand" and thus lower prices. Workingmen in Britain had nothing to fear from such a program.[67] In fact, there was much to be gained from it that went beyond the price of food. It would increase the exporting power of Britain and increase the demand for British labor. Under protection Americans received higher wages than British workers under Free Trade. Imperial Preference would improve the relative position of British labor. But for that to occur British trade had to improve. British workers had turned to trade unionism for individual protection, and now Garvin urged them to accept the idea of a tariff as a protection of trade.[68]

Given the correctness of Garvin's analysis, which others debated, the economic condition of Britain was precarious at best and dangerous at worst. Increasingly, it seemed that the country's economic position was eroding and if that trend continued, the country might find herself at the mercy of other nations for both imports and exports. Thus, Garvin devoted the third broad category of his writing on this subject to describing what the British had to do to improve their economic condition.

He prescribed a number of remedies. Free Trade, of course, had to be abandoned. Britain's competitive position had to be restored. "Efficiency," a much-discussed term in Edwardian Britain, had to be achieved. Free Trade would not guarantee "industrial efficiency" and protection would not prevent it, Garvin argued as he asked, "What has developed the industrial efficiency of our protected rivals?"[69] Indeed, one reason he so admired Chamberlain was that in him he detected "efficiency of mind and action."[70] That "efficiency" appeared in his programs. The tariff he proposed was not intended for "protection"; it was aimed at fostering "development." The issue, as Garvin saw it, was between the "drift" of laissez faire and the "dynamic principles of public policy" formed in Chamberlain's proposals. Laissez faire had been rejected in social policy; the time had come to reject it as commercial policy.[71] On the people's ability to recognize the need for the type of development offered by Chamberlain's program, he believed, rested the country's future security and the maintenance of its empire.

In fact, the future of the Empire was a topic that ran throughout Garvin's writing on Tariff Reform. He held that the "unpeopled parts of the King's dominions will be to the twentieth century what the Far West of the United States was to the nineteenth."[72] His concept of Empire far exceeded mere commercial considerations, though they were central to it. It involved the "English idea" and "British power." Continued life of the "English idea" depended on increasing the fabric of Empire, and mere sentiment and interest could not accomplish that end. Garvin claimed that Cobden "believed and hoped that Free Trade would be the dissolvent" of the British Empire.[73] Believing that the "age of separation" was over and that "the organization of the world" was proceeding, Garvin said that the breakup of the Empire would occasion "the greatest question of redistribution known to history" and would "plunge the world in war." On the other hand, "the final consolidation of the British Empire would be by far the greatest step ever taken towards the ultimate integration of mankind."[74] Only strong nations, he claimed, could serve humanity. What we have learned of the past, we have learned from nations during epochs of their political greatness or national vigor. This, his argument ran, was true since the days of Greece and Rome. Garvin spoke of how people in their aggregate numbers compose humanity and seem to "strengthen or decay according to variations in their national vitality and national achievement." A nation contributes to humanity by its example and by pursuing ideals "in the process of . . . [its] own development."[75] Therefore, the fiscal reformers who now sought to reconstruct imperial relations were trying to serve humanity by serving their own country. They were slaves of no universal panacea, he reflected.[76]

Garvin's sensitivity to the theme of imperial decline was pronounced. Would the Empire survive even another century? The question disturbed him. Observing not only the emergence of Germany and the United States as great powers but also what he called the "Asiatic renaissance" and the Russia of a generation hence, he foresaw either the breakup of imperial Britain or its greater consolidation. Chamberlain's program would give the Empire the chance it needed to continue its existence. His fiscal reforms would maintain and develop its political power. Therefore, Garvin concluded, Chamberlain's ideals on Empire were the greatest to appear since the time of Chatham. With them the colonies could be developed, the sea secured, and the homeland economically revived. A reorganized imperial economy could lead to imperial self-sufficiency. Canada, he felt, was the keystone. If Britain rejected Imperial Preference, then Canada would accept American reciprocity and the Empire would "become for all moral purposes a myth."[77] Gone would be that noble "Shakespearean vision of an Imperial sea-state with England at the center."[78] If Cobdenism were allowed to remain the economic principle for the Empire in the twentieth century, it would produce its demise. "We can have free imports without an Empire," Garvin warned, "but we can have no Empire without preference."[79]

As we have seen, Garvin's articles at this time appeared in several journals and newspapers. His articles in the *Daily Telegraph* deserve special mention. Seventeen in number, these long expositions later were published collectively in book form. After reading his article of 15 July 1903, Chamberlain told the Duke of Devonshire, "I do not see any answer to it and it puts my case better than I have seen it stated elsewhere."[80] Indeed, some people believed that Chamberlain himself had either written or inspired those articles. He made this comment about the series when it was reprinted in booklet form:

> In my opinion they constitute a conclusive indictment of our present one-sided system of Free Imports. They make clear to every impartial reader the changes which have taken place in our commercial relations and positions since our existing fiscal policy was first established. They indicate the conditions which justified that policy at the time when it was accepted, and which now call loudly for its modification to bring it into harmony with modern requirements. . . .
>
> All the points here mentioned [by Chamberlain in this letter] are developed with a wealth of facts and figures and original illustrations in the articles now reprinted. These form a complete popular hand-book on the subject and will be most valuable to students and speakers in the coming campaign.[81]

In retrospect it is impossible to deny the contribution Garvin made to the great debate over Tariff Reform. Whether he was right or wrong, the force, sweep, and intelligence contained in his writing on the subject made his pronouncements ones with which journalists on the opposite side of the debate would have to reckon.

ST. LOE STRACHEY

The editor and proprietor of the *Spectator* was a leader in providing that reckoning. Strachey's journalistic style differed sharply from Garvin's, as did his views on Tariff Reform. Yet like Garvin, he saw much to admire in Chamberlain. In fact, Strachey felt a "very warm affection" for Chamberlain personally and recognized that in him there was much in which the nation could take pride. "He was a good fighter and an unwearied worker, and he spent himself ungrudgingly in the service of his country." As a politician he was above "grumbling," Strachey claimed, and he admitted Chamberlain's "genius for friendship," even his qualities as a "natural chieftain."[82] From the late 1880s until 1903, Strachey reflected in his memoirs, he and Chamberlain were on intimate terms. "I think he was fond of me. I know I was fond of him," he wrote.[83] There is no reason to doubt his sincerity in making that statement. Chamberlain once told Strachey that he could not be offended by "honest newspaper criticism" and hoped that differences between himself and the *Spectator* would not emerge.[84]

Personal feelings notwithstanding, differences did appear. Strachey believed that "a newspaper at a moment of political and national crisis is obliged to adopt a definite line and without delay."[85] When Chamberlain delivered the speech that launched his great challenge to Free Trade on 15 May 1903, Strachey felt that such a moment had arrived. Adamant in his convictions on the fiscal question, he made the *Spectator*, as Garvin said, "the principal Free Trade organ in the country."[86]

During the great debate over Tariff Reform, the *Spectator* was the most influential journal of the Unionist Free Traders and, aside from the *Edinburgh Review*, the only one. Composing the ranks of the Unionist Free Traders were old Whigs such as the Duke of Devonshire, old guard Tories such as Sir Michael Hicks-Beach and Lord Balfour of Burleigh, and several promising young Unionists, most notably Winston Churchill (until he switched to the Liberal party) and Lord Hugh Cecil. The Unionist Free Traders represented the opposition to Tariff Reform within the Unionist party. Although their numbers were sharply reduced after the Election of 1906 and dissolved in 1910, they composed a vigorous group with sixty-five members in the House of Commons during the early years of the Tariff Reform controversy.[87] Strachey attempted to articulate their position in the press, but since he was an old Liberal Unionist, his advice, especially his efforts to be conciliatory toward Liberal Imperialists such as H. H. Asquith and Sir Edward Grey, did not always please the Conservatives among the Unionist Free Traders.[88] Still, the *Spectator* remained their main outlet in the press. The Tariff Reformers had no greater opponent in British journalism than Strachey, who was a doctrinaire Free Trader.

He believed the Chamberlainite position was fallible in all of its parts. For instance, Strachey dismissed the statistical analysis that Chamberlain, Garvin, and others advanced as an "Abuse of Export Trade Statistics." To be certain, Strachey admitted that Britain's exports had not grown as rapidly as its production, but he argued that such observation overlooked the importance of internal trade. Britain, he claimed, produced five or six times as many goods as it exported.[89] Moreover, he claimed that trade had not been stagnant for the past thirty years but that, to the contrary, it had been "going up by leaps and bounds." By citing the increase of capital investment both at home and abroad, the increase in wages, and improvements in housing, he demonstrated that many signs of prosperity existed. Go into any workingman's house, Strachey suggested, and decide whether or not the conditions of its residents were better or worse than they were thirty years before.[90] At one point, he even advertised: "WANTED: AN INDUSTRY RUINED BY FREE TRADE." After searching for a month, he had been unable to find one, so he invited the *Spectator*'s correspondents to help in the search by submitting information about any such ruined industry known to them.[91]

The counterarguments that Strachey raised in the *Spectator* struck the Chamberlainite position at many points. To the claim that the British accepted Free Trade in the first place believing that the rest of the world would follow, Strachey charged there was no proof. Free Trade, he said, had been adopted for two reasons: to terminate "endless varieties of taxation" and to respond to the mass of the people who "would no longer endure the inhuman taxation of their food." As a matter of fact Strachey noted that Chamberlain was "no historian, or he would not talk such nonsense about the causes of the decline of Spain and Holland; and we may pardon his scorn for the history of England in consideration of the glowing picture he draws of England's future."[92]

The *Spectator*'s position was that protection and preference had ill-served Britain when they existed in the past and that they represented a false hope for the financial, industrial, and social well-being of the country in the future. They would not supply the steady source of money needed to finance social reforms such as the introduction of old-age pensions; they would not produce the increased prosperity the Chamberlainites promised.[93] Moreover, the introduction of tariffs as a weapon of retaliation to use when threatened by protectionist powers was a dangerous remedy because there were better means of retaliation. Should the need arise, say against Germany, Britain might retaliate by refusing to act in common with Germany in any part of the world or by denying Germany use of coaling stations. But why prepare to retaliate against Germany by taxing the British poor?[94] Did the colonies actually urge Britain to grant preferential duties to them? Strachey produced evidence in the form of a number of recent statements by various colonial premiers to the effect that they were willing to give Britain preference while expecting nothing in return.[95] Free Trade had restrained corruption "in the citadel of the race"; it had enabled "the poor man to exchange his hard-earned wages for the fullest amount of food with which the world can supply him"; and it had given the nation a vital position on the sea. Why should such a successful policy now be changed?[96] With arguments such as these Strachey turned his paper into a major vehicle of opposition to Chamberlain and his supporters.

Yet to be considered, however, is the imperial argument that Strachey used. With it the core of his thinking on the subject can be appreciated. Simply stated, Strachey believed that, despite all the claims to the contrary, Tariff Reform would be detrimental to the Empire. In this belief he was adamant, and the imperial argument remained a prominent part of his writing throughout the controversy.

In his first major commentary after Chamberlain's Birmingham speech, Strachey announced his views in defense of Free Trade. "We are Imperialists first and Free Traders afterwards," he proclaimed, "for Free-Trade is but a counsel of economic perfection, while the Imperial Union is, in our view, vital to the race." Would Chamberlain's proposals prevent "the decay of the Empire," increase its wealth, foster its unity, or secure its future? Strachey refused to believe they would. Instead, he contended that although it was possible that the colonial secretary's scheme would bring a momentary flash of apparent prosperity to the Empire, in the long run it would be a "deadly blow" from which the Empire would begin "to die at the heart." "It is, therefore, because we are Imperialists, and not because we are Free-Traders, that we oppose Mr. Chamberlain in this matter, and urge the nation to reject his advice," he reiterated. The proposals forwarded by Chamberlain, Strachey claimed, raised false hopes, did not serve the needs of the great variety of interests present throughout the Empire, were potentially disruptive, and would destroy the freedom of action that had come to characterize imperial relations. Strachey concluded this page-and-a-half-long initial denunciation of the Chamberlain program by labeling it "Tied-House" imperialism. "The Empire can be great and strong," he said, "without the Mother-country making the Colonies, or the Colonies making the Mother-country, a 'tied house.'"[97]

Strachey returned to this theme many times. In the process, he projected the Free Trade Unionists into the center of the controversy in the press, and he made the *Spectator* a major voice in the party and thrust of political debate on the issue. For instance, when Chamberlain charged that Unionist Free Traders were imperialists only in theory but in practice "Little Englanders," Strachey replied that their Free Trade imperialism was the only "truly Imperial cause." By comparison, he accused Chamberlain of favoring an "antiquated and illiberal policy—the panacea of the 'tied house,' derived in its essentials from the policy of the men who lost us America." If such a policy, which Strachey claimed was nothing more than a mixture of preferences and "old fashioned" protection, were adopted, "it would strike both at the heart and at the extremities of the Empire."[98]

In a similar fashion, his view of the imperial past and present was quite the opposite from that which the Chamberlainites were fond of advancing. He claimed that once before, Britain had colonial links similar to the ones Chamberlain now favored. "Some eighty years ago . . . the Mother-country and the Colonies were bound fast by the preferential system . . . [and it] galled, irritated, wounded, and cut in to the flesh. . . . Not till they were abolished did the tumult of accusations of unkindness on one side and of disloyalty on the other die away." Following the abolition of that system Britain adopted a policy of Free Trade, which in turn became the guiding principle for relations between

Britain and the colonies. Under its banner, links of a new sort developed in the Empire, links of "brotherhood, of a common loyalty and of a sense of pride and gratitude." These ties, which the Chamberlainites were so ready to dismiss, Strachey claimed, were the ones that encouraged the colonial support given Britain in her recent effort to hold South Africa. Moreover, the colonies were developing each according to their particular needs as young self-governing parts of the Empire, or as Strachey preferred to call them, "free nations." Closer union could only come in time, when "great free nations within a free Empire, . . . [had] grown to sufficient wealth and population and power to enable them to enter upon a closer union with the Mother-country on something like equal terms." Chamberlain, however, wished to reverse this development and force union now by methods that lost the thirteen American colonies for the British and had, after that, caused friction with Canada.[99]

Strachey believed that the Empire of the past half century had been marked by a "Sane Imperialism" that allowed both political and commercial freedom to flourish. A new attitude that centered on development and maintenance of Empire, thanks to Free Trade, now had replaced older exploitative notions about imperial relations. Such was the imperial image that he developed in numerous *Spectator* articles. In summary, he held that Free Trade, as a guiding principle of Empire, was sound according to "the teachings of history," and that it produced not only a "minimum of popular hatred" but also "the best possible foundation-stone for the Empire" of the present and for imperial unity in the future.[100]

Contemporaries recognized Strachey's defense of the Empire and Free Trade, unabashed though it may have been, as an important factor in the Tariff Reform debate. "I confess it has been a much greater shock to me than usual to read in my *Spectator* of all papers that Free Trade is superior to all moral, social and political considerations," Valentine Chirol, *The Times'* foreign editor, complained to Strachey when the debate was only a few weeks old.[101] No matter, Strachey continued his line, as the Liberal J. A. Spender said, "unflinchingly and most courageously."[102] In fact, Strachey's defense of Free Trade and his utter rejection of Chamberlain's program was the most serious break he ever made with the bulk of Unionists. But looking back on that rupture many years later he wrote, "I believed that the policy of Tariff Reform, if carried out, would end by breaking up instead of uniting the British Empire, which I desired above all things to maintain 'in health and strength long to live.'"[103]

Regardless, it is important to grasp the difficulty of Strachey's position, estranged, as it became, from the main body of Unionists. After leaving the Liberal party over the Irish Home Rule issue in the mid 1880s, he became, in his own words, "a Liberal-Unionist and then an unhyphenated Unionist and a loyal supporter of Lord Salisbury, Mr. Balfour and their administration." People, he said, were surprised that he became "so strong a Unionist."[104] Nevertheless, he found it impossible to remain in sympathy with the bulk of the party once it began to accept Tariff Reform. So he became prominent in forming and then in leading the Free Trade wing of the party. The Unionist Free Traders, however, were not strong enough to form a party of their own, though in years to come they toyed with the idea of uniting with moderate Liberals to form a new Center party. When that failed, they were left to fend for themselves in retaining or finding an effective political role to play. Strachey himself was more willing than some other Unionist Free Traders to cooperate with the Liberals. In the Election of 1906, he even advised Unionist Free Traders to vote for Liberal candidates in constituencies where no one of their own persuasion was running. Yet in the post-election years, he, and the Unionist Free Traders, for whom he spoke, found themselves in a treacherous bind. As their influence waned among the majority of Unionists, they were unable to create a new counterbalancing position for themselves among Liberals. The latter, whose parliamentary majority was great during the three years following the election, saw little reason to accept advice from Unionist Free Traders who opposed most of their programs except for Free Trade. Therefore, it is easier to think of Strachey as an editor committed to principle rather than to party in the coming years.

J. A. SPENDER

In Spender's case, commitment to principle and to party were one. Liberal though he was, he could never be called an enemy of the Empire. He made his *Westminster Gazette* a bastion of defense for Free Trade and for a Free Trade Empire. Writing in his memoirs nearly a quarter of a century later, he could remember "nothing quite like the sensation caused by his [Chamberlain's] speech at Birmingham on May 15th, in which he declared food taxes and Preference to be essential to the Empire, and said flatly that he intended this to be the issue at the next Election."[105]

Spender had good reason for recalling that dramatic moment, for it was then that he launched one of his own campaigns. From the middle of May until the end of the year, his *Westminster Gazette* attacked Tariff Reform constantly. Hardly a day passed without the paper addressing a leading article to the subject. He later claimed he was well served in this effort. Others on the staff contributed according to their own expertise. Charles Geake mastered the statistical side of the argument, while F. Carruthers Gould, the *Westminster*'s gifted cartoonist, reduced tangled arguments to simple, humorous portrayals. The paper became a forum not only for Liberal Free Traders anxious to lend their support but also for disgruntled Unionist Free Traders. Some of the latter even wrote unsigned articles in the paper on the subject. Lord Cromer, the much heralded proconsul of Empire who had been so successful in his administration of Egypt and who was a doctrinaire Free Trader, also helped. He invited Spender to see him and after that initial meeting, wrote numerous letters to him on specific points of arguments, "the substance of which the editor conveyed into the *Westminster*."[106]

In reading through the *Westminster* for 1903, one cannot help but be impressed by the clarity and persuasion of its leading articles. They reveal Spender's own genius.[107] Every time Chamberlain delivered a speech on Tariff Reform, a *Westminster* leader examined it and exposed its perceived fallacies and contradictions. When *The Times* ran its long series of pro–Tariff Reform articles by an "Economist," the *Westminster* delighted in criticizing them and frequently turning the arguments advanced therein against the cause for which they had been written. When the *National Review* published the "Economics of Empire" by its assistant editor, the pseudonym Garvin used when writing for that journal, the *Westminster* analyzed that formidable pro-Chamberlain discourse and concluded that it was only in the "Imperial Economics" of a "Fiscal Wonderland" that such an argument made sense. It termed the arguments advanced in the "Economics of Empire" mere "nonsense."[108] It is no wonder that when the *Fortnightly Review* published a pro–Tariff Reform article in June 1903 by "Calchas" (another of Garvin's pseudonyms), which appeared to be "irrefutable and conclusive," the publication invited Spender to answer it in the next issue.[109]

His leading articles, renowned in their day, were read by both Liberals and Unionists. Always the main feature of the paper because of their prominent front page position, these articles gave the *Westminster* its reputation. In them Spender examined all sides of the Tariff Reform issue. Sometimes he would approach the subject from a mainly domestic perspective. Unionist leadership, for example, was not of one mind on the position the party should take on the issue and Spender exploited that situation.[110] Likewise, the taxes entailed in the program were a political liability, and the *Westminster* was quick to observe that working-class voters, who only recently had resented a one-shilling duty on corn, would now have to endure a tax on corn, meat, and other food supplies as well as on raw materials that Britain imported from the colonies. Meanwhile, imports from foreign nations were also to be taxed. Thus, said the *Westminster* , the three-fourths of the nation's trade which was with foreign countries would be taxed so that a significant amount of taxes could be remitted for the remaining fourth of the trade that was with the colonies.[111] Regarding Chamberlain's claim that the taxes on foreign imports could be used for old-age pensions, the paper retorted that if the Empire became self-sufficient, as Chamberlain hoped, duties would decrease to a point of insignificance and that the workers would then have to pay for their own pensions.[112] Tariff Reform simply involved too many risks. The country would lose its best markets in the hope of encouraging the development of "inexhaustible resources" in Canada, Australia, and other colonial areas where the population was far too small to develop those resources.[113] Chamberlain's plan, it charged, would force the forty million inhabitants of the United Kingdom into a perilous economic position.

It is also clear that Spender rejected both the view of the past and the interpretation of the present that Chamberlain and his supporters were fond of advancing. He argued that the British people were asked to accept a false view of Richard Cobden and John Bright, the great nineteenth-century radical spokesman, one that portrayed them as merely acting in the behalf of manufacturing and middle-class interests while leaving untouched their humanitarian impulses. Moreover, the last fifty years, or the Free Trade period, was quite the opposite from that which the Tariff Reformers claimed. It was a time during which Britain had amassed a foreign and shipping trade "unique in the world," had avoided great depressions, and had given its people the benefits of "cheap food and cheap commodities." Now, Chamberlain asked the nation to set aside all that prosperity.[114] Moreover, he and those who endorsed his scheme had allowed themselves to be misled by an erroneous interpretation of statistics. They dated the decline of Britain's position from 1872, an unrepresentative year to use as a basis for comparison. British trade in that year was swollen abnormally by circumstances produced by the war between France and Germany and by a boom in Britain's own iron and coal industries. The proper way to deal with such figures was to use quinquennial averages, which allowed for temporary fluctuations, the *Westminster* cautioned. Accordingly, it produced figures to show that in spite of ups and downs, the tendency had been "upwards." Mr. Chamberlain's idea that British trade had been stagnant was therefore "fantastic and illusory."[115]

Those words also described Spender's opinion of Chamberlain's perception of the present. Of course, improved methods and machinery might make Britain's productive machine still "more efficient" but there was a limit "to what a given population in a given area will produce" and the United Kingdom had "very nearly reached it." As for the industrial rise of the German Empire and the United States, that was a fact to be expected "unless we seriously expected the rest of the world to stop still and rely on us for production." The British, contrary to the claims of Chamberlain, had performed well in the face of the new competition and still were ahead of both Germany and the United States in terms of the total export of manufactured goods. Accordingly, Chamberlain's panic about the signs of a decaying Empire was needless.[116]

But, as was the case with Strachey, the argument Spender returned to more, perhaps, than any other was the imperial one. Like Strachey, he developed it from the moment of Chamberlain's Birmingham speech of May 15. Simply put, he contended that Chamberlain's scheme was "as bad Imperial policy as it . . . [was] bad fiscal policy."[117] Throughout the months that followed he argued that if accepted, the plan would promote disunity between Britain and the colonies. It would "plunge us into controversies between various interests in different Colonies"; it would make the colonies a burden for residents of the mother country and thus encourage ill-feelings about the Colonies among the Englishmen; and it would divide the country and parties on the issue of

Empire.[118] Chamberlain's plan for imperial consolidation, consequently, was one that would place the "material interests of its [the Empire's] various parts into perpetual conflict" and would lead to "Imperial disruption." Free Trade, on the other hand, had contributed to the peace and prosperity of the Empire, and the *Westminster* advised economists who talked "glibly" about imperial consolidation to "study the history of old Colonial Preferences." Such a study would show that "true industrial spirit" then had been discouraged.[119] "We cannot imagine anything more threatening to the Imperial connexion than an attempt to reimpose this policy upon vigorous and rising Colonies." There was ample evidence that the colonies did not desire Chamberlain's "artificial devices" and that "friction and danger . . . [could] come from the proposed bargains and the effort to thwart Colonial growth for the benefit of British manufacturers."[120]

It is interesting to observe how Spender handled the matter of retaliation in his indictment of Tariff Reform. To him the question of retaliation was linked to the nature of imperial relations. Some Tariff Reformers, including Prime Minister Balfour, advocated some degree of fiscal reform as a means of giving Britain the means to retaliate. If "after a short and sharp bout of retaliation," an economic war between the two conflicting countries were ended with a peace based on Free Trade principles, Spender speculated, there might be some merit in using it occasionally. He did not, however, believe that would be the case, for he was convinced that trade wars would become chronic, that there would be no swift or decisive victory, and that both parties in the conflict would suffer.[121] But beyond that he reasoned that the principle of retaliation would change the nature of imperial relations.

The then-current economic embroilment between Germany and Canada was a case in point. Trade relations between those two countries had been in dispute since 1898 when Canada granted a preference of 25 percent to Great Britain but not to Germany. In response, Germany withdrew the previous privileges she had extended to Canada and subjected the Canadians to her maximum tariff. The tariff battle between Canada and Germany lasted until 1910, and, consequently, was a topic of concern during Free Trade–Tariff Reform controversy. Tariff Reformers argued that Britain should be able to aid Canada but was helpless to do so. As Garvin put it, "Only the paralysis of the Mother Country by her inability under Free Trade to use the tariff, even as a defensive weapon, makes German action possible."[122] Nevertheless, Spender argued an opposite position. Why did Canada ask for most-favored-nation treatment from Germany while she refused to grant it in return? Why should Canada expect help from Great Britain in an instance such as this one? If the colonies were fiscally autonomous, as claimed, they must be treated independently. "Reduced to its simplest form," the *Westminster* announced, "the argument is that the British Colonies cannot have it both ways—cannot . . . enjoy all the advantages of self-government and fiscal independence, and yet, when they discriminate against foreign countries, claim to shelter themselves behind the British Government, which in its turn, has always declared that it does not control them." Moreover, if Great Britain would retaliate against a country who retaliated against a colony then the British must have a say in that colony's fiscal policy.

Therefore the *Westminster* concluded that the German-Canadian question was a revealing one to study. It showed that in the end the retaliation aspect of Tariff Reform endangered not only fiscal independence but also "the freedom and self-government of the Colonial Empire." Other systems might be more logical and might enjoy occasional advantages in conflicts with the British imperial system, but it was "pure demagogy to suggest that we can have all the advantages with none of the drawbacks of our chosen system."[123]

Clearly, while rejecting the imperial ideas of the Tariff Reformers, Spender defended imperial ideas of a different sort. He rejected the charge, common among Tariff Reformers, that Free Traders were, in fact, "Little Englanders," and he attempted to project a different concept of Empire in his paper. "The Little Englandism which neglects the Empire is certainly not to be encouraged, but the Imperialism which neglects Little England, recklessly piles burdens on it, and treats the affairs of its forty millions with high-flying contempt, is Imperialism gone mad," is a comment that typifies how the *Westminster* responded to such a charge.[124] Accordingly, an image clearly emerges in the paper's leading articles of Chamberlain's desired self-contained Empire obtained through Imperial Preference as nothing more than protectionist imperialism that would penalize colonial industry in the hope of aiding the agriculturists. Such a formula would rest on restrictive and risky ties and imperial economic development both at home and in the colonies. Even more important, it would destroy the fiber of the Empire: "The British Empire is unique precisely because it exists independently of these material ties and because, though elements of a mechanical union are wanting, it finds its own unity in race, sentiment, tradition, and common history."[125]

Spender's campaign against Tariff Reform penetrated far into the public debate on the issue. At one point he even received this unusual compliment from the Radical journalist H. W. Massingham, who was perhaps the most feared and caustic critic among the Edwardian publicists. "I feel impelled to write . . . to congratulate you on the really remarkable success and power of your Free Trade propaganda [i.e., publicity and commentary]. Not only does it seem to me to be by far the best thing in journalism, but it is, I am sure, turning out to be a very notable service to the State. It is the theme of universal praise. . . ."[126] Spender was justified in being proud of this particular word of praise from among the numerous others he received at the time, for on other occasions, he was the recipient of Massingham's wrath.

. . .

In the words of the *Annual Register* for 1903, the year ended in "an atmosphere absolutely undreamed of at its outset."[127] The great debate over Tariff Reform created the atmosphere of which it spoke. Once launched, the debate continued in some form for many years. It was, of course, partly responsible for the Unionist debacle at the polls in 1906, and after that remained fixed in political thought and action for the remainder of the Edwardian period. After 1903, however, it never again so eclipsed the political outlook as it did then. Variations of the argument naturally appeared, but the main themes of the imperial aspect of the argument all were established in the first year of debate.

Chamberlain's last great political battle became his greatest failure. One might ask, aside from uniting the previously divided Liberals and dividing the previously united Unionists, what did he accomplish? Very little, it would seem. Yet he did succeed in making Britain's world position, and with that its imperial position, an issue of public debate. The imperial journalists entered that debate in a way that confirmed their commitment to high-quality political journalism. Neither governmental pressure nor commercial influence interfered with the shaping or presenting of their opinions. Taken collectively, their writing on the subject indicates that there were no periods of editorial silence, no failure to pursue the issue fully and for as long as it was deemed important to keep before the public's attention, no hesitancy to probe into detail or into matters of history or into sophisticated levels of argument, and no tendency to elevate concerns of circulation over those of political commentary.

Their various styles remind us too that there was no one form for the political journalism they espoused. The leading articles of *The Times* were still long and untitled columns crowded with every word needed to develop a point in detail. The length of its editorials along with the way they covered the width of the column, from edge to edge with only the barest space between columns, gave them a monumental appearance of authoritative statements based on sturdy blocks of words. They had yet to undergo the changes in style that would appear before the Edwardian era ended. In contrast, Spender's leading articles were in keeping with the tradition of the small, influential evening papers of the day. With their brighter typography, headings, and paragraphs, those articles were attractive to read, and Spender's crisp and lucid style of writing made them more attractive yet. Strachey's leading articles could rival those of *The Times* in length, but like those in other weekly journals, his *Spectator* articles were laid out to produce a brighter effect than that of *The Times*. Each was titled, and although paragraphs ran long, they were separated by a line of space that enhanced their readability. Manifested in his writing was Strachey's own proper, evenhanded but always definite political persuasions. They gave the *Spectator*'s leaders an air of certainty that sometimes became pontifical.

Garvin, whose writing was polemical, provided yet another variation to Edwardian political journalism. What he wrote in the *Daily Telegraph* and various reviews and pamphlet literature was always engaging journalism, and in terms of vigor and range of knowledge, it prefigured his later writing as editor of the *Observer*. His forceful style created a sense of motion conveying urgency. More than the other imperial journalists, Garvin understood that style as well as content, format, and layout could enhance one's chances of reaching a wider audience during a long struggle for a cause.

Week after week, month after month, the imperial journalists engaged in prolonged debate about the cause of Tariff Reform. The subject dominated political journalism through 1903 and on into the early months of 1904, and it was impossible to isolate it from other serious political concerns. Consider how it related to the Irish Home Rule movement. Unionists among the imperial journalists believed that Tariff Reform was a program designed to bring greater economic security and prosperity throughout the Empire. Ireland would share in that prosperity as part of the metropolitan center, and in that way the Anglo-Irish Union would be strengthened. Besides, if Tariff Reform would build a strong imperial union, it made no sense to them to encourage disunity at the heart of the Empire by granting Home Rule to the Irish. A Liberal like Spender, however, took just the opposite position. He failed to see how imperial unity depended on Anglo-Irish unity. Part of his defense of the doctrine of Free Trade was that it fully recognized the existence of dominion nationalism and the dominions' right to self-government. Was not the Irish Home Rule movement a true national movement and did not the Irish, if they wished, have a right to self-government equal to that of Canada or New Zealand? Accordingly, Spender appreciated the logical continuity between Free Trade and Irish Home Rule. Strachey, on the other hand, denied a logical relationship between the two ideas. He was devoted to the Anglo-Irish Union and also to the doctrine of Free Trade. His imperial ideal was that of an Empire open and free at its fringes but containing a strong United Kingdom at the center. While accusing Chamberlain of "Tied-House" imperialism, he failed to perceive any "Tied-House" quality to the Anglo-Irish Union. Whatever their views on Irish Home Rule may have been, they were ones that, for one reason or another, reinforced the imperial journalists' thought on the Empire.

To them, nothing less than the nature of the Empire was at stake. Beneath all the charges and countercharges, beneath the battle over statistics and beneath all those thousands of columns of exposition, of agitated discussion, lay the assumption that the outcome of the debate on this issue was crucial for Britain's imperial future. The Empire could perform a constructive, even great, function in world affairs. The imperial journalists still held to such a view. But how could it survive to perform? Indeed, there was much at stake in this discussion.

These men often spoke of two imperialisms, by which they meant two imperial ideas. Men like Spender and Strachey envisioned an Empire loose and organic in nature, evolving according to liberal principles. But in those principles might well reside seeds of its own disintegration. Garvin, with the men at Printing House Square some distance behind, perceived the need for a new structure for new times. In a sense they were attempting to develop a belated logic for the Empire. Was it already too late for that, or, considering its heterogeneous composition, had it ever been possible? "I am more than ever convinced that we have reached a critical point in British history," Chamberlain mused at the end of 1903. "We may yet be in fact as well as in name, the greatest Empire that the world has ever seen—on the other hand we may, if we fail to take the present opportunity, drift into a condition of apathetic indifference which must in the long run be the precursor of separation."[128] The Empire *was* at a critical point, but which imperial idea would or could guide it to longer life? The imperial journalists would return to that question in earnest within a few years, but first problems in South Africa affecting the future of the Empire demanded their attention.

4

Chinese Labor in South Africa: Part I, 1903-1904

The Tariff Reform debate dominated politics in 1903, but it failed to gain an exclusive hold on public attention to imperial subjects. Even then, another imperial problem, one related to the economic reconstruction of postwar South Africa, began to grow in importance. Specifically it dealt with the importation of Chinese indentured labor to work the gold mines in the Transvaal. Like Tariff Reform it was an issue conducive to political controversy. Like Tariff Reform it could be blurred by emotionalism. Like Tariff Reform it lingered on for years after appearing in 1903, and like Tariff Reform it became a major reason for the Liberal landslide victory at the polls in 1906. Some background about British-Afrikaner relations in general and about the postwar economic condition in the Transvaal in particular is needed to explain the emergence of this issue.

THE SOUTH AFRICAN PRELUDE TO RECONSTRUCTION

Historians have frequently analyzed nineteenth-century South Africa and its many vicissitudes. In the web of themes that compose it, the long antagonism between the Boers and the British forms the centerpiece, from an imperial perspective.[1] It unfolded, of course, amid many other realities involving the land and its other inhabitants.[2] Yet it was the struggle between the Boers and the British that led to the South African War of 1899 and formed the context for the later British reconstruction policies.

The British arrival at the Cape has been called an "ideological earthquake."[3] That description provides a major clue for understanding the ensuing struggle between the Boer and the Briton. The Boers, who long predated the British at the Cape, tended to see the British as harbingers of a culture different than theirs, one that with its currents of humanitarianism and evangelical Christianity would disrupt their way of life. When the British abolished slavery throughout the Empire in 1833, the Boers perceived that act as the culmination of a long series of deeds regarding native policies that undermined what they believed to be their biblically sanctioned attitude toward the indigenous people of the area as well as toward the slaves who had been brought there. They felt the British held erroneous ideas about how "white-black, master-servant" relations should be conducted so as not to offend the law of God.[4] Consequently, many of them decided to leave Cape Colony and to migrate inland. The resulting Great Trek that began in 1836 involved about ten thousand Afrikaner men, women, and children. More than that stayed in Cape Colony, but those who left and plunged deep into the South African interior did so to escape the British and to find their promised land. They were, then, not only fleeing British rule; they were also following their own natural impulse to find land, space, and freedom.

After the Great Trek the history of the two white societies of nineteenth-century South Africa became a type of duel for land, position, and sovereignty. The Boers, individualists that they were, fought to survive, but they seemed to cause disruption wherever they went. To make matters worse, the instability of their frontier tended to spread into the coastal areas occupied by the British, who wished for order throughout all of South Africa. The Boers were more than a quaint anachronism; to the British, who valued South Africa for its pivotal position on ocean trade routes, they were a nuisance that somehow had to be contained. During the century, British policy toward the Boers varied sharply. At times they extended their sovereignty over them, and at other times they withdrew it, not wishing to enlarge their commitments abroad and believing that the Boers, located in the remote interior, no longer threatened their dominion in South Africa. Despite occasional talk about federation of all the South African white communities, separation between them became a fact. The Boers managed to establish two republics, the Transvaal and the Orange Free State, north of the Orange River, while the British remained at Cape Colony and acquired a second coastal colony, Natal. Throughout all the oscillations of policy, the British intended to retain some degree of paramountcy over all of South Africa, though confusion persisted about the precise meaning of that term.

Toward the end of the century, it became urgent for the British to establish a more defined position regarding the republics. After the Boer victory over the British at the Battle of Majuba Hill in 1881, Afrikaner nationalism became a more cohesive and aggressive force than it previously had been, and the change affected both the Africans and the British. That victory fell between two important events: the discovery of diamonds in 1866 in an area just outside the Transvaal border, and the discovery of vast gold deposits in the central region of that republic in 1886 on a ridge about thirty miles south of Pretoria known as the Witwatersrand and popularly called the Rand. These discoveries promised to transform the Transvaal, to give it wealth, and perhaps to make it the economic and political center of gravity for all of South Africa. Moreover, as this transformation occurred within South Africa (i.e., Africa south of the Limpopo River), imperial activity increased in tempo among the British, Germans, and Portuguese throughout southern Africa (i.e., Africa south of the Zambesi).

In the 1890s tensions mounted between the two white communities. Key figures (Paul Kruger, president of the Transvaal since 1883; Cecil Rhodes, premier of the Cape Colony from 1890 to 1896; and Sir Alfred Milner, high commissioner for South Africa and governor of the Cape after 1897) engaged in a duel for control of the Transvaal and perhaps for the fate of South Africa too. Kruger feared the transformation of his state into an Anglo-Saxon community. He had to deal with the influx of thousands of "Uitlanders," as they were called, men from America and Australia but mostly from Britain, who had come to the Transvaal to work the gold mines. These people provided labor for the republic, but it was feared that in time they would outnumber the Boers there. They paid 80 percent of the taxes, but they enjoyed few rights of citizenship. Attempting to discourage their permanent settlement, Kruger restricted the franchise for these immigrants by extending voting requirements to unprecedented levels.[5] Furthermore, he harassed the gold-mining companies in several ways, including making dynamite manufacturing a local industry and later a state monopoly, which meant higher prices for the mineowners. Such actions, of course, gave the British grievances to champion. Before the decade ended the Boers and the British were at war.

The Anglo-Boer War (1899-1902) lasted for three years and caused the deaths of tens of thousands. Although eclipsed in history by the world wars of our century, it was a formidable event that influenced how the Edwardians thought about the Empire. We have already seen how it affected the Tariff Reform crusade of 1903. The causes of that war, which have remained a subject of controversy to this day, fall beyond the scope of this study.[6] Nevertheless, several observations about the opposing attitudes of the combatants are in order. The British believed that the Transvaal was establishing local hegemony and with that might extend its influence throughout South Africa. In terms of imperial security as well as the area's economic development and for the future of the indigenous races, such a growth of Afrikaner influence was intolerable. Milner believed that it should and could be broken. No doubt, those men who controlled imperial policy also believed that as a result of the war the Uitlanders would become an extended basis for British influence in South African affairs. On the other hand, the Transvaal and its ally, the Orange Free State, believed they were fighting defensively, but they surely bear part of the responsibility for the state of affairs that led to war. In the end, they began the hostilities by issuing an impossible ultimatum and then by invading British territory.

Bitter though the conflict was, the terms of the peace signed at Vereeniging in 1902 were generous. At that time the two republics had to acknowledge British sovereignty; yet, in defeat they received many assurances that this was no Carthaginian peace. The British agreed to replace military rule with civil government as soon as possible, to repatriate the Boers and their families, and to help rehabilitate their farms, many of which were devastated by the war. They received the promise that their language would be assured limited protection in the schools and courts. In terms of future government, the British guaranteed that in time representative institutions would be established leading to self-government. A particularly sensitive question was that regarding the native franchise, since the condition of the natives in the Transvaal had been part of the British complaints before the war, and since Africans and the Coloured were part of the electorate in the British Cape Colony and to a much lesser extent in Natal. The peacemakers now postponed that question until after the establishment of self-government, a provision which gave the Boers a voice that would prove to be a decisive one in determining native policy. So that which was generous to the Boers was neglectful of African interests. By such leniency the British hoped to reconcile the Boers and to encourage as many of them as possible to become supporters of the imperial cause. It is possible to reason that the new South Africa that they hoped to build would "ensure some measure of fair play for the black peoples of the land," but a sense of practicality stayed the British hand.[7]

Following the war, the economic development of the two conquered republics, particularly the Transvaal, became a matter of crucial importance. Behind the colonies' economic reconstruction, and associated with it, administrative changes occurred. At the end of the war, Milner accepted the responsibility for the administration of the two Boer republics. Consequently, while retaining the title of high commissioner, he relinquished the governorship of Cape Colony and moved to Johannesburg. As governor of the Orange River Colony, as it then became known, and of the Transvaal, he was assisted in each colony by a lieutenant-governor. In each colony there also was an executive council and a legislature composed of officials and nominees. The administration of the two Crown colonies during reconstruction was crucial to the Empire and an undertaking of immense proportion; in performing it Milner had great authority. He exerted powerful influence over imperial policy.

Everything associated with the early years of reconstruction revolved around Milner. Thus, he is an interesting and necessary figure to contemplate before proceeding further. A committed imperialist who equated the Empire with international order and the advancement of civilization, he personified the storm center of imperial debate on South Africa both before and after the Anglo-Boer War. Impatient with parliamentary politics, which he distrusted, he wanted a more efficient and progressive Empire and believed that popular opinion would in time recognize the value of programs directed toward that end. He lacked neither critics nor devotees either during his lifetime or after death.

Milner believed that the Empire was both incomplete and insecure in his day. Imperial development and unity were needed; South Africa was a weak link. He had forced events in South Africa before the war in the belief that there was "no way out of the political troubles of South Africa except reform in the

Transvaal or war."[8] Later, as he prepared to leave South Africa after presiding over its reconstruction for several years, he claimed his work to have been directed toward "a great and distant end—the establishment in South Africa of a great and civilized and progessive community, one from Cape Town to the Zambia—independent in the management of its own affairs, but still remaining, from its own firm desire, a member of the great community of free nations gathered together under the British flag."[9] That is what he meant when he claimed to be "an Imperialist out and out."[10] When it came to the subject of race relations, he claimed that he held to Rhodes's old slogan of "equal rights for all civilized men," which did not endear him to many Boers. Whatever the degree of his assimilationist views, and however slight they might appear from today's perspective, he said he was "prepared to rely, for a return of what . . . [he] believed to be the true path, upon a gradual change of opinion in this country itself."[11]

Understandably, there have been as sharp differences of opinion among historians as there were among Milner's contemporaries about the success or failure of his work in the reconstruction of the two defeated republics. This much, however, is clear: that work was conducted, as it was undertaken, with the future in mind. By his policies he hoped to attract to the area large numbers of permanent British settlers who would mingle with the Boers, temper their opposition, and establish a new social foundation for the two colonies. In short, he wanted an Anglicized South Africa. To accomplish that goal the economic development of defeated republics was imperative, and although his efforts in that realm produced impressive results, it appeared in danger of foundering in 1903 due to a labor shortage in the gold mines of the Transvaal.[12]

The problem was involved. Before the war the Transvaal's gold-mining industry had grown from an insignificant output in 1886 to producing 25.5 percent of the world's gold in 1889. Even then there was a serious effort made to contain production costs in order to create the necessary market confidence to balance off the sharp fluctuations that were characteristic of speculation in the mining industry. The mineowners believed that the best way to reduce the costs of production lay in reducing wages paid to African laborers. Moreover, aside from the rich yields of ore in the so-called Central Rand area, the Transvaal mines yielded a generally low-grade ore. Deposits worked in Australia and Canada were much richer. The development of sophisticated machinery and processing methods, however, made possible the large-scale mining of low-grade deposits. Consequently, as the enterprise expanded, profits were reduced. Waste and production costs had to be restricted. That frustrated any hope of raising wages to attract additional African unskilled workers.

During the war mining conditions worsened. Little or no production was permitted on the Rand in 1899 and 1900, and after that it was severely restricted. Production plunged to 1888 levels and capital subscription fell 75 percent. The labor supply collapsed as the closing of mines caused African workers to disperse. Anticipating that reopening the mines after the war would entail increased expenses, the mineowners announced a wage reduction to become effective upon the conclusion of the war. That made the procurement of new labor difficult enough. Once the war ended, moreover, the demand for labor increased throughout the Transvaal and elsewhere in South Africa. Many African workers had no wish to return to the mines and were able to find other employment. A series of good harvests in African areas made the prospect of entering the mines even less appealing. Before the war the supply of African labor had fluctuated. After the war it seemed promising at first, as 38,631 and 43,625 African unskilled laborers were recruited in 1902 and 1903 respectively. Yet it was feared that those levels could not be maintained, and the recruitment figures for 1904, which dropped to 27,633, would justify that fear. The recruitment effort for that last year extended all through southern Africa (up to 22 degrees south latitude). The problem as the mineowners perceived it was twofold: where to find more labor, and how to secure it without increasing wages.[13] Moreover, the problem was urgent. In 1903 the Chamber of Mines, which represented the various mining groups in the Transvaal, announced that, irrespective of future needs, 197,644 laborers were "required" at once.[14]

Where could the necessary labor be found? It should be understood that in South Africa white workers did not engage in unskilled manual labor. Convention forbade their doing "Kaffirs' work." White labor, moreover, would be more costly than native, and there was no great surplus of white workers in the area. It seemed unlikely that emigrants could be attracted to a far-off land by the promise of hard labor and low wages. One mine manager, F. H. P. Creswell of the Village Main Reef Mine, did experiment with the use of white labor, but the results were less than encouraging.[15] He claimed, however, that with changes in the interior organization of the industry the mines could be worked as cheaply by unskilled white labor as by native. Other mine managers and engineers rejected that claim. Heeding their advice, Milner, who had been interested in Creswell's scheme, failed to push for a white labor solution for the problem. There were too many doubts and variables involved. He also came to acknowledge the inadequacy of the supply of native laborers. During the previous year, with characteristic vigor he had sought and achieved improvements of the conditions under which the native miners lived and worked. Improved conditions made little difference to the recruitment of natives. By March 1903, Milner reached the conclusion that another source of labor would have to be found and that the only available source lay in China. Indentured Chinese laborers could be contracted to work the Transvaal mines. Also, by that time, the British press had given its initial response to the prospect of importing laborers from China.

CHINESE LABOR: STIRRINGS OF DEBATE, 1903

Given the fact of the strong imperialistic sympathies of the leaders of *The Times,* we would expect that paper to have taken a vigorous interest in postwar South Africa. As the question regarding Chinese labor in the Transvaal developed, an inclination in favor of that policy appeared among those men who directed its policy. Moberly Bell supported the experiment. Amery was a devotee of Milner, and after at first preferring the use of white labor in the mines, followed his lead.[16] As for Buckle, he supported the imperial policy of the Balfour ministry, and there is no reason to suspect that he made this case an exception. Interestingly, not long before the Chinese labor question emerged as a proposition of political discussion, Buckle stated that he believed it would be easy to blunder in South Africa if "the views of local loyalists and the Man on the spot" were overruled.[17] In this connection it is significant that Buckle considered Milner an old friend.[18] Only Chirol, the paper's foreign editor, had misgivings about it.[19]

Nevertheless, *The Times* was slow to endorse importation of Chinese laborers for the Transvaal. In fact, when the idea of the use of Chinese labor first emerged, the paper voiced misgivings of the most serious nature. Early in January 1903, it received reports from Johannesburg to the effect that "in the opinion of many, Chinese labour . . . [was] the only remedy." Who were the "many," *The Times* queried in response. The British at home, it warned, would regard such an act with "repugnance and distrust," and Canada and Australia were apt to ask if it were for this that they had sent troops to South Africa in the recent war. It went so far as to state, "In the whole Empire, nay, in the whole English-speaking world, we do not know where to look for any body of opinion worth considering that would frankly approve the introduction of Chinese labour into South Africa." It would find disfavor even in South Africa itself "outside of mineowning circles," and, worse yet, increase the Boer objections to British rule and result "in driving into opposition many whom we should otherwise conciliate." Only "overmastering necessity" could justify such recourse, but the need for it had yet to be proven. There was still no satisfactory evidence that the mines could not be worked by white labor. Or, consider the case of native labor. *The Times'* correspondent had reported that the natives were unavailable in sufficient numbers to assure the prosperity of the mines. To that the paper retorted: "There are only two rational ways of treating them. One is to clear them out of the white man's country; the other is to make them gradually into useful citizens of that country." Predicting that the problem of the native population either would have to be faced now or would be "dearly paid for at a future time," *The Times* saw no reason why the mines could not be worked in the old way, by recruiting native labor from the area south of the Zambesi, and pleaded that more time was needed to allow "normal conditions" to return. "We did not undertake Imperial responsibilities in South Africa merely to run mines on the cheap. We undertook them in order to carry out our mission in the world, to bear the white man's burden, to evolve order out of chaos, and to build up a state," it argued. More time was needed for the return and growth of prosperity, but at this point there were "two honourable paths" from which to choose. Either accept white labor or bring the "black community into line with the white men as an efficient constituent of a State from which it cannot be expelled."[20]

At this point, the *Spectator* shared *The Times'* concern over this matter. It agreed with *The Times* that scarcity of labor in the Transvaal was a serious question and believed it was one for which a hasty solution should be avoided. Warning that it would be a mistake for the Transvaal to be "committed to a policy of importing Chinese labour while it . . . [was] still in the Crown Colony stage," it urged that the importation of Chinese workers should be decided only after the colony received self-government.

Like *The Times*, the *Spectator* thought that remedies other than the use of Chinese labor should be tried at this time. "We believe," it stated, "that the solution of the problem is to be found in the combined use of white labour and of labour-saving machinery." In other British colonies, it reasoned, goldmining was carried on either by white labor or by white and black labor together and there was "no reason why the same thing should not be accomplished in South Africa." It understood that the mineowners preferred native and non-white labor because white labor could be "troublesome and unreasonable." Black labor, on the other hand, had "no unions and no trade rules, and, best of all, . . . [had] no votes which . . . [could] interfere with the management of the mines." The *Spectator* had no wish to "attribute a double dose of original sin to the mineowners" but felt that the imperial government should not "surrender to their views." White laborers were needed on the Rand not only for economic reasons but also to solve the "Dutch problem" and to make the future secure. To make the Transvaal a white man's country in a true sense would be very greatly to benefit the whole Empire." But it would be a "retrograde and sinister" decision to make it "a yellow man's country" and the imperial government must avoid that at all costs. "In any case," it concluded, "it is quite certain that Parliament . . . [would] not consent to permitting the importation of Chinese labour as long as it is directly responsible for the government of the Transvaal. Of that we feel as certain as we can feel of anything in the region of politics."[21]

Spender's *Westminster Gazette* also sensed the seriousness of this matter and early in 1903 made it the subject of a series of five leading articles. Some type of labor shortage did exist in the Transvaal, it reasoned, but two things influenced and confused the perception of the problem. First, Milner had encouraged "extravagant hopes" about the economic future of the colony and had led South Africa to think in terms of an expanded prosperity following the war. Then there was the influence of the mineowners to consider. These magnates, it claimed, contemplated a colony dominated by one or two industries, "controlled by themselves" and supported by black labor and only a few whites, who would be employed as foremen or managers. The *Westminster* shared the *Spectator*'s belief that the magnates did not want a large number of white immigrants who might introduce "trade-unions and democratic politics."[22] The *Gazette* considered this attitude a damaging and unacceptable form of "colonial exclusiveness." "We look for a populous and thriving community with all doors freely open to immigrants, and nothing less will be fair or just to the people of this country," it declared.[23]

Neither did the *Gazette* accept the fact of native labor shortage. While rejecting as repugnant suggestions sometimes advanced to the effect that the natives were lazy and some means should be found to force them to work, it claimed that no government "which considered the interests of the natives" could wash its hands "of the whole affair except so far as to insist that there shall be no slavery or anything that can be called slavery in British dominions." The administration had ended the old "touting" system that was unfair to both the mineowners and the natives. Accordingly, the *Westminster* suggested that the Labour Associations, which the administration had introduced to replace the old touting system, should extend their operation into British territories north of the Zambesi.[24] In that way recruitment could be supervised, contracts carefully explained to the natives, and a fair means guaranteed for their return home. Such a policy would make it unnecessary to recruit in foreign territory where the British had no jurisdiction and would avoid leaving the problem in the hands of the mineowners.[25]

This early and limited reaction to the prospect of importing Chinese laborers to work the mines was but a brief flurry. It occurred six months before the subject became a major public controversy in England, and during that interim the Tariff Reform debate dominated the attention the press gave to imperial issues. However, the arguments advanced by those papers that engaged in this initial response to the idea of importation prefigured ones that appeared in the press when the subject acquired greater urgency. Before that time, late in the fall of the year, a number of things happened that shaped the progress of the idea. At the end of March, a public campaign began in the Transvaal in favor of importation, but it met with opposition based on several grounds. Simple prejudice against the Chinese, apprehension that the restrictions on the laborers would be too lax, and doubts that an adequate search for additional native labor had been made, combined to make the opposition formidable. Some of the opponents even formed organizations such as the White League and the African Labour League as vehicles of protest. Various groups protesting importation forwarded to the authorities resolutions stating their opposition. In Cape Colony the House of Assembly and the Legislative Council passed resolutions unanimously expressing their strong opposition to the importation of Asiatic labor. The advocates also were active. In July they organized the Labour Importation Association to aid the movement. The association held meetings throughout the Rand and elsewhere in the Transvaal, passed resolutions favoring importation, and in general sought to persuade opinion. It enjoyed the full support of the Chamber of Mines.

Milner held his ground. Having arrived at his own decision that importation of Asiatic labor was the only solution to the problem, he believed that white opinion in the Transvaal would accept the proposal once it understood the relevant facts. He appointed a Transvaal Labour Commission to make a comprehensive investigation into the area's labor problem. Then he left South Africa for five months to visit England and did not return until December. While at home he took his case for Chinese labor to his friends, to the cabinet, and to Alfred Lyttelton, Chamberlain's successor at the Colonial Office. He also approached some notable Liberal Imperialists, Asquith, Grey, and Haldane, about it and there is some indication that he believed he had their support.[26]

While Milner was away, the Transvaal Labour Commission accomplished its work. After meeting from July 21 to October 6 and hearing reports from numerous people (e.g., administrators, recruiting agents, mineowners, missionaries, farmers, tribal chiefs), it submitted a report that was published on November 19. The commission actually produced two reports, a majority report signed by all but two of the twelve commissioners and a minority report signed by the remaining two. The majority report included testimony that indicated that there were at present 68,280 laborers at work in the mining industry but that 197,644 were needed, a figure that ultimately could rise as high as 368,500.[27] It also stressed the testimony provided by Jacobus Nicholas DeJong of the Transvaal Chamber of Mines. He emphasized the inability of the African labor market, including the areas north and south of the Zambesi, to supply the Transvaal with adequate numbers of workers and suggested the best solution was to seek labor from some source other than Africa. The two commissioners who submitted the minority report believed that the above figures were exaggerated and that the mineowners were more concerned about making quick profits than about achieving a stable economy.[28] Milner accepted the majority report, and a summary of it appeared in the British press on November 23.

With the publication of the report, the campaign in the Transvaal reached a new stage. There the Chamber of Mines, the Stock Exchange, and the Chamber of Trade made unanimous declarations in favor of importing Chinese labor. Opponents made a last effort by calling a meeting to ask for a referendum on the issue. Members of the Labour Importation Association also attended that meeting and managed to wreck its proceedings. Meanwhile, William Monypenny, the editor of the *Johannesburg Star* and a champion of white labor, resigned his position because of his strong disagreement with the paper's mine owning proprietors. Wilfrid Wybergh, the commissioner of mines, also resigned at this time citing as reasons his sympathy with the white labor view and distrust of capitalist influence. Monypenny's motives were beyond question; Wybergh's may have been mere pretense or they may have been justified.[29] In any case, the resignations attracted the attention of critics of importation in London.

In Britain, press commentary on the importation of Chinese labor into the Transvaal reemerged in the fall of 1903. Serious statements about it actually predated the publication of the Transvaal Labour Commission's report in November. They began to appear in October and correspond to the end of Lord Milner's visit to England. Since the fact that Milner favored importation was known by this time, to oppose the policy was tantamount to opposing him. That was a factor of some consequence for the leaders at *The Times*. Buckle, as previously mentioned, thought of Milner as an old friend.[30] Chirol, whose support for an importationist policy was not nearly as pronounced as Moberly Bell's, wrote Strachey a friendly letter a few months before. It contained these lines of gentle persuasion:

> I thought merely of appealing to you privately not to prejudice the question of importing Asiatic labour into the Transvaal against the opinion of a man who has rendered such service to S. A. as Milner. Surely if he considered Asiatic labour necessary and inevitable, he must have good reasons for doing so. But then it struck me that the same argument ought to hold good about Chamberlain and his proposals, viz. that if the man who more than any other had twice saved the Empire, in the Home Rule crises and in S. A., comes forward and says that a certain policy deserves consideration in the interests of the Empire, he is entitled at any rate to a hearing. But unfortunately the *Spectator* does not see things in this light.[31]

The thinking of the leaders at Printing House Square about the importation proposal was changing.

Toward the end of October, *The Times* addressed a leading article to the fact that the Transvaal was suffering from "temporary economic stress." Economic conditions there were not what the paper had hoped they would be a year before. "The inhabitants [of the Transvaal] have as little wish to import the Asiatic as ever, if only they could get on without him," it observed. "They seem, however, to have come to the conclusion that they can no longer get on without him. The mines must be supplied with abundant labour unless the whole country is to continue to languish." More labor had to be found, but "for the present neither mining nor agriculture can obtain anything like the supply they require from South African sources."[32]

The Times now approached the subject from a different point of reference. Setting aside its own earlier misgivings about importation, some of which were moralistic, it no longer spoke of the possibility of recruiting additional labor in Africa south of the Zambesi. A few days after the publication of the Transvaal Labour Commission's report, the paper began to editorialize about "the labour famine" that crippled the gold industry in the Transvaal and of how it had "been clear for some time past" that it could not be remedied by "modification in the laws under which the Kaffir" worked, or by introduction of "white labourers, British, Colonial, or Continental." That the Transvaal magnates were in part responsible for the problem of attracting white labor, it admitted: "Fear of strikes," *The Times* said, had "done even more than fear of expense to prejudice the mineowners against white labour." Nevertheless, the paper expressed no surprise at the findings contained in the report of the Transvaal Labour Commission. If the Chinese were brought in, it contended they should be supervised, and prevented "from engaging in any trade or industry except those specified in terms of their labour contract." *The Times*, however, refused to accept importation as a permanent solution for the labor shortage. It was merely a "temporary means." The paper hoped that some way could be discovered to reduce the demand for labor either by "mechanical ingenuity" or by applying "chemical knowledge."[33]

Any doubt regarding where *The Times* stood disappeared with its reaction to the resignation of Wilfrid Wybergh from his post as commissioner of mines. The paper's own Johannesburg correspondent reported that Wybergh opposed the introduction of Chinese labor and did not wish to be involved in dealing with importation. Wybergh also complained about the political influence on behalf of the financial interests. *The Times* expected that the critics of importation would "exploit his resignation for all its worth against the findings of the Labour Commission report." His comment about the influence of financial interest, it believed, lent itself "with fatal facility to those denunciations of the mining industry as a sordid . . . concern which we have grown accustomed to hearing." Consequently, *The Times* hoped "that nervous people . . . [would] not let their imagination run away with them in the matter." The development of the mines affected the entire colony, that development depended on an adequate supply of labor, and other resources of labor offered no solution for the problem. With "great reluctance" the expedient of Chinese labor now had been suggested and "we feel confident that the people of the Transvaal will decide it for themselves." In this matter *The Times*, with some restraint, began to construct a defense for importation.[34]

As reports of the closing sessions of the Transvaal Labour Commission reached London, Strachey's *Spectator* also wavered from its earlier opposition to the importation of Chinese labor. As it did so, however, its continued uneasiness about the entire proposal remained obvious. It attached a particular importance to the testimony given by F. H. P. Creswell, the manager of the Village Main Reef Mine who had experimented with the use of unskilled white laborers until ordered by his directors to discontinue the experiment. In his comments before the commission, Creswell stated he believed that the mining industry could be reorganized and different methods used to make the extended use of white labor feasible. That, however, would cause a delay in operations and necessitate a new capital expenditure, and the mineowners were unlikely to agree to either. More important, Creswell explained that the mineowners feared a large white industrial population that "would make the labour element too strong a factor in economic questions, and when representative government . . . [was] given, in political question." The *Spectator*'s previous fears about hostility to the use of white labor thus appeared confirmed and it exploited the point. "No free Colony can arise from the ruins of war unless free industrial conditions exist," it warned. "To stereotype one form of subject labour in order that the mineowners may have less trouble in the management of it, and in order that the political stream may flow smoothly, is to postpone the birth of a free nation forever." To suggest that white labor would culminate "in the tyranny of the working man," the journal observed, was to make "the most odious of imputations" against the British people as well as against those residing in Australia, New Zealand, and Canada. Yes, it admitted, with the increase of white labor, strikes and lockouts would occur on the Rand as they did in any industrial city in England, but it would be better "to have in a British city a free and vigorous British population than to bolster up the chief industry by an exotic labour system." The introduction of white labor was the goal sought, and the *Spectator* believed it must be emphasized in order to stress the temporary nature of the introduction of imported labor.

Nevertheless, the *Spectator* recognized that some immediate relief had to be found. The Transvaal had a debt of £65,000,000 to pay and to remain solvent its railway and custom revenues could not be allowed to diminish and the direct taxation of the mining industry had to be increased. Moreover, subsidiary industries and the agriculture of the area awaited the return of the gold industry to a "proper basis," and the prosperity of that industry depended upon the immediate procurement of more labor. Such arguments, it admitted, were sound. The *Spectator*'s uneasiness with the choice forced upon the Transvaal by necessity was apparent. "If, in deference to the Report of the Commission [which had yet to be published], the importation of Asiatics is undertaken," it cautioned, "it must be on a very clear understanding, and with a distinct object in view." The temporary character of such a measure would have to be stressed; and "the result can only be achieved by insisting that any experiment in imported labour must be made under the strictest conditions as to seclusion and repatriation, and by keeping white labour constantly in view as the only final settlement." While continuing to hope for a "large influx of white men" into the Transvaal as soon as possible, the *Spectator* concluded that the "temporary development of the mines by a strictly guarded use of Asiatic imported labour" would have to be accepted.[35]

The *Westminster Gazette* entered the fray by charging that "real grounds for anxiety" existed. The predicted "boom" had failed to materialize, and it was "foolish" to have expected it. Difficulties, which should have been anticipated, abounded in the Transvaal, and the administration "always actuated by good intentions, has rushed rather crudely at legislation and expenditure and is certainly not popular at this moment with the British inhabitants." Turning its attention to the labor problem it reasoned: "Black labour is scarce, being drawn from the mines by railways, irrigation, and the work of restoring and rebuilding after the war. White labour is not being developed and, owing to the obstinate prejudice of South Africa, is not likely to meet the case. Very reluctantly but on pain of great financial disaster or prolonged depression, the white population finds itself being driven into the acceptance of Chinese labour." Even if a majority of colonists gave their "painful consent" to Asiatic immigration, there remained a "stubborn and hostile" minority against it. The *Westminster* , then, while recognizing that the importation of Chinese labor might occur, refused to accept it as anything other than an odious decision that, if it had to be made, should be the responsibility of the colonists themselves and not the work of the imperial government.[36]

With the publication of the Labour Commission's report, it became more probable that the importation of Chinese laborers would be adopted as a policy. The *Westminster Gazette* sensed the direction in which things were moving when it noted that although the report made no mention of Chinese labor as such, it made it clear beyond doubt that no other remedy existed. It also observed that when *The Times'* Johannesburg correspondent cabled a summary of that report to London, he appended this comment to his message: "Thus the path is prepared officially for the introduction of Chinese labour." The *Gazette* failed to express surprise at the point the Transvaal's labor crisis apparently had reached since it believed that Chamberlain had failed to anticipate what the results of war would be in that fatal year of 1899. The war had left the country in debt, removed the restraint that "the agricultural Boer put upon the mineowners," and encouraged exaggerated expectations regarding the quick development of the Transvaal as a prosperous area. What could be done at this point? "It is useless at this stage merely to throw up our hands and attribute everything to the wickedness of mineowners," the *Westminster* said. "They, no doubt, have aggravated the mischief by their endeavor to cut the native wage, and certainly they . . . [were] at no pains to relieve the situation." Commercial considerations guided the mining companies, not "philanthropic or patriotic" ones, and the paper understood this fact, even if it wished it were different. Nevertheless, it strongly objected "that the mining industry, having South Africa at its mercy, should throw upon the Imperial Government the invidious task of forcing Chinese labour upon reluctant Colonies." South Africa itself had to take responsibility for such a policy. The people of that area must not afterwards be allowed to say that "we compelled them to this course by a despotic exercise of our administrative power." Therefore, need dictated that either the Transvaal be given autonomous government or some means be implemented to take into account the opinion of the self-governing colonies in South Africa and of white men in the Transvaal.[37]

Still, the *Westminster* appreciated that a serious impasse would be reached if sufficient labor could not be found, and it tried to approach the question "without prejudice." So serious had the likelihood of importation become by early December that the paper insisted the two "proofs" be provided before allowing matters to proceed farther. Was importation absolutely necessary? Would "South Africa" agree to it by "her own free will"? The *Westminster* doubted that proof existed at this time to allow those questions to be answered in the affirmative. Then it probed into what the outcome would be if Chinese laborers were introduced in the Transvaal. Ultimately it meant "a barren country containing little but mines which financial persons of mixed nationalities exploited with the aid of Chinamen." Was the hope of making South Africa "a white man's country" to be abandoned? Agricultural settlement had attracted few immigrants. Now, after claims had been made that mining was "no fit occupation for a white man in a black man's country," it was "really the last blow to be told that the black man himself refuses to go down the mines." With black labor, there still would be one white foreman to every ten black laborers, but the "Chinaman would come with his own foreman and his own army . . . of camp-followers to provide him with necessities and luxuries of life as understood in China." Under these circumstances the *Westminster* said the Rand would be a "dismal failure." The importation of Chinese laborers represented the "parting of the ways for the Transvaal, one way leading to financial ascendency with the aid of Chinese labourers, the other to the development of a white man's country."[38]

THE QUESTION DEBATED: 1904

At the end of 1903, the proposal to introduce Chinese labor in the Rand acquired rapid momentum. On December 30, after several days of discussion in which it examined the Labour Commission's report, the Transvaal Legislative Council passed a motion made by Sir George Farrar, the president of the Chamber of Mines, for the "importation of indentured unskilled coloured labourers" by a vote of 22 to 4. Meanwhile, a petition in favor of importation already had been signed by 17,000 white male workers. By the end of January the signatories of this petition, described by critics as "skilfully organized" and by supporters as "carefully authenticated," numbered 45,000 out of a population of 90,000 male white adults in the Transvaal. Considering that both 15,000 government employees and most of the Boers abstained, the figure, if at all accurate, was impressive.[39] The same conclusion could be reached about the evidence of support for importation in the Transvaal. Even allowing for exaggeration and manipulation, when viewed in the aggregate it was difficult to dismiss. Having been endorsed by the Legislative Council, Milner's policy of importation now awaited approval from Westminster.

During the first five months of 1904, Chinese labor became a prominent subject of controversy in the British Parliament and press. On January 16, the colonial secretary Alfred Lyttelton announced the government's decision to sanction the importation of Chinese labor in the Transvaal, and on February 10 the Transvaal Legislative Council passed the Labour Importation Ordinance, which the Parliament at Westminster then debated until late in March. Finally, the ordinance received royal assent on May 11. The press closely followed and tried to shape the outcome of the issue through this period. *The Times*, for instance, made it the subject of thirteen leading articles while seventeen leading articles about it appeared on the front page of the *Westminster Gazette* . Strachey left no doubt about where his sympathies lay on this issue. Among the imperial journalists only Garvin failed to offer distinctive comment. He would, however, speak out before the issue receded.

To the men at *The Times*, a moment of "overmastering necessity" had arrived. As supporters of Lord Milner and his work in South Africa, they defended him now. Harboring no doubt that the Chinese labor policy would encounter a strong opposition in England, they developed as convincing a case as possible for the measure. They defended it as a reasonable experiment reluctantly adopted in the face of pragmatic circumstances that left the government no choice in the matter. Having originally voiced their own misgivings when the idea first appeared early in the previous year, they now endorsed it by stressing two arguments, necessity and the force of colonial opinion in the Transvaal. "Necessity" was the core around which they built their case. About midway through this period of debate on the subject, the paper defined its position in this way:

> We have seen it alleged against ourselves with an air of triumph that we formerly opposed the introduction of Chinese labour. Of course we did. So did Lord Milner, so did Mr. Chamberlain, so did thousands of people who have since yielded to the evidence of necessity. We wanted the black men to be utilized and civilized in the process; but it turns out that they cannot be induced to work in sufficient numbers except by the Boer methods of compulsion. We wanted everything done to extend the use of machinery and to make room for white labour. Everything has been done in that way, but there remains an enormous quantity of labour which must be manual and which our workmen will not perform on any terms. Therefore Chinamen must be employed or the Transvaal must stand still. Therefore we are in favour of employing Chinamen under proper restrictions. It is not that anybody wants to introduce Chinamen out of mere perversity, but that they are a necessity for the progress of the country.[40]

Such an argument, of course, indicated that *The Times* had accepted Lord Milner's appraisal of the problem. It also showed that it refused to accept the idea that importation was "a device invented by impatient money-getters."[41]

The "necessity" theme was convincing, at least to a degree. It allowed one to argue against the coercion of Africans into the mines. Many Afrikaners in the Transvaal apparently approved of some form of coercion. Some were in favor of coercing the natives to work by strictly enforcing the Squatter's Law; others, by massive increases of the poll tax, which subsequently might be remitted for Africans in white employment. Every Afrikaner who appeared before the Labour Commission as a witness stated approval of measures such as these.[42] By rejecting such ideas, *The Times* could speak out in behalf of the Africans playing a considerable part in the larger economy of the Transvaal by producing foodstuffs, a task that they preferred to mining. The argument also allowed it to defend importation as a response to an urgent problem that could not await the slow development of other resources of manpower that, after all, might never occur. It could also argue that it was a constructive imperial policy because it could restore prosperity to the Transvaal and improve the economy of all of South Africa. If, as Milner claimed, South Africa was the weak link in the Empire, here was a temporary policy that could speed its economic development and with that, and never without it, the way would be opened for true administrative independence and eventual self-government. Consequently, a strong link would replace the weak one and the Empire would gain sturdiness.[43] The argument, therefore, did have some persuasive value.

The Times also stressed the idea that colonial opinion in the Transvaal favored importation. It based this claim on several sources of information beyond reports from its own correspondent. There were the statements from Lord Milner to consider, and *The Times* always accorded great weight to his pronouncements. Then there was the action that the Legislative Council, which in the paper's judgment was as "representative as possible," to weigh. It had arrived at its decision in favor of importation after three days of "free" debate and, according to *The Times*, there was "no shred of evidence" that the members had voted under pressure. Moreover, the council's action had the support of a petition then circulating in favor of importation.[44] Various government Blue-books published on the question only served to confirm *The Times* in its contention that public opinion in the Transvaal favored the policy.[45] By March, the paper was so convinced on this point that it stated, "The first question for us is whether we are to repeat the blunders of colonial policy in the eighteenth century by overruling the opinions and wishes of a colony upon strictly domestic affairs." Of course, technically Britain could intervene because the colony had not yet been granted self-government. But such an exercise of power, *The Times* reasoned, would "ruin all prospect of amicable relations in the future."[46]

Such arguments, however, failed to persuade Strachey. The guarded approval of importation that his *Spectator* voiced late in 1903 now vanished. When Parliament began its review of the ordinance in February 1904, the *Spectator* announced, "No issue of more momentous import, Imperial and Ethical, is likely to be debated in the House of Commons in the whole course of the twentieth century than that . . . of sanctioning the introduction of Chinese Labour into the Transvaal." Moral and economic questions of "great gravity" disturbed the journal about the use of Chinese labor. Since the employment of the Chinese as "ordinary free labourers" was beyond consideration because public opinion in the other South African colonies would not allow it, the mineowners had only managed to disarm the hostility toward importation of the Chinese by promising to subject them to the "discipline of a convict settlement." That was the *Spectator*'s opinion of the Code of Regulations regarding the Chinese in the Transvaal that Parliament had received. Could a "Christian State" be justified in imposing such conditions? "Surely it is *contra bonos mores*," it stated, "for a nation to authorize the organized invitation of human beings, . . . to enter upon a state of life which it recognizes for its own members as inherently undesirable, and truncated in respect of the essential requirements of human progress." The *Spectator* also feared that an "odious demoralization from the employment of numbers of Chinese without their womenfolk" could occur. It even worried that the Chinese compounds would become "nests of vice."

Economically speaking, the *Spectator* believed that the advocates of the policy were moving too fast. It questioned whether "sufficient evidence" had been produced to show that the people of the Transvaal favored it. On 27 July 1903, Chamberlain had stated that the majority of the people of that colony opposed the importation of Chinese, and the *Spectator* now observed that a half-year was "a very short time indeed to allow for the conversion of a community to a line of action by which its whole future may . . . be affected." The report of the Transvaal Labour Commission, it said, indicated that the labor shortage would last for years. That being the case, it appeared that the imported laborers (or, since the plan stipulated the Chinese would be repatriated after three or five years, relays of laborers) from China would remain in the Transvaal far into the future. Consequently, "sooner or later" some cause would be found for "whittling . . . away" the restrictions and the country "would become alive to the fact that it had adopted a Mongolian element." "We can hardly believe," the *Spectator* concluded, that Parliament would sanction the experiment for this reason "even if it does not, as in our judgment it ought to, reject it on moral grounds."[47]

When the measure received the royal assent in May 1904, the *Spectator* expressed its dismay in forceful terms. "A profound mistake has been made by the Imperial Government in sanctioning the Transvaal Ordinance," it announced. It was a "dangerous and most retrograde step" for the Empire, which would "fall like the great Empires of the past" if liberal principles were forsaken. The *Spectator* believed that the imperial government should have refused to move when it became obvious that its action offended both colonial and home opinion. It should have refused to "break away from the principles on which the Empire has been reared—principles which have brought emancipation to subject races, and have prevented the grave demoralization of the white race that comes through holding men in any form of servitude." There had been no cause to hurry action; indeed, a slow development of the mines would have served better the economic health of the Transvaal. "The true duty of the Imperial Government," it argued, was "to build up a sound and healthy English-speaking community in the highlands of South Africa, not to develop low-grade mines in haste." The *Spectator* was willing to make one concession to the use of Asiatic labor on the Rand at this juncture. It did not oppose the use of laborers brought from India where the process would have been supervised by the "vigilant protection" of the Indian government. Under those conditions, there would have been "strong guarantees against the system partaking of the nature of serfage." That alternative, however, was not used. The Indian government refused to agree to it. "Surely," the *Spectator* reasoned, "the Ordinance stands condemned. We have had to go to China for coolies because the Indian system of indentured labour could not be reconciled with the demands of the Transvaal."[48]

In the course of this controversy, Strachey wrote to Moberly Bell suggesting that *The Times* showed partiality on the Chinese labor issue as well as on Tariff Reform. Bell replied in a manner indicative of his own growing adamancy on the question. "On the Chinese Question I feel more strongly than on any other," he told Strachey. "I think your line deplorable—an abnegation of every rule of right—an abdication of every tradition I hold dear—but I should never dream of accusing you of a want of impartiality! You have formed your ideas as honestly as I have formed mine."[49]

Among the critics of Chinese labor, none raised its voice in louder protest than the *Westminster Gazette* . During the first half of 1904, Spender's daily became an arsenal of arguments against importation. It refused to accept the evidence of "necessity" that *The Times* found so convincing. It brushed aside the petition signed by forty-five thousand people that had circulated in the Transvaal favoring importation, noting it had been circulated by the Importation Association, neither an "official nor an impartial authority." Rather it supported those opponents who were now asking for an official referendum on the question in the colony. Moreover, it cautioned that it was a mere "juggling with words" to call the Transvaal "a free country with a free press." It was not popularly governed and its press appeared to be subject "to certain severe qualifications, if we may judge from the recent history of some of its newspapers."[50] So from the beginning of this chapter in the debate, the *Westminster* doubted the very premise of consent upon which both Lord Milner's administration in the Transvaal and the imperial government in London justified their policy of importation.

In the months that followed, the *Westminster* repeated and hardened most of the criticism it had made in 1903 against importation. It continued to portray the introduction of Chinese labor in the Transvaal as favoring financial rather than imperial interests. "The Imperial interest is not to work out the mines in feverish haste and then leave the country to the Boers but rather to prolong the period while the gold lasts until a British community with other industries and interests can be built up," it insisted. Consequently, it urged the government, using Chamberlain's slogan no less, to "think imperially."[51] It still believed also that the entire case had been exaggerated in order to placate the mineowners. The

Westminster still maintained that alternatives to using indentured Chinese labor were available. Labor from India, recruited under supervision, could be used, it claimed, or if need be the imperial government could guarantee a deficit in the Transvaal. Perhaps the British government could forgo the £30,000,000 that it intended to have the colony pay as a debt. In return for that the mineowners could do without Chinese labor and the Transvaal Executive could reduce the cost of administration. Then the cost of living in the Transvaal could be cheapened by reducing tariffs and railway rates. Beneath it all, the *Westminster* quarreled with the government about "time." Slower, but steady and lasting, economic development was the remedy the Transvaal needed, not an industrial boom supported by the crutch of Chinese labor.[52]

The new emphasis appearing in the *Westminster's* criticism was a humanitarian one. Disturbed by the restrictive terms of the ordinance, it charged time and again that it would make the Chinese workers mere "animated implements." It had little patience with the idea that the Chinese should be excluded because they were Chinese and considered as mere pretence the argument that it was in the interests of the Chinese workers themselves to be brought to South Africa. The *Westminster* opposed the type of life that they would be forced to endure in the Transvaal. Nor did it mitigate circumstances to have the Chinaman's life there compared to life in the army. "Tommy Atkins submits cheerfully," it argued, "to the discipline imposed on him in serving his country, but we wonder what he would say if it were proposed to indenture him for service to mineowners on terms that are proposed to the Chinese."[53] For several months the paper searched for just the right phrase to express the confined conditions under which the Chinese would be allowed to live. "A system indistinguishable from slavery," "animated implements," and other such expressions were tried and used.

Then in the middle of March, it stumbled upon its most effective label. "It is not for us to dictate to the Transvaal whether it shall have Chinese or not, but we have a fair right to say that while we are responsible for the policy of the colony it shall not have them as serfs." To support this claim it referred to three treaties the British had made with the republic. The terms of the Sand River Convention of 1852 forbade slavery in the area while the Convention of Pretoria of 1881 and the Convention of London of 1884 forbade "slavery or apprenticeship partaking of slavery." No one could deny, the *Westminster* said, that the present ordinance created conditions "partaking of slavery" since, although the laborer entered voluntarily into the agreement, during the time of his indenture he was deprived of rights and privileges and if he left his employer he was to be treated "as a fugitive slave."[54] On the very day that the *Westminster* presented this argument, Campbell-Bannerman moved a vote of censure of the government in the House of Commons, claiming that the policy was an outrage. The state of labor prescribed by the ordinance, he said, was "very like slavery. . . . 'Indentured labour' no doubt sounds better, but do not let us haggle over words: let us see what the thing itself is."[55] Defenders of the ordinance delighted in comparing it to a previous ordinance passed by a Liberal government regarding labor for British Guiana. The *Westminster*, however, made short work of such comparison. While admitting that the British Guiana Ordinance was far from satisfactory, it claimed that it was substantively different from the Transvaal ordinance since in the case of Guiana the laborers were not "forcibly repatriated" but rather encouraged to remain "to take [their] place in the life of the community."[56]

In fact, the *Westminster* contended that the government had lost touch with public sentiment and was making a "disastrous mistake." It was far from being a matter of party warfare as the defenders claimed. The government, the paper said, had failed to prove its case for Chinese labor, alternatives existed, and even if the case could be proven, "we are not entitled to import them [the Chinese] under the conditions of the Ordinance."[57]

THE TIMES AS RESPONDENT

As the debate over importation proceeded during the first half of 1904, *The Times* assumed the responsibility of answering critics' questions on the subject. These responses represented an effort to force the debate to recognize the facts of the case, but the facts were open to interpretation.

Consider the criticism that importation would impair the future of South Africa as a "white man's country." That term meant that the area should remain attractive to British laborers who wished to emigrate there. Consequently, when critics charged that this policy would destroy all hope of the colony becoming "a white man's country," they had future opportunity for labor in mind. Sometimes the idea that Chinese labor was harmful to the prospects of British labor was mentioned directly. The idea, of course, was part of the general indictment of the mineowners. *The Times,* claiming that such a proposition could not withstand "serious examination," dismissed it categorically. The present labor shortage in the colony hindered all other branches of industry there and also kept the cost of living high because it allowed agricultural production to lag. Chinese labor not only would restore the mines to prosperity but also would increase railroad traffic and "free Kaffir labour for work on the land." Agriculture in the colony, the paper reminded opponents, was at a standstill just as much as its mining industry. Chinese labor, consequently, would restore prosperity throughout the colony and create conditions attractive to British labor. In the mines, for instance, where it was estimated that one skilled white laborer was needed for every eight men working as unskilled laborers, the opportunity for British labor could only be widened.[58]

Then there were questions about the indenture system itself. In an attempt to reassure the public on this aspect of the question, *The Times* offered several types of observations. Regarding the loose talk about the "vices of the Chinese," for instance, it observed: "The vicious Chinaman is no worse than the denizens of our own slums; the average Chinaman is as decent as the average of other races. The Chinese merchant or banker could teach honesty to a good many company directors in this country; and the Chinese labourer does more work, asks less pay, makes less fuss, and turns his hand to a far greater number of things than the ordinary white labourer."[59] Moreover, the laborers to be recruited were of the best class of workers in the north of China, and the terms of contract were "more liberal than anything hitherto offered to the Chinese."[60] While in the Transvaal they would be "decently and comfortably housed" and would live under restrictions freely agreed to in the contract.[61] Those restrictions, which guaranteed that South Africa would not become a "Chinaman's country," as well as fulfillment of the terms of contract, were fair and businesslike, *The Times* contended.[62] They protected the South Africans from a great influx of Chinese immigrants and were not debasing to the Chinese laborers themselves. Yet opponents raised the cry of "slavery." *The Times* left no doubt as to what it thought of that accusation. "The cry of slavery is, perhaps, the silliest that has been raised in this controversy," it stated. No race on earth could "take care of itself better than the Chinese." They were informed about the conditions offered, their government approved of the arrangement, and the workers themselves made a contract for three years. Yet, it observed, "we have good people at home who call the result slavery."[63] The Opposition when in office had passed a similar ordinance for the use of Chinese laborers in British Guiana; thus, *The Times* charged that the "slavery" cry was just so much "cant" voiced by "pretending philanthropists."[64] Accordingly, it claimed the Opposition was attempting to create an "artificial hysteria."[65] It even charged that "a more unblushing and unscrupulous appeal to ignorance and prejudice was never made" than that which the Opposition now made by advancing the label of "slavery."[66] So the critics of Chinese labor held no corner on hard language.

Toward the end of this phase of the debate, Milner expressed his doubts about the future of the Empire and South Africa, as he did from time to time. "I don't know whether we shall succeed in saving the British Empire," he said on this occasion. "There are not quite enough of us, who care enough, and the nation are *such Fools*!! But it is quite clear that we shall not save it if we muddle South Africa."[67] He could not fault *The Times* for the effort to prevent "muddle" as he perceived it. Yet the mounting tide of opinion in Britain against him and his Chinese labor policy indicated that his definition of "muddle" failed to find wide acceptance among the politically astute.

The first phase of the debate on this issue ended in the spring of 1904. Following the Chinese government's acceptance of the experiment in May, the indentured servants began to arrive in June. They contracted themselves to work as unskilled workers in the mines. Their contracts were for three years and could be renewed for another three by mutual consent. After that, repatriation was mandatory. The mineowners assumed the cost of transit, and the workers could bring their families also at company expense although the high cost of living on the Rand makes one doubt the sincerity of that offer. While working in the Transvaal they had to reside in compounds, which they could leave for forty-eight hours if they procured a permit, and they were subject to a number of regulations. Thus began an experiment in economic development that would pester imperial discussion for several years to come.

5

Chinese Labor in South Africa: Part II, 1905-1906

After the initial controversy over the issue of the use of Chinese laborers in the Transvaal, a lull occurred in the debate. It reappeared, however, as an issue in 1905 and assumed major dimensions at the time of the Election of 1906. After that it remained a source of hostility between the parties for several more months and a subject that could touch political nerves for several more years. J. L. Garvin entered this second phase of the debate. During the previous year, Tariff Reform preoccupied his personal contributions to the imperial cause. Late in that year Sidney Goldman acquired the *Outlook* and appointed Garvin to edit it. Like the *Spectator*, whose influence the "new" *Outlook* intended to counter, it was a weekly review of politics, letters, science, and the arts. Garvin announced its purpose in the first issue, on 7 January 1905. It would be an "organ worthy of the Unionist party and the Imperial cause."[1] A little later he described it as a journal of "Constructive Imperialism."[2] Faithful to his word, Garvin at once addressed imperial subjects in the journal. In the case of South Africa, he discussed the area mainly in terms of its wider political and economic problems—those that went beyond the issue of Chinese labor. Yet there was ample support for Lord Milner and his achievement to imply where Garvin would stand on the issue of Chinese labor should it again become a topic of major controversy. Another imperial journalist would now accompany those at Printing House Square in defending the Milner program.

RUMBLINGS OF THE ISSUE: 1905

Was prosperity returning to the Transvaal with the aid of Chinese labor? The imperial journalists examined that question in the early months of the new year. Those on both sides of the issue employed figures to document their cases. *The Times* was quick to claim that Chinese labor benefited the Transvaal.

Between June and October 1904 the native labor force in the mines rose from 74,632 to 78,491. "It is clear, therefore," the paper observed, "that the Chinese coolie, who was to be a disruptive force in the social economy of South Africa, has not even caused a permanent disturbance in the Kaffir labour market." Moreover, it stressed the fact "that 2,130 more white men were employed in November than were in January 1904." Consequently, *The Times* began to speak of the "returning prosperity" of the gold-mining industry.[3]

Opponents of Chinese labor, however, were apprehensive about the results. The *Westminster Gazette* cited the figures released by the colonial secretary as reason for disappointment. It observed that between May and October of the previous year 14,000 additional unskilled workers had been employed (13,000 Chinese and 1,000 Coloured) but the increase in white employment during that period had been only 1,400 and they were not necessarily engaged in gold mining. Such evidence convinced this paper that arguments used to secure British assent to importation were proving false. Similarly it recalled that "the Government led us to think not merely that [Chinese] women and children could come, but that in point of fact they would." Only two wives and twelve children had arrived.[4] The *Westminster*, moreover, refused to abandon its previous protests at this time. Aside from humanitarian arguments, which always merited consideration, it still claimed that Chinese labor on the Rand was an artificial crutch and that resort to it was harmful to the Empire. It returned to the idea that imperial policy should have been designed with the aim of making the colony "a country for British white men," a hope that "depended on breaking down the repugnance of white men to manual labour" in the Transvaal. That attitude was "an old inheritance from the days of slave labour." It was a "social prejudice." But shortage of labor represented a great chance to break down that prejudice.[5] Consequently, the *Westminster* continued to view the employment of the Chinese as fundamentally wrong and would not be persuaded otherwise. Meanwhile, the *Spectator* warned that as the Chinese workers became more proficient, the mineowners might resort increasingly to hand labor rather than to the use of machine drills. What would then be the future of white skilled workers on the Rand?[6]

The critics had raised a significant point. In fact, the ratio of white laborers to others employed on the Rand was dropping. Moreover, many of the whites there were only temporarily employed to build compounds. In January 1905, the Emigrants' Information Office announced there was no demand for white miners on the Rand and that those who were already there were encountering depressing employment prospects. To this discouraging news could be added the fact that of the British emigrants who had gone to various parts of the Empire in 1904, none had emigrated to the Transvaal.[7] The effectiveness of the use of Chinese labor to enlarge opportunities for white labor and to stimulate emigration from Britain, indeed, could be questioned.

Nevertheless, the Chinese labor question failed to achieve major proportions at this time. When it did experience a revival of serious proportion some months later, the nature of the argument had shifted. It then focused on reports regarding the maltreatment of the Chinese. Indeed, in August Lord Milner's successor Lord Selborne acknowledged the fact that some illegal floggings had occurred.[8] About that time a number of disturbances took place in the Transvaal involving some Chinese who had deserted. Crimes and "outrages" had been committed, and a state of uneasiness spread among the white inhabitants of the area.

Then, on September 5, the bishop of Hereford wrote a letter to *The Times* that received considerable attention in the press. What had caused such a state of affairs on the Rand? The "natural inference," he suggested, was "that the condition of things in some of the mines must be very bad, or the wretched men would hardly have deserted in such numbers as to become a danger to the country. The only alternative explanation . . . is that many of these 50,000 Chinamen must belong to the lawless or criminal classes, and that our Government have allowed the Colony to become the dumping ground for these dangerous undesirables." The bishop charged that the government had made a "stupendous political blunder" in sanctioning the ordinance and suggested that it be ended. He lamented that "this ugly blotch of 50,000 serfs on the fair face of our Empire" brought discredit to the British nation and was injurious to British workers and abhorrent to traditions cherished by them all. Claiming that "men and women of all parties" opposed it, he declared, "We object to this yellow labour ordinance, because its conditions partake of slavery."[9] The letter indicated that a state of affairs deeply disturbing to the British people had been reached.

The Times devoted an entire leading article to the bishop's letter and, in that manner, to the revival of criticism against the Chinese on the Rand in general. It was an interesting article that synthesized much of the Conservative defense of the ordinance at this point. Claiming that the actual amount "of grave crime committed by the coolies" was relatively small, *The Times* tried to show that opponents of the use of Chinese labor in the mines had exaggerated the issue. "Only sixty-eight Chinamen are now serving sentences of more than six months. That does not strike us as an appalling proportion in a mining population of over 40,000," it observed. While it was correct, it admitted, that there had been "a good many convictions" for "riot" and "assault," few of them were of a serious nature as the sentences indicated. Furthermore, the paper acknowledged that desertion was a serious problem but stressed that authorities were bringing it under control. The bishop's statement had occasioned other letters to the paper and in one of these the correspondent argued that Chinese labor should be as free on the Rand as it was in Singapore. *The Times* disagreed with that contention on the grounds that the Transvaal was a "white man's country" and Singapore was not. The paper admitted also that, although the original ordinance that the government introduced was a mild one, the laborers lived under restricted conditions. Under pressure from the "clamour of their opponents" in England and South Africa, the government had made the terms more stringent. Therefore, it did not behoove those very critics who had demanded greater restrictions, "whether as avowed political enemies or under the cloak of devotion to particularly exalted ideas of humanity and of moral purity," now to denounce the results of their own remonstrance. *The Times* suggested the bishop had based his protest on unexamined sources and on an exaggerated interpretation of news reported in its own columns. "We believe that the great majority of the Chinese labourers are, on the whole, content with their lot," it maintained, and that the bishop erred when he predicted that the ordinance would be repealed. "His own party was challenged in the House to say they would repeal it, and they refused to say so." The system, *The Times* concluded, was successful and "essential to the prosperity of South Africa."[10]

The rationale offered by *The Times* little appealed to the *Westminster Gazette*. It agreed with the bishop that the government had made a "grave blunder." Regarding the causes the bishop had given for the wave of crimes, the *Westminster* found them reasonable and suggested that "the real explanation is that both alternatives . . . [were] in part true." Even if the Chinese were well fed and sheltered, as *The Times* had claimed, there remained not only the evidence of illegal punishment but also evidence that "particularly the earlier contingents . . . contained a considerable proportion of undesirables" to consider. The *Westminster* did agree with *The Times'* retort that the Transvaal was "a white man's country and Singapore . . . [was] not," but insisted that an essential difference existed: in the Transvaal the Chinese became "human implements" as compared to Singapore where they were welcomed to participate in "the ordinary forms of trade and commerce." Furthermore, it claimed that *The Times'* attempt to make Liberal critics of the policy responsible for the addition of more stringent provisions to the ordinance was a "travesty of the facts." They had not flogged the Chinese in an unauthorized way. The ordinance was simply "an unnatural and un-English measure, alien to our traditions and bearing within itself the seeds of trouble and mischief."[11]

Traces of the bishop's protest also appeared in the *Spectator*'s leading article on the subject at this juncture. Even if one allowed leeway for possible exaggerations of the reports from Johannesburg, it argued, sufficient evidence remained to prove "that the experiment of employing Chinese labour has broken down from the point of view of law and order as completely as we believe it has from the economic standpoint." Chinese laborers working in Hong Kong, Singapore, and throughout the Malay Peninsula did not behave as they did in the Transvaal and the Chinese were known as people who had "a strong sense of justice and a great deal of pride of race." Why, then, had they resorted to lawlessness in this case? The answer probably could be found in antecedents or treatment or in some combination of the two. Perhaps the Chinese had been recruited from among undesirable elements at home or perhaps they had been "demoralized" by their employers and the whites of the area who treated them with "dislike and contempt." Was it not "quite conceivable" that injustice encouraged them to desert and after that "to act with complete lawlessness in order to obtain food"? The *Spectator*'s commentary had touched part of the truth of the matter since once a deserting laborer left the Rand he was technically an outlaw and had to live as such to remain alive. "The essential thing now," it concluded, "is to send back the Chinamen as soon as possible, and to make an honest attempt to employ white labour as the necessary supplement to Kaffir labour on which hitherto the industry has been based." Because of the influence of the mineowners and the failure of statesmanship, that solution never had received a fair trial.[12]

Unquestionably, the combination of maltreatment of the Chinese plus the lawless conduct of the deserters had revived the Chinese labor question. It would be erroneous, however, to suggest that, either before or after this revival, the question was a dead issue. To the contrary, fixed in the political attitudes of the imperial journalists, it emerged from time to time in their commentary and awaited the moment when political circumstances would make it a major question once again. Balfour's resignation, Sir Henry Campbell-Bannerman's subsequent formation of a Liberal government, and the ensuing Election of January 1906 provided the necessary circumstances. At the beginning of that year the issue resurfaced as a major question.

CHINESE LABOR: 1906

Not since 1904 had there been such a flurry of debate over Chinese labor as there was in the opening months of 1906. The focal point of the renewed interest was the general election in January. As an election issue, this subject was second only to that of Tariff Reform. After that, controversy revolved around what would be the policy of the new government regarding the Chinese on the Rand. Finally, a few months after the election, Lord Milner became the center of a discord that caused the imperial journalists to address the question once again.

During the month of the election, supporters of the Chinese labor policy were angered by what they contended was the mendacity the Liberals displayed in exploiting the issue for political profit. They had done so since the beginning, but now the subject was being used against the party that prided itself in being most identified with the interests of Empire. Believing that the late government had saved the imperial cause in South Africa, they now found it galling to be portrayed as the wreckers of Empire. *The Times*, for example, charged that "no subject of recent years . . . [had] been treated by the Liberals with more colossal and wilful dishonesty." They had known all along that it was false to say the Chinese were "slaves" used to take employment away from white men, or to claim that the Chinese might "overrun South Africa," or to contend that other alternatives existed for the Transvaal's development. "The object," *The Times* concluded, "was to catch the votes of the same ignorant voters whose confidence has been so shamelessly abused, and the mischief that might be done in South Africa counted for nothing in the party maneuvre."[13] An ally now joined *The Times* in publicizing that sentiment.

J. L. Garvin did what he promised. He made the *Outlook* into a major voice in imperial affairs. His touch made a difference: after ten weeks of his editorship, the circulation of the *Outlook* tripled. Garvin then claimed that his "serious intention" was to make it the best political weekly in the world.[14] Yet despite his own success, he was in one of his periodic phases of despair about his craft as the election approached. "The state of the newspaper world generally is terrible," he told Lord Milner. "Never have I admired journalism as an institution all my heart being in sustained work and sustained thinking; but the cowardice, ignorance, the tacit corruption of newspapers now fills me with more amazement than I know." Regardless of the performance of others he declared to Milner, "Upon Chinese Labour we shall fight with every fibre."[15]

True to his word, Garvin entered the fray with an article bearing the unmistakable imprint of his own hand. "If it had been possible by any means to avoid the importation of Chinese coolies we should have been the first to advocate their exclusion," he announced. Native labor could only be had "by taxing the natives into the mines," a policy unworthy of consideration. White men in the area refused "to work in company with the black man." Moreover, the Rand was not a second Comstock Lode "rich enough to pay its unskilled workers the four dollars a day of the worst-paid Comstock mines"; its profits were difficult to maintain. The white population of the Transvaal had consented to the importing of Chinese workers, and "we cannot break our bargain to that effect and allow the latter-day Cobdenites to write 'Perish South Africa' in place of 'Perish India.'" As for the men who were stomping over England proclaiming "Chinese slavery," he said he had "small patience" with such "unreasoned emotion."[16] Later in the month, when news of the Liberal triumph became known, he made this bitter observation: "To the vision of peak-cowled inquisitors and twopenny loaves was soon added another—that of the Chinamen in chains. For all the other tools known to Mr. Birrell's department, Chinese 'slavery' was the handle that fitted. It was the lie of all work."[17]

Such charges left the opponents of the Chinese labor policy unmoved. Although Strachey, who remained personally opposed to it, withheld the *Spectator* from the controversy at this point, Spender could not allow the issue to remain dormant at a time when an election was at hand. During the month of campaigning that preceded the polling, he devoted five leading articles to this subject. All of the paper's old arguments were revived for the effort. The government's labor policy for the Transvaal was one of mischief and mistake, based on the false ideal of servile labor, and deeply resented by the English people.[18] "The mineowners wanted the Chinese; the Boer, the storekeeper, the miner and the artisan would not let them come in as free men." Accordingly, his

Westminster concluded, the imperial government approved the ordinance when it should have helped the colony to a better choice.[19]

A new dimension of speculation also entered the issue at this time. What would the Liberals, who had long abhored Unionist policy on this matter and considered it a departure from British traditions, do about it once they gained the power to act? Both supporters and opponents of the ordinance had to face that question on 4 December 1905, when Sir Henry Campbell-Bannerman formed his Liberal government and later when the Liberals received their record majority in the General Election of January 1906.

Beginning in late December and continuing through the first two months of the new year, the Liberals developed their policy on this question. Campbell-Bannerman came uncomfortably close to making a false start on this issue. On December 21, he delivered a keynote speech for the coming election at Albert Hall in which he announced it had been decided "to stop forthwith—as far as it is practicable to do it forthwith—the recruitment and embarkation of coolies in China and their importation into South Africa; and instructions have been given to that effect."[20] However, when the government learned that licenses had been granted for 14,700 coolies who had yet to leave China, it realized that some qualification of the Albert Hall statement would have to be made, or else it would appear that Liberals were revoking the already issued licenses by *ex post facto* legislation. Consequently, on the eve of the election, the cabinet decided to respect those licenses and to allow the importation of the 14,700 additional coolies.[21] Thus a Liberal policy on this imperial question began to emerge and it commanded public attention for the next several months. The policy can be reduced to four basic points: (1) to respect existing licenses but to issue no more, (2) to attempt to modify the existing regulations in order to improve the conditions for the Chinese who were there, (3) to arrange for the repatriation of those Chinese who wished to return home, and (4) to reserve the final decision on the question for the Transvaal itself after it received self-government.[22]

Such a policy disturbed and angered the previous supporters of Chinese labor such as *The Times*. Concerned about what it interpreted as uncertainties revealed by the government's pronouncements on the subject, it believed that if Campbell-Bannerman and his colleagues failed to recognize realities and allow the Chinese to stay in the Transvaal, they would "cut the tap-root of South African prosperity, which is also the tap-root of South African tranquility."[23] It bothered *The Times* that the Liberals did not appreciate how important the Chinese laborers were to the continued prosperity of the Transvaal, to the continued employment of 18,000 white men who were indirectly dependent on the mines, and to the maintenance of the colony's basis for revenue. Rather than concentrating on this central proposition of the problem, the Liberals appeared more concerned with "queries about imaginary grievances" and in the mitigation of supposed "servile conditions."[24] Accordingly, *The Times* declared: "The new Administration has cut a very sorry figure in the debate on Chinese labour. It has been driven to shuffle, to wriggle, to prevaricate, to take refuge in petty quibbles and verbal tricks, and, in spite of it all, to confess that there is a flaw in its mandate, and that it cannot defend the statements upon the strength of which it obtained a very substantial proportion of its total support."[25]

The Liberals found it difficult to deter criticism of their handling of the Chinese labor problem. As the controversy moved into February, for instance, Lord Elgin, the new colonial secretary, expressed his regret that the term "slavery" had been used in connection with the ordinance and Winston Churchill, then the under secretary of state for the colonies, announced that the term "slavery" only could apply to the conditions specified by the ordinance at the risk of "terminological inexactitude," a phrase that deserves to be ranked among his more famous utterances. After it became clear that the Liberals had opted for gradual measures on this subject and would await the time when the Transvaal would receive self-government and could repeal the ordinance itself, a new proposition appeared in debate. Suppose the Transvaal acted contrary to Liberal expectations when its time came, and imported more Chinese or passed a new ordinance offensive to the Liberals. Would the imperial veto be employed in such a case? Several Liberal leaders stated in Parliament that they would favor the use of the veto if that occurred.[26] So *The Times* was able to continue its criticism. "On the Chinese labour question," it explained, "while driven ignominiously to withdraw the charge which formed the sole basis for interference, the Government seem bent upon claiming the right to intervene." The imperial government, of course, had the right to intervene, but the paper questioned if it would be prudent action for the Liberals to take after making numerous declarations about their wish for the colony to have self-government. "But the present is bad enough, without anticipating the future. What we have to complain of in the present is the utter uncertainty in which the Government has plunged South Africa."[27]

Garvin's *Outlook* reacted in a similar fashion to the Liberals' expression of regret regarding references to the indenture system as one of slavery. "We welcome these kindnesses as evidence of the chastened repentance which responsibility brings . . . . But the belated disclaimer of Lord Elgin and others does not absolve the Government."[28] Nevertheless, the *Outlook*, showing considerable restraint for the militant journal it was, abstained from exploiting the subject at length. It was more interested in the new constitution being proposed for the Transvaal.

The *Westminster Gazette*, however, devoted a number of its leading articles to justifying the Liberals' evolving policy on this issue. "Unqualified Satisfaction" was the title of its December response to the new government'shandling of the Chinese labor problem. Although the government was reserving its "opinion in the matter," it had chosen the wise course of not agreeing to further importation and seeking the opinion of "an elected and really representative Legislature, and they have accordingly decided that recruiting, embarkation, and importation of Chinese coolies shall be arrested pending a decision as to the grant of responsible government to the Colony."[29] This statement came on the day following Campbell-Bannerman's Albert Hall speech. A few days later, as the new prime minister shifted his ground somewhat on this issue, the *Westminster* adjusted its defense. The mischief, it claimed, was done when the Chinese were introduced in the first place and the Liberals had a right to indict the previous government for that act while doing all in its power "to wean the Transvaal from Chinese labour" under present conditions.[30] The paper's position was that the new government recognized the impossibility of any immediate and violent reversal of the policy of its predecessors, and, therefore, it was suspending further importation while conceding that the question would have to be settled ultimately by the responsible government of the colony.

When the new Parliament gathered in February and the Chinese labor dispute emerged once again in that forum, the *Westminster* continued to give the government its complete support. On the thorny question of whether or not the imperial government should intervene if the future government of the Transvaal should decide in favor of the ordinance or some similar measure, the paper tried to steer a middle course. In a rather ambivalent statement it reasoned along these lines: "If the Colony decides ultimately that the Chinese are a necessity, we may regret it but we shall not dispute their decision, but at the same time we shall say to them that one of the tests of their necessity must be their readiness to receive the labourer under a contract which is really free."[31] Regarding the exchanges in Parliament revolving around whether or not the ordinance created a condition of slavery in the Empire, the *Westminster* showed little patience. Was it "the equivalent of slavery," "a servile" condition, or something merely objectionable? Such discussion, the paper claimed, went wide of the mark. "What has been condemned," it insisted, was "not the word but the thing—the whole policy."[32] The *Westminster* charged that the Opposition had lost touch "with ordinary sentiment. During the first weeks of the session, the Opposition forced the question to turn on the legitimacy of campaign rhetoric and pledges. Later it suggested that the Transvaal would not yield and a disastrous conflict would ensue with the new colonial government that it planned to establish. Puzzled by such argument, the *Westminster* declared that the ordinance was a source of trouble for the imperial government, for the colonial government, and even for the Chinese government, which could terminate the entire system. Furthermore, to attract the investor and to create confidence in the future of the gold industry, the industry needed "some more permanent and stable foundation than reliance on Chinese coolies." It was, therefore, "bad business as well as bad politics."[33] The *Westminster*, then, did not care to be bothered by troublesome details of the case; it preferred to focus attention on the greater thing involved, the evolving sound Liberal policy that gradually would correct the damage done by the previous government in this matter.

THE ENTRAPMENT OF LORD MILNER

In the midst of this continuing debate on the Liberals' evolving policy on Chinese labor, a trap ensnared a giant. It was fitting that Milner, the proconsul returned from years of service in South Africa and now sitting in the House of Lords, should become the center of controversy in the last phase of debate on this subject, for he had long been a symbol to both sides. While to Conservatives he personified vigorous imperial statesmanship and appeared heroic, to Liberals, particularly to the Radicals, he represented all that was rash, dangerous, and destructive in imperial policy. The Radicals detested him and made him the scapegoat for all South African misfortunes since the time of the Jameson Raid. On February 26 Milner, whom the Conservatives hailed as the great authority on South Africa, delivered his maiden speech in the House of Lords. In it he reviewed his entire South African policy. The following day, the Liberals sprung their trap. It was then that Lord Portsmouth referred to some Blue-book statements to show that, in fact, abuses of the Chinese laborers had occurred, and drew attention to an admission by Mr. Evans, the superintendent of foreign labour, to the effect that he had sanctioned "slight corporal" punishment at the mines for minor offenses and that he had informed Lord Milner of that action. Lord Milner, in turn, had not objected to it. Lord Portsmouth then asked Lord Milner whether or not that account was correct. As Alfred Gollin has observed, Milner's response was "straightforward and manly." He answered that he had been informed.

> He fully recognized that he took upon himself the whole responsibility. He thought in the light of subsequent events that he was wrong. Shortly afterwards, the Lieutenant Governor, Sir Arthur Lawley, was informed that on one or two of the mines ill-treatment of the coolies had taken place, and he immediately forbade all corporal punishment whatever at any of the mines. If he himself had been there he should have done exactly the same.

Lord Portsmouth then proceeded to read a dispatch sent from the Colonial Office to the Foreign Office on 5 March 1904, stating that "Lord Milner pointed out that any labourers imported would be amenable to the law of the land by which everybody, including whites, is liable to corporal punishment for certain offences, and in these cases could only be inflicted after trial and sentenced by a magistrate or judge."[34] It appeared, therefore, that Milner had sanctioned illegal flogging.[35]

The admission, manly or not, caused a sensation. Several weeks later the House of Commons debated a motion of censure expressing "its high disapproval of the conduct of Lord Milner . . . in authorising the flogging of Chinese labourers, in breach of the law, in violation of treaty obligations, and without the knowledge or sanction of his Majesty's Secretary of State for the colonies." Afterwards several amendments were made to the resolution including one for the government introduced by Winston Churchill, whose language throughout this skirmishing did little to smooth tempers. It stated, "That this House, while recording its condemnation of the flogging of Chinese coolies in breach of the law, desires in the interests of peace and conciliation in South Africa to refrain from passing censure on individuals."[36] The amendment, despite Chamberlain's charge that it was "a cowardly" one, was accepted, and the motion as amended was carried with a majority of 220.[37] What did this mean? The *Annual Register* termed it an "implied censure," and that remains an apt description of the action. Regardless, Milner's supporters in the press were irate.

From the time of Milner's speech of February 26 through the Commons' debate on his censure, he became the subject of an angry exchange of views in the press. Naturally, the pro-Milner papers rushed to his defense. Radical extremists, *The Times* said, were

> clamouring fiercely for the censure of the House of Commons upon that eminent public servant [Lord Milner], because he yielded to the representation of some harassed official that he could not maintain discipline among the coolies without resorting to corporal punishment. People whose prejudices against the Chinese are so strong that they would not have them in the Transvaal on any terms whatever profess to be profoundly indignant because a few Chinamen underwent what public school boys habitually suffer, and what has only within the last few days been abolished in the Navy. What are eight years of fearless effort and tireless devotion in his country's cause, what are the defeat of Krugerism and the saving of South Africa for the Empire to politicians of this kind?[38]

The *Outlook* spoke of the treatment of Lord Milner as an action of "little motives, led by little men, [that] called forth little emotions. It was conceived in hatred indeed, but its effect was as futile as its end was cowardly. It was a pitiful attempt to assume the functions of the judge, and to bias the verdict of posterity. Malignity could no further go." The Radicals, it claimed, could not understand Milner's "profound sense of responsibility," and they were playing with the British people and the Empire for party purposes. They were "pigmies" who dealt a blow against all the administrators who served the nation. "The ingratitude of England to men who had made her what she is has been told again," the *Outlook* reflected. "The reward of a lifetime of brilliant service . . . is malignant hostility at Westminster, ending in a vote of censure on a single error."[39]

The idea of censuring Lord Milner was even more than Strachey could accept. Although he had not featured the Chinese labor issue in his *Spectator* since the previous fall, he took this opportunity to convey his thoughts to Asquith, the chancellor of the exchequer in the Liberal government, shortly before the debate on censure began. "I hope you will not think me a busybody," he began, "if I venture to express some considerations on the subject [the censure of Milner]." Then he continued:

> As you know, I have been a very strong opponent of Milner's, not only as regards Chinese labour, but of his attempt to suspend the Cape Constitution, and other matters. Indeed Milner, I believe, regards me as one of his arch enemies, and if it is a sign of enmity to regretfully consider that in many respects he is not a statesman of the best Imperial kind, but is far too much of the bureaucrat who hates representative government, and thinks people ought to be ruled by intelligent officials, and not to govern themselves, then in that sense, I suppose, I am an enemy. At the same time, I feel, as I am sure you must feel, that it is an enormous mistake for the House of Commons to weaken the sense of responsibility in the Ministers of State by censuring their subordinates. It seems to me like the proprietor of a newspaper censuring, not the editor who publishes a bad article, but the man who wrote the article.

Strachey preferred to place the blame on the late government for "allowing Milner a free hand, or if you like, for choosing a bad High Commissioner and keeping him in office." He admitted that the flogging episode, which was contrary to a treaty, was a peculiar case, but he felt that "the Government would gain a great deal in consideration if they were to take the high line of refusing to censure the underling, and insisted only on dealing with the master, or at any rate the man who took the responsibility of calling himself Milner's master. . . . If the Government puts him in his proper place by protecting him, as the subordinate ought always to be protected in our system, I think they will score heavily."[40] Asquith replied forthwith, on the day when the censure resolution and the amendments were introduced, and said, "I agree with you about the Milner. . . [motion]. It will be met by a suitable amendment."[41]

The *Spectator*'s article on this subject reflected the substance of the thoughts Strachey had communicated to Asquith. Furthermore, that article, while lamenting Milner's grave mistake, went so far as to state, "Though we disagree so profoundly with certain of Lord Milner's actions, we can never forget, not only that his intentions have always been patriotic, single-minded, and self-sacrificing in high degree, but also that he has rendered great and notable services to the nation."[42] So amid all the passion of the moment, Strachey and the *Spectator* took to the high ground.

There were, however, other responses to Milner's predicament. Spender's *Westminster Gazette*, while remaining restrained in its reaction, tried to place what it called "the Milner episode" in its proper place "in the history of the matter." His role, it explained, should have been to carry out the policy of the imperial government but it became one of championing his own policy of Chinese labor. "In his anxiety to make it work, he did not realise that the illegal flogging which was alleged to be necessary and which he appears to have considered harmless, was a violation of an international obligation and a wrong to the Imperial Government."[43] Regarding the government's maneuver that resulted in the "implied censure" of Lord Milner, the *Westminster* expressed satisfaction. One section of the government's followers, it reasoned, demanded the censure of Milner, but the government wished to refrain from censuring an individual and desired to do everything possible to advance conciliation in South Africa. All things considered, Spender's paper termed the government sponsored resolution moderate, even mild. "Envy, malice, and all uncharitableness have been read into this resolution, but one would have supposed that even an Archbishop would have been content with it," it stated. As a parting word on the subject, it offered the reflection that Whig statesmen of fifty years ago probably would have taken a sterner course when dealing with a "departure from legality."[44]

A final act in the Milner episode remained to be played. Just five days after the Commons accepted the government-sponsored amendment on the censure, the House of Lords took a contrary action. On March 29, it approved a resolution stating, "That this House desires to place on record its high appreciation of the service rendered by Lord Milner in South Africa to the Crown and the Empire."[45] *The Times* and the *Morning Post* were urging some action of this sort and, of course, were elated by the resolution while Radical papers deemed it cause for attack. Nevertheless, despite the far-reaching implications of the House of Lords' statement, the controversy in the press over Chinese labor was drawing to a close.[46] Since the decision to allow a self-governing Transvaal the right to render the final verdict on the use of Chinese labor had been made, the subject could not be divorced from the attention given to the drafting of a new Transvaal constitution. Therefore, the issue stayed alive in that context. Yet although it continued to attract sporadic comment until the Chinese departed from South Africa in 1910, it ceased to be a major item for concentrated examination in the press after the attempt to censure Milner.

PERSPECTIVES ON THE ISSUE

The controversy about using Chinese indentured labor on the Rand remains a fascinating one in the history of the Edwardian Empire. It hardened imperial views that dated back to differences over South Africa policy before the Anglo-Boer War; it engendered doubts and hostility about the Unionists' reconstruction of South Africa and their imperial policy in general; it played a major role in the mounting difficulties Balfour's government faced; and it emotionally charged the Election of 1906. Furthermore, it called into question the need for great proconsuls who towered over party politics to administer the affairs of Empire. A belief in the force of personality seldom has been stronger than it was among

Edwardians of strong imperial persuasion. That is one reason why the attempt to censure Lord Milner was so important. By condemning him, the Liberals were showing their disdain for the imperial idea that he personified.

The imperial journalists found it a difficult issue to handle. Their task was one of response to Lord Milner's initiative. Supporters of the policy like *The Times* had to set aside imperial idealism, which could have popular appeal, and argue in a pragmatic and defensive manner. They had to make the best case for an unpopular policy. Was there any question, as the *Westminster Gazette* said during the last stages of the debate, about how the people would respond if they were asked if they approved of the Chinese labor ordinance? *The Times*, of course, claimed it was a necessary measure, needed to bring about the economic reconstruction of South Africa and to secure its place in the twentieth-century Empire. Opponents believed it unnecessary, but they had the same general imperial goals in mind for South Africa. So it was an imperially divisive issue.

In terms of political consideration, the ordinance was a risk. Even the senior staff at *The Times* was not in accord about it. Buckle wished to support Milner and that probably gained his support for it. There was, however, little need to convince or push Moberly Bell on this issue. He thought that any policy of resorting to "exclusion" was "wholly wrong. . . . If that much-buttered Anglo-Saxon race can't dominate a continent without resorting to exclusion, we had better stop talking about our governing genius. Exclusion is a Russian and childish way of shirking the difficulty." Moreover, Bell disdained the thought of considering white labor as an alternative. His private comments regarding it became crass. "Personally," he told one correspondent, "I look forward to the time when, not in its Colonies only, but here in England, it shall be regarded as disgraceful to employ a white man on mere manual unskilled labour, and when the lower races shall be the universal hewers of wood and drawers of water."[47] Buckle's moderation and Bell's own sense of what was politic kept that aggressive tone out of *The Times'* commentary on the subject.

On the other hand, there is evidence to suggest that Chirol had serious reservations about the policy. "Nor can I imagine anyone with statesmanlike grasp of the situation denying that the economic advantages of Chinese labour have been ruinously outweighed by the disastrous political consequences—both in this country and in the Transvaal," he wrote several years later. "I may perhaps be somewhat biased as I always had very grave misgivings as to the policy of Chinese labour, but even those who had none at the time are, I think, now for the most part prepared to admit it has proved a great and grave blunder."[48] Chirol's point regarding the outweighing of economic advantage is significant, for by premising its argument in behalf of the ordinance as economic necessity, *The Times* had made a serious mistake. The idea of importing Chinese laborers entailed much more than economic consideration. It involved social and imperial traditions dear to the English. Besides, as the opponents were able to show, even the correctness of the economic argument could be debated.

Strachey was quite willing to play down the economic argument. He would accept a much slower economic development of the Transvaal than Milner and his supporters deemed necessary. Political considerations, however, led him to practically abandon the subject after September 1905 and he only returned to it in March of the following year to urge fairer treatment for Lord Milner. The reason for his dropping the subject, however, had nothing to do with his opposition to the ordinance. That continued to the end. It probably resulted from Strachey's own involvement in politics at the time. He made his only attempt to seek an elected position by standing for Parliament in the Election of 1906. He did so as a Unionist Free Trader. Considering the fact that he was then taking a conciliatory line in the *Spectator* toward the Liberals, particularly toward the Liberal Imperialists, and that on January 6 he urged electors to vote for Liberals in constituencies where there were no Unionist Free Trade candidates, one can conclude that he had done enough already to offend the more conservative Unionist Free Traders. It would have been impolitic for him to have pushed his opposition to the ordinance at a time when Unionist wrath was being aroused by the cry of "Chinese slavery," which jeopardized any chance they might have for success at the polls.

No one wanted a Unionist victory in the Election of 1906 more than J. L. Garvin. To him the Unionist party was the imperial party, and one would expect him to be emphatic in defense of its imperial policy. Emphatic involvement, however, was precisely what he avoided in this instance. The *Outlook* did not approach the question of the ordinance directly until the Election of 1906, a year after Garvin assumed command, and it did so then mainly to protest the Liberals' abusive "Chinese slavery" language. His journal only took an emphatic stand in March 1906 and then more in defense of Lord Milner than in support of the ordinance. It might be well to remember that Garvin was Chamberlain's great champion in the press and that from the start Chamberlain had misgivings about the introduction of Chinese labor on the Rand.[49] Bearing this in mind, it can be observed that Garvin's explosive defense of Lord Milner in the *Outlook* on March 24 came just three days after Chamberlain delivered a masterful if hopeless defense of Milner in Commons and that the article repeated with emotive forcefulness some of the same arguments the statesman had employed with dignified restraint. In fact, by his own admission, Garvin believed that Balfour had underestimated the "Chinese slavery agitation" and later wrote that the issue was "as fitted as any ever known to madden popular prejudice."[50]

Opponents of Chinese labor suffered difficulties of their own. The issue was a yawning trap for overstatement, and it caught a number of Liberals. The Unionist charge that their opponents exploited the issue for political profit was accurate. Their substitution of the term "slavery" for "labour" and their subsequent apology for doing so proves the point. Even J. A. Spender, who had attempted to remain fair-minded in his many critical statements on the subject at the time, later wrote that it was a subject in which "ugly party spirit mingled with sincere indignation." "Ardent Liberal politicians who had writhed under the Unionist attack at the Election of 1900 now took their revenge."[51] He made that comment about the years 1903 to 1905. About the Election of 1906, he said it was a time when "Liberal and Radical partisans took a malicious pleasure in exploiting Chinese Labour against opponents."[52] That being the case, it bears mentioning that the partisan journalists considered here, who opposed the experiment, showed greater restraint in handling the "slavery" theme than did some of the partisan Radical and Liberal politicians and journalists responsible for election speeches, leaflets, and posters in 1906. Suggestive though their language could be, it appears almost moderate when compared to election posters depicting coolies in chains.[53] Regardless, considering the context of political discussion of the times, the implication of what they said exceeded the precise meaning of the words they used.

Chinese labor was also an issue that marred the chances of resolving differences among British imperialists, to whatever degree that was possible, that dated back to before the Anglo-Boer War. Everyone interested in the Empire favored a generous reconstruction and hoped for a British-Boer reconciliation. Furthermore, there were many parts of that program that Liberals and Conservatives alike could endorse. Liberals, for instance, supported Milner's policy of repatriation and resettlement of the Boers after the war. They supported his creation of an Agriculture Department as an important contribution to the future economic life of the colonies, and they approved his establishing the Inter-Colonial Council in 1903 to deal with matters of common interest between the two colonies. Moreover, the Liberal Opposition in Britain approved of the £35,000,000 guaranteed loan that Milner wanted to finance the general reconstruction of the colonies including railway development and public works construction. His imposition of a 10 percent tax on mining profits also received the Liberals' consent, though some preferred an even higher tax. One element of his reconstruction program, his educational policy, was a potential issue for debate at Westminster. Since it met with Afrikaner resistance when it challenged the teaching of their own language and traditions in school, it might have become a serious discord between Unionists and Liberals in Britain. It failed, however, to become a major source of controversy at home. All things considered, it can be said that under any circumstances his policy would have been watched carefully and some differences about it no doubt would have appeared, but it is possible to suggest that there was much in Milner's reconstruction program that could receive support from imperialists in both of the major parties at home. Chinese labor made it difficult for that degree of support to materialize.

What was there about the Chinese labor experiment that made Milner's most respectable critics in the press so hostile to it? Based on the idea that extreme circumstances necessitated extreme measures, the policy might have been a feasible one. Most historians have accepted the fact that an economic crisis existed in the Transvaal at the time of the inception of the policy. That being the case, Milner searched for the clue to all the economic difficulties the colonies faced and found it to be labor. An adequate supply of labor for the mines, he came to believe, would secure both the economic recovery and the reconstruction of the colonies. He also believed that the number of laborers who were needed could only be found in China and the Labour Commission Report appeared to substantiate his conclusion. His critics, however, believed that other alternatives existed. They suggested that more white men should be employed in the mining industry, that more natives could be attracted to the mines, and that improved machinery could be used. As we know, in making these suggestions, they brushed aside a number of important considerations. White immigration to the Transvaal was not materializing, and if it did, there still remained the fact that the barriers that kept the white man from doing "Kaffirs' work" were ever formidable. As for native labor, which after all was cheaper than Chinese, it failed to develop in necessary numbers, despite the improved conditions in the mines resulting from the reforms Milner began in 1902. Improved machinery would have been expensive, but most of the Rand's mines were of low-grade ore and worked on a slim margin of profit. Furthermore, some of the mines were so narrow that no machine drills of any sort could be used.[54] Perhaps in time such problems could be mitigated, but Milner perceived the problem as an immediate and urgent one. He believed economic stagnation was approaching that would imperil the entire reconstruction program. So he turned to the Chinese.

He had no intention of introducing a system "partaking of slavery." Chinese indentured workers were employed elsewhere in the Empire. In the Transvaal, although restricted, the Chinese were to live under conditions as generous as possible. It is true that they lived in compounds, but it is easy to have a distorted idea of those living areas. They were large, up to three miles long, and were in no sense enclosed. A coolie could leave the compound with a pass, and forty-eight-hour passes were procurable for anyone not at work.[55] One might suppose that when approached in this manner, Milner's policy was reasonable. Why, then, was it so opposed in England?

In answering that question, the views of Spender and Strachey are revealing. They were men of moderate persuasion when compared to their Radical contemporaries, and they thought of themselves as supporters of the Empire. Yet neither Spender nor Strachey accepted either Milner's alternatives or his rationale for his policy. Though men of different political party preferences, they shared similar views when it came to criticizing Chinese labor. First of all, they believed that Milner exaggerated the circumstances and that he was rushing the economic recovery of the Transvaal. That led him to rely too heavily on the possible results of a quick exploitation of the gold fields, which led him, in turn, to link imperial policy to the mineowners' quest for the greatest profits procurable. Milner was wrong, these journalists contended, in believing the problem was so urgent as to require an immediate, large-scale solution. To them the problem appeared a long-range one that South Africans along with new immigrants, who would remain there on a permanent basis, would have to solve with their own resources and perhaps with the help of natives from other parts of Africa. Consequently, they spoke of accepting a slower pace of economic development in the Transvaal. Once they established the idea of a slower pace, they could continue to advance their solution of using additional white laborers. Time would allow for overcoming the immediate obstacles that stood in the way of this solution.

The idea of attracting additional white men to the Transvaal directs one's attention to the term "a white man's country." That phrase appeared frequently in the arguments advanced by both the defenders and critics of Chinese labor. Spender and Strachey used it repeatedly in their journals. It is an interesting phrase that introduces a note of unreality into the debate since the natives of the area far outnumbered people of European descent and since their population was increasing at a faster rate than the white. South Africa could never be a "white man's country" in the true meaning of that phrase. As Arthur Balfour once observed, it could be a "white man's country" only in the sense that it was a land in which white men could thrive.[56] The British-born and highly regarded South African journalist and politician Edmund Garrett explained that the idea of a white South Africa meant that it would be a land of white civilization where white men could flourish in the professions, in business, and as skilled labor. "It has never yet meant," he said, "a South Africa of white unskilled labour, whether British or other."[57] However, Spender's *Westminster Gazette* and Strachey's *Spectator* suggested a somewhat different meaning when they used that phrase. The *Westminster* spoke in terms of the doors being opened to perhaps a hundred thousand white immigrants, while the *Spectator* talked about the possibility of placing two hundred thousand white laborers on the Rand.[58] Moreover, the *Westminster* referred to a stream of free white laborers into the Transvaal capable of introducing a spirit by which it would "no longer be deemed an offence against accepted canons for a white man to work with his own hands" if he so chose. The *Spectator* said that "the plea that you cannot ask British workmen to do unskilled labour in the mines is the merest piece of clap-trap invented to cover the determination of the capitalists to use Chinese labour."[59] Both journals admitted that decent wages would have to be paid and thereby the mineowners' profits would be reduced. Such suggestions give credence to Garrett's claim that Milner's opponents in England were counseling an overturning of the unwritten social law of South Africa which reserved unskilled labor, cheaply rewarded, for native workers.[60] The suggestions advanced by the *Westminster* and the *Spectator* did, in fact, call for a social and economic revolution in South Africa. It is clear also that they sanctioned a large influx of British immigrants into the Transvaal, which in 1904 had a total white population of about three hundred thousand.[61] The point is of particular significance for the *Westminster* because it shows that it paid little heed to the argument advanced by some of Milner's

Liberal critics that he was trying to pack the Transvaal with British immigrants in order to secure British political supremacy.[62]

At least two other fundamental differences existed between Milner and moderate critics like Spender and Strachey. As we have seen, he believed that economic recovery had to precede the political reconstruction of the colonies. A prosperous economy would secure peace, lay the basis for a Boer-Briton reconciliation, and guarantee British supremacy in South Africa. It would attract British workers and farmers to the Transvaal. British immigration was essential to the entire plan, though the Liberals exaggerated the case when they accused him of wishing to flood the area with British settlers. Spender and Strachey advanced a different priority. They believed that real reconciliation between the Boer and Britain would result from the application of the Liberal imperial policy of granting self-government. That should take precedence over a hasty economic recovery and it would form the basis of a new loyalty. At the very least, the ordinance should not be sanctioned until the Crown colonies received responsible government. It is worth noting that the *Westminster* and the *Spectator* advanced this idea months before the Opposition introduced it in the Chinese labor debates in Parliament.[63]

Finally there was the indenture system itself. To Milner it was a necessary expedient, and there is no reason to doubt his belief that the terms of contract and the condition of the coolies' lives both at work and in the compounds should be made as agreeable as possible. Although some form of a Chinese indentured labor system had been used in the British Empire since the 1840s, and although Liberals had not opposed it before, it appeared to Spender and Strachey as fundamentally wrong at this time. Perhaps that was due to the sheer numbers involved, or to the fact that they would work in mines and live in compounds, or to the fear that they would become a permanent element in South Africa's already mixed population. The opposition, moreover, of other colonies in South Africa and throughout the Empire, which was made clear by the publication of the much-discussed official Blue-books on the question, must be considered. Regardless, once the terms of the ordinance were published early in 1904, the Chinese labor articles in the *Westminster* and the *Spectator* became sharper and more adamant. Undoubtedly, Spender and Strachey believed that an indenture system of this nature called into question the entire liberal tradition of an Empire where freedom and autonomous development were guiding principles. Milner never appreciated the full depth of commitment on this point, and he underestimated public opinion in England from start to finish on this all-important consideration. Both Strachey and Spender, in their respective journals, repeatedly warned that Milner was making a serious mistake by overlooking British public opinion. As the *Spectator* put it, "A great Imperial statesman . . . should have made it his business to consider public opinion in England."[64]

In many respects, the case of Chinese indentured labor on the Rand remained unsolved. Any experiment can be judged in part by its results, and by 1906 the mines were in full production supported by a force of 163,000 laborers (18,000 whites, 94,000 natives, and 51,000 Chinese). Nevertheless, the results were a subject for disagreement.[65] Bearing in mind that this study deals with imperial thought and not with the resolution of debate, several observations might be made before we examine the next imperial problem that the Edwardians encountered. That it was the wrong policy at the wrong time seems clear. At best, it was an anachronistic solution to a twentieth-century problem; at worst, the imposition of a social evil. It ran counter to what the Empire represented at its best. In opposing it, publicists, particularly men like Spender and Strachey, demonstrated a fundamental grasp of reality and, in this case, of historical change. *The Times,* on the other hand, became an apologist for the government's policy.

The entire episode of the experiment with Chinese laborers represents an unpleasant chapter in imperial history. There is no reason to suppose that it was anything other than that for the men who argued over it at the time. Both *The Times* and J. L. Garvin admitted that it would not have been introduced if any other solution were possible. Moreover, the entire matter obviously was a vehicle by which a disruptive imperial problem intruded into domestic party politics. It impaired any hope for a consensus policy for South Africa, and it captured attention that otherwise might have been directed toward arresting the drift in South African native affairs. Regarding the last point, surely it is at least possible to suggest that the mineral wealth of the Transvaal was the property of both the European and African population of the area, that both black and white labor could have expected a decent wage for their work in the mines, and that the labor shortage represented an opportunity to reorganize the mining industry and perhaps even to remove or reduce the economic color bar on the Rand. Enough traces of this line of thought appeared in the thousands of words that British journalists put to paper on this subject, to remind us that such thought at least stirred in their minds.

While the commentary on Chinese labor excited a vigorous, even at times impassioned, controversy over the various elements of the issue, it also involved many expressions of concern about the image and the future of the Empire. In the vernacular of the day, South Africa may have been perceived as the "gilt-edged asset" of the Empire, but in reality it held a much more important place than that in serious imperial thought. Implementing the proper reconstruction policies for South Africa was a matter of anxiety for the imperial journalists as they pondered the future of Empire. What does the future hold for South Africa and for South Africa within the Empire was a frequently asked question associated with their writing on Chinese labor. Their many references to the "hope" of South Africa, to its "promise," and to the "far-reaching considerations" involved in this issue remind us that there was a broad imperial perspective in their argumentation. The economic recovery of the Transvaal was crucial to this line of thought. It was the springboard to a firm Boer-British reconciliation, to a closer union of the South African colonies, and to South Africa's becoming a second Canada in the association of British settlement colonies. Would Chinese labor, even if some policymakers deemed it an unavoidable expedient, help or hinder the long-range imperial hopes for a viable and unified South Africa in the Empire? That was the larger question that hovered over this controversy. It was a question of means not of ends. The Liberal government that assumed office at the end of 1905 believed the goal could be reached by stressing political rather than economic reconstruction. A new constitution, they thought, would work the necessary magic, but they would soon discover that imperial dissension over the proper way to proceed with the reconstruction of South Africa was far from silenced.

6

The Political Reconstruction of South Africa: Part I, 1905–1906

The dissension that appeared in the ensuing dialogue in Britain about South African reconstruction should not blur the fact that a general consensus prevailed about long-range goals. First, the Transvaal and the Orange River Colony were to receive self-government in time as the Treaty of Vereeniging promised. Furthermore, a widespread hope existed that the four South African colonies would unite to form a new state, which the British imperialists hoped would become a strong component in the Empire. With these aims in mind and while the Chinese labor dispute rumbled on, discussion began about the political settlement that would replace the early form of Crown colony government the British installed in the two defeated republics for the purpose of carrying forward the reconstruction of those colonies.

The settlement itself was not all of one piece. It proceeded over a five-year period first under Unionist, then under Liberal auspices. Although it ended with the formation of the Union of South Africa in 1910, most of the discussion about it centered on a new constitution for the Transvaal.

Milner was in no hurry to change the form of government for either of the two ex-Boer republics. To him, "development" was the "trump card" to play. "Every new railway, every new school, every new settlement, is a nail in the coffin of Boer nationalism," he told Alfred Lyttelton, who replaced Chamberlain as colonial secretary in 1903.[1] Believing that he and Lyttelton had saved the Transvaal and the Orange River Colony from "a first class financial mash" by carrying through the labor importation experiment, he now hoped for time to allow the expected industrial growth to take hold. "As regards that blessed constitution," he confided to Lyttelton, "my strong advice is, unless political conditions at home make immediate action necessary, *not to hurry*. I never felt very greatly enamoured of my own suggestions on this point—it was a distasteful task."[2] But political conditions, doubts about how much longer the Unionist government in London could cling to office, did force the issue.

Initially, differences emerged over the question of time. On the one hand, Milner counseled a patient evolution toward self-government. He favored first the granting of representative government to the Transvaal and then, two or three years later, establishing a system of responsible government there. By responsible government he meant "a system, under which the people of the Colony choose the Legislature and the Legislature appoints the Government," that would be "to all effects and purposes independent."[3] That definition complied with the general usage of the term at that time. Milner feared the consequences of a premature grant of responsible government. "Impatience is one of the commonest forms of human error," he claimed.[4] The cornerstone of his policy was "to defer responsible government until the Boers, or at least a large proportion of them, had learned to acquiesce—it must needs be many years before they rejoice—in membership of the British Empire, or until the British element of the population had been so strengthened as to make separation impracticable."[5] Too rapid a move to responsible government, far from accomplishing that goal, could place the Transvaal's legislature in the hands of men hostile to the imperial connection. Representative government, however, would draw together approximately equal numbers from the British and Afrikaner populations into an elected legislature. Moreover, Milner wished to introduce representative government in the Transvaal first and then at some later date extend it to the Orange River Colony. Boer and British voters were about equal in number in the Transvaal, but in the Orange River Colony the Afrikaner element was overwhelming. To him that difference controlled the order of action; he wanted the Orange River Colony to have what he hoped would be the constructive results of the experiment in the Transvaal to use as a guide in its own constitutional advance. Unionists at home supported Milner's gradualist approach.

Others opposed it. Speaking at Dundee on 17 November 1904, the Liberal leader Sir Henry Campbell-Bannerman announced that if and when the Liberals were called to power at Westminster they would grant "a full and encouraging measure, an honest measure of self-government" to the Transvaal.[6] Moreover, part of the British population in the Transvaal favored the immediate implementation of responsible government without an intermediate step of representative government. So did the leaders of the Afrikaners. Toward the end of 1904, a number of these leaders, including Louis Botha and Jan Christian Smuts, both of whom would have great political roles to play in the years ahead, met with Lord Milner and told him that they could not accept representative government. Only full responsible government would satisfy them.[7]

Before proceeding farther, some explanation of the various political organizations that now appeared in the Transvaal is in order. The best-known of these groups was the Boer organization, *Het Volk* (The People). Meetings leading to its formation began as early as May 1904; it formally organized in January 1905.[8] The *Het Volk* had exceptional leaders in Louis Botha and Jan

Christian Smuts, two Boer commanders of repute in the recent war, and behind it loomed the force of an Afrikaner revival.[9] It opposed a constitution granting only representative government and even threatened to boycott it. Among the Transvaal British two organizations of political consequence appeared at this time: the Transvaal Responsible Government Association and the Transvaal Progressive Association. Both formed in November 1904. The former was led by E. P. Soloman, brother of Sir Richard Soloman, the attorney-general of the Transvaal. As its name implied, it favored responsible or self-government. It was based in Johannesburg and in 1905 had about five thousand members. The Transvaal Progressive Association was larger. Active in Johannesburg, Pretoria, and throughout the Rand, it claimed thirty-two thousand members in 1905. Sir Percy Fitzpatrick and George Farrar led this organization, which urged the granting of representative rather than responsible government for the Transvaal.

THE LYTTELTON CONSTITUTION OF 1905

Lord Milner and colonial secretary Alfred Lyttelton began to consider the need for a new political arrangement for the two colonies in the spring of 1904. They believed the time had come to fulfill Article VII of the Peace of Vereeniging, which specified "as soon as circumstances permit, representative institutions leading up to self-government, will be introduced." After talking with Prime Minister Balfour about the future prospects of the government, Lyttelton reported to Milner that it could not be expected to survive beyond the following spring. It appeared certain that the Liberals would form the next government and the colonial secretary feared that they would "extricate themselves from a painful dilemma [their own overstatement of the case against Chinese labor] by granting self-government to the new Colonies *sans phrase* [without needless words]." It would be better, he continued, if the first step toward self-government were "taken under your and our guidance than under that of men who seem very reckless of the essential interests of South Africa."[10] Several dispatches from Lord Milner on the same subject crossed Lyttelton's message in transit. Milner's thinking on the subject was clear and direct. He believed the material aspects of his reconstruction program would be completed by the end of the year and that the industrial and agricultural development of the area would continue if the labor problem were solved. A longer wait would risk alienating particularly the British population of the Transvaal. Moreover, Milner explained that he planned to retire from his South African position by the spring of 1905 and would like to settle "the next step in constitutional development" before departing.[11]

At the proconsul's urging the colonial secretary then made a public declaration about the government's plan to introduce a constitution for the Transvaal. On 21 July 1904, he announced at the House of Commons that the time had arrived for the colony to receive elective representative institutions as promised by the Vereeniging terms. Controversy about representative versus responsible government had already begun in South Africa, and within a few months after the Lyttelton declaration the previously mentioned political organizations appeared in the Transvaal to champion one idea or the other. In England there was scattered commentary in the press about the proposal, mainly around the beginning of the new year. The document was promulgated by Letters Patent at the end of March 1905, and its terms were made public on 25 April 1905.

The instrument that became known as the Lyttelton Constitution applied only to the Transvaal, not to the Orange River Colony. In short, it converted the Transvaal's Legislative Council into a Legislative Assembly composed of 6 to 9 official members and 30 to 35 members elected by qualified white male voters. The franchise was actually liberal. All the ex-burghers over twenty-one who were on the old voting lists of the republic could vote regardless of monetary qualifications.[12] The constitution provided for seats to be distributed on a voters' basis rather than on population. This principle of "one vote, one value" favored the British, many of whom were bachelors as compared to the Afrikaners, who normally had large families and who would have benefited from a distribution based on population. There was to be an automatic redistribution every four years. Intended as a temporary measure, the constitution provided, to use Lyttelton's description, "a school for self-government, a means of bringing citizens together in political co-operation, and a sphere for the natural selection of the men most fit to lead and ultimately to undertake the responsibility of administration."[13] Milner's ideas again had prevailed, but they occasioned a mixed reaction in the Transvaal. There, as one historian explained it, "the Progressives announced that they were grateful for the constitution, Het Volk announced that it was unacceptable, the Responsibles announced that they would make it unworkable."[14]

In England scattered press commentary on the new constitution began around the first of the new year. At that time some attention was given to the idea of representative government for the Transvaal, which it was understood the forthcoming constitution would provide. In a series of three editorials, *The Times* expressed its approval of the idea that representative government had to precede responsible government and concluded that wisdom supported Milner's preference for the automatic redistribution of seats and for basing the allotment of seats on the number of voters rather than on total population. Regarding the last point, it observed, "Giving voting power in respect of people who do not vote is likely in practice merely to swell the power of the political parsons of the Dutch Church, who are one of the most retrograde forces in the Transvaal."[15] It pronounced the demands of the Transvaal Responsible Government Association "outside the area of profitable discussion."[16] As for the Boer opposition both to representative government as an intermediate step toward responsible government and to the idea of basing the suffrage on the actual number of voters, the paper saw little value in such negativism. The Boers merely were being uncooperative and trying to avoid "the doom of their old political monopoly."[17]

Garvin's *Outlook* argued along similar lines. It approved of the main features of the forthcoming constitution, as they were known, and complimented the Transvaal Progressive Association for being "a sensible body of opinion." Regarding Mr. Soloman and his Responsible Government Association, who wanted "full Responsible Government, practically by return of post," the *Outlook* labeled such opponents "Irresponsibles" who could be disregarded "were they not so obviously supported by the great body of the Radical party in this country." It believed the average Transvaaler would reject the urgings of that association in favor of the more sage advice of the Progressive Association. "We will offer the Johannesburger a sound argument which has, probably, occurred to him," it concluded. "He is interested in finance, and has various loans in prospect. Upon what terms does he suppose that any commercial house in Europe would finance him? We had the curiosity to ask this question of one or two great financiers in the city a day or two since, and they met the inquiry in silence, but with looks more eloquent than anathemas."[18]

The *Spectator*, too, expressed its satisfaction at this preliminary stage. It announced that there were "very many and very cogent" reasons for granting a "modified autonomy" at this time. There were risks to be run in doing so, but it really came down to a "case of competing dangers." The Transvaal, it reasoned, scarcely had recovered from the war and the influx of the British population was not yet large enough to make the colony secure. But the Transvaalers were anxious to receive a system of free representation, and it ran counter to British traditions to deny such wishes. The present system of a nominated legislative council had worked smoothly enough, but it was not intended to be permanent and should not be perpetuated. However, "the chief reason for the grant is that it provides a safeguard to the Colony against the vagaries of our party politics." Although it had no wish to offer precise comment on the scheme until the government published it, the *Spectator* did say that it was in agreement with the general principles that Lord Milner favored. It suggested, moreover, there were two principles that should guide the formation of the constitution itself. First, it must establish a real system of representation and provide for "freedom for popular opinion on all public matters, and [for] popular control over legislation." No scheme representative only on paper would suffice. Second, since the idea was to establish a "modified autonomy," "the modifications and safeguards must be equally real." Great Britain still bore the responsibility to "ensure that no harm . . . [should] come to the Colony or the Empire during such an experimental era." The *Spectator* hoped, as it believed, that the "education in the responsibility which complete self-government" would bring could begin now and that it would "lay the foundations of the self-government, which we hope will not be long delayed."[19]

The *Westminster Gazette* shared the hope that the forthcoming constitution would mark the beginning of the move toward self-government in the near future. Beyond that it had little to say on the proposal at this time, thus separating itself from the biting criticism of the Radical press that portrayed it as a sham. All things considered, the chance of the forthcoming constitution receiving the support of the imperial journalists seemed encouraging.

On April 25 the government published the constitution both in England and in the Transvaal. During the interim since the issuance of the Letters Patent nearly a month before, Lord Milner retired from his position in South Africa. Lyttelton wrote a dispatch explaining the circumstances and reasons that led the government to settle on this particular constitution as the best one for the Transvaal at this time. His statement appeared in published form accompanying the Letters Patent.

A thorough response now could be made to the constitution. These were, however, crowded times for international news. Reports of the Russo-Japanese War, which was then raging, filled the papers. Japan recently had defeated the Russians at Mukden, and that event was still receiving wide attention. In the West, a confrontation between the powers that would become known as the First Moroccan Crisis was at its height. A dispute over the military administration of India had emerged between top British authorities there, and that problem edged its way into the news. Nevertheless, imperial journalists made an immediate and emphatic response to publication of a new constitution for the Transvaal.

As one would suspect, the constitution pleased *The Times*. The masters of Printing House Square labeled the new instrument of government a "great proof of our trust." As it had done at the beginning of the year, *The Times* once again endorsed the idea of a gradual development leading to self-government. That approach, it reasoned, fulfilled previous pledges the government made on the subject and had behind it the force of precedent since such a system had been followed in the case of Canada, the Australian colonies, the Cape Colony, and Natal. Moreover, the effects of a long and bitter war still lingered in the Transvaal and there was "strong reason to fear that the leaders of the defeated race" still held ideals that were "incompatible with the welfare and the peace of the Empire." Then there was the fact that the native population there greatly outnumbered the white inhabitants, another reason, claimed *The Times*, for a gradual and cautious move. Regarding this point, it observed, "The representation of this population [the native] is expressly withheld by the terms of the peace until responsible government has been established, but any Bills passed by the new elective Assembly subjecting coloured subjects to exceptional disabilities are to be 'reserved' by the Governor." Regarding specific provisions of the instrument, the paper chose to comment on two items: the formation of new constituencies and the use of the number of voters rather than the total white population as a basis for representation. *The Times* approved of both of these decisions. The old constituencies had been designed to give the Boer farmers preponderance over the non-Boer populations of the towns, while to base the electoral districts on the total number of white inhabitants would have secured supremacy for the Boers because of their traditionally large families. Although "Boer reactionaries" favored the use of the old constituencies as well as the use of total population for the purpose of distribution of seats, neither seemed practical or wise in the view of *The Times*. Even as things stood with the provisions of this constitution, risks abounded, and the paper stressed this point.[20]

Garvin's *Outlook* also voiced its strong approval. "There is no parallel in political history for the magnanimity with which the Boer population of the annexed territories is dealt with in the scheme of representative institutions which we have now proposed," it announced. Without commenting on specific provisions of the scheme, the *Outlook* offered a strong defense of granting representative rather than responsible government at this time. To award responsible government without this transitional stage would have been "to bestow a malignant gift" because, as Lyttelton had explained in his dispatch, responsible government meant party government. The latter would have created an unacceptable political environment. It would mean "a political vendetta between the races [Boer and Briton] and would stereotype their divisions." Noting that it desired the domination of neither race by the other, the *Outlook* mused that a union of the races was the hope of the future and believed that this constitution promoted that hope. It also believed that considerable risk existed in the grant of representative government. "In conceding representative institutions to a community in which a positive and cheerful loyalty has not yet been substituted for sombre acquiescence, we are taking—it would idle to disguise it—a considerable risk. We take that risk without grudging . . . . The only hope for the Imperial future in South Africa lies in convincing the Boer race that our racial will and fibre are as stubborn and tough as their own, and that British power is as little to be manoeuvred out of its positions as to be swept out."[21]

Strachey also brought the *Spectator* into line with support of the new constitution. His commentary, of course, was more subdued in style than that of his rival, the *Outlook*. As always, the *Spectator* attempted to provide reasonable advice on this imperial matter. "Though we should not have been afraid to grant the Transvaal the privileges of complete self-government at once and without limitations, it was not only natural, but according to precedent, to take two steps instead of one, and to begin by the grant of representative government," it stated. "The custom of the Empire has always been to conjure the full right of nationhood within the Empire gradually, and no harm will be done in the case of the Transvaal in this case." It is clear, however, that the *Spectator* wished that the transition to self-government would be quick. "We want to see responsible government established in the Transvaal as quickly as possible because we believe it to be the great antiseptic of Empire." With that idea in mind, it devoted most of its space to explaining how "unfettered self-government" had smoothed imperial relations elsewhere in the Empire and how it had the power "to sterilise" colonial disloyalty. It agreed with *The Times* that the Colonial Office acted wisely in granting representative government only to the Transvaal at this point. The Orange River Colony, its reasoning went, "just because it was a more homogeneous, an older, and a better-governed state than the Transvaal, was also a deadlier antagonist of the British Empire" when it was the Orange Free State. Moreover, the Boers in that colony vastly outnumbered the British. The Orange River Colony, therefore, should receive the grant after the Transvaal. The *Spectator* noted the blemish in the constitution regarding the suffrage. Although it was right that the former Boer burghers should have the right to vote, it was equally right that newcomers should receive it as well. The constitution provided a six-month residence requirement, but it also specified that a new voters' register would be prepared every two years. In effect, that meant that the newcomers would find the qualification for voting was "more like eighteen months." Consequently, the *Spectator* favored compiling a new voters' register every year. As for the "one vote, one value" stipulation, that was "thoroughly sound."[22]

Spender's Liberal *Westminster Gazette*, however, found little that could be termed sound or even satisfactory in the constitution. At best it was "a small first bite." But it had not come as a surprise, for it remained true to the pledge that Joseph Chamberlain made to the House of Commons in July 1902 when he said self-government would be established in a series of steps (i.e., first step, a Crown colony; second step, the adding of a nonofficial element to its legislative council; third step, the substitution of an elected assembly for the nominated legislative council; fourth step, self-government). Surprised or not, the *Westminster* faulted the instrument on a number of points. It disapproved, for instance, the idea of basing the allotment of seats on the number of voters. Large families were the rule in rural areas of the Transvaal while in town a number of young unmarried men lived. In his dispatch Lyttelton had reasoned that to base representation on the total population would make it disproportional to the wealth of the land. To the contrary, the *Westminster* believed that "a man with a large family has certainly a very definite stake in the country and has shown that he has thrown in his lot with it much more definitely than the young unmarried man. We should have thought it possible to have arranged that the basis of the electoral districts should be a function of the two variables—population and number of electors." It also expressed regret over the fact that the Legislative Assembly received no power to initiate taxation nor did it receive authority to legislate on matters such as the control of railroads and the South African Constabulary that had been placed under the International Council. The decision to withhold the granting of representative government to the Orange River Colony it labeled "profoundly unsatisfactory." This constitution would have a short life, it predicted, because it would satisfy neither the Boers nor the Transvaal British who were agitating for responsible government.[23]

Far from having said its last word on this subject, the *Westminster* returned to it in a second leading article. It did so to examine "a great precedent" in which it discovered "a warning from the past." In discussions about a constitution for the Transvaal, the Durham Report of the previous century became a frequent reference point. When Lord Durham went to Canada in 1838 as governor-general, part of his task was to gather information and make recommendations about the troubled condition of the Canadian colonies. His *Report on the Affairs of British North America* of 1839 stands as one of the great documents of imperial history. It represents a milestone in the development of responsible government in the Canadian colonies and in their evolution toward union. In that report Lord Durham warned of the dangers inherent in a system of government in which an elected assembly had no control over its rulers. "It is difficult to understand," he said, "how any English statesman could have imagined that representative and irresponsible government could be successfully combined." The *Westminster Gazette* now claimed that anyone who read the Durham Report would be struck by the "ominous resemblance between what we are now doing in South Africa and what Lord Durham condemned in such remorseless terms in Canada." Bearing that in mind, what could one say of the constitution that Lyttelton now tendered to the people of the Transvaal? Only that it was a transitional instrument and a poor one at that. "For our part, we advise both the Dutch and the British advocates of responsible government to adapt it as such [i.e., as transitional] and to work together with as much forbearance and practical wisdom as possible for its conversion into complete self-government." Moreover, it could not offer even that advice were it not for the fact that the days of the present government were numbered and that another government soon would be in office at Westminster, one that it hoped would be "careful to see" that this constitution would "not under any pretext whatever be allowed to continue a day longer than is necessary."[24]

The Lyttelton Constitution need not detain us further. Technical reasons made it impossible to implement it immediately, and before they could be resolved the Unionist government fell from power in Britain in December 1905. The new Liberal government under Campbell-Bannerman, which then assumed office, had different ideas about the political reconstruction of the two ex-Boer republics.

PRELUDE TO THE LIBERALS' TRANSVAAL CONSTITUTION OF 1906

When the Liberals gained office late in 1905, they immediately addressed the matter of the Transvaal Constitution. In the Transvaal both the *Het Volk* and the Responsible Government Association found the Lyttelton Constitution unacceptable. It also failed to satisfy Radicals, or even to fulfill the hopes of many Liberals in England. Campbell-Bannerman, his recent biographer tells us, "never wavered in his belief that self-government and trust was the right policy in South Africa."[25] He had reiterated his intention to restore self-government to the two colonies as soon as possible, and now that he was prime minister there was widespread feeling that something would be done to implement that idea. When Balfour's Unionist government fell, the *Het Volk*, sensing that an opportunity for a more generous constitution had arrived, dispatched J. C. Smuts to London to press for a better settlement. He carried with him a persuasive memorandum favoring responsible government and written in language that would appeal to Liberals to consider several questions about the suffrage in the Transvaal, points that the Lyttelton Constitution had overlooked. It appeared that due to deficiencies in the old burgher rolls, which now were to be used in determining the franchise, some men would be excluded from voting. There was also the question of whether or not soldiers should be allowed to vote. The Liberals had several alternatives of action. They could allow the Lyttelton Constitution to stand. They could amend it, or they could scrap the whole instrument and offer a constitution of their own. In the end, they selected the last of these courses of action and drafted a new constitution that gave the Transvaal full responsible government.

The unfolding of Liberal policy regarding the Transvaal Constitution has provided the grist for some fascinating history. When Smuts came to England he saw Churchill, Morley, Elgin, and Lloyd George and was far from pleased with the outcome of these meetings. Then he saw the prime minister. His meeting with Campbell-Bannerman occurred on February 7. It was then, according to Smuts, that after listening to him Campbell-Bannerman said, "Smuts, you have convinced me." The next day the prime minister met with the cabinet and in a dramatic ten-minute speech persuaded its members to accept the policy of granting immediate self-government. Historians now tend to disregard this "legend" and accept a different, more involved version of what Smuts accomplished. They underscore that though significant, his role was not decisive. On the basic question of granting immediate self-government it appears he was "preaching to the converted."[26] If Smuts exerted any influence, it was probably on two points that Campbell-Bannerman introduced for the first time in the cabinet meeting of February 8: the desire to scrap the Lyttelton Constitution rather than to amend it, and the procedure of sending a commission to the colony to establish the basis for a new constitution. The Smuts memorandum had urged both points.[27]

This revised account of the meeting between Campbell-Bannerman and J. C. Smuts is a prelude to broader considerations about the grant of responsible government. Was it, in fact, the "magnanimous gesture" that it so often has been portrayed as being? Some historians, Ronald Hyam and Ged Martin in particular, doubt that it was. They claim that far from being motivated by "magnanimity," the Liberals were guided by realistic considerations. To disassociate themselves from the Lyttelton Constitution and to seek British supremacy in South Africa by another means was their intent. They believed that the first election under a new constitution would produce a small British majority and that Sir Richard Soloman, who was then the acting lieutenant-governor of the Transvaal, would become the first prime minister. Consequently, British interests including the quest of supremacy would be secured. When their expectations about the election failed to materialize, the idea of a "magnanimous gesture" that would lead to a true Boer-British reconciliation became a convenient device used by the Liberals to explain their action. According to this interpretation, the Liberals even distrusted the Afrikaners. "They based themselves on Gladstone's formula: Britain did not give Home Rule because colonies were loyal and friendly but colonies might *become* loyal and friendly because they were given responsible government. Responsible government was the last desperate remaining hope of making the Transvaal loyal. And so they tried it: but this was expediency—it was not magnanimity."[28]

It took the Liberals almost the entire year to design and present the new constitution. Many of the deliberations surrounding the forming of that document, of course, remained private, but at several points important public statements about the constitution appeared. First of all, the public learned of the government's decision to abrogate the Letters Patent for the Lyttelton Constitution and to send a committee of inquiry to the Transvaal on 19 February 1906.[29] After spending several months in South Africa, that committee, under the chairmanship of Sir Joseph West Ridgeway, submitted a report which the ministers received, but the government never published. On July 31, however, the government outlined a new constitution for the Transvaal to both houses of Parliament, just five days before adjournment. Naturally those proposals became a source of public discussion. Then, on December 6, the government issued a new constitution establishing responsible government in the Transvaal by Letters Patent. The publication of the new constitution in London appeared on December 12. Press commentary on the subject appeared mainly at two times: during the early months of the year and at midsummer. Beyond that some commentary of a rather anticlimactic variety accompanied the publication of the constitution in December. We shall consider first the general themes that shaped the press response during the months preceding the government's presentation of constitutional proposals at the end of July.

PRELIMINARY RESPONSES TO THE LIBERALS' CONSTITUTION

To the men of Printing House Square, there appeared little reason to applaud the Liberals' initiatives regarding a new Transvaal constitution. Their South African correspondent, Geoffrey Robinson, who was also the editor of the

Johannesburg Star, the most important newspaper in South Africa, fortified their misgivings a number of times. Despite the Boers' "pious appeals for co-operation galore" and all the assurances that they were "the only true friends of the working men and . . . of the natives too," which appeared in their speeches, and despite their conciliatory approach to Lord Selborne, Milner's successor, Robinson warned that the Boer traditions were unchanged.[30] His main correspondent at *The Times*, Leo Amery, had little reassurance to report to him from London. "As far as I can make out," he told Robinson, "the Government is only too anxious to leave South Africa alone, and to let the new Constitution start, and wash their hands of responsibility, but the fanatical section, I fear, are not likely to give them much peace." Dismayed about the Liberals' control of Commons, he confided to Robinson that he thought the time was approaching when those "keen on Imperial matters must definitely begin agitating for some common Imperial body outside of the House of Commons of this country."[31]

During the early months of the Liberal government, *The Times* continued its normal steady interest in South African affairs. Several definite themes appeared in its commentary on the Transvaal at that point. To begin with, it worried about the influence the Boer leaders might have over British Liberals and sensed the need to remind its readers that among the Liberals at home there were a handful of "political fanatics" who, unmindful of necessary imperial interests, were willing to accept "the protestations and assurances of the Boer leaders at their face value." Since Transvaal problems had so entered the fabric of British politics, the work of these "political fanatics" had to be watched. "But we feel certain that the opinion of these doctrinaires have but little weight either with the statesmen of the Liberal party or with the great mass of their adherents in the country," *The Times* said. The Liberal leaders understood that there were "hundreds of their own followers who . . . [were] as sound Imperialists as their Unionist fellow-citizens."[32] The paper had less faith in the Boer leaders who, in its opinion, remained unreformed. "Whatever the changes in tactics, the object of the Boer leaders remains the same—to undermine British supremacy and to deprive this country of all that it fought a costly war to secure." These leaders, it believed, played upon the emotions of the average Boer farmer, to whom *The Times* always attributed a good deal of common sense, and tried to create divisions among the Transvaal British.[33]

Securing British supremacy in the Transvaal was the all-important goal, *The Times* said, a theme that permeated all of its South African articles. Feeling as it did about the Transvaal Boer leaders and knowing that the Liberals, who now controlled the British government, would have to formalize their thinking on a constitution for that colony before long, what did *The Times* believe to be the irreducible minimum needed to safeguard the British position and hopes for the future? It was not representative government. Just after the General Election of 1906, a week and a half before Campbell-Bannerman's much-heralded cabinet meeting of February 8, *The Times* announced:

It appears that the colony [the Transvaal] is to have responsible government without the transition stage of representative government. That is not the solution we have favoured, nor do we now feel assured that it is wise. Still there may be a good deal to be said on both sides, and opinion is divided in the colony itself. But what will rob the Government of all independent support, and will assuredly be bitterly resented by the country in the long run, is any attempt to gerrymander the new constitution to the disadvantage of the loyal British element, upon which depends not only the progress of the colony but its retention as a loyal portion of the Empire. One vote one value is a Liberal and Radical principle which the present Government cannot abandon . . . . Its abandonment . . . would mean handing over the colony to the most reactionary and disloyal portion of its population. It would mean throwing away for nothing, but the satisfaction of partisan spite, what this country has secured by an enormous expenditure and by the blood of many thousands of her sons.[34]

Considering the timing of this statement, it was an important pronouncement. It came when J. C. Smuts was in London trying, as *The Times* said, "to induce the Liberal Government to modify the Constitution" their predecessors granted to the Transvaal. Among the items he and the other Boer leaders wished to have excluded from the constitution was the principle of "one vote, one value."[35] In the months that followed, defense of the "one vote, one value" principle became the bedrock of *The Times'* argument on the subject. The question no longer was would the Transvaal have representative or responsible government. It was rather what form of responsible government would be granted.

There was also an economic aspect to consider. As always, *The Times* developed its arguments regarding the Transvaal with one eye focused on the colony's economic development. Now it noted that the colony's economy was "paralysed" and hundreds of its shopkeepers and artisans had been ruined. Why? Not because of an ending of Chinese labor, for the Liberal Imperial government had stopped short of taking that step. Rather, the present economic difficulty in the colony was due to uncertainties about how the home government might interfere with and disregard the Transvaal welfare in the future. *The Times* accordingly reasoned: "The British inhabitants of the Transvaal are thirsting for self-government at the earliest possible moment, because they feel that there can be no real improvement in the economic situation as long as they do not know from one day to another what intolerable or ridiculous *ukase* may be sprung upon them at the bidding of a handful of fanatics in Parliament who may threaten to make themselves unpleasant to a timid Government. Yet, . . . they would rather continue in their present state than barter away the principle on which, they are convinced, British supremacy in South Africa so largely depends."[36] Claiming that the Transvaal British community was unanimous in its support of that principle of "one vote, one value," *The Times*, therefore, contended that only a settlement that recognized that arrangement would be acceptable.

Toward the end of July, speculation about the constitution that the Liberal government soon would propose reached its peak. The government had received the Ridgeway Committee's report, but the public had no information about its contents. Also, Sir Percy Fitzpatrick and several of his colleagues were in London at this time as delegates of the Transvaal Progressive party. They hoped to influence the home government about the need to maintain British supremacy in the Transvaal. To this end the Progressive delegates met with the colonial secretary, Lord Elgin, with the Liberal members of Parliament, and with the South African and Colonial Parliamentary Committee.

In July, as the moment approached when the Liberals would reveal their new Transvaal Constitution, *The Times* reiterated its deepest concerns. It said that the next few days would be ones of "strained anxiety" for the Transvaal. That description fits *The Times'* own disposition at this crucial point. Why had the prime minister refused to publish the Ridgeway Committee's report? The question troubled *The Times*. It feared that the committee had recommended that the system of representation proposed by the Lyttelton Constitution should be modified in favor of the Afrikaners. Precisely, the paper contended that it had been suggested that the low franchise requirements that Lyttelton had advanced now were to be replaced with the even lower requirement of manhood suffrage. What reason could justify that change, *The Times* demanded to know. Lyttelton's franchise was low by South African standards; it excluded no class; it created no injustice. "To remove it would redress no grievance; it would simply mean the increasing of the Boer vote by the enfranchisement of dependents and squatters on the Boer farms."[37] The introduction of a franchise based on manhood suffrage it charged was "simply a concession of additional voting strength to the Boers." Moreover, the application of that principle would complicate matters by raising the question of whether or not Coloured persons were to have the vote.[38] Yet even that complication was a minor consideration. The essential point was the safeguarding of British supremacy. What was at stake? "It is the issue of British or Boer supremacy in the Transvaal, and not only in the Transvaal but in the whole of South Africa, and closely connected with it, the issue of unity of the British Empire." *The Times*, therefore, placed its full weight behind the efforts that Sir Percy Fitzpatrick and his Progressive colleagues were making in behalf of retaining British supremacy in the Transvaal. Finally, on July 30, when the government announced that it would make public its program for a new constitutional settlement the next day, the paper made its last appeal on the subject. "Like Sir Percy Fitzpatrick, we do not wish to question the good intentions of Ministers; but we are filled with genuine anxiety as to their decision in view of the extreme narrowness of the margin between British and Boer supremacy in the Transvaal at this moment, and of the incalculable dangers involved if that margin is allowed to disappear. It is the whole future of South

Africa, and to a large extent of the Empire, which the Government has to decide to-morrow."[39]

The *Outlook* believed there was still hope that British goals in South Africa could be realized. A fair constitution for the Transvaal and prosperity in its mines would allow the loyal element there to prevail. However, it feared that the home government, oblivious to the "lessons of a hundred years," was about to provide a ballot that favored the Afrikaners with their large families at the expense of the unmarried British electors living on the Rand. Thus "the ballot" would bring "the triumph of Boerdom where the bullet failed."[40] Essentially, it believed, two guarantees were needed to prevent this calamity. First, since Chinese labor had been necessary to preserve the imperial tie, as a policy it should not now be reversed. When it became clear that Radicals were pressuring the Liberal government to abrogate the ordinance altogether, the *Outlook* urged, "Leave the whole question to a Transvaal Parliament elected on a basis which will not deliberately subordinate British to Boer opinion."[41] The second guarantee it demanded returns us to the "one vote, one value" principle. The *Outlook* thought that the application of that principle for the division of constituencies, rather than dividing them on the basis of gross population, was the only feasible way to secure equal representation between the British and Boers.[42] Clearly, its line of argument indicated that even for the most devoted Unionists the battleline had shifted from representative versus responsible government to the question of whether or not representation would be based on population or on the "one vote, one value" principle.

During the early month of sparring about the Liberals' intention to introduce a Transvaal constitution of their own, Garvin's *Outlook* agreed with much of what *The Times* said. It had little doubt about the Afrikaner character or aims. "The eternal Boer has not changed his character any more than the average Briton has lost his incapacity to understand him," it warned, arguing that the same impulses that moved the Boers to embark on the Great Trek and to rebel in 1881 and 1899 motivated them now. There was something to be admired in such determination, but the *Outlook* feared it ran counter to imperial interest. However, it reserved its harshest comments for the British Liberals. They were "woefully devoid of information" and caught in the web of their own "irresponsible chatter."[43] The government, it believed, lacked perspective in its imagination. It was unable to see South Africa as a whole. "They gaze at the spectacle of two white races, first cousins in ethnology, coalescing into a white whole, and all they can see is Smuts. Smuts has been received as an ambassador and has returned home rejoicing. They cannot see that, after all, the racial animosity of Boer and Briton is a minor matter in comparison with the underlying feud between white and black." This statement appeared in the wake of a native rebellion in Natal, and fears that one might occur in the Transvaal remained alive. Consequently, the *Outlook* expressed its anxiety about the ramifications of the Liberal opposition to Chinese labor. If the mines of the

Rand were to become dependent on native labor, then "men of many tribes, near akin though dwelling apart," would meet in the mines. Should that happen it would be difficult to imagine "how the proposed great reserve-system, an obvious application of the Imperial maxim *Divide et Impera* [divide and rule], could be carried out." It believed that the Afrikaners had a solution of their own for this problem. They still cherished "the Kruger idea of a South African slave-power" that the war had invalidated. Regarding the British Liberals, it offered this thought: "The time will come, no doubt, when the great untravelled party in this country will advocate the grant of political equality to the Kaffir. They were anti-Chinese yesterday. They are pro-Boer again today. To-morrow they will be Negrophile. Then they will remember that the war was waged to give the Kaffir equal legal rights, but not either social or political equality."[44]

At the end of July when the London papers produced a final flurry of articles on this subject before the Liberals produced their program, the *Outlook* became more explicit than ever in defining its position. "The attitude of the future government of the Colony toward the Chinese Ordinance, inconvenient as Liberals may find it for a time," it said, "matters little in comparison to its attitude on a thousand other questions intimately affecting the predominance of British ideals in South Africa." The constitutional settlement, therefore, was crucial. Garvin's journal had now arrived at a position not only of accepting self-government for the Transvaal but even contended that the sooner the grant could be made, the better it would be for all British interests. "The grant of a bad Constitution would be better than further delay, which can only serve to emphasize the feeling of insecurity now paralysing industry in every form." Concerned about the exodus of British from the Transvaal, the *Outlook* urged, "The Transvaal must have self-government at once, but, if South Africa is to remain British, it must have it on lines securing a just preponderance to the British majority." Retaining its apprehensions about Afrikaner past actions, it believed that an Afrikaner supremacy in the Transvaal had to be avoided at all costs. As for the Orange River Colony where Afrikaners vastly outnumbered the British, if self-government were forced on that colony which, according to the *Outlook*, neither desired it nor would profit by it, the strictest safeguards would have to be included in the grant.[45]

The *Spectator* could shift its ground with greater ease than the *Outlook*. As soon as the Liberals made public their intentions in February that they planned to grant self-government to the Transvaal and the Orange River Colony, Strachey's journal had little difficulty in adjusting itself to that policy. A year before it had supported the Lyttelton Constitution and thought it wise that a new constitution would be withheld from the Orange River Colony at that juncture. Even then, however, it had stated that, while the granting of representative government to the Transvaal was a sound move, it would have welcomed giving that colony self-government immediately. Consequently, the *Spectator* offered its support for the new policy when the Liberals announced their intention to make that grant. Admitting that "difficulties and dangers" might result from implementing self-government in those colonies, in a forthright manner it stated, "We hold . . . that the government have done right in choosing the course that they have chosen." It even set aside its own earlier misgivings about granting self-government to the Orange River Colony and said that, although it was a "bold course" to do so now, the government was now acting wisely in making that move. "The gift of self-government tends to sterilise the dangerous forms [i.e., political agitation] of hostility," it reflected. The *Spectator* assumed that men of British race and sympathy in the Orange River Colony would be protected in the constitution and said it was "pretty obvious that there. . .[would] be a pro-British majority" in the Transvaal so long as there was no gerrymandering in favor of the Boers. As for Lord Milner, who recently had spoken in the House of Lords opposing granting responsible government to the Transvaal so soon and who had warned that if South Africa were lost it would be "lost forever," the *Spectator* had this to say: "If Lord Milner had such grave doubts and anxieties as to the condition of the Transvaal and the Orange River Colony, and as to the temper of the Boers, surely it would have been the part of statesmanship not to have yielded to the cry of the mineowners for the importation of Oriental labour into South Africa under conditions which were bound to excite extreme hostility and indignation in the British democracy."[46] So Chinese labor continued to cast its shadow across all questions of imperial thought about South African politics.

After declaring its position on the Liberals' projected policy, the *Spectator* made no further major statements about the subject until July. Its leading articles at that time pulled into synthesis the basic elements composing its position and added several new ones as well. First of all, it set to rest all thoughts that the government wished anything other than that the Transvaal become a free and contented community within the Empire. "The notion that the Prime Minister or the Cabinet" entertained any anti-imperial ideas or that they wished to place the Transvaal British at the mercy of the Afrikaners, the *Spectator* said, was "utterly ridiculous." Then it considered the matter of representation and suffrage in the Transvaal. British voters in that colony outnumber Afrikaner voters, it reasoned, and even without regard to imperial expediency they should have the majority of representatives. Electoral power should be distributed, therefore, on the basis of "one vote, one value." Even so, the distribution of seats would reduce the British majority since the greater portion of their numbers lived in one area. The best the British could hope for was a majority of two or three representatives. To prevent the majority from being placed in the position of a minority, the journal suggested that a safeguarding device existed—the referendum. Already in use in Switzerland and in a number of localities in the United States, this "poll of the people" would guarantee the rights of the majority by having all legislation of great importance receive popular sanction before it would become law.

Regarding the question of suffrage, it hoped the government would produce a formula fair to all. "We should like to see 'one man one vote' and 'one vote for every white man' adopted as well as 'one vote one value.'" Nevertheless, it admitted there were problems involved in introducing manhood suffrage in the Transvaal. Since no other South African colony used that standard in determining suffrage, its use in this case would create a stumbling block for union. The basic reason for using some alternative other than universal manhood suffrage, of course, was the presence of a large native population. Although the *Spectator* favored giving the right to all Coloured men, it said "it would be madness to give the natives the suffrage *en bloc*." On the other hand, if some property and education qualification were employed, most natives would not receive the franchise, "which they would certainly misuse, and yet the educated and property-holding native" would not be disfranchised. So the *Spectator* hoped that some plan could be discovered which would make "the suffrage qualification just to all."[47]

The *Spectator* rounded out its arguments on this subject by addressing a number of additional points. How should the British, the British Liberals in particular, react to the Transvaal Progressive leaders then in their midst? "We feel bound to point out," the *Spectator* said, "that the situation, perilous though it is to themselves, and we fear, also to the Empire, is very largely due to their own fault." They had asked for Chinese labor and "that unhappy policy poisoned the relations between the progressives of the Transvaal and the majority of the British people." Nevertheless, it continued, "we are sure that Sir Percy Fitzpatrick and his colleagues are acting patriotically and with no sinister idea of duping the British public opinion into a policy in favor of Chinese labour." Maintaining that the views of the Progressives on Chinese labor ought not to influence the cabinet in its designing of an electoral system, the *Spectator* urged that the labor problem be resolved separately and that the Liberals bear in mind the fundamental facts from an imperial perspective.

At the bottom of its argument lay the conviction that the Empire had to be maintained "strong and inviolate." "Disruptive tendencies" within the Empire could not be permitted to grow; representative and responsible government reflecting the majority will had to be established in the Transvaal; and the Liberals had to understand that the "Transvaal Dutch" felt "no particular gratitude of loyalty toward" them. The last point was an interesting one for this journal to make and led it to point out that the Afrikaners were in no sense Liberals, nor did they make any "pretence of holding Liberal principles." Moreover, "the whole history of the Transvaal under Dutch rule shows that the Boers entertain what we may euphemistically call old-fashioned ideas as to the rights of minorities, or, for that matter, majorities if they do not occupy the seat of power." In fact, so concerned was the *Spectator* with the fate of the Transvaal British that it introduced an entirely new point although realizing it was too late to have it become part of the discussion. It recommended that the Transvaal and

Natal be amalgamated into a single state. Such an arrangement would secure a British majority, provide the Transvaal with an outlet to the sea, and assist Natal in solving problems (i.e., the native question, the Asiatic question and the railroad question) that were beyond its "size and numbers."[48]

During the first half of 1906, no London paper showed more interest in South African affairs than the *Westminster Gazette*. Beginning January 25, it urged the new government to "take steps immediately for the establishment of responsible government." Like *The Times'* similar pronouncement of the same day, the timing of this statement is significant since it preceded the cabinet meeting of February 8 by a week and a half.[49] The *Westminster* showed its firm resolve to support responsible government for the Transvaal as the new policy for the new government, and it also wished to confirm that the Liberals were dependable defenders of the Empire.

In its defense of the new Liberal policy, the *Gazette* proceeded to portray the government as strong, moderate, and sensitive to imperial interests. Feeling that the Unionists had for years paraded before the Transvaal the idea that the Liberal party was anti-imperialistic, this paper now sought to reassure the Transvaal British. "What we have now to ask of the British in the Transvaal," it stated, was that the present government was "just as much concerned as its predecessors for Imperial interests in South Africa." In making that statement, it partly had in mind the Chinese labor problem, for although "the new Government has realised the impossibility of any immediate and violent reversal of the policy [Chinese labor] of its predecessors," there now was a difference to be considered. The Liberals had suspended the ordinance and said that the question would have to be settled by the responsible government of the Transvaal once it was established. That was a moderate approach to the problem, considering the way that the question had been excessively treated in the recent British election. Nevertheless, the election had produced proof enough of the anti-Chinese-labor feelings of the British people, and that was the difference to which the *Westminster* referred. "If the Home Government cannot in the last resort prevail against the responsible Government of the Colony, it can at least make it quite clear that the continuance of the Ordinance would in its opinion be a very great disaster both on its own merits and because, as the election has shown, it must alienate the Colony from a formidable mass of British opinion."[50]

Throughout its handling of the topic of responsible government for the Transvaal, the *Gazette* continued to interject comments about Chinese labor. Behind its thinking was a tendency, common enough among Liberals of that time, to suspect that if the Transvaal British came to power in that colony the Progressives, who had defended the ordinance, would contrive to continue it in the future. Hoping that a political settlement fair to all parties could be found, and making known its own views about the "disastrous" Chinese labor policy and its support for Liberal posture regarding it, the *Westminster* did "not want to gerrymander the Constitution for or against Chinese labour."[51] One can surmise that it believed a fair constitutional settlement would allow public opinion, both in the colony and at home, to guide a responsible Transvaal government toward extricating Chinese labor from that colony.

The *Westminster* avoided being dogmatic about the provisions regarding electoral districts and voting regulations for the new constitution. It left it to the statesmen to produce a document fair to all parties. On the much debated "one vote, one value" versus population question, it reasoned: "There is no sanctity and universality in either principle. A Liberal may approve of both or either principle according to circumstances, and in the present case the unqualified adoption of either principle . . . [was] likely to work injustice." Doubting the assumption that the Transvaal British would be a united party and believing that Transvaal political relations would be wrecked from the start if the new constitution began "with a race quarrel at the base of it," the *Westminster* urged that a compromise be found on this question.[52] Such was the predominant tone of its articles on the framing of a new constitution.

It might be added that Spender's paper labored under no illusions about Afrikaner affection for the British. "We rely on gradually creating contentment by giving proof that British government is good government and free government, and by strictly keeping our word, as given at the Peace Conference."[53] Nor had it forgotten about the matter of imperial supremacy. To the *Westminster* it was not the imperial object to secure the ascendency of any party in the Transvaal. "In giving responsible government," it concluded, "we give internal freedom, and rely on our capacity to maintain our Imperial supremacy, whatever results it may yield."[54]

Late in July, the *Westminster* reiterated this argument. At the time, it appeared that the Ridgeway Committee favored the "one vote, one value" principle along with converting the franchise to manhood suffrage. The paper found that solution palatable. It desired only "absolute fairness" and expressed scepticism about "fine calculations" which the parties in the Transvaal were making about their electoral prospects. Moreover, in contrast to the pleas made in *The Times* and the *Outlook* for a settlement that would secure the British future in South Africa by guaranteeing a safe voting margin to the Transvaal British, the *Westminster* argued a different line. "British supremacy will not depend on the balance of voters in three of four constituencies, and at the worst the Colony will have a second Chamber to guard its material interests against rash innovations. In giving Responsible Government, we are obliged to contemplate the possibility of either party winning, and whichever wins, we do not believe that the consequences will be as formidable or as decisive as both parties seem at present to suppose."[55] Finally, when Sir Percy Fitzpatrick and his colleagues presented the Progressives' case in London urging the Liberals to avoid restoring the Afrikaners to power in the Transvaal, it refused to accept the Progressives' argument. If we really "thought that the British case would be destroyed by the defeat of the Progressive party, we should oppose . . . granting a constitution or proceeding to grant responsible government," the *Westminster* countered. That was far from what it, in fact, believed. In a phrase, it rested its case by contending there were "good and patriotic" men on both sides in the Transvaal, and should the Progressives fail to gain power with the grant of responsible government, these men would do their best to prevent disaster.[56]

. . .

The preliminary debate among the imperial journalists on the forthcoming Transvaal Constitution had been as thorough as circumstances allowed. Details of arguments and arguments themselves varied among them, but they all agreed the Transvaal should receive responsible government at some point and that a tranquil and loyal South Africa was essential for the Empire and its future. On those broad propositions, at least, agreement existed. It is even possible to detect some tentative consensus among them on granting responsible government to the Transvaal at this time. Would that tentative consensus grow when the Liberals delivered the instrument itself?

7

The Political Reconstruction of South Africa: Part II, 1906-1914

Granting the Transvaal a constitution was only the first in a series of steps involved in the implementation of the Liberals' South African policy. It took them several years to introduce all parts of the policy that provided constitutions for the Transvaal and the Orange River Colony and union for all four South African colonies. Concern about that policy and its ramifications continued throughout the remainder of the Edwardian era. Midway through the summer of 1906, public consideration about the policy began in earnest with the sharp response accompanying the presentation of the Transvaal Constitution in Parliament.

On July 31 the public learned of the government's decision regarding the political settlement for the Transvaal. That was the day on which Winston Churchill, then under secretary of state for the colonies, presented the "outline and character" of the settlement to the House of Commons. His speech, moderate in tone, was a carefully constructed explanation of the government's plans and how it had resolved the basic questions involved in the settlement. Churchill tried to place the entire matter above party politics. "After all," he said, there was "no real difference between the two great historic parties on this question." The previous government had stated it would extend representative and responsible institutions to the colony. "The only question in dispute was, when?" He even quoted Chamberlain, who, though absent this day, had stated: "The responsibility for this decision lies with the Government now in power. They have more knowledge than we have; and if they consider it safe to give the large grant, and if they turn out to be right no one will be better pleased than we. I do not think that, although important, this change should be described as a change in colonial policy, but as continuity of colonial policy." Thus Churchill began this crucial statement by extending the open hand.

He then proceeded to outline the provisions of the constitution. There would be an elected assembly composed of sixty-nine members and an upper chamber of fifteen members nominated by the governor. Either Dutch or English could be used for speeches in the legislature and proceedings would be published in both languages. Regarding the question of the franchise, the Boers had argued that the Lyttelton formula disqualified many day laborers and farmers' sons from voting in rural areas. Sympathetic to the point, the government made provisions for all adult, white males who were twenty-one years of age or older and who had resided in the Transvaal for six months to vote, except for the officers and men of the British garrison. In arriving at this decision, the government had considered including suffrage for women, but as Churchill explained, it decided "it would not be right for us to subject a new young colony, unable to speak for itself, to the hazards of an experiment which we have not had the gallantry to undergo ourselves" and, consequently, left it for the new legislature to decide.

Would the seats for the assembly be distributed on the basis of voters or population? It will be recalled that the Transvaal British favored the former; the Boers with their large families, the latter. As was the question of franchise, this was a crucial matter. The new constitution would use the "one vote, one value" principle. That was the major decision. As the electoral districts were designed, they fell into three groups: the Rand, Pretoria, and the rest of the Transvaal. The government decided to allot thirty-four seats to the Rand including Krugersdorp Rural (a secure Boer seat), six to the Pretoria area, and twenty-nine to the rest of the Transvaal. The constitution would also provide for the automatic redistribution of constituencies by three commissioners as circumstances changed. Clearly the government had attempted to design an instrument in accord with the balance of interests of the Transvaal British and Boers.

In some other respects, Churchill's speech reminds us of the full scope of issues involved in the settlement. According to the Peace of Vereeniging, no franchise could be given the natives until after the grant of self-government. Nevertheless, the government stipulated that "any legislation which imposes disabilities on natives which are not imposed on Europeans will be reserved to the Secretary of State and the Governor will not give his assent before receiving the Secretary of State's decision." Moreover, legislation affecting native lands would be reserved, and the government also reserved Swaziland to the direct administration of the High Commission. Another section of the speech dealt with Chinese labor. On 30 November 1906, the arrangement for recruiting Chinese laborers in China would be terminated. The new Transvaal Constitution would abrogate the existing ordinance "after a reasonable interval" and Churchill added, "I earnestly trust that no British Government will ever renew it." Then he explained that the Transvaal Assembly would need time "to take stock . . . and to consider the labour question as a whole." However, he explained the government's intention to include this statement in the Constitution: "No law will be assented to which sanctions any condition of service or residence of a servile character." In the course of his other comments, Churchill also promised there would be no "unnecessary delay" in granting a constitution to the Orange River Colony.

The address, a formidable achievement for the young statesman, ended, as it began, on a lofty note. Addressing himself to the Opposition, he asked them to place aside party considerations and join with the Liberals in making the granting of the constitution "something of a national sanction. With all our majority," he said, "we can only make the gift of a party; they can make it the gift of England."[1]

Judging from the tenor of the Unionist responses that followed, it appears that Churchill's effort to place the constitution above party politics failed. Alfred Lyttelton wanted to know if it were right "without a single published paper, that the discussion of this important subject should be relegated to one day in the dog days of July, when the Government themselves, through the Prime Minister, had admitted a few months ago that they themselves were lacking full information upon it, and had appointed a Commission to supply that information." Furthermore, he said it would have been "fairer" if the government had made that information available to its critics. Balfour's comments were more piercing. He admitted that both parties shaped the ultimate goal of autonomy for the Transvaal, but that they differed on approaches to that goal. He thought the approach contained in the plan just presented was faulty and proceeded to argue that manhood suffrage rested on the theory of natural rights. That being the case, "how are you going to deal with the question of the natives at all?" Since the Cape Colony had a qualified franchise, the introduction of manhood suffrage in the Transvaal could only form a barrier to future federation. His comments began in a rather calm manner, but they became angrier as he continued. "I think the Government are attempting an experiment of the most dangerous description," he said as he asked that the constitution be deferred. "No human being ever thought of such an experiment before—that of giving to a population equal to, and far more homogeneous than our own, absolute control of everything, civil and military," Balfour charged. In closing he gave Churchill this answer to his offer: "I refuse to accept the invitation so kindly offered that we on this side should make ourselves responsible with the Government for what I regard as the most reckless experiment ever tried in the development of a great colonial policy." To that, with only one minute left for him to speak, the prime minister rose and retorted that he had never heard "a more unworthy, a more mischievous and a more unpatriotic speech." Applause, cheers matched by counter-cheers, and shouts of "Shame," "Withdraw," and "Order" buried his rebuttal, as an emotional outpouring of feeling and expression filled the House of Commons.[2]

Simultaneously with Churchill's speech, Lord Elgin presented the constitution to the House of Lords. Lord Milner made the most formidable reply in that chamber. "I hold that a great and capital error was made" when the government reversed the policy of its predecessors. Charging that the Liberals had "rushed . . . with precipitate speed" to granting self-government while at the same time imperiling the Transvaal's material prosperity by tampering with its labor supply, he stated his conviction that "mischief has been done which can never be retrieved." Now the future of the Transvaal depended only on "the chances of this experiment." He particularly attacked the electoral arrangements, which, despite their voting majority of about twenty-two thousand, gave the British Transvaalers a doubtful majority of seats at best. He went on to attack the land settlement provisions in the constitution. Though he remained more subdued in his comments than Balfour, Milner left no doubt about his rejection of the constitution, nor about his lingering apprehensions regarding the Boers.[3]

RESPONSE TO THE LIBERALS' TRANSVAAL CONSTITUTION

Considering the heated commentary that Churchill's address occasioned in the House of Commons, *The Times'* reaction to the new constitution he outlined was restrained. Upon announcing its decision "on the momentous issue of the Transvaal Constitution," the government was "entering upon a great experiment of whose magnitude they [the Government] seem to be conscious," *The Times* began. The paper expressed its satisfaction about the inclusion of a second chamber in the constitution and was heartened to find that the principle of "one vote, one value" would be applied. As to the allocation of seats, the paper believed that the arrangement might, but only might, produce a slight margin in favor of the Transvaal British, yet it was reassured on this point by Milner's successor, Lord Selborne, who pronounced it a fair settlement. In awarding manhood suffrage, *The Times* claimed that the Liberals had made a significant departure from the Lyttelton Constitution, one that the Boers, whose position it would strengthen, had advocated. Manhood suffrage, it also observed, created several other difficulties. It made the problem of the Coloured vote far greater, and since qualifications for voting were common elsewhere in South Africa, the introduction of simple manhood suffrage in the Transvaal could create an obstacle to federation. The franchise qualifications stipulated in the Lyttelton Constitution had been liberal by South African standards. Why change them? Although the paper declined to comment at length on the "subsidiary points" of the constitution, it did mention that the decision on the use of the Dutch language was "gravely open to question" and that the labor problem was "dealt with under home control as was to be expected." Although it felt that good reason existed for anxiety, *The Times* concluded with the hope that the Transvaal British would do their best under circumstances created by the proposed constitution. "They have a great task before them—a more uphill task than a perfectly wise Government would have set them."[4]

Garvin's *Outlook* was more caustic. It opened its article on the subject with this foray: "Warned by a growing acquaintance with the facts, but fettered by engagements given with unpardonable freedom while yet in total ignorance of the facts, the Government has crowned its South African policy with what passes on the surface for a compromise." The *Outlook* viewed the new constitution as simply a new phase in the general South African malaise that the Liberals had caused. By creating an atmosphere of uncertainty by its earlier actions regarding the Transvaal, the government had hampered the colony's industry, had impaired its handling of recent Chinese disorders there, and had encouraged the growing exodus of British settlers now leaving the area. Consequently, it announced: "We accept absolutely no responsibility for these new features in the situation, . . . we are ready to acknowledge that that immediate grant of responsible government has become inevitable as the only possible outlet from the present *impasse* . . . and we decline on any ground to share with Liberals the responsibility for the new phase of South African history which the decision inaugurates." Here was one Conservative's answer to Churchill's offer to make the new constitution "the gift of England."

As for the settlement itself, the *Outlook* recognized that it "might have been far worse." There were even some "concessions to the Imperial case" contained in it. Into that category it placed the application of the "one vote, one value" principle, the introduction of a second chamber, and the delay in granting a constitution to the Orange River Colony. However, the *Outlook* looked askance at other features of the constitution. It found the clause on Chinese labor "a perfectly unwarrantable infringement of the very principle on which the whole policy is based, the principle of trust." It condemned the introduction of manhood suffrage because it enfranchised "a considerable number of worthless Boer dependents," complicated any future adjustment of the native problem, and created a "grave obstacle" to federation. Beyond that, the grant of manhood suffrage established a "logical case for womanhood suffrage," which, if it were adopted, would enhance the Afrikaner position at the expense of the British. The *Outlook* much preferred the Lyttelton Constitution. With the new constitution, it believed, Milner's reconstruction had been "frittered away in the blindness of partisan demands, and the future of the Transvaal . . . [was] thrown once more into the melting pot." Everything now depended on the "doubtful turn of an election." It concluded, as had *The Times*, with words directed at the Transvaal British. "We can only pray," it said, "that every settler of British origin will realise the responsibility as far-reaching and supreme as any in the long annals of our Colonial history. South Africa is at the cross-roads, and its fidelity to British ideals can only be maintained if British Afrikanders [settlers], one and all, will close their ranks, stamp out the curse of disunion, and work for federation on Imperial lines."[5]

Even Strachey's more moderate *Spectator* had serious misgivings about the Liberals' constitution. It might be recalled that this journal had supported the Liberals' ideas regarding a Transvaal constitution earlier in the year when it spoke of how "the gift of self-government tends to sterilise" dangerous political hostility. Of course, it had based its previous opinion on the assumption that there was a British majority in the Transvaal, and it still believed that was true in the case of the adult males residing in the colony. It claimed the British adult males outnumbered the Afrikaner adult males in the Transvaal by over twenty thousand. Churchill had stated that there were "undoubtedly" more British than Dutch voters in the Transvaal. The test, by which the constitution should be judged, it therefore observed, was a simple democratic test. Did the will of the majority prevail? "Unhappily, the plan for the distribution of electoral power under the new constitution cannot be said to stand this test successfully," it claimed. The Boer minority might even receive a majority of two or three in the Transvaal Assembly while the most the Transvaal British could hope for in that chamber was a majority of three or four. To make matters worse, "we are bound to confess that we are running not a small, but a very great, risk of installing a minority in power under representative institutions, . . . in a country where its interests of the British Empire make it essential that the will of the minority shall prevail." The *Spectator* expressed less concern with the introduction of manhood suffrage although it feared that "without property qualifications many difficulties may arise in withholding the vote from the native and coloured population." That could work a "grave injustice." Nevertheless, it found other parts of the constitution more to its liking. It particularly endorsed the clauses protecting the natives and reserving Swaziland. As would be expected, it also expressed its pleasure with the clause on Chinese labor. "We desire," it said in conclusion, "to express our earnest hope that the British section of the colony, even though they may be disappointed and may feel that the rights of the majority have not been fully respected, will honestly endeavour to work the constitution fairly and straightforwardly and in a practical spirit."[6] The *Spectator*, then, pleased though it may have been with some important clauses of the constitution, found its electoral provisions unfair.

The *Westminster Gazette*, on the other hand, believed the constitution provided an altogether fair settlement. By coupling the "one vote, one value" principle with manhood suffrage, it claimed, the instrument gave equal opportunity to Boer and Britain alike in the Transvaal. Regarding the allocation of seats between the Rand, the Pretoria district, and the rest of the country, the *Westminster* sensed that the arguments of this arrangement were too intricate for the "home population" to appreciate. Therefore, it assured its readers that the distribution represented the nearest point of agreement between the various Transvaal parties that had emerged in their discussions with the Ridgeway Committee. Like *The Times*, the *Westminster* attached particular meaning to the fact that Lord Selborne pronounced it a fair division. It also expressed its pleasure with the introduction of manhood suffrage and commented that "the advantage in simplicity of manhood suffrage is so great and the difference in the result between manhood suffrage and any other qualification . . . so slight that we see no reason to question the decision." Nor did it believe, as some critics suggested, that it would result in the inclusion of the natives (a reference that probably included the Coloured as well). In the future they could be admitted in two ways, it reasoned, without "a swamping of white voters." Either an "educated franchise . . . consistent with manhood suffrage" could be introduced or a limited number of native constituencies could be established. Either method would be satisfactory, and it hoped that one or the other would be "adopted hereafter." Regarding apprehension about the forthcoming elections upon which some critics said everything now depended, it offered this comment: "Unless we were prepared in conceding self-government to contemplate a possible victory of either party, we should not have been prepared to concede it at all." The *Westminster* itself thought that the election would produce a balance between "Boer and British forces" in the Transvaal. All things considered, it believed that the settlement was "carefully designed to guard the essentials of British supremacy against the dangers" foreseen by pessimists.[7]

On December 6, the government issued the new constitution establishing responsible government to the Transvaal. Following that, on December 12, it published the document in London. It occasioned only slight press response. In fact, the papers had offered scant comment on it since its initial reception during the previous summer. Considering how fervent the party disputes were earlier in the year and how important both sides felt was the framing of the new Liberal constitution, its final form of presentation appeared anticlimactic. At that point, however, the basic decisions involved had been known and commented upon long before, and the final version faithfully reproduced the features that Churchill had outlined on July 31. Furthermore, there was nothing to prevent the Liberals from proceeding with their new instrument.

THE TRANSVAAL CONSTITUTION IN RETROSPECT

For nearly two years, discussion about a constitution for the Transvaal held a significant place in the imperial debate. During that time all the imperial journalists acknowledged it as a subject of commanding presence, even a "momentous" one, as *The Times* labeled it. Naturally, differences among them on the subject appeared, and at times they were sharp. They dealt with particular provisions first of the Lyttelton Constitution and later of the Liberals' constitution. Beyond disagreement over particular provisions, however, their commentary on this subject provided evidence indicating that a good deal of consensus existed among them about the wider setting surrounding the constitution.

The imperial journalists, for example, argued little about long-range British goals in South Africa. They all agreed that federation, or some form of union, of the South African colonies was the end toward which all else should be directed.

That end would benefit both the Afrikaner and the South African British while securing the imperial connection. To achieve it, all believed that the Transvaal, the home of the idea of an independent South Africa, was crucial. Transvaal loyalty, therefore, was imperative, and to have that the British had to demonstrate their trust in their recent foe. The grant of responsible government would be the hallmark of that trust, and it would attract the Boers to British ideals. No one doubted that. The question separating the imperial journalists in London was one of timing. When would it be appropriate to make that grant without imperiling the whole British position? Throughout 1905 and 1906 there was a great deal of talk in the papers about maintaining British supremacy in the Transvaal. After Milner's departure from South Africa, however, little chance remained for the success of his policy of anglicization. Gradually the imperial journalists, following Spender's lead, began to seek a settlement that would allow the Transvaal British and Boers to cooperate in a mutually constructive manner. They also hoped the political settlement would provide the seedbed for the best imperial ideals to grow in that land. As the months went on, they had to acknowledge, with regret in some cases, that the type of political settlement they wanted could be best achieved by the grant of responsible government. Interestingly enough, with the advent of Campbell-Bannerman's government, even *The Times* and the *Outlook* were ready to accept the fact that the time had come for that grant to be made, even if they wished that circumstances could be other than they were.

The reaction of these journalists to the Liberals' constitution underscores the point. Clearly, it was more moderate than that of the Opposition leaders and critics in Parliament. One is forced to the conclusion that the portion of informed public opinion these journals represented accepted the introduction of responsible government at this time. That had been clear since the beginning of the year. Even J. L. Garvin accepted that policy.

From the beginning of the year, indeed before Smuts's meetings with Liberal leaders, there was little doubt that the Liberals would grant responsible government. In the months preceding the publication of the constitution, the controversy in the press turned mainly on the implementation of the "one vote, one value" principle. The main thrust of the response to the July 31 announcement of the constitution centered on the franchise and electoral provisions it contained, not on whether or not the time had come to deliver responsible government to the colony. Consequently, the hope Balfour expressed on that day that the experiment would be deferred was out of step with the assumption upon which the imperial journalists based their arguments. This does not mean that someone like Garvin had ceased feeling that the grant of self-government was premature. Rather it suggests that men of his persuasion recognized the political shift that had occurred and the need to accommodate themselves to new political realities.

Consider, too, the case of the *The Times,* which attempted to be judicious in its comments about the political settlement. By the summer of 1906, it realized that a Transvaal constitution could be delayed no longer. Such a postponement could only endanger the British position in the colony. An exodus of British Transvaalers already was occurring there. *The Times* felt that the people who left had little faith in Campbell-Bannerman's Liberal government and blamed it for the "present stagnation and paralysis" of the colony's industry. Among these people, it reported, there had been a "general unrest and apprehension" caused by "the Government's attitude at the beginning of the Session" in February. The *"speedy grant of a Constitution"* (italics mine) was "imperatively called for," otherwise the chances of British supremacy would be damaged severely. Political and industrial confidence had to be restored in the colony.[8] It is significant to note that *The Times* spoke of the need for "a Constitution." In the spring of 1906 Leopold Amery, then the paper's colonial editor, thought he detected in government a tendency to be "much more delicate in their handling of the Transvaal question than they originally showed signs of being."[9] So there was reason to hope that the Liberals would not be wreckers of all that had been achieved in the Transvaal if only the Radicals among them could be controlled.

Amery provided an additional clue to the context in which the men at *The Times* placed the grant of responsible government. He considered the subject of the Transvaal Constitution in his *The Times History of the War in South Africa, 1895-1902*, published in 1909. In it he explained how the Transvaal Afrikaners and some of the Transvaal British attacked the Lyttelton Constitution and created a danger of the development of a "systematic effort to make the constitution unworkable." Consequently, circumstances worked against its implementation. On the other hand, a constitution providing full self-government would be received by the Boers as a gesture of friendship that could far outvalue "another two or three years of increasing administrative efficiency, or . . . a few thousand more British voters." He also mentioned that reasons other than altruistic ones motivated the Campbell-Bannerman Liberals in their desire to grant responsible government. A responsible government in the Transvaal could relieve the Liberal party from possible embarrassment regarding a final decision on Chinese labor. All of these points, of course, had been mentioned a number of times in the press commentary on the two constitutions. The significance of Amery's account, however, lies in the following statement: "The argument in favour of the direct grant of responsible government was one which, on general grounds, could reasonably appeal to the most sincere Imperialist. It was true that the risks involved were tremendous. Still, the most venturesome policy might sometimes prove the wisest."[10] Considering that these were the words of a staunch Unionist and a disciple of Lord Milner, they indicate that there was probably more of a base of support for, or at least a willingness to accept, the Liberal constitution than one might expect.

The fear was that it would be a reckless document. That fear, however, failed to materialize in the summer of 1906. There was almost a sense of relief in *The Times'* response to the Liberals' constitution as it appeared on July 31. It incorporated as many safeguards for the British position in the Transvaal as political expediency would allow. After the formal promulgation of that instrument, Geoffrey Robinson wrote to Amery from Johannesburg, "You all seem to have taken the constitution lying down in England, but I expect the B. P. [i.e., the British public] is sick to death of South Africa and all its works."[11] It would be more feasible to assume that *The Times* saw the Liberal constitution as sound a compromise as the Liberals were apt or able to give. There were, indeed, a number of reasons behind the imperial journalists' acceptance of the grant of responsible government for the Transvaal.

As their commentary on the constitution unfolded, it also recognized the need to reconcile the Afrikaner and British populations of the Transvaal. Some constructive balance between them had to be found. Imperial policy had to reconcile the Afrikaner, for, rhetoric aside, the British could not be successful in South Africa without them. All of the imperial journalists desired that reconciliation. Differences between them went beyond this basic point and centered on the extent to which the Boers could be trusted, on what constituted a fair treatment for the Transvaal British, and on the safeguarding of imperial interests. As the emphasis of commentary shifted from debate over representative versus responsible government to the "one vote, one value" versus population argument and then to the concern about the distribution of political power provided by the Liberal constitution, the nature of the balance of power between the Transvaal Boers and British remained a cause for anxiety. In structuring that balance the Liberals, of course, were more inclined to trust the Boers than were the Unionists, and the papers reflected that difference according to their party preferences.

This manner of "trust" was not exactly the "magnanimous gesture" it has sometimes been portrayed as being. *The Times,* for instance, even spoke of the risks involved with the Lyttelton Constitution while the Liberal *Westminster Gazette* admitted that it was not in human nature to expect the Boers to regard the British with affection and found it necessary to explain that there were always risks involved in "making experiments." Nevertheless, the *Westminster* believed the time had come to try the experiment.[12] Papers on both sides, indeed, wished the experiment to proceed although, as we know, they quarreled over its form.

Several tangential themes also surfaced in the London journalists' discussion of the constitutional settlement. The most obvious of these was that of Chinese labor, which both sides injected into their commentary. Long into the debate, it remained a type of verbal springboard to use, one that could release political prejudices and emotions. The final Liberal solution, to allow the new Transvaal government to decide the matter for itself so long as the outcome conformed to the clause in the constitution prohibiting servile labor, was probably as reasonable a formula as could be formed. At least with that the issue of Chinese labor made its exit from public discussion.

Throughout the debate of the political settlement, the imperial journalists made a number of references to the native factor. Sometimes, but not always, the term "native," as it appeared in the press, included both Coloured and Indians as well as African people. In the long run, the way in which the settlement dealt with these people was of greater importance than how it handled the Chinese labor problem. As we know, the Transvaal Constitution of 1906 provided white manhood suffrage, but it left the political color bar untouched. Racial discrimination had been a founding principle of both of the Boer republics. On the other hand, the British had more enlightened views about the non-European majority in South Africa than did the Boers. Franchise disqualifications imposed by the South African Republic (i.e., the Transvaal) on non-Europeans had been one of the grievances the imperial government had against the republic on the eve of the recent war. During the war a number of imperial statesmen including Chamberlain and Milner had spoken of enfranchising qualified natives at some point after the war. At the end of the war, however, the imperial government had to choose between laying the groundwork for a Boer-British reconciliation and promoting the welfare of the non-European people in the conquered republics. Believing that the two goals could not be approached simultaneously, the imperial government chose the former. Consequently, Article VIII of the Treaty of Vereeniging stated: "The question of granting the franchise to the natives will not be decided until after the introduction of self-government." That proved to be an epoch-making decision, but at the time it appeared the surest way out of the dilemma presented by racial relations in the two republics. It is important to understand that, although the Unionist party in power at the time of the treaty made the decision, during the Parliamentary debates on the peace negotiations the Liberal party made no dissent to Article VIII. Both parties accepted the idea that there were too many risks involved in defending the cause of the non-Europeans at that time.[13] In 1906, the Liberals included no stipulation in the Transvaal Constitution for the enfranchisement of natives.

Although the "native problem" was not part of the mainstream of press commentary on the Transvaal Constitution, it did receive some attention. That is not to say, however, that it was thought to be of little consequence. To the contrary, the context in which the journalists placed their opinions on this problem indicated that they perceived it as one of far-reaching significance. Several assumptions governed whatever consideration they gave it. First of all, most of the imperial journalists agreed that Article VIII of Vereeniging placed the matter of giving the franchise to the natives outside the bounds of discussion. Strachey's *Spectator* was an exception. Claiming that Article VIII did not bind the government to exclude the Coloured from the franchise, the journal urged that it be extended to them now. Other papers stopped short of going that far. They all hoped, however, that the franchise would be extended to some portion of the non-European population in the future. Moreover, a number of hints appeared in their commentary indicating there was reason to believe that the white population of the Transvaal showed signs of becoming more enlightened in their attitude toward the native element. Along with hoping for better things to come for the non-Europeans, all the imperial journalists wanted that part of the Transvaal population to be protected from unfair legislation, and that protection the constitution did guarantee.

In 1906 Lord Milner referred to the Liberals' South African initiatives as a "fearful mischief."[14] The imperial journalists refused to go that far in their commentary. Campbell-Bannerman's South African policy, of course, pleased Liberal journalists like J. A. Spender. Writing in his biography of Campbell-Bannerman some years later, he had this to say about the prime minister's Transvaal policy: "Looking back on these events after the experience of a far greater struggle [World War I], we may be tempted to think them of relatively small importance, but it is not the size of the scene which determines the values of political action, and the story of what Sir Henry Campbell-Bannerman endured for South Africa, and what he wrought for her and for the British Empire, may shine out in history as one of the great examples of human wisdom and courage."[15] Spender's commentary about the Transvaal Constitution in 1905 and 1906, though more restrained and pragmatic than that later assessment, reflected the same confident affirmation of its correctness. Unionist imperial journalists too could find some grounds for approval, despite the reluctance and even apprehension about it that remained in their minds. Publicists of strong imperial persuasion to a man, they knew that South Africa was the hinge of Empire. Moreover, after the Liberal electoral rout of 1906, they understood that, given the political arithmetic of the times, their opinion could not sway British South African policy from its Liberal course. As Leo Amery confessed to *The Times'* Johannesburg correspondent, "The luck has been so steadily against us economically and politically [in South Africa] the last few years, that it is bound to have a turn."[16] Amery, however, as we have seen, was willing to make the most out of the Unionists' unfortunate circumstances and found positive things to say about the grant of responsible government in 1906. Most of all, the commentary of the imperial journalists, both Unionist and Liberal, on the Transvaal Constitution revealed the broad agreement that existed among them on long-range goals. Regarding those goals (i.e., the timely grant of responsible government to the ex-Boer republics, the unification of all four South African colonies, and the integration of a unified South Africa in the Empire) the question was one of means rather than ends.

BRITISH INDIANS IN THE TRANSVAAL: 1907-1908

After the granting of the Transvaal Constitution at the end of 1906, events in South Africa proceeded at a fast pace. The first Transvaal election of February 1907 produced a *Het Volk* majority, after which Louis Botha became prime minister. The Orange River Colony received self-government, as everyone anticipated, in June of that same year. Nevertheless, aside from scrutinizing the Afrikaner presence at the Imperial Conference of 1907 and following the progress toward unification in South Africa, the London press paid relatively little attention to South African problems. After the grant of self-government to the Transvaal in 1906, the center of political debate on South African affairs shifted to South Africa itself. Moreover, London was reluctant to impose its imperial authority on those affairs. To have done so would have questioned the trust extended to the South Africans.

The ordeal suffered by the Indians in the Transvaal is a case in point. They began arriving in South Africa in the mid-nineteenth century, mainly as indentured servants. Many stayed on after their contracts expired. Then, beginning in the 1870s, a new class known as "passenger" Indians came on their own initiative. As traders and shopkeepers this latter group was successful in business throughout the towns of Natal and the Transvaal. With success, however, came discrimination. Before the Anglo-Boer War, the British had protested the Boers' injustice to the Indians, and their mistreatment even became a cause of the war. After the war, however, old restrictions remained and additional disabilities were imposed. By that time there were perhaps twelve thousand Indians in the Transvaal. Under an old republican law, they had been registered, and when the validity of that registration was questioned, they agreed, on Lord Milner's advice, to register a second time. They were told that no further registration would be required, but that reassurance proved to be an empty gesture. In 1906 the Transvaal Council passed a new law requiring yet another more stringent registration. Colonial Secretary Lord Elgin at first balked at that measure, but later, in 1907, when the new responsible legislature in the Transvaal returned it to him, he assented. The Indians, whose residential, trading, and immigration rights were already restricted, now were required to carry passes bearing, as if they were criminals, their fingerprints. Sadly *The Times* said, "As a nation we have little reason to be proud of the treatment now being meted out to our Indian fellow-subjects in the Transvaal."[17]

What was "the problem"? At this point the trouble lasted for more than a year until a temporary solution was found. One might think that a problem of such duration would be a major question for public debate in the press. It was not. Some editorials did treat the matter and were by no means insensitive to the grievances of the British Indians. *The Times* and the *Westminster Gazette* provided the best coverage, but even Strachey's *Spectator* was disturbed by the indignity and cruelty of the new registration act, which not only compelled fingerprinting but even sanctified deportation of recalcitrants. Yet it did not emerge as an issue of major dimension in the London press. Several reasons help to explain why. Surely, the overarching one was the fact that at its core the issue rested on a dilemma. A self-governing colony claimed the right to make its own immigration laws. On the other hand, Britain guaranteed the rights of British Indians. No one argued that the Indians should be granted unrestricted immigration, but in this case, British subjects were suffering discrimination on grounds of color. Intervention in the behalf of either party would alienate the other; consequently, the British imperial government respected the right of the self-governing Transvaal to regulate its own policy and used its influence to urge that a fair solution be found for the problem. Anglo-Boer reconciliation remained the chief priority of British policy in South Africa, and the imperial press declined to challenge that priority at this time.

There is, however, another reason that explains the mild press response to this question. *The Times'* foreign editor Valentine Chirol explained it frankly, as was his habit, and his explanation deserves quoting at length. To the paper's correspondent in Johannesburg he wrote:

> The feeling here concerning the harshness with which the Indians have been treated [in the Transvaal] is one to which only partial expression could be given in the press, but amongst Imperialists there has been very keen and bitter disappointment that the British element in the Transvaal should have shown itself as callous as the Boer element of the deplorable consequences which this wretched business will have in India, especially at a time when the relations of the ruling and subject races in India have entered into such a critical phase. One had hoped that some leading Briton would at least have protested against so signal a breach of the solemn promise given by Milner himself to those Indians who registered under his advice that they would never again be subjected to fresh disabilities on that score and that the act of registration to which he advised them to submit would be absolutely final. Your telegrams which no doubt accurately reflect British opinion on the subject, have shown unfortunately that, though the grievances of the Indians were a useful political weapon in the old days against the Kruger regime, they no longer command a market now that their usefulness for purposes of party warfare is exhausted. It has been altogether a very deplorable episode which, I fear, has estranged a good deal of sympathy from the Progressives of the Transvaal amongst thoughtful Imperialists in this country. The answer, I suppose, is that as the mother country has done so little to protect the British element in the Transvaal against the Boers, she cannot expect much consideration for Imperial interests in a question which would involve renewed antagonism to the Boers.[18]

It is difficult to escape the conclusion that racial prejudice in the Transvaal was by no means limited to the Boers.

SOUTH AFRICAN UNIFICATION: 1909-1910

After the grant of self-government to the two ex-Boer republics, the imperial journalists mainly focused on the movement to unite the four South African colonies. They all endorsed the movement. Spender, of course, could applaud it as a culmination of the Liberal policy of trusting the Boers. The moderate Strachey believed that Botha and Smuts were "perfectly sincere in their reconcilement and in their abandonment of any desire for a Dutch Republic." He saw that reconciliation as an application of a Whig policy regarding the colonies and professed his belief that such a policy was still the best hope for the Empire.[19] In fact, the movement toward unification progressed so rapidly that it would have been, as Geoffrey Robinson said, "hopeless to fight it even if one wanted to."[20] Some questions did emerge regarding the form the union should take and whether or not it would force conservative elements in the Transvaal to reassert themselves, but no imperial publicist wished to resist the movement. Even Leo Amery, the conservative imperialist who wrote most of *The Times'* South African leaders, reflected privately: "From all I hear the movement is advancing very rapidly in South Africa. . . . The Dutch are quite keen because they see their way to a majority in the Federal Parliament. But I am sure the English are quite right in pressing it on. The only thing which can bring about a real increase in the British element is prosperity, and Federation even under a Dutch majority is bound to spell prosperity."[21]

The work of the National Convention that produced the Union of South Africa began in 1908 and culminated in 1910. Starting in 1908, the convention met successively in the various capitals of the South African colonies. By 1909 a draft constitution was ready. In the summer of that year both houses at Westminster approved it, and it received the royal assent on September 20. In the end, the Act of Union provided for a consolidation based on a unitary rather than a federation principle. Accordingly, the colonies became provinces, each one with its own council. Among its provisions, the act created a Union Parliament consisting of a senate and a house of assembly. The executive power was vested in the king (i.e., the governor-general) and an executive council could advise him. Up to ten ministers would be appointed to administer departments of state. The constitution would be amended by a majority of both houses of Parliament in joint session at the third reading. As was the case with the other dominions, the constitution forbade legislation that was contrary to any act of the Imperial Parliament. It established the right of appeal to the Privy Council in London. The Imperial Parliament could amend or repeal specific clauses of the act, though it never used that power. Regarding the question of the franchise, only whites were eligible for election to the Union Parliament. The voting privileges the non-whites had in Cape Colony would be retained and could not be abolished without the agreement of a two-thirds majority of both houses sitting together. To extend the Cape's system of franchise northward required no special procedure.

It was possible, therefore, for Cape Liberals to think that theirs was the system that would spread in the future. At this time, however, each province would retain its own franchise laws. The Union itself would become operative on 31 May 1910, eight years to the day after the signing of the Peace of Vereeniging.

As the final round of negotiation and ratification of the South African constitution proceeded, *The Times*, fulfilling its function as a newspaper of record, provided detailed and reserved commentary on every stage in the process. Other journals of strong imperial persuasion tended to treat the subject either sporadically or as an item of decreasing priority in the news. By this time Garvin had acquired the editorship of the *Observer* (an appointment that will be covered in detail in the next chapter), but even he relegated this subject mostly to editorial page paragraphs reviewing the week's news. As he explained in one of his articles in *Fortnightly Review*: "The Conference upon South African Union is passing with comparatively little notice, so earnest and so crowded are the times; yet it might well have deserved at a less preoccupied moment a great share of the attention not only of this country but of the world at large."[22] Garvin had a point. It was a crowded time for news—domestic, international, and imperial—and little space was available for a circumstance that the British basically approved of and could little control in any case.

One thing did trouble Conservative imperial publicists during the time of constitution-making for the Union. They feared that the Liberals would walk off with all the laurels for initiating the imperial policy that fostered the rapid achievement of South African unification. Conservatives balked at that idea. As Geoffrey Robinson wrote from South Africa:

> Nothing seems to me so thoroughly hollow as the claim, which is constantly put forward by Asquith and others, that South African Union is the result of the premature grant of self-government to the two new colonies. No doubt that hastened it a little; but it is not the real condition that has made the Union possible. That condition is the war and the annexation, and the Liberal Party must accept and even take a pride in the war and the annexation if they are going to plume themselves on the present condition of things.

Robinson even spoke of the Act of Union as "the Crown of Lord Milner's policy."[23] Amery, to whom Robinson reported at *The Times*, pushed this same line of argument. To Lord Grey he wrote: "From South Africa all the news I hear is good. The Union is likely to go through . . . and I believe we are on the edge of a new period of expansion based on the sound work done in Milner's time, the fruits of which are only just beginning to show themselves."[24] On July 1, when the last volume of Amery's *History of the War in South Africa* appeared in print, dealing with the period of reconstruction, *The Times* took the occasion to praise the work of Lord Milner. Speaking of the proconsul's "patient and far-seeing statesmanship, with errors here and there such as no human statecraft can avoid," it predicted that history would recognize the contribution of the Liberal party to the great achievement in South Africa but would "look first and foremost to the statesmanship of Mr. Chamberlain and Lord Milner."[25] Such was the counterpoint they made to the Liberals' claim, proudly announced by the *Westminster Gazette*, that the course of events in South Africa was the vindication of a principle—a Liberal one, of course. The Gazette, indeed, went so far as to speak of trusting in colonial self-government as "the saving principle in British Imperialism of which the Liberal Party is the special trustee."[26]

Accordingly, as the Union of South Africa became a reality, imperial publicists of all persuasions were able to applaud the achievement. Now that the work of union was accomplished, *The Times* said, praising all that had been achieved, it now remained for those who had accomplished the Union to complete their work by making South Africa "a single nation." But even at this point the Union marked "the end of a stage in the evolution of Empire," it proclaimed.[27] Garvin's *Observer* praised the Union and compared it to the United States after the Civil War in this manner: "South Africa . . . has been not only unified, but deepened, strengthened, raised to a far larger and nobler existence by the struggle, which taught two great nations at last how to live together."[28] Strachey's *Spectator* took the occasion to recognize the work of the Liberal government in achieving unification, "a truly Imperial work."[29] Spender's *Westminster Gazette*, while maintaining that the Union was a vindication of Liberal principles and courage, proclaimed that South Africa was "at last free to govern itself in an atmosphere of peace and goodwill." In its enthusiasm, this Liberal journal even made a slight bow to Lord Milner's contribution. "We had occasion to criticise his political action," it admitted, "but after the war, despite some mistakes, he rendered great service in the difficult and often thankless task of reconstruction." Particularly, it added, guarding its Liberal integrity, this was so in "such a matter as railway organization."[30]

Amid all of this acclaim, was there any lament? Was there any sense of disappointment or any note of disapproval struck by the publicists? The answer is yes, and though it came in the twilight of the public debate about South Africa, it carries us to the core of the dilemma involved in this imperial episode. The problem dealt with the "native question." Because the Act of Union established a political color bar, it appeared to disregard principles of tolerance and political equality. At the end of the war, hope existed that the limited franchise enjoyed by the Coloured and Africans in Cape Colony would be extended northward into the two ex-Boer republics while they were under British administration. It was not. The Treaty of Vereeniging concluding the war had stated: "The question of granting the franchise to natives will not be decided until after the introduction of self-government." The British kept that promise, but the Transvaal and the Orange River Colony now had self-government, and the constitutional foundation for a united South Africa was being laid at this juncture. Accordingly, the moment to deal with the question of native franchise had arrived. Yet the Act of Union restricted that franchise to the Cape alone and forbade the presence of non-European legislators in the new Union Parliament.

Those restrictions were at variance with British imperial principles. It was common enough for the nation's leaders to think of the British as custodians of the South African native people. A humanitarian conscience, after all, had long existed in the British imperial outlook. At the time of the debate over the Transvaal Constitution, Winston Churchill, as under secretary for the colonies, pledged the government to "advance the principle of equal rights for civilized men irrespective of colour."[31] His statement was in accord with Liberal policy, and also expressed the belief of British Conservative statesmen and publicists. In 1906, however, an uprising occurred among the Zulu in Natal. They were protesting Natal's stiffening policy regarding Zululand. In defeating the initial rebellion, the Natal authorities condemned a dozen Zulu leaders to death. Thereupon the British government intervened to prevent the executions. As a result the Natal ministry resigned and the colonies of Australia and New Zealand protested the interference of the British government in the affairs of Natal, a self-governing colony. Consequently, the British withdrew their protest, and the Natal ministry resumed office and carried out the executions. That occasioned a more serious Zulu uprising, which, in turn, was suppressed. So the British effort at imperial intervention received a jarring response, and the memory of that rebuff was not forgotten by the authorities in London.

Returning to the passage of the Act of Union of 1909, one might ask if reason existed to lead one to expect that something would be done to protect native rights in the new constitution. This much is clear. The Cape refused to relinquish its liberal native franchise while the Transvaal and the Orange River Colony refused either to have it extended northward or to have it apply to the Union Parliament. The Cape delegates made a determined fight for their franchise and Asquith's government let it be known that it hoped for some suffrage based on a "civilization qualification." When the act reached London, various advocates of a native franchise travelled to England to campaign for British help. W. P. Schreiner, a veteran Cape politician and a leader of the Cape bar who championed native rights, appeared and tried to influence the Liberal government. So did John Tengo Jabavu and Walter Rubusana, two Africans who were acknowledged leaders of native opinion, who headed an African deputation. A few Liberals and Labourites did raise a critical voice in Parliament, but to no avail. No amendment of the native franchise provisions was accepted, although the prime minister and the House made it clear that they disapproved of the color bar in the bill. The Coloured and African franchise would remain restricted to the Cape.

The imperial journalists, like Asquith, regretted the native franchise provisions in the act, but they accepted the prime minister's judgment on this matter. *The Times* offered the most comprehensive statement about the question. "We regret this feature in the Constitution, but we believe, in the circumstances, no other arrangement was possible," was the keynote of its argument. These provisions in the constitution were difficult to approve, it reasoned, but they represented a delicate compromise agreed to in South Africa. The compromise had to be respected, not only because in the spirit of the principle of self-government, South African wishes had to be respected, but also because any "attempt to bind the people of South Africa to measures in advance of their own views could only prejudice the native cause."[32] Yes, the imperial government had the power to amend those provisions, but what would be the result of such an action? Would the position of the Coloured and native population be bettered by amendments Britain had the right to make "but no power to enforce"? Would such action safeguard the Coloured and African people in the area or bring down upon them a more bitter reaction? *The Times* argued that one could not create a self-governing system and then interfere with matters "most vital to local interests." "We must either not create them at all, or else, having created them, trust them to the full in regard to their own affairs," it reasoned. Moreover, if amendments were made they would have to be considered by the various South African parliaments, and consequently the entire bill would be risked. So *The Times* accepted the color bar not as a permanent solution but as one reflecting the political realities involved. The white population of the Cape already had accepted the principle of "equality for all men, irrespective of race or colour, who attain a certain standard of civilization," it added. *The Times* trusted to time. "We trust that South Africans," it said, "aided by these debates, will realize how keen the feeling in the Mother-Country is that no man who raises himself to the same level of civilization as the average European should be debarred, merely by reason of his colour, from the attainment of equal political rights."[33]

Others shared that sentiment. Garvin's *Observer*, wishing not to wreck the entire scheme, proclaimed, "The freedom and independence of United South Africa with respect to all internal questions are complete and absolute."[34] Strachey's *Spectator*, with a respectful nod toward the opinions expressed by W. P. Schreiner and others of like mind, believed that amendment on behalf of native rights was the wrong course to follow. If the act introduced slavery or enforced labor, the imperial government should intervene. It did not impose such things. Therefore, to intervene by the process of amendment, would cost at least an indefinite delay in the forming the Union and might wreck it altogether. The *Spectator* sympathized with those natives who hoped for political rights, but pleaded for patience. "Downing Street can never help the native much in the long run," it argued. "His real advancement must come from humane and enlightened opinion in the country in which he lives . . . The apparatus for raising the native must be invented and perfected, not here, but in South Africa." In the end, it reflected, the natives' fortunes were "as dependent as those of every one else on the elevation of political thought—on catholicity and tolerance."[35]

The *Westminster Gazette*, as always the voice of the Liberals, admitted that the South Africans had to work out "their own salvation." Any attempt at coercion by the imperial government would be wrong, it said. As did most of

British public and press opinion, the *Gazette* expressed its great regret at the disability that even the Cape natives would endure by being disallowed from the Union Parliament. The solution on "the native question" contained in the constitution was not what it would prefer. "We should like to see it a fundamental law of the Empire that education and civilization, and not colour should be the test, . . . We have no illusions about admitting the negro populations wholesale to political privileges irrespective of their culture." Nevertheless, it claimed that the imperial government should not be expected to spoil its splendid work in South Africa by "insisting unreasonably on its own view of the native question." Counting on the influence that "sentiment and opinion" could have when reasonably stated, as was then being done, it predicted that South Africa "while claiming liberty, will, we are sure, in using its liberty be anxious to avoid any unnecessary collision with the feeling of this country."[36]

So, as the years of political reconstruction of South Africa came to an end the imperial journalists felt inclined to place their trust in liberal principles. The principles of self-government once granted produced a Union that both Conservatives and Liberal imperial journalists hoped would enhance the Empire. Beneath all the fanfare showered on belief in the redemptive qualities of self-government lay a deeper belief shared by Conservatives and Liberals alike. That was a belief, common in British thought, that man and society would progress. In this case, the progress they had in mind was that toward a realization of "British civilization." The theme ran throughout journalistic commentary on South Africa. To what degree was it a belief based on conviction rather than hope? No one can say short of acknowledging the presence of both conviction and hope in the expressed opinions of the time. Behind such beliefs, however, a measuring of alternatives can be detected. Who among the imperial journalists would have dared to suggest a goal other than self-government? What other course would have secured the Empire and been harmonious with the long development of English practical traditions? Perhaps a greater flow of British immigration to South Africa would be an alternative. Yet there was no guarantee of that either happening or changing the results in the long run. Perhaps political reconstruction could have been delayed. After the Liberal victory of 1906, there was little chance of that occurring. Both sides knew that the Liberals' gaining power in Britain encouraged Afrikaner expectations in South Africa. To delay the implementation of self-government would have endangered hopes of reconciliation between Boer and Briton. Similarly, several years later, to have delayed the movement of the self-governing South African colonies toward unification was an unrealistic gamble to take. Amending the constitution to protect in some way the present and future native franchise also appeared an unrealistic gamble. Asquith refused to take either and in that even the Conservative imperial journalists supported him.

Time was another factor in the British imperial outlook. It was generally assumed that with the passage of time the South Africans' racial rigidity would lessen. As Winston Churchill put it, within five or six years the "government of United South Africa will take a broader and calmer view of native questions because it will be above local panics." Moreover, he said, "The natives are gaining in education, civilization and influence so rapidly that they will be far more capable apart from force . . . of maintaining their rights, and making their own bargains."[37] The imperial journalists shared that sentiment.

Nevertheless, we can ask, knowing the fate that unfolded for the Africans in the Union with the passing of years, if the British acted irresponsibly in the case of the native franchise provisions in the Act of Union. So much appears to have stemmed from those provisions. The imperial journalists regretted those provisions, as did Prime Minister Asquith. Yet they supported the Act of Union. They left the fate of the Africans to the future, trusted the South Africans, and hoped for the emergence of more enlightened views there regarding the African people. What was the alternative? The hard facts of Empire were there and could not be wished away. Native franchise rights were protected where they existed, and it might be possible to extend those rights in years to come. Disliking the compromise on the native franchise contained in the Act of Union, they accepted it with the expectation, perhaps only a hope, that it would not be permanent. These publicists were, after all, men astute in the world of politics and were drawn to practical solutions. On the balance, approving the Act of Union appeared the practical thing to do.

AFTERMATH AND PERSPECTIVE

In the years immediately following the creation of the Union, a number of domestic crises erupted in South Africa that caused anxiety in Great Britain. They need not detain us long, for it is clear that after the passage of the Act of Union in 1909 a new imperial relationship existed between Britain and South Africa. It began, in fact, with the granting of self-government to the Transvaal in 1906. The premise of that relationship was that Britain would not intervene in South African affairs. This was surely the case in the Native Land Act of 1913, which failed to surface as a major question in the British press although it provided a drastic limitation of the right of Africans to own land in the Union and despite the fact that it provoked unprecedented political activity and protest among black South Africans. Two other problems, one dealing with the Indians in South Africa and the other with the cause of labor, stirred some commentary since they were problems involving repercussions elsewhere in the Empire. Nevertheless, the outcome was the same; the British government adhered to a policy of nonintervention that the press strongly endorsed.

The condition of the British Indians in South Africa, as we know, had been uneasy for years. In 1913 the hard hand of South Africa again fell upon them as the Union legislated new restrictions. Now they suffered the imposition of a three-pounds-per-person tax on all ex-indentured Indian laborers and they were forbidden to move from province to province. Accordingly, three thousand Indians followed M. K. Gandhi, who had become prominent among South African Indians, across the border between Natal and the Transvaal to court arrest. Their arrests occasioned a general strike among Natal's Indians in protest against the imprisonment of Gandhi's passive resisters. Some violence also occurred as rioters burned about 150 acres of Natal's prized sugar cane fields. The Indians were not disputing the closure of Indian immigration into South Africa, nor were they protesting the failure of the South African Bill to give them any political rights. Claiming to be subjects of the king, they were protesting their particular disabilities. Since the British Empire posed itself as the protector of the rights of all its subjects, the Indians made an excellent point. Moreover, their unfair treatment in South Africa was understood to be one of the reasons for the continuing unrest in India. What could be done? Very little, concluded the imperial journalists. They all expressed their regret about how the Indians were being treated in South Africa, sympathized with their grievances, and believed they should be redressed.[38] But beyond voicing such opinion with the hope that it would serve a constructive end, they concluded there was nothing to be done. Imperial intervention of any sort simply was out of the question. As the *Spectator* said, "The truth—and one cannot possibly escape from it—is that the right of self-government involves the right to do wrong."[39]

In their commentary about Prime Minister Botha's militant suppression of strikes in 1913 and 1914, the imperial journalists took a similar line. When Prime Minister Asquith declined to take any action against the South African measures, both *The Times* and the *Westminster Gazette* supported him. *The Times* captured the predominant sentiment in this instance when it reflected that the British people should not and did not condemn "self-government in the Dominions just because they disagreed with its effects in isolated instances."[40] It was, however, the *Westminster Gazette* that had the most explicit comment to make on this subject. "The right to self-government," it reasoned, "must include the right to do things which we dislike or which we think wrong. But it need not exclude our right to say freely and frankly how we are affected or how we think the Empire is affected by this or that action on the part of the self governing community."[41] That comment, which recognized the reality of the imperial relationship with South Africa dating from 1906, placed the *Gazette* in step with its Conservative journalistic brethren. They joined in regretting South Africa's using its liberty to crush liberty.

Such incidents as the two mentioned above might have been harbingers of a troubled future, but the imperial journalists hoped for a different sort of South African and imperial future. Their opinions about the political reconstruction of

South Africa since 1905 made it clear that nothing regarding it was more important than the reconciliation of the British and Boers. That would open the way for South African unification, which in turn would foster imperial cohesiveness and help to secure the future of the twentieth-century Empire. Once the Transvaal received responsible government, a new context surrounded imperial policy relating to South Africa. The fact of self-government, as we have seen, became the standard against which imperial intentions had to be measured. Coercion and intervention were ruled out because they were deemed harmful to the imperial cause and contrary to public opinion both in Britain and in South Africa. They were also ruled out because no other course was plausible. As Geoffrey Robinson confided to Leo Amery in 1907, "Your ambition I suppose is to Anglicise and imperialise Botha to such an extent as to make him drop . . . all this sort of racial nonsense." Robinson had in mind the anti-British racial bitterness that could still be found in the Transvaal. "Anyhow," he reflected, "it is the only hope."[42]

If the British imperial journalists hoped to see a transformation of Boer character in time, they did so with practicality in mind. As we have seen, after 1906 they were gentle in their criticism of South African legislation and action. They did advance some noteworthy criticism that was selective rather than steady. The latter would have become a source of antagonism. Moreover, it was of a firm but mild nature. Obviously papers like *The Times*, the *Spectator*, and the *Westminster Gazette* desired to convey their understanding of the difference particular circumstances made as they offered their disapproval of specific things. This was true in the case of the native franchise provisions in the constitution, as it was with commentary about the Indian and labor problems that emerged in South Africa in the wake of the passage of the constitution. Having ruled out other alternatives and having granted local authorities control over domestic affairs, now they hoped that persuasion would influence South African opinion, conviction, and policy. As the *Westminster Gazette* commented in its criticism of the South African Indian legislation of 1913, "In dealing with a self-governing Colony, the Imperial government can only use suasion."[43]

Was that preference for "suasion" mere sham? Several considerations should be examined in answering that question. First, this was still a time when men believed in the force of rational argumentation with greater confidence than they did after experiencing how it could be swept aside by the force of irrationalism. The appeal of fascism and nazism in the 1920s and 1930s proved how tenuous was Western society's belief in reason. Second, political structures as well as social conditions change all the time. The creation of the Union itself was a case in point. Was it implausible to think that once that great achievement became a reality, internal reforms would occur as Boer and Briton interacted with one another in South Africa and as the Dominion interacted with Britain and the other great units of the Empire in terms of its world engagement? Third, it was understandable that the imperial journalists, who were proud of the Empire, would expect the new South Africa to share in that pride and, in time, to wish to contribute to it by their own responsible and generous actions. Finally, it should be noted that Louis Botha, by his demeanor and rhetoric, both in South Africa from 1906 on and in London while attending the Imperial Conferences, increased the confidence of British imperial publicists about the prospect of change in South Africa. Accordingly, grounds exist for accepting the integrity of their belief in "suasion" while recognizing at the same time that, as men of practical bent of mind, they probably harbored no illusions about it. Most of all, it was the course that remained open to them.

In examining the work of the imperial journalists regarding South Africa and the Empire after 1906, one can recognize the emergence of a common attitude that helped to shape their commentary. It was an attitude sometimes explicit and at other times implicit in commentary about South Africa. Regardless, neither the substance of that commentary nor the diminishing space devoted to it leaves any doubt about its existence. Simply stated, the time had come to put to rest South Africa as an imperial issue. This was true even before the passage of the Act of Union, after which it became even clearer. Interest in South African affairs waned as alternatives of action there narrowed and as other imperial problems demanded greater attention. Since the prelude period of the Anglo-Boer War, South Africa received more attention than any other area of Empire. Now a united South Africa was in place in the Empire. Had British ideas also been secured there? No one knew how that question should be answered. The imperial journalists hoped it could be in the affirmative.

8

The Quest for Imperial Partnership: Part I, 1907–1910

Imperial problems other than those associated with South Africa produced, indeed excited, journalistic commentary of major proportion in the years after the Liberals gained power. They were related to the general effort to achieve greater unity between Britain and the self-governing colonies, or the dominions, as they would now be known. Sometimes the product of plan and sometimes a reaction to circumstance, this movement acquired prominent position among the great issues of the time. It involved a return of Tariff Reform to the center of the public debate as well as matters of imperial defense, communication, and organization. Previously Chamberlain's Tariff Reform crusade had made imperial unity a subject of utmost importance, but after the Election of 1906, when the Liberals were returned with every intention to implement their social reform program, there was a lull in the attention given to strategies for closer cooperation with the self-governing colonies. In 1907, however, the lull ended and the subject regained its place among the imperial journalists.

The revival of concerted discussion about imperial unity occurred in the midst of some of the most exciting years of modern British politics. Britain's Liberal government, which the 1906 Election confirmed in power, presided over a nation aroused by numerous and at times tempestuous political issues. The social legislation carried out by the triumphant Liberals, Lloyd George's "People's Budget" of 1909 and its subsequent rejection by the Lords, the two elections of 1910, the Parliamentary Act of 1911, and the introduction of the Irish Home Rule Bill in 1912 were all the focus of lively and intense political debate. It would be a distortion of reality if the partisan emotions and anxieties manifested in the political life of the times were overlooked. There existed an urgent edge to politics. The future nature of British political structure seemed to be at stake as Conservatives hurled charges of socialism at Liberals who, in turn, denounced them for their Tory obstructionism. The imperial publicists played major roles in all of these controversies not only because they were comprehensive in their commentary, but also because it was impossible to separate imperial and domestic issues. The subject of imperial unity, however, retained its place in their thinking and in their work throughout these years. Our coverage of it will span this chapter and the next and will begin with a consideration of the Colonial Conference of 1907.

THE COLONIAL CONFERENCE OF 1907

The idea of holding colonial conferences began in the late Victorian era. The first official one, that of 1887, owed its origin in large part to the Imperial Federation League.[1] Founded in 1884, the league had the object, as its name implied, of promoting imperial federation. Although the idea never reached fruition, the league did last for nine years, and before its demise it persuaded Lord Salisbury to call a colonial conference at the time of Queen Victoria's Golden Jubilee. That conference was a casual but large gathering of cabinet ministers and public men from Britain and the self-governing colonies who were attending the Jubilee celebration. Prime Minister Salisbury guided its discussions away from debate about the question of imperial federation and toward consideration of ways to improve imperial defenses and of other matters of mutual concern, mainly economic ones. Although the conference failed to achieve all that imperial advocates wished and disappointed the imperial federationists, it did establish a precedent for meeting. It was the first of a series of colonial and later imperial conferences out of which emerged the Commonwealth prime ministers' meetings of more recent times.

Two more colonial conferences met within the next fifteen years. After becoming colonial secretary in 1895, Joseph Chamberlain used the occasion of the queen's Diamond Jubilee two years later to summon a second colonial conference. A smaller affair than its predecessor, it was attended by the colonial premiers of the self-governing colonies. Earlier in this study, we described Chamberlain's role at these two conferences. It will be recalled that he presided over the conference of 1897 and attempted to have it address the political, commercial, and economic relations of the Empire. He especially tried to persuade the conference to create a "council of the Empire" that might "slowly grow to that federal council to which we must always look forward as our ultimate ideal."[2] The delegates, however, remained unconvinced of the need for such a council at that time, and were content to express their satisfaction in relations between Britain and the self-governing colonies as they then existed. They also expressed their desire to hold similar periodic conferences in the future. Chamberlain failed, therefore, to create any new foundation for imperial unity at that time, but he was not a man to abandon his conviction.

Five years later he renewed his efforts at the third colonial conference, held to coincide with Edward VII's coronation. In the interim, Britain fought the

South African War, and during that sobering conflict received the support of contingents of troops from Australia, Canada, and New Zealand in addition to those from the South African colonies that remained loyal to the Empire. Chamberlain again pressed the colonies to commit themselves to assisting in imperial defense in a regular way. Indeed, he garbed his plea in poignant language that touched many political nerves and spoke in phrases that his contemporaries would quote endlessly during ensuing years. "The weary Titan staggers under the too vast orb of its fate," he proclaimed. "We have borne the burden for many years. We think it is time that our children should assist us to support it."[3] More than the problem of imperial defense interested the colonial secretary. In a manner similar to 1897, he laid his concern about imperial political and economic relations before the conference. Once again he encountered major difficulties. For a second time the colonial premiers rejected the idea of a federal council. They countered his plea for free trade within the Empire, to be implemented in conjunction with tariff protection against foreign producers, with the demand for reciprocal imperial tariff preferences. Britain, as we know, was unable to participate in an imperial preferential system because of its adherence to the principle of Free Trade, and Chamberlain, as we also know, spent the rest of his political life trying to rectify that circumstance. The conferences did produce some positive results. The premiers agreed to renew, but not to enlarge, the colonial naval subsidy agreements with Britain, and they agreed to hold colonial conferences in the future at regular four year intervals.

By the time the fourth colonial conference met in 1907 some of the most disruptive occurrences that affected the imperial cause during this era had taken place.[4] Chamberlain's Tariff Reform and Imperial Preference campaign, the Election of 1906 in which imperial issues played so prominent a role, and the sharpest conflicts over policies for the reconstruction of South Africa, now were matters of history. Interpretation of them, of course, continued to provide abundant grist for the ongoing imperial debate. There was, however, reason to question how great a role that debate would occupy in post–1906 Edwardian politics. After their landslide victory in the Election of 1906, the Liberals held 377 seats in the House of Commons, a clear majority of 84. Besides that, they could count on their Irish allies with 83 seats and their Labour allies with 84 to support them in most cases. Unionists' fortunes were just the opposite. Now they could claim only a meager 157 seats. Since Unionists considered themselves more the custodians of Empire than the Liberals, how strong would the government's commitment to the imperial cause be in the foreseeable future?

Moreover, a curious political metamorphosis occurred within the Unionist party. After the election there was a desperate need to reconcile the Balfour and Chamberlain factions of the party. With the Liberals perched in power and prepared to begin implementing their social reform program, the question of revenue became crucial. Where would the money be found to pay for them? The same question could be asked of the expenditures that imperial defenses involved.

Unionists feared that they would involve a substantial broadening of the basis of taxation. Consequently, Balfour began to move toward accepting Tariff Reform as an alternate means of revenue, but as he did he allowed the broader imperial aspects of that policy to be de-emphasized. In July 1906, when Joseph Chamberlain suffered the stroke that ended his political career, he left the way open for Balfour's redefinition of the policy to prevail as that of the party.[5] What ramifications would these intra-party shifts have on the imperial cause?

Liberal imperial advocates, on the other hand, had problems of a different sort to face regarding the Empire. For years they had preached the value of an Empire held together by loose sentimental ties and a strong application of political practicality. Now, as the conference approached in which serious colonial problems would be discussed, the burden of proof was upon them to show that such ideas were workable and capable of maintaining the Empire.

The public discussion on the conference began months before it opened. Already by mid-February *The Times*, with its characteristic restraint of tone and suggestion, began to speculate about the imperial problems that needed to be addressed. It claimed there was a need to consider fuller colonial participation in imperial defense and spoke of fiscal reform, meaning Imperial Preference, being bound up with every question of imperial development.[6] As the conference drew near, it returned to the question of Imperial Preference on a number of occasions as it began to champion "some form of common council." *The Times* argued that if the Empire were to continue at all it had to be on "a basis of partnership, not on the basis of a trustee dealing with minors."[7] Nevertheless, Imperial Preference was the topic it cautiously brought to the forefront of its pronouncements on the forthcoming gathering.

Caution, however, was not part of J. L. Garvin's approach to the conference. He was between editorships at the time, having lost the *Outlook* at the end of 1906 and not yet in the chair at the *Observer*. He busied himself writing for the *Fortnightly Review* and for his friend, Leo Maxse, in the *National Review*. His major statement about the coming meeting, "Time and Contrast: A Foreword to the Colonial Conference," appeared in the *National Review* and was full of alarm and urgency.[8] Garvin considered the imperial record since the previous colonial conference as one of "missed opportunity" for which he blamed both of the major parties.[9] Were imperial advocates to abandon the dream of a stronger Empire held together by preferential tariffs and mutual economic prosperity among all of its parts?[10] Garvin told Maxse in private that the object of his statement was to point out "the terrible character of delay we are all contemplating." If Britain failed to act now, and Garvin had little confidence in the Liberal government acting in behalf of imperial causes, he thought Canada would negotiate trading treaties with the United States and Germany, thus "destroying the possibility of a strong preference policy." He told Maxse, "*That is the point*. The only one worth hammering on from our point of view."[11] Garvin, in fact, had little hope for the conference and confided to Maxse that it was "a foredoomed fiasco" and that only the "inevitable" swing of the political pendulum could save their program.[12]

No such sense of urgency or despondency can be found among the publicists who supported the government. Spender's *Westminster Gazette*, for instance, defended the Liberals against charges of indifference to the Empire. It chose to express its confidence in the existing strength of imperial relations by observing that, despite all of the predictions to the contrary fifty years before, "the bond between the mother-country and the colonies has, on the whole, grown firmer in the last generation." Ties of sentiment and pressure from the outside in the form of the emergence of other great colonial powers kept the Empire together, it felt. "The pressure from without," it argued, "is not likely to grow less in the years that are coming, and we regard it as an infinitely more important factor in holding the Empire together than any commercial ties that might be created by changing our Fiscal system."[13] The *Westminster* took a more open stand on matters of imperial defense and on the possibility of an imperial council, so long as it was consultative and not executive.[14] Nevertheless, from the first its main thrust centered on a defense of free trade imperial principles. "The Government has neither the desire nor the power to betray its mandate in regard to Free Trade, and the Colonies hitherto have recognized that this is a domestic question for the British people to which the answer can only be varied by the ballot."[15] When *The Times* suggested that the recent election failed to produce a clear verdict on Free Trade and had provided at best only a "mixed mandate," the *Westminster* argued against the point at length while finding it at the same time a "sufficiently absurd" contention that needed no response.[16]

St. Loe Strachey's *Spectator* followed the same path as the *Westminster* on this question of Imperial Preference. Let us recall that Strachey was a doctrinaire Free Trader and that his *Spectator* was not only one of Britain's most prestigious weekly journals but also the most important outlet in the press of the Unionist Free Traders, a group that, between its founding in 1903 and its collapse in 1910, was mainly within the Unionist party. As the chief publicist representing this group, Strachey had been at odds with both Balfour and Chamberlain regarding their Tariff Reform policies. Indeed, in 1906 he advised voters to support the Liberals in the absence of any Unionist Free Trade candidate. Moreover, he even stood, and lost, as a Unionist Free Trade parliamentary candidate and during the election went so far as to speak for Winston Churchill, no favorite among Unionists whom he deserted when he joined the Liberals in 1904. Since the Unionist Free Traders were a group rather than a major party, some perspective on their political fortunes after the Election of 1906 will help to explain their precarious and waning position during the years under discussion in this chapter.

After the election, they found themselves caught between "the devil and the deep sea," in the words of the old guard Tory, Lord Balfour of Burleigh (not to be confused with A. J. Balfour, the Unionist party leader and former prime minister). He pondered if the Unionist Free Traders should "go to the Devil of Protection with our friends, or the Deep Sea of Socialism with our political adversaries."[17] That dilemma became even more pressing later in 1906 as A. J. Balfour guided a reunited Unionist party toward Tariff Reform and as the Liberal government began to implement its social legislation. The growth of Tariff Reform within Unionist ranks left the Unionist Free Traders in a desperate position. Sheer numbers tell the tale. At one point sixty-five Unionist Free Traders sat in the House of Commons. After 1906 their numbers shrank to about thirty, and after January 1910, only one remained. Meanwhile, the citadel of Liberal power remained indifferent to their advances for influence there. So in the four years after 1906, they gradually slipped back into the Unionist ranks and even came to offer their support for Unionist Tariff Reformers whose control of the party was secure. Better that, a Free Trader like Strachey thought, than support for the Liberals' "semi-socialism."

Difficult though it was for Strachey to maintain his Free Trade advocacy, he refused to abandon the cause until other political circumstances simply overcame it. Accordingly, he placed his *Spectator* in league with the Free Trade Liberal press as the colonial conference approached and extolled the glories of Britain's Free Trade Empire. It was unnecessary, the *Spectator* explained, to seek a "premature tightening of the bonds of Empire." Rather than that, it favored looking forward to a true imperial union or alliance of equal states on equal terms that it predicted would occur within the next fifty or sixty years.[18]

The conference itself opened on April 15 and lasted one month. It was an interesting gathering that could be considered a source of pride by imperial statesmen and publicists of all persuasions. Not only was it the fourth of the series but it was also the first one scheduled to meet solely for the transaction of business. All the previous ones met in connection with imperial celebrations. It was, moreover, the first conference of the series that could be called public. At the opening of the conference the premiers asked that there be greater publicity of the proceedings. Their request resulted in the publication of a daily official report in time to be used by the next day's newspapers.[19]

It was the best-prepared and publicized conference to date. Shortly after he became the colonial secretary, Lord Elgin began to gather proposals for the conference agenda. Australia, Cape Colony, and New Zealand responded to Elgin's request for proposals as did some of the great departments of state. Moreover, both politicians and publicists had been promoting the need to improve imperial organization, so it now appeared the time had come to address and resolve that problem. The official agenda was circulated before the meeting opened, and it indicated that consideration of an imperial council, of imperial defense, and of imperial preferential trade would be the major subjects of the conference.[20] The gathering also had its interesting personalities. Among the most prominent of its delegates were Alfred Deakin and Sir Wilfrid Laurier, the premiers of Australia and Canada respectively. Both were outspoken nationalists who held definite but different views on the Empire. Deakin, unlike his Canadian counterpart, failed to see the incompatibility of nationalism and imperial commitment. Present also were two South Africans, Louis Botha and Dr. Leander Starr Jameson. The former, the ex-Boer general, was now premier of the Transvaal; the latter, the same Dr. Jameson who led the famous raid into the Transvaal in 1895, was now premier of Cape Colony. It is surely an ironic twist to imagine both of these men sitting together at a conference of Empire discussing matters such as imperial defense.[21]

The conference, over which Lord Elgin presided, was productive, though not as productive as the Unionist imperial enthusiasts wished. Imperial preferences commanded a great deal of attention at the meeting. Despite the colonial sentiment in favor of the idea of a reciprocal, preferential, imperial trading system, and despite Deakin's energetic pushing of the scheme, Britain would not budge on the issue. Essentially the conference changed nothing on that topic. Imperial defense also received ample attention, but nothing specific resulted from those discussions other than an agreement to hold a subsidiary conference two years later to continue discussion of the subject. It was on the matter of imperial organization that some definite strides were taken. Should there be an imperial council complete with executive and legislative powers? Protective of their own national autonomy, the colonial premiers opposed that idea as they had in 1897 and 1902. The discussion then turned to a proposal, which Deakin pushed particularly hard, for an imperial secretariat. The Australian premier thought it would minimize the role of the Colonial Office to have a new body devoted exclusively to dominion affairs, but Laurier balked at the suggestion, seeing in it the implication of a strong organization. Ultimately the delegates reached a compromise. A secretariat would be established as a division within the Colonial Office rather than as a separate organization. In time the secretariat became simply a Dominions Department within the Colonial Office.[22] The delegates also agreed to several changes in terminology: they decided on the use of the term "Dominion" as a designation for the self-governing colonies, and they agreed that the quadrennial conferences would be called henceforth "Imperial Conferences." During the month of the proceedings two contrasting views of what could and should be accomplished by the delegates appeared in the press. For purposes of delineation of these views, we shall consider the treatment the conference received, first in *The Times* and then in the *Westminster Gazette* .

The Times proceeded from the premise that the Empire was always a moving entity. That being the case, it urged that every chance of advancing the unity of Empire should be taken. "Every chance that is missed," it warned, "means, not that we are left where we were before, but that we are drifting further toward disunion."[23] Since the Liberal government would not give real consideration to imperial preferences, the best hope to strengthen relations lay in improving imperial machinery. For the first week of the conference, this argument, always generously stated, was the main focus of its leading articles.

When the delegates struck the compromise on the imperial secretariat, *The Times* seemed satisfied and understood why it was not possible with deference to colonial opinion to move farther at this time.[24] During the middle weeks the conference was in session, as the discussion more and more centered on the subject of imperial preferences, *The Times* voiced its disappointment, however politely, with the "reluctant Government." It found the various statements of the premiers favoring preference "full of hope and constructive imagination," suggesting engagement of the future and a "determination to mould it to their ends." In contrast, it turned to Asquith's responses to those statements "with a feeling of depression."[25] "What all sensible Imperialists hoped for, whether tariff reformers or not," *The Times* said, "was that the Government might find themselves in fuller sympathy with colonial statesmen." All of the Liberal rhetoric about freedom and self-government, it reasoned, was perhaps inoffensive, but it only related to what already existed within the Empire. Nevertheless, the point it underscored most of all was that the present situation called for more than words. It demanded "recognition of the practical efforts which are being made to fashion a closer imperial connexion."[26]

No "golden moment" had arrived with the opening of the conference, said the *Westminster Gazette* . There was no "crisis of our fate." The Empire was not "doomed to decay and disruption" if certain "gigantic problems" were not resolved immediately. Spender's paper deplored the appearance of such rhetoric about the conference and warned that such melodrama would only hinder the work of the conference. Why was such a crisis atmosphere created, it questioned, whenever the home government conferred with the self-governing colonies?[27] With that attitude in mind and with the determination to tackle subjects where practical achievement was possible, this journal immediately placed itself in favor of improving the machinery, or constitutional organization, of the Empire. Much on this subject, it claimed, deserved to be "talked out and thought out" by the colonial premiers.[28] For the moment it did not anticipate that an imperial council was at hand, nor that all of the colonies wished it. The idea of a secretariat was more appealing to the *Westminster*, and it stood ready to accept any reasonable compromise on the issues associated with establishing it.

By far the great focus of the paper's leading articles throughout the conference was on defending Britain's Free Trade policy. Day after day it returned to it. Of course, all parties including Britain were free to state their views on the subject, it said, and of course, Britain's position had been decided at the last election. Expounding on Deakin's expression that the problem the British peoples faced was that of combining liberty and union, the *Westminster* suggested that there could be "unity in difference." That theme became the main one the paper chanted, and it used a number of arguments to support it. For instance, there was always the mandate the Liberals claimed to have from the last election to consider. Then there was the principle of autonomy, one that applied to Britain as well as the colonies. The home government recognized that the self-governing colonies were protectionist. They, in turn, should recognize that Britain was for Free Trade and, indeed, that any change for Britain's fiscal system would be a much more massive undertaking than for any of the colonies. At any rate, Britain recognized the right of the others to have their own policy, and they, in keeping with the principle of autonomy, should do likewise. In the process of repeating their argument, the *Westminster* claimed that fiscal policy was really a matter of domestic politics. As for the argument that the British had nothing to offer colonies that granted preference to them, the paper pointed to defense as a balancing factor. It reasoned, "The mother-country provides the Navy, of which all the Colonies get the benefit; the Colonies lower the tariff wall against the mother-country when that can be done and the Colonial manufactures [are] still protected."[29] At the end of the conference, the paper was still offering firm defense of British Free Trade against all challenges and offered this summary of its position: "We hold that freedom is greater than Free Trade, and we have never attempted to force our policy on any self-governing Colony. But the freedom we give we ask for ourselves, and when the Colonies say that they cannot abandon Protection we are entitled to reply that we cannot abandon Free Trade."[30]

In retrospect the conference was worthy of the attention it received in the daily press. As W. David McIntyre writes, it was "the last of the pioneering colonial conferences and was in many ways an important landmark in the emerging trend of imperial cooperation."[31] There were, in fact, many references to a spirit of cooperation in the conference that appeared in the press. The genuine response the papers made to efforts to improve the imperial machinery is a case in point. So too was the general accord publicists gave to conference discussion about how to improve imperial communications and transportation. The sympathetic understanding they displayed in commenting on questions of imperial defense revealed again a willingness to be cooperative. The stumbling block, of course, was the issue of imperial preferences, but it did not close all paths to increased unity. The publicity the conference received, moreover, gave the dominion premiers the chance to gain recognition before the British public. That, in the opinion of *The Times,* was so much the better for the cause of Empire. Since the premiers could now voice dominion opinion at the metropolitan center of the Empire, *The Times* believed that it would become impossible for any informed person "to go about saying that the Colonies offer us nothing and want everything."[32] All things considered, it is possible to conclude at this point that the conference elevated the factor of imperial cooperation in the public debate.

The imperial journalists shared in the achievement and disappointments of the conference. They promoted the meeting and publicized its deliberations. They placed the main issues the delegates discussed in wider imperial perspective as they sharpened public perception of them. In the matter of reviving the Imperial Preference issue, they anticipated the proceedings and created momentum that affected the debate.

THE REEMERGENCE OF THE TARIFF REFORM ISSUE: 1907-1910

The best index to serious imperial thought in the years following the colonial conference can be found in expressions of opinion regarding Tariff Reform. Support for the program was on the rise during these years. In part, the colonial conference stimulated this expanded backing, but it was also due to the industrial depression of 1908-1909 and to the Liberal government's move to introduce its program of social reforms. Where would the money come from to pay for them? The same question would be asked of the increased revenue the naval rearmament program entailed. Liberals felt the money could be generated by increased taxes. That was the idea behind Lloyd George's famous budget of 1909. He proposed not only to raise traditional taxes (e.g., the income tax, death duties, and taxes on profitable luxuries such as alcohol and tobacco) but also recommended a super tax on incomes over £5,000, a small tax on underdeveloped land, and a 20 percent tax on capital gains on land to be paid whenever it changed hands. Angered by the new super tax and by Lloyd George's tax assault on land, the Lords rejected the budget on 30 November 1909. The House of Lords was a Conservative stronghold, and the Unionists depended on it to block the Liberal legislation, a situation that encouraged Lloyd George's remark that the upper house had become "Mr. Balfour's poodle." The Lords had rejected a plural voting bill in 1906 and a licensing bill in 1908 before taking action on the "People's Budget." Their repudiation of the budget, however, resulted in the Liberals making the reduction of the power of the Lords, as well as approval of the budget, an election issue in 1910.

Meanwhile, support for Tariff Reform grew as an alternate means of raising revenue. But as it did, support for imperial preferences became an issue. A number of Unionist M.P.'s, perhaps as many as 50 percent of the party after the Election of 1906, were dedicated to fiscal reform, but they were not necessarily drawn to the idea of imperial preferences. Known as "Whole Hoggers," this faction of the party was basically protectionist. By 1907 the party accepted Tariff Reform as its official policy. In the ensuing years it held the support of the majority of Unionists.

Before proceeding with our account of the Tariff Reform issue, however, it is necessary to describe briefly the events of 1910. That year stands out as one of the most politically intense times in modern British history. Two elections, one at the beginning and one at the end of the year, tend to enclose these turbulent months in a type of political parenthesis. Between those two elections political excitement ran high. The proposed reform of the House of Lords that followed in the wake of its veto of Lloyd George's budget produced a steady flow of debates in both houses on the subject. Then suddenly in May, the nation was stunned by the death of the king. Following that there was a five-month-long round-table conference on the constitutional question regarding the House of Lords' reform. It failed to resolve the issue. Tariff Reform remained interwoven throughout the political discussions of the day. It was a major issue in both elections of 1910, but after failing to win in the first election, Balfour agreed to submit the whole matter to a referendum should the Unionists win the second election. That referendum pledge probably did win a few additional constituencies for the Unionists in the Election of December 1910, but not enough to change the balance of power.[33] The Liberals and Unionists remained about equal in numbers, but the Liberals continued in power with Irish and Labour support. That dependency guaranteed both the passage of the budget and the reform of the House of Lords, the latter being needed if the Irish ever hoped to have Parliament pass a Home Rule act.

The imperial publicists were at the center of the resurgent Tariff Reform debate. They helped to make it the issue it became again. But now in several important cases their professional circumstances changed, and it is necessary to consider those changes in order to understand the conditions surrounding their work after 1907.

The men at Printing House Square, for example, faced serious journalistic problems throughout these years. The paper was straining under the weight of its own costly production. It remained the complete national newspaper as Bell and Buckle wished, and it was still a monumental enterprise compared to other papers of the day. The question was, could it pay for itself? Its daily circulation in 1908 hovered around 38,000. That was a weak figure compared to ones in the hundreds of thousands that the *Daily Telegraph* claimed or to its own circulation of thirty years before, which was upwards of 60,000. As the organs of the New Journalism entered the field of the morning daily press, things became increasingly difficult for *The Times*. By 1907 the paper reached the end of its resources and a number of its proprietors demanded that it be financially reconstituted. After a series of intriguing negotiations, Lord Northcliffe, the personification of the popular journalism and the most powerful figure in the British press, was appointed chief proprietor. His charge was to modernize the paper, and that he did.

It is only fair to Bell and Buckle, however, to point out that some aspects of that modernization preceded Northcliffe. Since the beginning of the Edwardian years, the paper began to acquire a more attractive appearance, if ever so slightly. Its editorial page is a case in point. By 1908 its leading articles were written in a more direct manner and had less spacious quotation than they did in previous years. More white space appeared between the articles with the introduction of headings in 1907 and the lengthy columns, which now were divided into paragraphs, became more readable. Northcliffe would carry the modernization farther yet in coming years, but because of his autocratic ways, he would make life difficult for Bell and Buckle. As they worked to retain *The Times'* place in national affairs, they also struggled to hold their own positions under Northcliffe. He was a man with his own strong views on national life and imperial affairs.

Lord Northcliffe, indeed, posed a several-sided problem for the senior staff at *The Times*. Bell, Buckle, and Chirol were great defenders of the traditions associated with the paper and of highly principled journalism. They tried to formulate careful, deliberate, and broad-minded positions for the paper on all prominent issues. They subordinated their own views to those that *The Times*, being the national institution that it was, should hold. By contrast, Northcliffe was much more impetuous by nature. Powerful force though he was in Unionist politics, he was really, by his own admission, a poor party man. His first loyalty was to what he called "the great outside public" whose great champion he considered himself to be. Throughout the Edwardian era, he was a foremost supporter of the Empire, but he could waver on specific issues, particularly if their popular appeal was a matter of question. Tariff Reform is the classic case of his wavering. In 1903 he had begun by condemning "Stomach Taxes," as he termed the proposed duties on foodstuffs, while offering some general support for Chamberlain and his program. Then he offered to conduct a press campaign for Lord Rosebery, the former Liberal prime minister and Liberal Imperialist leader, if he would place himself at the head of a Free Trade movement.[34] When Lord Rosebery declined that unorthodox offer, Northcliffe changed directions and supported Balfour's position of retaliationism.[35] After that he was definitely a supporter of Tariff Reform, and even threw much of that support behind Chamberlain, though at times he returned to backing Balfour and retaliationism. At the time of the Colonial Conference of 1907, his *Daily Mail* was emphatic in its endorsement of Tariff Reform as the correct policy to pursue "for the good of British trade and the greater unity of Empire." It even went so far as to admit at that point that it might be necessary to place a small tax on colonial food imports and a higher duty on foreign foodstuffs.[36] Such fluctuations were uncharacteristic of the policymakers at Printing House Square.

After the colonial conference, *The Times* became a consistent supporter of Tariff Reform, and its position corresponded quite well to the general inclination of Bell and Buckle on the subject. Moberly Bell had been loyal to the cause since 1903. He regretted the defeat it suffered in the Election of 1906 but that failed to surprise him.[37] Afterwards he remained committed to a new fiscal policy, though that commitment became increasingly linked to the defeat of "Socialism" (a term he used in reference to liberal legislation).[38] Buckle was more moderate in his views and declined to support extremist Tariff Reformers. Like A. J. Balfour, whose political opinions he continued to support, Buckle sympathized with the policy in general but kept his options open on details about it.[39]

Under their guidance, *The Times* offered a broadly defined support for the revived interest in Tariff Reform. Its leading articles made few specific recommendations about the shape the reform should take, but they gave clear indication of where the paper stood on the issue. In particular *The Times* advanced the argument that public support for fiscal reform had grown dramatically since the last election and that there was good reason to explain why. Tariff Reform, it said, was "widely different from protection particularly in being defensive, not aggressive" and that in their search for new revenue the time had come "for statesmen to understand that a great country cannot be governed by theories and catchwords."[40] The last point, a direct reference to the Liberals' attachment to Free Trade theories, led the paper to be critical about the Liberal government's failure to respond to needs of the time and to address the "dogmatic assertions" that had lost their power.[41] This line of argument became one of the most consistent ones advanced by *The Times* on the subject. It also championed the colonial factor as a "second branch of the tariff reform doctrine." The colonies had grown, so argued the paper, into self-governing communities, who controlled their own policies, and who preferred "to form a part of the Empire" and "to do business with the Mother Country" if they could.[42] By 1908 *The Times* felt that Free Traders were on the defensive. The problem, however, that Bell and Buckle faced dealt with Northcliffe. Would he remain steady in his advocacy of Tariff Reform? If not, what would be the consequences for the paper and its senior staff?

As it turned out, there was no apparent disagreement between Northcliffe and the senior *Times* staff on this question in the years immediately following his acquisition of the paper. *The Times* continued to take to task the Liberal government's insensitivity to the need to reform fiscal policy. Why do men, supposedly "conversant with affairs," it asked in a typical comment on the subject, "deny flatly and boldly the existence of conspicuous facts . . . . Do they imagine they can get rid of awkward facts by denying them?"[43] After 1908 the paper also continued to champion the imperial side of Tariff Reform and claimed that it was a means of securing the unity of Empire instead of its otherwise inevitable disintegration.[44] Its support for Imperial Preference was one of the strongest and most consistent arguments it made on behalf of Tariff Reform. Against the thrust of the "Whole Hoggers," those Unionists who were primarily protectionists, it had this to say: "The response which recent appeals to Unionists to drop or emasculate the policy of Imperial Preference have met with shows how solid the Unionist party is to-day on this the greatest of all national and Imperialist issues."[45] This is where *The Times* stood midway through the dramatic events of 1910. Before we can proceed to the end of that year, we must consider J. L. Garvin's new role, for he had become Lord Northcliffe's chief political consultant and foremost editor.

In January 1908 Northcliffe appointed Garvin editor of his Sunday *Observer* and allowed him to acquire a proprietary interest in the paper. The editor then embarked upon his years of greatest influence. For the first three years of his long editorship of that paper, which lasted until 1942, he worked in close association with Northcliffe, who remained the paper's principal owner. Garvin quickly converted the *Observer* into a paying journalistic property and made it a force of utmost significance in British politics. Seldom, if ever, in the history of the British press has an editor wielded the political influence that Garvin did in the early years of his editorship. Northcliffe shared in making the paper successful in the early months of Garvin's reign, not only because of his managerial skills and the extensive resources of his organization but also because he advised Garvin on the effective techniques of modern editorship. But it was Garvin's genius, which was so manifest in the paper's long, forceful, and compelling leading articles, that made the *Observer* the power it became. He wanted to be a molder of public opinion and a mover of the masses.[46] This delighted many of the champions of the Empire. They recognized his professional preeminence. Northcliffe, at this point, regarded Garvin as "the greatest journalist in England."[47] When Lord Grey, the governor-general of Canada, learned of Garvin's new editorship, he commented that he was "far and away the most brilliant living journalist in England." Lord Grey's only lament was that *The Times* had not secured Garvin's services.[48]

It was, in fact, a common enough rumor in Fleet Street that Garvin was earmarked to succeed Buckle at *The Times*, but the rumor was without substance. It is, moreover, difficult to imagine him as editor at Printing House Square. Garvin was, as David Ayerst has reflected, "an innovator, an individualist, a skirmisher in front of the line."[49] The *Observer* was the proper forum for his talents, and he made it a paper that embodied his own spirited and perceptive views on imperial matters.

Garvin became the epitome of the journalist as a political strategist after gaining the editorship of the *Observer*. In the great budget fight of 1909 and 1910, he and his *Observer* spearheaded the Unionist attack. That party, as Alfred Gollin has commented, lacked platform orators who could match the two leading Liberal speakers of the day, Winston Churchill and David Lloyd George, and it had to look to its press to provide the counterbalancing force in the public debate.[50] Contemporaries recognized this fact. The *Observer* became the most-quoted paper in the British press and Garvin the most-recognized editor. It was Garvin, moreover, who brought Northcliffe back into line on the budget in the summer of 1909. Northcliffe, at first, opposed Lloyd George's budget, but began to modify his thinking on the subject after a surprise meeting with the chancellor in the House of Commons. At that meeting Lloyd George applied a little of his Welsh wizardry, for which he was famous, on the press baron. Afterwards *The Times* noted that a change in favor of the budget was taking place in the country. The *Daily Mail* struck the same theme with even greater force. Garvin acted immediately to bring Northcliffe back into line.[51] In a seventeen page letter written on August 4, the very day that *The Times* reported the shift in attitude in favor of the budget, he warned that "a Unionist surrender" on the budget would create "almost the gravest situation that any of us has known in England politics." He told Northcliffe that "the whole of social, national and Imperial policy is indirectly at hazard in this business."[52] The letter was as strong and convincing as any editor, who was astute in politics, could or dared to write to his publisher. Garvin followed it by yet another one the next day. "The whole tone of *The Times* and *Daily Mail*," he said then, "seems to me utterly, utterly disastrous." He continued in terms measured both in doses of admiration, for there was much in Northcliffe's character and accomplishment that Garvin admired, and alarm. "You know my affection for you. You know I am not one of your suppliants," he said. "You know I want nothing from you at all; and that you can get from me the opinion of an honest and fearless man with a touch of prophecy in him and that kind better than flattery, 'priceless to Kings,' as someone said, ought not to be useless to you!" "The Budget," the editor warned, ". . . would ruin the Empire."[53] Garvin's bold, impassioned plea took effect and Northcliffe returned to his position in the Unionist opposition.

The editor's influence over Northcliffe remained for the rest of the year and for the extraordinary one that followed. "Nowhere in the history of journalism," wrote Alfred M. Gollin, a historian not known for overstatement, "can one find a more clear-cut case of an editor first modifying and then controlling the attitude and outlook, not simply of his proprietor but of the entire newspaper system controlled by that proprietor."[54] There is no need to quarrel with that statement, except to mention, as Gollin does himself, that *The Times* was not part of what could be called the Northcliffe press. Neither Northcliffe nor Garvin was beyond trying to influence the editorial policy of *The Times*; neither was completely successful. Papers like the *Daily Mail* that were the standards of the Northcliffe press, however, were quick to echo the line taken by Garvin and the *Observer*.

It was also in the midsummer of 1909 that Garvin began his close association with J. S. Sandars, Balfour's confidential secretary. Though he remained an unknown figure to the Edwardian public, Sandars was a man of influence in Unionist politics. While Balfour was prime minister, he acted as a type of cabinet secretariat and provided a link between Balfour and other Unionist politicians and publicists. He continued to perform that role for the Unionist leader after the party went into opposition in 1905. Garvin's association with Sandars gave him an indispensable entrance into the inner sanctums of Unionist politics. For months to come, the two men met often and also maintained a frequent and regular correspondence. Sandars asked Garvin to criticize Unionist campaign literature, sought his advice on policy, and asked for his counsel in matters of political strategy.[55] Garvin's association with Sandars, as well as the one he had with Northcliffe, is important to keep in mind when considering his role in the great political events of 1910. Such associations alert us to the fact that not only did he have his finger on the pulsebeat of Unionist politics but also that his influence was a private as well as a public reality.

Garvin, for instance, was a power in the first election of 1910. Late in May 1910, when the death of King Edward was suddenly announced to the nation, it was Garvin who, without consulting anyone, made a plea in the *Observer* for a political truce, "a truce of God," and called for a round-table conference including men of both parties to address questions of constitutional reform. That conference, though it ended in failure, remained in session from June 17 to November 10. As it approached its inconclusive end, it was Garvin who roused public attention for an even larger settlement.[56]

The larger settlement Garvin came to espouse was known as "federalism," and it had several roots. It was a broad proposal for a federal solution for the problem of Irish Home Rule. Garvin first allowed that idea to surface in the *Observer* on 31 July 1910, but he and others had contemplated it before then.[57] Toward the end of the constitutional conference, Lloyd George began to circulate a document that he had been preparing since August in which he called for the formation of a national government. He reasoned that such a government could deal effectively with major problems, including imperial unity as well as Irish Home Rule. Lloyd George also believed that the Imperial Parliament was overworked and that some of its responsibilities could be handled by local legislatures. He brought this plan to the attention of his cabinet colleagues and a few other people in early October.[58] Garvin was one of the few and the idea impressed him. Accordingly, on October 16, he proclaimed the need, if the present constitutional conference should break down, for a "wider and greater settlement" that would consider "the new programme of federalism."[59] He continued to advance that idea in powerful leading articles in subsequent weeks.[60] The *Daily Mail* fell into line behind the *Observer*, and on October 20 *The Times* began to publish a series of pro-federalist letters by 'Pacificus,' who was Frederick Scott Oliver, a well-connected publicist of the day who authored *Federalism and Home Rule* during this same year. Garvin and he were in contact at this time. They shared ideas and Oliver said he agreed with Garvin's views on federalism in the *Observer*.

Garvin also campaigned in private for federalism. He took his case first to Northcliffe and won him over and then tried to persuade Balfour.[61] The Unionist leader, whose reputation had been made originally in Ireland, refused to budge on his position against any type of Home Rule for Ireland. He and Garvin exchanged fascinating political epistles on the subject, but the exchange failed to advance the case of federalism with Balfour.[62] Finally Sandars told Garvin on November 4 that the campaign for federalism would have to be abandoned due to Balfour's intransigence on the subject.

In retrospect some form of the idea of federalism appears to have been one of the more promising schemes of the time for solving the Irish Home Rule problem. Garvin also perceived it as a promising step for the cause of imperial unity. At any rate, it was no exaggeration for Lord Grey, who had been attracted to the idea of federalism since the beginning of the year, to write to his various correspondents that "Garvin has done a big thing."[63]

With the failure of federalism and the conclusion of the constitutional conference without any agreement only a week later, the "truce of God" also ended. Party politics were resumed with the questions of Irish Home Rule and Tariff Reform being pushed into the foreground by the Unionists. The leaders of that party were puzzled, however, by how to present Tariff Reform to the public. In the first election earlier in the year, that issue had helped Unionists to acquire about equal strength with the Liberals in the House of Commons, but it had not given them the majority they wanted. Now as another election grew near, Balfour was approached by a number of people including both Buckle and Garvin, who told him that they failed to see how the Unionists could win with the food duties entailed in a full Tariff Reform program. The Unionists, however, found the solution to their worries over the power of Tariff Reform to attract additional voters in another maneuver. Toward the end of November talk increased in political circles about using the referendum as a device for resolving great issues regardless of which party was in power. Garvin, who as we have seen had been searching all year for the most reasonable way to pursue Tariff Reform, was again instrumental in leading the new departure. Acting alone he introduced what became the new Unionist policy. He suggested that the referendum be used for Tariff Reform in one of his most powerful leading articles. It appeared in the *Observer* on November 27, and two days later, in a much-acclaimed Albert Hall speech, Balfour declared that he had no objection to submitting Tariff Reform to a referendum. It was the reaction of the Unionist press to Garvin's November 27 article that created the momentum for the referendum suggestion. That was a fitting end to a year in which Garvin and the *Observer* had played so large a role in the great events of the times. "The *Observer* during that year," Alfred Gollin writes, "had reached a peak of influence almost unparalleled in the history of the Press."[64] Though his appraisal of the editor may seem excessive, there is good reason, as the evidence shows, to agree with it.

Garvin's Tariff Reform advocacy included a strong commitment to imperial unity. His personal correspondence, in which he normally expressed himself with both candor and passion, bears eloquent witness to the attachment he felt to that goal. A few examples from that record during the years we are considering will suffice. "The question of Imperial integrity and power is and always has been decisive for me," Garvin wrote to St. Loe Strachey on one occasion.[65] In another letter to Strachey, with whom he was then engaged in one of those frank but ever so delightful Edwardian private intellectual skirmishes, he wrote: "The unity of the British Empire is to me a matter of 'conversion,' and the strength with which I have endeavoured to struggle for the wider union of the Empire is the real index of the energy with which I would resist any attempt . . . to impair the measure of unity which after the conflict of centuries we have established in these islands."[66] On another occasion while corresponding with Sandars about future Unionist policies, Garvin began to express his thoughts about Ireland. He indicated he was flexible on the subject. "If the Irish would give real Imperial guarantees . . . [such as] the fleet, preference, Ulster, . . . closer Imperial Union, the dearest wish of my life would be fulfilled, and I could then render nearly as much service to the Empire as any person in it outside the great ones."[67] His private comments about his imperial commitment reveal the same passion for cause and broadness of mind that can be found in his many public references to imperial unity.

Although he continued to write for the *Fortnightly Review* on a regular basis as well as occasionally for other journals, the *Observer* is the best gauge to his public commentary after 1908. His leading articles there, masterpieces of effective journalism that they were, provide clear evidence of the line of his argument in the political debates of his day. Of course, he used those articles to advance the cause of Tariff Reform. He claimed that in the minds of its adherents it was nothing less than "a supreme faith."[68] Garvin was ill-disposed to treat the subject in the narrow terms of a simple tariff policy and surely did not present it as protectionism. He tried rather to place Chamberlain's tariff policy in its wider setting. In his opinion it was an integral part of social reform and the soundest means for financing an expanded social system. But how did he present the imperial side of the issue? Through all the reorientations that the Tariff Reform argument took in 1909 and 1910, did Garvin continue to stress the imperial element in it? As the "Whole Hogger" protectionist faction of the Unionist party became more clamorous, did Garvin continue to use the imperial argument for Tariff Reform? These questions can be answered in the affirmative. It remained either implicitly or explicitly a major part of his arguments on fiscal reform. To use his words, it was one of the "first principles" that defined the proposal.[69]

Garvin was never more effective than when he thought a crisis imperiled the nation. So it was in 1909 and 1910. He believed, indeed, that the Empire as well as the nation faced a crisis. To him the question was one of choice. Britain could select either a path that would lead to imperial union or one to wider separation. The advocates of free food, Garvin said, actually supported an imperial policy of "'wider separatism'—antagonism, that is, to Imperial union upon a preferential basis."[70] He presented imperial preferences as one of the potential "Foundations of Empire," a means of providing closer union between Britain and the dominions, a type of "wider patriotism." Without it Britain had only to wait for the "dissolution of the Empire." This theme permeated a number of the *Observer*'s leading articles on the subject. "Cobdenism means utter fiscal separation within the Empire," Garvin wrote. "It means the complete economic disintegration of the Empire. It means practically fiscal federation between British territories and foreign nations."[71] He sensed that imperial sentiment both in Britain and the dominions was greater now than at any time since 1903, but Britain was yet unable either to reciprocate or even negotiate preferential trade arrangements with the dominions. This led him to warn that Canada, in particular, could soon drift into trade arrangements with the United States that would lead her to develop a fiscal policy "upon a North American basis." Garvin said that would be disastrous to British capital and labor alike, and would be an "almost mortal" blow to the "imperial idea."[72] A systematic consideration of Garvin's commentary in the *Observer* throughout these years reveals no weakening of his commitment to the imperial side of that argument. Moreover, he made it an integral part of his appeal for federalism in October 1910. A "larger settlement with Preference left out" was not what Garvin had in mind at that time.[73] He already had his eye fixed on the imperial conference scheduled to meet the following year and on the hope of being able to deliver some type of fiscal preference for dominion trade at that time.

The positions of Strachey and Spender regarding Tariff Reform and Imperial Preference between 1907 and 1910 were less involved than Garvin's. In the case of Strachey, he may have maintained some hope for the growth of Unionist Free Trade ranks after the Colonial Conference of 1907. Indeed, we find his *Spectator* at that time denouncing the arguments of Tariff Reformers as "absolutely bankrupt" and the damage that Balfour had done to the party after the last election and the "Valentine Letters."[74] It spoke of the "baleful influence of his tactics" on Tariff Reform and had this to say about the Unionist leader: "Mr. Balfour was an exceedingly bad Free-trader. We are bound in honesty to say that he is even a worse Tariff Reformer."[75] Regardless, Strachey's defense of the Unionist Free Trade position would soon be crushed from opposite directions. On the one hand, he found he was unable to influence the programs of the Liberal party despite the fact that he had urged Unionist Free Traders in 1906 to support it in constituencies in which they had no candidate of their own to back. Strachey still described himself as a defender of the "left centre" position and as a "Whig by conviction, temperament and heredity."[76] Nevertheless, he was hostile to social reform because he felt it would necessitate financing by means of direct taxation. He believed that since the Unionist Free Traders had turned away from preserving Unionist principles and voted for Liberals in the last election because "the duty of supporting free trade was higher," it was now incumbent on the Liberals to make a similar sacrifice. The Liberals, he contended, had accepted their help but in turn were actually damaging Free Trade by their social reform program, which, because of its costs, was entirely incompatible with it. Strachey reasoned that those reforms could only result in state socialism or Tariff Reform or in some amalgam of the two. At the very least, he said, the Liberals had "smoothed the way for Tariff Reform and made it possible."[77]

The premise of his argument was far from convincing, and Margot Asquith told him why. The wife of the prime minister was a lively Edwardian personality whose letters were as spontaneous as her mind. Strachey enjoyed his correspondence with Margot, even when they disagreed. She was not one to mince words. In this case she probed to the weak basis of his argument when she told him that she resented the idea "that *we* [the Liberals] have betrayed Free Trade." She explained, "I mean you can't expect a genuine Lib. government returned not at all on a snap vote but returned on several issues . . . to act in accordance with your views. . . . Did you seriously expect us to do nothing with our big majority except sit still and speak of Free Trade? and pass Conservative measures to please Unionist Free Traders and make sure of their support?"[78] Margot grasped the fact that Strachey could not hope to sway Liberals to his way of thinking. He recognized it too, but that did not mitigate his predicament.

Unable to influence Liberal policy, could he hope to regain influence among Unionists? Tariff Reformers now controlled the party. Strachey, like other Unionist Free Traders, found himself in the position Balfour of Burleigh previously described as that of being between "the Devil [Protection] and the Deep Sea [Socialism]."[79] That being the case, Strachey decided to place himself in league with "the Devil." With the ranks of the Unionist Free Trader M.P.'s diminishing to insignificance (and after Lloyd George introduced his budget that meant impending socialism to Strachey), he made his peace with the party. The fact that he could champion most Unionist causes with ease, especially their opposition to Irish Home Rule, gave him the leeway to reorientate his position. Toward the end of 1909, as the general election approached, he wrote to Balfour, "You may probably have seen, that though I remain an impenitent Free Trader, I have thought it my duty to urge, in the strongest possible terms, that Unionist Free Traders should rally to their Party at the general election and vote for Tariff Reformers, on the principle of the lesser evil."[80] Balfour welcomed him and other Unionist Free Traders back into Unionist ranks and promised to discourage any ill-feeling toward them on the part of Tariff Reform Unionists.[81]

During the hectic political year of 1910, Strachey remained in that position fighting against the Liberals and particularly against Irish Home Rule. When the idea of federation began to grow, he took a definite stand against it. "I cannot believe that it would be wise if indeed possible to begin the federation of the Empire by breaking up the United Kingdom," he said. "I am as strong a Unionist as ever I was, and on many grounds. . . . If you begin to break up the United Kingdom on grounds of justice or expediency, then you must in fairness break up Ireland into North and South and Britain into Ireland and Scotland and England and Wales, and possibly England into North and South." But if the United Kingdom were maintained "one and indivisible," that would be the "essential foundation" of some "future scheme of [imperial] federation."[82] Consequently, when Garvin and *The Times* began to push federalism, Strachey explained that his *Spectator* "alone stood up strongly [in the Unionist press] for Union and denounced the folly and immorality of this Home Rule all around and the new aliases for breaking up the United Kingdom."[83]

Strachey was again a publicist of influence among Unionists. His success at rallying Unionist opinion behind the idea of a referendum on Tariff Reform late in 1910 made this clear. Garvin's *Observer* proclaimed that Strachey had "done more than all other publicists put together to advance the idea of the Referendum."[84] In fact, Strachey had supported the referendum since 1894 when A. V. Dicey, the most influential constitutional authority of the time and a man with whom he frequently corresponded through the years, converted him to it.[85]

In this case, however, it is difficult to escape the conclusion that Strachey hoped that the device would kill Tariff Reform hopes, if it were ever implemented on the issue, by rendering a people's verdict for Free Trade.

He remained a Free Trader at heart throughout these years. Yet his defense of it in the *Spectator* was basically one of criticizing Tariff Reform as protectionism. He no longer considered the Imperial Preference side of the issue as worthy of attack. The issue became for him one to be treated increasingly as a domestic fiscal controversy. As for the Free Trade Empire in which he so believed, he wrote to Garvin in private that he did not believe it would perish "because at bottom I am an optimist and believe in the star of the British Empire."[86] Little of the restrained spirit implicit in that comment could be found in J. A. Spender's commentary at this point.

The political circumstances that so impaired Strachey's Free Trade position had just the opposite effect on Spender. Never was he closer to the machinations of Liberal politics than he was at this time. Like Garvin, he was the classic political journalist on the inside of affairs. He was on friendly terms with most of the Liberal leaders including Campbell-Bannerman, John Morley, Lord Rosebery, and a number of others.[87] He was particularly close to H. H. Asquith, and that relationship continued after Asquith became prime minister in 1908. Edward Grey and Richard Haldane, whom he saw regularly when they were in London, were his intimate friends. With Winston Churchill, he remained in more or less close association. Contemporaries considered his *Westminster Gazette* not only as the stalwart Liberal paper that it had always been under his editorship, but also after 1906 the voice of the Liberal government in the press. Asquith's ascendency to the prime ministership in 1908 and the fact that Grey, Haldane, and Churchill held such important cabinet offices confirmed Spender's reputation as an insider in the minds of other publicists. Moreover, the rising appeal of Tariff Reform among Unionists that had so frustrated Strachey gave Spender a clear target to attack, and month after month, attack it he did.

His *Westminster Gazette* missed no chance to criticize Tariff Reform and to praise Free Trade in the years following the colonial conference. All arguments, both domestic and imperial, were employed in the process as well as spunky language at times when it could embarrass Tariff Reformers in their various shifts of course. In the opinion of the *Westminster*, the proposed policy of Tariff Reform was simply protectionism. When Balfour stated that he believed that revenue could be raised by Tariff Reform at an insignificant cost, the *Gazette* retorted: "His alternative is thus a revenue and not a protectionist expedient. But, since the needs of the Exchequer are great, the revenue raised must be large."[88] So, his concept of Tariff Reform failed to provide a viable alternative to direct taxation. On the one hand, the *Westminster* charged that Tariff Reformers were unclear and uncertain regarding what they meant by their ideas on the subject; on the other, it claimed that they reduced all political subjects to this one. It had spirited advice to offer about such reductionism.

That we may observe, is always the remarkable thing about a quack remedy as advertised by its inventor. Do you suffer from rheumatism? Our pill will cure you. Have you a headache? There is nothing like our pill. Is your heart weak or your digestion out of order? Take two of our pills. Do we want to cure unemployment? Tariff Reform alone will do it. Is the Empire in danger? Tariff Reform must be taken at once. Do we want a big Navy? Tariff Reform alone will give it us. . . . But do not let us forget that the habit of mind which sees that same thing everywhere and groups everywhere in relation to an *idée fixe* is sometimes called monomania.[89]

As to the charge Strachey advanced about the Liberals actually ruining the cause of Free Trade by introducing social reforms that would heighten the nation's revenue needs, the *Westminster* failed to see the consistency in it. To the contrary, it answered Strachey's charge by showing how during their first three years in office the Liberals had reduced taxes and paid off about £40 million from the debt. A far better record, it declared, than the Unionists had achieved in their two previous governments. Now the government had to raise approximately £6 million for old-age pensions and additional funds for the navy. The *Spectator* predicted that between £20 and £25 million would be needed in extra taxation. The *Westminster* said that was "pure moonshine." Moreover, it also argued that while the *Spectator* despaired over the costs of old-age pensions, it urged the country to adopt universal military service. In the *Gazette*'s estimate the cost for that would be at least £10 million a year.[90] Yet for one reason or another additional revenue was needed. So, the following year when Lloyd George proposed his budget, the *Westminster* supported it without reservation as the best expedient available for raising additional money for both social reform and defense.

In the stormy political debates of 1910 the *Gazette* continued to defend Free Trade, including supporting it as an imperial policy, and to attack Tariff Reformers in their various maneuvers. "We rejoice," it stated, "that our Empire is one which is broad—based upon 'freedom, justice, and peace.' . . . If we had to secure loyalty by a system of preferential tit-bits it would be an unpleasant necessity; as a fact we believe no such necessity exists."[91] In the summer of this year, the paper expressed its delight when Sir Wilfrid Laurier, the Canadian prime minister, advised his Canadians to go as far as they could toward establishing the Free Trade policy of England, which was "a shining example to the world." And, it played up the recent declaration by Canada's Western farmers that their current system of protection was "a grievous burden."[92] With leading articles such as "Trade Tariff and Empire" and "The Fiscal Test for Empire," it emphasized its continuing belief in a Free Trade Empire and in the eventual harm that imperial preferences could cause.[93] As for Unionists, and particularly the *Observer*'s shifting tactics regarding Tariff Reform in the fall of the year, the *Westminster* had this to say: "To plead that their views on men's character or on the general principles of policy can be turned on or turned off at a moment's notice to suit their electioneering convenience is merely to expose once more that incurable levity which has done so much to ruin Unionist politics in the last few years. There are no such dangerous demagogues as the Unionist cynics or zealots, who treat the public as children or fools to be duped by electioneering games."[94] In making that charge, Spender's paper had to make no apologies for any of its own uncertainty or wavering on its Free Trade views or on its faith in Free Trade as an imperial principle. In this case, if consistency is a virtue in politics, the *Westminster* personified purity.

IMPERIAL NAVAL DEFENSE

The resurgent Tariff Reform–Free Trade controversy did more than any other subject to revive the issue of imperial unity in press commentary between 1907 and 1910. The debate surrounding it was by no means over at the end of 1910. Before we can proceed beyond that point, however, there are other subjects that engaged the imperial press to consider. To do so, it is necessary to retreat a bit in terms of time. Naval defense was the greatest subject other than Tariff Reform that stimulated the imperial debate during these years, and at certain times it even overshadowed the ongoing commentary about Chamberlain's program. Imperial communications also received some simultaneous and well-deserved attention, but we shall first consider the naval problem.

Naval security had long been a matter of the gravest concern to the British, but there were particular reasons that explain why it became so crucial and electrifying a question especially in 1909. Since the proposition has received detailed treatment by historians, only a review of its basic elements is needed for the purpose of our inquiry.[95] First of all, the naval crisis of that year occurred against a backdrop of shifting international relations. The Anglo-French Entente of 1904 and the Anglo-Russian Accord of 1907 underscored the fact that Britain's traditional rivalry with those two countries had diminished. Meanwhile, Anglo-German ill-feeling increased. Relations between Britain and Germany had been uneasy since the "Kruger telegram" incident of 1896.[96] They became more precarious with the passage of the German Naval Law of 1898. That law was the result of the efforts of the German secretary of the navy, Admiral Alfred von Tirpitz, who shared the kaiser's interest in building a great navy, and it was a new departure in naval construction for Germany. By proposing to include battleships, which were the symbolic units of measure of naval power, the law made the German fleet much more of an international factor and much more a potential threat to Britain. Two years later, in 1900, Tirpitz engineered another bill calling for an even greater naval building program through the Reichstag. It proposed the building of thirty-eight battleships to be completed in twenty years.

The threat mounted. Britain's protection from a possible naval blockade or even an invasion as well as her imperial connections and links to other trading partners depended on her command of the seas. Then in 1906 the British launched a new type of battleship, the HMS *Dreadnought*. It was a fast-moving vessel equipped with powerful twelve-inch guns and capable of outshooting any other battleship afloat. The naval arms race therefore became increasingly more dangerous, for with older types of battleships now obsolete, all questions of naval security and supremacy depended on which country could most quickly produce the most Dreadnoughts. Admiral Sir John Fisher, the first sea lord, was convinced that Britain would be able to stay well ahead of any other country in this respect.

The Anglo-German naval arms race took an ominous turn in 1908. That was the year that both the Young Turk Revolution and the first major crisis in Bosnia occurred, sending unsettling repercussions throughout Europe.[97] It was also the year the Admiralty learned that Germany was accelerating its Dreadnought building program. The British Sea Lords came to the conclusion that Germany could have seventeen Dreadnoughts and battle cruisers by 1912 instead of the thirteen previously predicted. They even recognized that by using maximum figures it might be possible for Germany to have twenty-one capital ships by 1912. Reginald McKenna, the first lord of the Admiralty at this time, became convinced that Britain would have to respond by increasing its own naval construction program for 1909-1910 in order to maintain superiority over Germany on the seas. During the Election of 1906, however, the Liberals had promised to reduce what they termed the excessive Unionist expenditure on armaments. That pledge was a serious matter to many Liberal politicians, and the government, having received a decisive vote of confidence at the polls, took steps to implement it. It reduced both the Dreadnought building program and naval expenditures every year until 1908.[98] When the first lord recommended an increase in naval construction for 1909-1910, a cabinet crisis occurred. Lloyd George and Winston Churchill were adamant in their rejection of the proposed increase. They would agree to the construction of only four Dreadnoughts. McKenna, with the support of other cabinet colleagues including Grey and Haldane, supported the construction of six, the minimum number the Admiralty wanted. When the estimates were published on 14 March 1909, and debated in Commons several days later, the subject shocked the nation and plunged its way into the public debate.

Behind the controversy within the government and behind the public debate, navy propaganda was at work. Much of it was the work of Sir John Fisher, the first sea lord since 1904. This pugnacious and determined man (who was a little eccentric too) resolved to overhaul the British navy. Having pushed the Dreadnought construction at the time of its inception, he now led the fight to pressure the cabinet to approve the construction of not only six but eight new Dreadnoughts in the coming year. Fisher sought press support in his campaign and became a practitioner of the strategic leaking of information. He had corresponded, for instance, with Spender irregularly since 1904, and during the cabinet debates early in 1909 communicated to him his pleasure at the position the *Westminster* had taken on naval expenditures. "Repetition is the soul of journalism!" he declared to Spender in his typical flamboyant language as he urged the editor, after sharing a secret with him, to "keep on pegging away."[99] But it was with Garvin that Fisher maintained his most interesting journalistic liaison. Throughout much of the first half of the year, the admiral was in almost daily correspondence with the *Observer*'s editor, and during that time he supplied Garvin with practically all the secrets of the government that he knew.[100] Fisher's strategy was twofold. He believed that Garvin was the editor who could best lead the fight in the press for eight Dreadnoughts and that he was also the person best positioned and able to keep Northcliffe in line during the fight. The admiral was correct in both cases.

Garvin's own correspondence reveals that he was in accord with Fisher. Writing to W. T. Stead at the peak of the crisis, he stated: "The governing classes in Germany mean to end us if they can. It must be my work to say so so long as the naval security of this country seems likely to be jeopardised."[101] And he told Northcliffe: "With regard to Fisher don't think for a moment I am losing my patient head. Nothing of the kind. Before we met at all my broad conviction was formed that the Admiralty revolution was . . . right and splendid. . . . Upon every issue which has arisen *since we began to work together* there has been no difficulty, nor is there likely to be."[102]

The naval "scare" of 1909 may have been caused, at least in part, by exaggeration or even by misrepresentation on behalf of the admiralty, as some writers have claimed.[103] By 1912 the German navy had nowhere near the twenty-one Dreadnoughts of which proponents of a larger navy originally spoke. In fact, it had only nine while the British navy had fifteen. From the beginning of the controversy, Radicals in the Commons and in the press protested against new naval expenditures, claiming they were unneeded and unwarranted. H. W. Massingham called them "monstrous."[104] Lloyd George, the chancellor of the exchequer, and Winston Churchill, then president of the Board of Trade, led the Radical attack in the cabinet, much to the dismay of Prime Minister Asquith. Indeed, at one point he privately confessed: "Winston and Lloyd George by their combined machinations have got the bulk of the Liberal press in the same camp . . . . [They] go about darkly hinting at resignation (which is bluff) . . . but there are moments when I am disposed summarily to cashier them both."[105] In the end, Asquith and Sir Edward Grey, the foreign secretary, stood firmly behind McKenna, and he would not retreat from his defense of increased expenditures.[106] Should four, six, or eight Dreadnoughts be built? In the solution one can sense Asquith's political skill at work. The government decided to have four Dreadnoughts built immediately and four more later in the year if needed.

Critics of the new naval estimates, then and later, frequently accused the portion of the press that supported them of being jingoistic. Based on exaggerations about German naval strength, the critics' argument runs, the pro-Big Navy press inflamed public opinion and pressured the government to enlarge the naval building program. The charge is partly true, particularly as it relates to the popular press. It fails, however, to address the fact that many responsible politicians in both parties perceived the German threat as real, and in retrospect, there appears to have been a good deal of substance in that perception. Moreover, if their intentions were misrepresented, German leaders did little to alleviate those misgivings either before or after the crisis.[107] For our purposes, it will suffice to say that the imperial journalists believed that a crisis existed, and that their concern about the comparative strength of the Royal Navy continued to appear in their commentary in the years following 1909.

When the naval crisis peaked early in 1909, it sent repercussions throughout the Empire. Imperial security seemed imperiled. The Empire responded in several ways. Following the spontaneous lead of New Zealand, the Federated Malay States and, after considerable debate, Australia offered to contribute the cost of a Dreadnought. Canada announced plans to establish a local navy force and said she would assume more responsibility for the protection of her coastlines and harbors. These gestures, however, energized already existing controversies, particularly in Australia and Canada, over whether the dominions should contribute in some way to the British navy or have local navies of their own. The situation called for consultation between the home government and the dominions. Accordingly a special or supplementary Imperial Defence Conference met in London in July and August of 1909.[108] The main outcome of the conference was the proposed remodeling of the Pacific fleet into a force composed of three squadrons (i.e., the East Indies, Australian, and China squadrons). Australia would own and operate its own squadron while New Zealand would contribute toward that squadron's maintenance. Meanwhile, Canada contemplated building a small force to protect her coastlines. Subsequently, in 1910, Canada passed a Naval Service Act and Australia passed a Naval Defence Act, as those two dominions began to realize their hopes for local navies. But there were many technical, tactical, strategic, and command questions yet to be resolved regarding how those local navies would be coordinated with the British. All of these developments, as well as the naval crisis itself, are chapters in the longer story of imperial naval defense during this era that occurred against the growing strength of dominion nationalism. It began before the Colonial Conference of 1907 and lasted beyond the Imperial Conference of 1911.

It would take a separate volume to consider the press and imperial naval defense through all the webs of its history in this era. Even a complete rendition of how the press participated in the crisis of 1909 would involve a separate, lengthy narrative. It is important for the purpose of our inquiry, however, to appreciate the close involvement that the imperial publicists had with the

Admiralty and with Whitehall at the time of the crisis of 1909. The Garvin-Fisher connection and the Garvin-Northcliffe association were of the greatest significance in the unfolding of that crisis. Garvin's *Observer* led in the demand for the building of eight Dreadnoughts, and Garvin himself was responsible for keeping Northcliffe in line on the subject. Northcliffe, in turn, mobilized his powerful popular press, particularly the *Daily Mail*, in the campaign. He was always chauvinistic when it came to the defense of the United Kingdom and the Empire, and this crisis occasioned one of his most energetic efforts to guarantee the security of British defenses. Today, in reviewing the role the *Daily Mail* played in the naval crisis, it is difficult to discount the fact that Northcliffe helped to raise the sense of alarm that spread through the public in March.[109] Nor was Garvin blameless in spreading that alarm. Nevertheless, most of the leaders of the government and the Opposition as well as the imperial journalists recognized the seriousness of Germany's evolving naval policy, and when the crisis became public it demonstrated the importance of the dominions to imperial defenses. Consequently, the attention the imperial press paid to this subject as well as the air of urging that surrounded it can be understood.

Several themes dominated the protracted response of the imperial journalists to this problem. They all recognized the need for strong defenses and applauded the various contributions the dominions said they would make to it. They also acknowledged the right of the dominions to determine the nature of their own contribution. As the *Spectator* observed in retrospect: "Two years ago the principle was laid down that 'each of the Dominions should contribute in the fashion most appropriate to its resources and its internal public opinion to the strength of the Empire. Some would do it by direct contribution to the power of the British fleet, either by annual payment or by gifts of ships or by both. Others by the development of fleets of their own.'"[110] Furthermore, as the dominions developed their naval policies in the years immediately following the crisis, the imperial journalists took pride in the progress they were witnessing. The *Westminster Gazette*, for instance, expressed its pleasure at the efforts it detected on the part of both Britain and the dominions to work out an effective imperial naval policy, each according to its own needs, and cited it as an example of the "practical unity" that it had always claimed characterized the Empire.[111] The *Spectator* said that it was "one of the most inspiring signs of our day, . . . of how the Empire works out its salvation."[112]

The imperial journalists seemed to derive a particular lesson from this entire episode. It provided substance to their own belief in the need for Britain to maintain its sea supremacy. Accordingly we find the *Spectator* announcing: "To-day the whole Empire is alive to the fact that to talk about maintenance of the Empire is idle unless we maintain our command of the sea, and, therefore, a supreme moral force. This is the great Imperial fact of the last few years."[113] The *Westminster Gazette* pondered at one point if it were right for the British to claim a command of the sea that no power demands on the land. "The answer," it said, was "that we claim nothing more than is necessary for our security, and that we have given most abundant proof that our sea-power is unaggressive. We claim no commercial monopoly . . . we have grudged none of our rivals and competitors the same trade privileges that we have gained for ourselves."[114] Since this statement was consistent with earlier ones in this journal, it is obvious that it was quite willing to link together the causes of imperial defense and Free Trade.

Supporting arguments for naval supremacy varied from journal to journal, but they all favored maintenance of British sea power for imperial as well as national purposes. The *Observer* had always joined imperial defense to the banner of imperial unity and Tariff Reform. *The Times,* always the defender of Britain's world position, never doubted that "the British Empire . . . [was] determined at all costs to preserve its mastery of the seas."[115] Like all the imperial journals it also frequently spoke of how the dominions' response to the crisis was an illustration of imperial solidarity. In 1909 Britain alone was almost entirely responsible for maintaining imperial naval defense. Two years later the dominions had agreed to assume a proportionate share of the burden, the greater part of which Britain still shouldered. Details of working out dominion participation still remained an open topic for discussion. J. L. Garvin, for instance, who had done so much to start the "awakening of empire" based on the naval problem, failed to see how the policy of separate navies served the greater imperial purpose. Yet he conceded that, given the state of opinion in Britain and the dominions, "no other course was possible."[116]

Surely the advancement in imperial naval cooperation they were witnessing pleased the imperial journalists. They were also impressed by the public attention given to the nation's need to retain its position on the seas. So the needs of home defense and imperial defense combined to produce a consensus of opinion among them on naval policy, at least on the general premise that they desired a sufficiently strong navy to provide both needs. This is not surprising since pride in the Royal Navy was an old tradition and also since the British public as well as politicians and publicists desired a strong navy and had no wish to see their country lose its naval supremacy. Even most Radicals who favored naval retrenchment shared that belief.[117]

IMPERIAL COMMUNICATIONS

Another imperial matter, for which there was broad consensus of opinion, received a good deal of publicity in the midst of that accorded imperial naval defense. That was the subject of imperial communications, and it resulted in the Imperial Press Conference that met in London in June 1909. Communications between Britain and the various parts of the Empire had long been considered important not only for practical purposes but also, as Austen Chamberlain once said, "as a step in the direction of promoting closer business and political relations" in the Empire.[118] Discussions about them occurred periodically at the colonial conferences since 1887. Cable communications also received considerable attention around the turn of the century because of strategic needs. Between 1899 and 1901 a new cable line to South Africa was laid.[119] In 1901 another line was laid from Durban to Perth and then on to Adelaide. This completed the cable route known as the "All Red-Cable," connecting England to Australia while touching only British soil. These additions to the imperial cable network, like the earlier lines, were built under private management. Early in the century, however, the demand for state ownership increased, and colonial governments expressed their willingness to be partners in such enterprises. Consequently, in 1912, Britain, Canada, Australia, and New Zealand joined in establishing a state-operated cable between Vancouver Island and New Zealand and Australia. All the governments involved shared in its ownership and subsidized its operation.

At the Colonial Conference of 1907, Sir Wilfrid Laurier moved a resolution for the establishment of a new imperial mail service. It involved establishing a line of steamers to Canada, a fast crossing of Canada by rail, and reshipping from Vancouver to New Zealand and Australia. The proposed "All Red Line" could reduce service between Britain and Australia or New Zealand from thirty to twenty days. All admitted that it would be an expensive undertaking, but the resolution passed and it was referred to the appropriate experts. "We hope," the *Westminster Gazette* responded when Laurier first made his proposal, "that . . . the Imperial Government will give it most careful and sympathetic consideration."[120] When the conference passed his resolution, *The Times* applauded the action, saying it should not be considered on the grounds of simple "profit and loss." It pointed out that the national experience of Britain, Germany, and Italy confirmed the idea "that few things contribute more powerfully and more directly to the consolidation of national sentiment amongst scattered communities of the same blood than easy and constant communication between them."[121]

At this point Harry Brittain entered the scene. He was a journalist of sorts who in time became the director of numerous daily and weekly newspapers.[122] Brittain was also a great imperial enthusiast and incurable world traveler. While he visited Canada in 1907, the idea of organizing an imperial press conference occurred to him. He believed, as he later recalled, that it might "bring into closer unity and understanding the constituent parts of the Empire."[123] For two years thereafter, he devoted himself to turning that idea into a reality. He sought and received the assistance of many of the most influential journalists in the country to help him organize the unprecedented meeting. Brittain formed an organization with Lord Burnham as president, Lord Northcliffe as treasurer, C. Arthur Pearson as chairman of the Executive Committee, and himself as secretary. Moberly

Bell, J. L. Garvin, J. A. Spender, and St. Loe Strachey were all members of the organization's General Committee.

Altogether there were ninety-one British journalists involved in the organization of the conference, and they include most of the leaders of the profession. Buckle was a noteworthy exception. He thought the conference was "utterly wrong," but on journalistic rather than imperial grounds. "Journalists should do their own business behind the scenes, and not edify—if it be edifying—the public by reading papers and discussing their affairs in speeches before reporters, for all the world as if they were minor politicians," he said. Traditional journalist that he was, he thought "all this vulgarises journalism, tends to rob it of its mystery, . . . and only panders to the vanity of Mr. X of the Daily Howler and Mr. Y of the Oracle." He did not wish to participate, especially not as a speaker, in the conference because he felt "it would be entirely against my whole practice as Editor, and would not be good for the paper."[124]

The vast majority of journalists did not share his reservations and most of the imperial journalists supported the conference. Indeed, it must have been a striking thing to contemporaries to observe both Lord Northcliffe and J. A. Spender so deeply involved together in this common cause. Northcliffe, in fact, said it was "one of the most important gatherings that has ever taken place in England."[125] He was probably sincere in making that statement, for the conference was just the kind of meeting that he could appreciate. Furthermore, in his post-conference correspondence and later writings, Brittain was more than generous in his comments about Northcliffe's contribution to its organization.[126]

The conference itself was successful within the boundaries of what was possible to achieve. Fifty-four journalists from Australia, Canada, New Zealand, South Africa, India, Burma, the Straits Settlements, and the West Indies attended. They were welcomed with a "Welcome Home" address by Lord Rosebery that was full of his wit and charm. On subsequent days a number of British political leaders, both Liberals and Unionists, addressed the visitors.[127] The array of speakers would have impressed any gathering. Beyond that the visitors were treated to a military display and simulated skirmish at Aldershot and a magnificent review of the fleet at Spithead. Their hosts provided various entertainments for them including a luncheon with Northcliffe at Sutton Place, his home in Surrey. The Prince of Wales invited them to a garden party at Marlborough House. They toured England's industrial and university cities and its places of historic interest. Aside from the goodwill engendered by these meetings and entertainments, the conference did provide a forum for the discussion of serious imperial matters such as defense, and it addressed itself to the proposition of improving imperial communications. It was in regard to the latter that it made its most tangible achievements: the establishment of an Empire Press Union to advance press interests throughout the Empire, the organization of a permanent committee to arrange for further imperial press conferences, and the promise by the Pacific Cable Board that cable charges would be lowered.[128]

Historians have tended to ignore this conference, but it deserves a place in the present inquiry. While it may not have satisfied all the imperial journalists in terms of specific achievements, it was successful in elevating the importance of imperial communications. That was a worthwhile factor to address not only for practical reasons but also because of the bearing it had on imperial unity. Both of the major parties agreed on that point, and it ran throughout the press commentary on the subject. Of course, improved communications would serve the press as well as the Empire, and one must make allowance for the romantic and sometimes exaggerated rhetoric that journalists can employ when describing the power of the press. Nevertheless, while it does not have the power to shape public opinion, the press can influence it. Edwardian publicists and politicians believed that influence was a significant factor in the political life of the nation. The record of their private correspondence is clear on this point. In this case, it is also clear that the imperial journalists believed that an efficient press, well served by effective imperial communications and by well-informed journalists, could be a factor of consequence in fostering imperial cooperation.

9

The Quest for Imperial Partnership: Part II, 1911–1913

The three years following the December 1910 election were troubled ones for both Liberals and Unionists. If one compares the Liberal position after this election with its stance after that of 1906, it is evident that a major change had occurred. According to the political arithmetic of the day, the party held power now because of Irish and Labour support. If the Liberals hoped to carry through their own legislation and to provide Home Rule for Ireland, they had to destroy the veto power of the House of Lords. To that end, they reintroduced their Parliament Bill, and it passed its third reading in Commons in May. The Lords then were free to pass or reject it. Unremittent Tories, the so-called "Diehards," organized a formidable Lords resistance to the measure, but Balfour, knowing that the king was ready to create five hundred new peers if necessary to defeat them, repudiated their resistance. The bill passed in August by a vote of 131 to 114. That act "reformed" the House of Lords by trimming its power. It stipulated that money bills no longer needed the assent of the Lords and that other bills would become law without the Lords' assent if passed by Commons and rejected by the Lords three times in two years. From start to end, the bill's passage had been conducted amid heated debate, and in the end the Liberals won a flawed victory in its passage. The Lords were left with the power to obstruct by delaying non-money bills for two years. Thus, the Conservative-dominated House of Lords would be able to frustrate the will of Commons for a specific period, and that period could be crucial.

Moreover, the Liberal government had to confront serious domestic and international unrest. A series of strikes and protests began to plague the government as militant civil strife emerged to challenge parliamentary democracy. The major industrial disputes, indeed, involved the government itself since the Board of Trade functioned by this time as an agency of conciliation and mediation in such instances. At the same time suffragettes became increasingly violent and destructive in their efforts to win the parliamentary franchise. After the Commons passed the Irish Home Rule Bill of 1912, which the Lords delayed for two years, domestic politics acquired a dangerous edge of adamancy and bitterness. Ireland seemed to be drifting toward civil war over the fate of Ulster Protestants under the proposed Home Rule Bill. The Ulster Protestants, of course, had no wish to have the Union with Britain end. Supported by the British Unionists, they were determined to maintain it. Meanwhile, international tension increased to an alarming degree. In 1911 the Second Moroccan Crisis took place, and beginning in that same year a series of crises and wars rocked the Balkans. The possibility of avoiding a major conflict between the great powers diminished as strains between them mounted and alternatives for maintaining peace narrowed.

Unionists found little solace in this atmosphere. The same range of international problems affected them, and the threat of Ireland's receiving Home Rule challenged them at the core of their political beliefs, the preserving of the Union between Ireland and Britain. Moreover, their divisions over the tactics to use in pursuing Tariff Reform and apprehensions about whether or not that program, including imperial preferences, could attract additional support among the voters haunted them. They needed all their collective strength to fight Irish Home Rule, at least to be in a position to support Ulster Unionists.

Considering the range of problems Britain faced during these years, it is almost surprising that imperial issues received the public attention they did. But the politics of a great power are always multi-dimensional, and there were pressing imperial as well as domestic and foreign circumstances to consider. India remained the vexing problem it was, even after the major reform of 1909, and the problems of imperial preferences and defense received another round of attention. In the midst of it all, Canada emerged as a major imperial concern.

ANXIETIES ABOUT CANADA

The imperial journalists gave more attention to Canada than to any other dominion in 1911. Several reasons explain why. First of all, both Liberal and Conservative imperialists regarded the Dominion (i.e., Canada) as the keystone to Empire. Liberals looked with pride to Canada where their policy of implementing self-government within the Empire had worked out so well in the mid-nineteenth century. Rather than lament the growing American influence in the Dominion as the Unionists did, they welcomed it. They thought it was bound to grow because of the geographical proximity of the United States and Canada. "Far from there being anything to be deplored in this peaceful invasion," the *Westminster Gazette* once explained, "it is good for the Dominion." It reasoned that the American farmers who were migrating into Canada brought with them capital, knowledge of farming, and an individualism that was necessary for successful agriculture in the Canadian West. They found there cheap land in abundance, banks willing to support them, and good government.[1] All things considered, it was a fortuitous situation for Canada. That was also Strachey's opinion. He never shared "the fears expressed in many quarters that the immigration from America is going to de-nationalize Canada." The "attractiveness of law and order," he believed, would draw good citizens to Canada, and when such people encountered the fine conditions that could be found in the Dominion, they would be "naturally inclined to support the status quo."[2] Liberally inclined imperial journalists also failed to see why imperial preferences were needed to keep Canada in the Empire, but they did appreciate the need for colonial subjects of all types to receive greater publicity in the British press. Strachey, for instance, who wanted his *Spectator* "to be not merely the literary paper of England but of the Empire," attempted to give colonial poets preference in the journal. That was, he said, the "only type of Colonial preference" he could tolerate.[3]

More conservative imperial journalists took an opposite view. They saw Imperial Preference as a necessary device to keep Canada in the Empire. Men like Garvin and Northcliffe were apprehensive about the Dominion's imperial future. Both appreciated the importance of Canada to the Empire. The Dominion captivated Northcliffe. He believed the "Americanization of Canada" ranked as "grave a danger as Indian unrest or German preparation [for war]."[4] On one occasion he explained his views in this manner. "I never forget what van Horne said to me many years ago—that the future of the British Empire will be decided in Alberta and Saskatchewan. Australia and New Zealand have to be loyal anyhow. South Africa would rather have us than the Germans any time. Canada troubles me greatly."[5]

His actions confirmed the sincerity of his words. He visited the Dominion often and encouraged not only his journalistic associates but also a number of the country's public figures to do likewise. He did all he could to publicize Canada as a land of opportunity in his *Daily Mail* and even said that he acquired *The Times* to make it an instrument for helping both Canada and the Empire.[6] Like Garvin, Northcliffe corresponded with Lord Grey, the governor-general of Canada, in order to keep the British press informed about Canadian opinion and affairs. Lord Grey's imperial fervor and hopes for Canada's imperial future, and sometimes his romantic rhetoric, surfaced in those letters, especially in his correspondence with Northcliffe, who visited him during his various trips to Canada. After seeing the press baron in action during one of those visits, Lord Grey observed: "He is magnetic and volcanic, full of nerves and energy. He appears to be genuinely possessed by the religion of the Empire." Northcliffe, he said, "has appeared like a Napoleon on the scene."[7] Northcliffe traveled widely throughout Canada and from his own observation perceived the growing American influence there in a manner quite different from that of his Liberal contemporaries. He believed that Canada suffered from an influx of news, people, and products from the United States, and told Buckle in private that "the condition of the Canadian mind to-day, as far as I can judge . . . , is somewhat similar to that of the American colonists about the year 1760." The real danger to the Empire, he said, was "much greater in Canada than in India."[8]

The second reason for the attention Canada received centered on the subject of Canadian-American trade reciprocity. When Canada and the United States negotiated a reciprocity agreement on 26 January 1911, Liberal imperial journalists were not disturbed. They believed the mutual lowering of tariffs between the two countries provided by the agreement was a natural arrangement beneficial to both Canada and the United States. The *Westminster Gazette* even noted that a previous reciprocity treaty between the Canadians and the republic to the south, that which ran from 1854 to 1866 and is well known in Canadian history, had brought prosperity, not annexation, to Canada.

The *Westminster*, consequently, questioned, "Are the reasons [now] any the less cogent or are the consequences likely to be any different?"[9] To Unionists, however, it was, in the words of Arthur Balfour, an "Imperial disaster." Northcliffe's *Daily Mail* had been warning the public since the previous September that such a step would weaken imperial ties. Now it exploded with the cry,"Exit Imperial Preference," and announced that without Canada that part of the Tariff Reform program was dead.[10] The *Daily Mail* was only carrying out his orders, for on the day previous to the appearance of that outburst, he said in private that "Preference was dead, and that if it still lingered, he would give it the death blow."[11]

At times of crisis, Northcliffe wanted all of his papers to pull together. *The Times* took up the desired position. "The remission of American duties on Canadian wheat [provided by the treaty] must necessarily emasculate, at any rate in its present form, the policy of Imperial Preference," it announced.[12] Garvin was the problem. Previously he had been able to hold Northcliffe in line on the question of imperial preferences. But Northcliffe, with the tempestuous side of his nature aroused, was now adamant on the subject. "My views are based on twenty years personal knowledge of Canada and the United States and the apprehensions I have often expressed to you are being more rapidly and smashingly materialized than I ever expected," he told the *Observer*'s editor. "I hope you will not misunderstand me when I say that I cannot possibly be associated with a policy that I believe by its hopeless ignoring of new facts would certainly help to lose Canada."[13]

Garvin replied at once. He knew his editorship was at stake and perhaps his career too. His letter was as courageous as any ever written by an editor to his proprietor. Reflecting as it did his integrity and passion as well as his views, it merits being quoted at length:

This is a matter of conviction upon as grave a question almost as can ever arise. You know my record and my character. I, of all men would be left without a rag of the world's respect & without a vestige of self respect—if I were to throw over the cause to which I have given the best years of my life; and if I were now to echo *The Daily Mail* in views which you know me to believe disastrous and wrong. I came into journalism meaning to live and die in that profession, an honest man; and upon that basis I stand hitherto, no matter what the cost may be . . . . For me the effect of your view means quite plainly the destruction of Unionist policy, the fiscal impotence of England, the complete alienation of Canada, and the certain loss of Empire.

I differ from you utterly and upon strictly reasoned grounds . . . . You are not to be influenced by me, and upon the other hand nothing can confuse my convictions. . . .

The reciprocity project is still not fully understood here . . . . Large numbers of Canadians including Aitken . . . disagree with you about its effect upon the present situation and the future . . . . It would not matter a brass farthing to this country if, under Imperial Preference and Reciprocity (working together in a quite practical way), some United States food supplies came in free with the overwhelming bulk of Canadian supplies. That . . . could only help the English speaking idea as well as the Imperial Idea. There's where the *Daily Mail* articles, in my judgment have made one fundamental error . . . . If Imperial Preference were dead indeed there would, in a few years, be a further and wider reciprocity arrangement wiping out the British preference still maintained . . . and practically separating Canada from the Empire. More than ever is it life and death to fight for Imperial preference to the last. These views are not unworthy of consideration by what is still a great people with an Empire yet to save. I mean to give quiet and reasoned expression to these views. I am certain they will prevail in the Unionist party. I hold them with unalterable conviction. If I could not express them according to my mind and conscience, my public usefulness would be at an end. If you like I will sign my article in the *Observer* and make it purely personal but 'I can't be silent and I will not lie' by concealing or weakening my different view.[14]

When Garvin proceeded to publish his views in the *Observer*, Northcliffe wired him: "Either you get out or I do."[15] The proprietor was holding to his views too and even confided privately that "Garvin, Leo and others make one weep. Studio landscapes are nearly always bad pictures."[16] The affair ended with Northcliffe giving Garvin three weeks to find someone to purchase the *Observer*. He found William Waldorf Astor, the famous American millionaire who had lived in England since 1890. Astor had recently been elected to Parliament, and not only wished to purchase the *Observer* but also wanted to have Garvin edit his *Pall Mall Gazette*. The indications were that the issue of Imperial Preference was far from dead now that Britain's leading supporter of that policy in the press had received new journalistic life not with one but with two papers. But the unexpected is never absent from politics, and before long Imperial Preference would receive a death blow. Before that occurred, however, another imperial conference met.

UNSETTLED DOMINION RELATIONS: 1911-1913

The Imperial Conference of 1911 was less publicized than the previous one in 1907, but it did continue the series. Attended by the dominion premiers and their selected cabinet ministers, it was held at the Foreign Office (previous conferences had convened at the Colonial Office) and the British prime minister presided with the colonial secretary acting as his deputy. As was the case four years before, pleas to admit the press to all but confidential meetings were denied. The most striking difference between this conference and its predecessor was the absence of any serious discussion of Imperial Preference. This time the topics that received the most attention were those of imperial organization and defense. The "All Red Route" idea and various matters related to cables received some, but lesser, attention too. Sir Joseph Ward of New Zealand, who introduced a plan for an imperial council of state, was responsible for the consideration given to improving imperial organization, although neither Asquith nor the dominion premiers accepted his proposal.

Imperial defense, on the other hand, did receive serious consideration, probably because the threat of war in Europe seemed increasingly possible. Accordingly, the delegates met with the Committee of Imperial Defence, a practice begun at the time of the special Imperial Defence Conference of 1909.[17] This time Sir Edward Grey, the foreign secretary, presented an exposition of British foreign policy and the European situation. Asquith actually brought the dominion representatives into three sessions of the Committee of Imperial Defence, thus underscoring the government's commitment to consultation with the dominions. As for imperial naval defense matters, the essential questions had been resolved in 1909 when the policy of separate dominion navies had been approved. Now the delegates directed their discussion to specifics and tactics of cooperation between the fleets and to matters of common training standards. In general, press commentary on the conference was mild, stressing the continuity between this and previous conferences and the fact that the principle of imperial consultation had become a reality. Liberal imperial journals found reason to applaud these results, but the *Observer*, while admitting the conference was valuable "because it has been a conference," concluded that it was the "least distinguished of the series." The exclusion of preference, it claimed, had "sterilised" the conference as a stimulus for closer partnership.[18] After reading that statement and believing it wrong, W. T. Stead wrote to Garvin: "It [the imperial conference] has done more to give Great Britain the leadership than anything that has happened in our time. I wish that you had not adopted as your ideal the Grand Llama of Thibet. You certainly live up to that ideal better than most men live up to any ideal. Thou unapproachable one!"[19] Garvin respected Stead but he would not change his opinion on the conference.

At this point several major changes occurred among the figures who played a major role in Edwardian politics and journalism. Within a little less than one year both A. J. Balfour and G. E. Buckle resigned their respective posts. Both resignations came as a result of pressure exerted by others—in the case of the former, from the Unionist party, and in that of the latter, from a Unionist proprietor. Balfour had long been a subject of criticism among members of his own party for his lack of firm leadership. He had failed to win three consecutive elections, and in the summer of 1911 he failed to stop the Parliament Bill that curtailed his party's power by limiting Unionist Lords to delaying legislation for only two sessions. With the prospects of an Irish Home Rule Bill before them, many Unionists wanted more definite party leadership. Balfour resigned in November 1911, and Andrew Bonar Law became the new Unionist leader. Instead of the subtle, urbane, and detached Balfour, the party now had, in Robert Blake's words, "the ordinary man writ large."[20] Yet Bonar Law possessed considerable assets. His honest and direct, indeed even aggressive, parliamentary ways impressed the party as just the qualities they needed in a leader to fight Home Rule. Moreover, he took a much more active role in party management than Balfour, and also more than Balfour, he took an active interest in the press. For the most part, J. S. ("Jack") Sandars handled Balfour's press relations but as his private correspondence shows, Bonar Law dealt with leading figures in the press more directly.

The case of G. E. Buckle's resignation was a more personal matter. He would have preferred to stay on through the next election, but Northcliffe decided he wanted a new editor for *The Times*. By then Moberly Bell had died and Valentine Chirol had resigned, so Buckle's departure would remove the last of the old senior staff, "the Old Gang" and "the giant tortoises" as Northcliffe called them, from Printing House Square and allow him to continue the paper's rehabilitation as he wished.[21] It was a painful thing for Buckle to relinquish his position under these conditions, but he did so on 31 July 1912, thus bringing to an end his twenty-eight-and-a-half-year editorship of *The Times*. It also marked the end of his struggle since Northcliffe became chief proprietor to protect the senior staff and the traditions of the paper from his proprietary interference.[22] As befitting the editor of *The Times*, Buckle maintained close relations with most of the party leaders of the day, particularly with the Unionists. His close professional association with Arthur Balfour and sympathy for his views remained firm until both men departed from their positions. "I feel the passing of Arthur Balfour very deeply, as I have been on terms of personal friendship with him for five & twenty years," he told Bonar Law as he moved quickly to establish a compatible association with the new Unionist leader.[23] When the time came for the editor to introduce his own successor, Geoffrey Robinson, to Bonar Law, he explained that he was "one of Milner's band of clever youngsters, & has been working for *The Times* for several years, first as our correspondent in South Africa, and afterward in the editorial department at home. I think he will be a great success as he is very keen & blessed with a cool head & a good judgment."[24] Before turning over his post to Robinson, Buckle could tell the new editor that he had recommended him to the leading Unionists including Bonar Law, Arthur Balfour, Lord Lansdowne, Austen Chamberlain, Lord Curzon, Lord Milner, and Lord Selborne and that he also would find a "good reception" from Liberal leaders including H. H. Asquith, Sir Edward Grey, Richard Haldane, and John Morley.[25]

So *The Times* would continue in its unique position. The change in editorship pleased Northcliffe, who had struggled with the old senior staff of *The Times* over the paper's editorial policy. "Congratulations on your appointment," he wrote to Robinson. "I hope and believe that we shall work well together. I do not think either of us are unreasonable people, and I know that we have many Imperial ideas in common."[26]

Northcliffe no doubt did appreciate having a new editor at *The Times*, for he had grown weary of struggling with Buckle and his old colleagues. This was evident in regard to this paper's policy on naval defense. Northcliffe had used various methods, direct and indirect, to try to control *The Times'* policy since becoming its chief proprietor. But in the spring of 1911 when it advocated the Declaration of London, which attempted to specify articles that would be considered contraband in time of war, Northcliffe was furious. He opposed the declaration and his *Daily Mail* had taken its position in accord with his view. This was more than he could tolerate, and he conveyed his displeasure to both Buckle and Moberly Bell. Buckle replied that the pro–Declaration of London article represented no new departure for the paper, and reversal of its position now would call the paper's independence into question. It would imply that *The Times* was following the lead of the *Daily Mail*.[27] Northcliffe, in turn, exploded: "I thought Nicholson had made it clear, that I will not devote one farthing of my fortune to supporting that which I know would be an injury to this country, and this, therefore, is to acknowledge, with much regret, the receipt of your letter and is my final communication on this subject."[28] The editor resolved the problem by having *The Times* remain neutral on the subject. Regardless, the place of naval defense policy in the public debate extended far beyond differences over this treaty within the walls of Printing House Square.

In the spring of 1912, Anglo-German naval rivalry again captured the public's attention and heightened its anxieties over imperial defense. It was then that Germany adopted a supplementary navy bill that, by increasing the strength of the German navy, forced Britain to raise her naval strength as well. The German plans to build three additional Dreadnoughts and to form a third active squadron appeared, in the words of the *Observer*, "as a direct aggression aimed at us."[29] Such responses were widespread in the imperial press, and they called into question the polycentric idea of imperial naval defense agreed upon at the 1909 Imperial Defence Conference. In the face of a mounting challenge in the North Sea, British sea strength appeared to be spread thin. Might the dominions make a more direct contribution to the imperial navy? The answer to that question evolved mainly out of naval debates in Canada.

The Canadian prime minister Sir Wilfrid Laurier provided the Dominion's initial answer to the German naval threat in 1909. Canada would construct her own navy, which could assist the Royal Navy in time of crisis. That navy would be small and, of course, built to suit Canada's own needs. Robert Borden, the Conservative leader in Canada and Laurier's rugged opponent, called it a "tin-pot navy" and charged that it would be of little use in war. After Borden swept into power in the Election of 1911, he visited England for consultation on defense, and then developed his own naval policy. He was willing to offer a Canadian contribution of capital ships to the Royal Navy, and he asked in return that the Dominion receive a voice in determining foreign policy. The British replied that a Canadian member could be added to the Committee of Imperial Defence. Borden, knowing that the CID was only an advisory body, continued to hope for a more definite Canadian voice in imperial policy decisions. Nevertheless, on 5 December 1912, the Canadian Parliament received his proposal for an appropriation of $35 million for the British government, to be used for the construction of three battleships for the Grand Fleet. Debates on that proposal dragged on for months. Eventually the resolution passed the lower house but the Senate rejected it at the end of May 1913. Canada's naval problem, and Britain's, remained unsettled.

To understand the opposition of Laurier and his supporters to a direct naval contribution, it is necessary to grasp the fervor of Canadian nationalism around the turn of the century. During his tenure as governor-general of Canada, Lord Grey had enjoyed friendly relations with Laurier, and toward the end of the navy debates the two men corresponded about the subject. It was a revealing exchange of opinions. Lord Grey told Laurier that he was mistaken in assuming that there was no emergency and also pointed out that "the evidence of the strength of Empire, revealed by the gift of the New Zealand and Malay Dreadnoughts, and again by the offer of 3 Canadian Dreadnoughts as an Emergency contribution . . . [was] an accession of strength to the Empire just when such an accession was most needed." Then Lord Grey continued by offering Laurier this piece of unwanted and undiplomatic advice: "Now what I am afraid of is that if your Party force a general election upon this Emergency contribution you would lose the support of many English-Speaking Liberals who will feel uncomfortable at your proposal that Canada should abstain from giving any immediate assistance to the overtaxed people of the United Kingdom in their effort to carry the Imperial burden."[30]

Sir Wilfrid answered with a rebuff. It illustrates the opposite forces involved in imperial problems in the early years of this century. "I feel a new sense of sorrow and regret," he began, "that upon a question so fundamental as the imperial question we stand so far apart." In an effort to warn Lord Grey of what would follow, he then said, "Let me tell you my whole thought." The way was now open for an exposition on Canadian national feeling. "You speak of empire [not Lord Grey's Empire with a capital "E"], your letter is full of it, and yet, if you read it again . . . you will realise that your conception of Empire is purely insular. You think of Britain and Britain alone, and for you Britain is the whole empire." Laurier did not dispute Lord Grey's reference to the heavy burden that the British people were making for defense, but he did question the idea that it constituted an emergency. "If this be emergency by what name would you call actual war? In these considerations is to be found the basis of our own dissenting views," Laurier continued. Should young nations such as the major dominions be placed in line behind England in matters of diplomacy and armaments? He did not think so. "They [the advocates of such a policy] forget," he explained, "that there is a very natural repugnance within these young communities to be drawn into a field for which they are not prepared, and which must singularly impair their growing resources. Between Britain and its young nations there is a vast distance; all conditions are at variance, and to force these young nations into the militarism in Europe will cause a tremendous shaking up some day." To emphasize his point, Laurier reached into history for a comparable example. Accordingly he told Lord Grey with the utmost candor: "Let me remind you that a similar attempt was made in the 18th century, and the result was the secession of the American colonies. The imperialists of this day will not proceed by brutal methods of the 18th century, but tell me frankly if the thought is not the same as it was then?"[31]

The attention the Canadian naval debates received in the British imperial press represents an interesting ending to its commentary on imperial naval defense of 1909. Prime Minister Borden's visit to England and subsequent advancement of his proposal for a direct Canadian contribution in 1912 stimulated a great deal of grateful praise and talk of partnership through defense among the imperial journalists. But as the debates about Borden's program dragged on in the Canadian Parliament, the subject gradually became overshadowed in Britain by other issues of greater emergency. Imperial Preference reclaimed its lofty position in the public debate; Turkey's defeat in the Balkan wars made international relations regarding southeastern Europe more fluid and dangerous; and after the introduction of the Irish Home Rule Bill in 1912, the Irish problem began to encroach upon all others as the predominant one of the time. Moreover, from the British perspective the needs of imperial defense had to be measured against the reality of dominion priorities and national sentiment, as indicated in the above exchange between Grey and Laurier. The *Westminster Gazette* was indeed correct when it described the premise of the discussion on the subject in this way: "For the Dominions, as for the Mother Country, the maintenance of British sea power is the supreme cause, and the problem to be solved is [how] to create an effective system of mutual aid and support that shall not imperil the Empire in its political aspects."[32] Colonial autonomy and the free institutions that had evolved from that principle placed definite limits on what the dominions could be expected to do, if anything, for imperial defense.

It was with this restraint in mind that the British imperial journalists discussed the Canadian naval debates. Two underlying themes characterized their commentary on the subject. The first comes as no surprise and simply put, was a confirmation of the fact that Canada had the liberty of choice in this matter. The second theme reminds one of the continuing pull of the idea of imperial unity. It ran along the line that Canadian political dispute over this subject was, in fact, proof of an evolving imperial partnership since both Canadian parties, though they differed as to means, favored some type of imperial naval aid.[33] With the defeat of Borden's program major discussion ended on the subject in Britain, but hope for the development of that partnership remained. The *Westminster Gazette* expressed what would be the final word on the subject quite early in its comments about it. Speaking about the possibility of a Canadian representative on the Committee of Imperial Defence, which none of the imperial journalists opposed, it offered this reflection: "Now, the development of a true Imperial government may ultimately come this way, and we are prepared for a transition stage in which some ultimate questions must be left unsettled."[34] In the end, the form of the Canadian contribution to imperial naval defense remained an open question. Can the same be said about the problem of imperial preferences that so permeated Edwardian politics?

THE DEMISE OF IMPERIAL PREFERENCE: 1912-1913

Our previous discussion of Tariff Reform and Imperial Preference ended with negotiation of the reciprocity agreement between Canada and the United States in January 1911. Prime Minister Laurier, whose government had negotiated the agreement, found it his undoing. Designed to become effective only when approved by concurrent legislation in both countries, the agreement was endorsed in the United States, where President Taft pushed it through Congress. In Canada, however, both the agreement and Laurier went down in defeat in the Election of September 1911. That election, a hard-fought one between Laurier and Borden, was an emotional contest filled with talk of anti-continentalism and abundant pro-British publicity. Boastful and galling statements made in high places in the United States, which implied that the republic to the south harbored annexationist aspirations, only heightened the patriotic rhetoric running through the election campaign. To the British, the Canadian election and the defeat of reciprocity had particular meaning. It was proof of the Dominion's appreciation of its imperial connection.

The Canadian repudiation of reciprocity cheered Tariff Reformers in Britain. Moreover, just several months after that, in November 1911, Bonar Law became the new Unionist leader. Since he was a much more confirmed Tariff Reformer than Balfour, the cause he avowed might well appear to stand on the brink of a new and major campaign. Instead, Unionist leaders decided to readjust their Tariff Reform program in the hope of making it more popular for the next general election. That readjustment occurred late in 1912 and early in 1913, and it involved the imperial journalists with Unionist attachments.

Immediately after his election as Unionist leader Bonar Law was "beset by letters" pleading with him to abandon food taxes.[35] Many Unionists believed that the food duties contained in the Tariff Reform and Imperial Preference program represented a burden they were unable to overcome at the polls. These Unionist "Free-fooders" now wanted the proposed food taxes to be abandoned. After Prime Minister Asquith introduced the Irish Home Rule Bill in April 1912, the need for Unionists to resolve their party differences and to broaden their appeal among voters became more urgent. By the summer of 1912, some devoted supporters of the complete Tariff Reform program including Imperial Preference feared the party might "wobble" on the issue of preference. Bonar Law reassured them that this was not the case and that the party's position would remain steady.[36] Nevertheless, late in the fall of that year, there were clear indications that some changes would be made. Already in April the Unionists decided in public to drop the referendum pledge that Balfour had made at the time of the last election. Actually, when Balfour made that pledge, he had said that the Liberals should hold a similar referendum on the question of Irish Home Rule. Since they had chosen to disregard that invitation and had introduced a Home Rule bill, Unionists were technically free to abandon the pledge themselves. That they did in April. By November, Bonar Law and Lord Lansdowne, the Unionist leader in Lords, decided the time had come to make the decision public. Lansdowne made the announcement in a widely publicized speech delivered at Albert Hall on 14 November 1912. When this speech caused unrest in the Unionist ranks, Bonar Law undertook to clarify matters in a speech of his own at Ashton-under-Lyne. There he reaffirmed the decision to abandon the referendum pledge and then attempted to elaborate on the party's position on food taxes, a point Lansdowne had only briefly treated. The party, if returned to power, would not impose food taxes. Instead, it planned to call a colonial conference to consider the question of preferential trade. Food duties would be imposed only if the dominions insisted.[37] It appeared at this point that Law was remaining true to his commitment to the full program.

The Ashton speech, in fact, became a source of confusion for Unionists.[38] It failed to pacify the growing unrest in the party among anti-food taxers who were increasingly convinced of the tactical disadvantages of that element in Imperial Preferences. Even Law admitted in private that "the great bulk of our members are agreed in desiring to get rid of food duties."[39] As the anti–food taxes campaign in the party grew in strength and adamancy, Unionist Free Traders like Strachey added their criticism of the lingering sentiment among some Unionists that those duties might still be needed. Recall that Law said in his Ashton speech that food taxes would be introduced if the dominions wanted them. Strachey tried to be subdued about the subject in his *Spectator*, but he told Law that he felt "bound to point out . . . that the ultimate result of the policy set forth must be that Food Taxes will not now be proposed by the Unionist Party." "I am certain," he went on to say, "that the Colonies will never ask for them."[40] Still a Free Trader at heart, he had no wish to see food duties, or tariffs of any sort, imposed. But the cause of union was his overriding concern, and he wanted most of all to have the party be as effective and unified as possible as the Irish problem assumed the dimensions of an impending crisis. Just recently, he had told Law that he was "prepared to sacrifice not only my Free Trade views but also my views about Taxes in order to save the Union."[41] Accordingly, he now told Law that although his *Spectator* would "be unable to avoid some mention of the subject [food taxes], . . . I am sure that whatever is said will be said in as little of a provocative spirit as possible."[42]

Northcliffe, on the other hand, had no desire to be subdued. He seized this moment of policy redefinition as an opportunity to foist his views on the party. Although he had misgivings about food duties dating back to 1903, he had generally supported a full Tariff Reform program despite instances of fluctuation. Now he bolted completely on the issue and conducted a vigorous campaign in his *Daily Mail* against food duties throughout December and January. More important, *The Times'* new editor Geoffrey Robinson agreed with Northcliffe on this issue. Prodding from the chief proprietor was unnecessary in this instance.[43] Robinson was originally in favor of "keeping this millstone [food taxes] round our necks instead of publicing [*sic*] throwing it away," but Edward Grigg, then the colonial editor of *The Times*, urged dropping it. In Robinson's words, there was a "terrific controversy" at Printing House Square over this issue. He held to the position that the issue should not be raised while the Unionists were still in Opposition. Consequently, the paper withheld comment on Lansdowne's speech, but Bonar Law's Ashton speech forced a response. Robinson believed that Law's speech actually suggested, which it did, "that the imposition or abandonment of 'food taxes' should practically be left to the decision of the Dominions." That, he thought, would be "absolutely disruptive of the Empire." After the speech, he observed, the "general uprising against 'food taxes' by nine-tenths of the party" simply "drowned" the point. That demonstration of opposition surprised him, for he had no idea that hostility to such duties ran so strong. Accordingly, Robinson concluded that the "only possible course was to drop these duties altogether, so far as the next election" was concerned.[44]

Robinson had his own long-range views about what policy should be on this subject, and he intended to press them when an opportune time came. He believed that the correct course to follow would be to tell the people that "we want authority to alter the present fiscal system and that we propose to frame a new one primarily in their interest." All talk about "sacrifice" should be abandoned and stress should be placed on how Britain could give preference to the dominions. It might be done under the present or the new fiscal system and it could be "assisted by other means than a tariff." Regardless, that was the positive approach to the problem that he wished to use in the future.[45] For the present the strategy he employed in *The Times* was to stress that the policy of Imperial Preference entailed more than food duties. Unionists, *The Times* said, were in agreement about the policy of preference in general; they were only divided on the proposition of taxes on foodstuffs.[46] Therefore, *The Times* advised that food taxes be laid aside for the present.[47] For that, Robinson said in private, "we have been vilified and bismirched in every possible way, notoriously by Garvin in the *Pall Mall Gazette* and *Observer*."[48]

There is no disputing the fact that Garvin attacked *The Times* for its position on food taxes. He did it both in private and in public. Convinced in his own mind that Bonar Law was remaining steady regarding his Tariff Reform and pro-preferential views, Garvin directed his efforts to check the anti–food duties tide at Northcliffe. To Law he wrote this warning about the press baron:

> Our only real trouble is that by comparison with the Radicals we have not a reliable party press fighting on day by day, and owing to the nature of Northcliffe's system we can never have one. The difficulty is not with this or that question. He lets us down on every question in every crisis; and likes letting us down to shew his power—this is the . . . element which makes him delightful in private life and a deadly danger in public. I am *very very fond* of him *as a man;* he fascinates me in a sense by his thousand attractive ways; but I have always denied to him that he had any political power whatever except temporarily to 'queer the pitch.'[49]

He was more intemperate in some of his other correspondence with his references to the *Daily Mail* as "Rag Times" and to the combination of Northcliffe's two papers as "Mail-Times." Garvin told his new proprietor that "repudiation of the food duties on *Mail-Times* lines (Rag-Times!) will leave us perfectly helpless in the Counties."[50] To his friend Leo Maxse he wrote: "B. L. is coming to Second Election. You and I may see all the dangers of that [the idea that if the Unionists came to power that they would not impose food taxes without consent at a second election]. But the *Mail Times* ("Hello Ragtimes!") will try to make it 'food duties not an issue at that Election.'"[51]

Garvin guided the *Observer* and the *Pall Mall Gazette* into a collision course with *The Times* and the *Daily Mail*. Even when Arthur Steel-Maitland, the Unionist party manager, personally asked Garvin to be silent on this subject in order to avoid a display of party differences, the editor proceeded with his attack. Toward the end of the crisis, the *Observer* offered this short statement about the Northcliffe papers that captured the essence of Garvin's views on their position. "The *Daily Mail* and its sad associate and victim *The Times* have both fought this question as though their real object . . . was to advance the interest, not of the Unionist Party, but of Mr. Churchill. 'No food taxes' shrieked the gramophone of Carmelite House [home of the *Daily Mail*] just as it had shrieked 'Canada Kills Imperial Preference' when it thought and hoped that Mr. Borden would lose; . . . *The Times* more furtively said, 'Preference without food duties!' urged in different words the 'banged, barred and bolted door.'"[52] Nevertheless, Northcliffe was riding with the tide of party sentiment and would win this contest.

The crisis ended in January 1913. Bonar Law, who was contemplating resigning over the issue, decided that to do so would impair party unity. Instead he accepted a memorial from the party signed by all but six Unionist M.P.'s, requesting him and Lansdowne to remain in their offices and to accept a modification of the party's Tariff Reform policy. The memorial, in Law's own words, meant that the party was "determined to continue Imperial Preference on the understanding that any preference which is possible without food duties should be carried immediately [when] we obtain power; that any further preference including food duties could be arranged by us but would be subject to approval at another election."[53] His acceptance of the memorial signaled the end of the full program of Tariff Reform and Imperial Preference as envisioned by Joseph Chamberlain. Garvin waged the vigorous fight to the end. This time he lost. He attributed the defeat to the behind-the-scenes influence of Sir Max Aitken, Law's confidant, and referred to him as "the Hermit Crab."[54] Garvin had devoted ten years to the Chamberlain program as the surest means to achieve imperial unity. One can appreciate his despair as he lamented to Waldorf Astor, "If there is to be no effective policy on food duties, then the present Cabinet is in a better position to realise Imperial unity than we are."[55] Strachey, on the contrary, rejoiced about the outcome. "Thank Heaven we can now show a united front to the enemy and are not in danger of losing votes over the food-tax prejudice," he wrote to Law.[56] At the end of the crisis, Northcliffe met with Law. The Unionist leader recognized even before this meeting that the press baron's campaign had been a major cause of the destruction of his position.[57] Now he confronted Northcliffe by saying, "You are my worst enemy." The indomitable Northcliffe responded, "Oh, no! I am your best friend. I have taken the millstone of food taxes off your shoulders. You could never have won an election on the food tax."[58] So the Tariff Reform campaign ended for Unionists as it began, in conjunction between the press and politics.

THE REVIVED IMPERIAL DEBATE: 1907-1913

Most adamant imperialists feared that the Liberals would devote little attention to imperial affairs when they took office in 1905. Those apprehensions continued throughout the following year as the new Liberal government moved quickly to resolve the problems associated with reconstruction in South Africa.

After that, would imperial interests be subordinated to all else? Quite the opposite proved to be the case. Debate over imperial problems continued to have a place in the nation's political life, and the imperial journalists helped to make them part of the public debate. Between 1907 and 1913 interest in imperial unity revived. Throughout these years the issue of Tariff Reform and Imperial Preference permeated further into the political fiber of the times than any other imperial subject. For publicists who felt a commitment to the Empire, that controversy was also about imperial unity and the proper approach to take in achieving it. It was about the nature of and the future of the Empire. Imperial unity was the coordinating concern that pulled together all the major imperial topics featured in the press between 1907 and 1913.

No single imperial subject, however, retained newsworthiness so long as that of Tariff Reform and Imperial Preference. In the hands of J. L. Garvin, it was also the subject of some of the greatest press campaigns in British journalism history. Yet the press is only one factor in the equation of modern politics, and however brilliantly its role might be conducted, it cannot always tilt the balance of opinion as it would wish. "I am sorry for you," the Liberal Winston Churchill wrote to Garvin, the leading Unionist editor of the era. "You try so brilliantly. If words could alter facts, how different it would be!" Churchill went on to say, "Tis a pleasure . . . to offer you my best congratulations upon the transformation which your management has effected already in The Pall Mall . . . I relish equally good journalism and a personality which dominates the mechanics of a paper."[59] Journalism, in fact, has known a no more dominant editor than Garvin. Yet even he failed to convert Chamberlain's program into a political success, thus reminding us of the falsity of inflated boasts regarding the power of the press. As vital as it is to political life in a modern democratic state, it bears repeating that the press wields influence not power.

Tariff Reform, of course, was the great imperial cause of Unionists. If they believed it to be the means by which imperial unity could be achieved, others disputed that claim. Since the Irish problem finally forced Strachey to modify his position as a leading anti–Tariff Reform spokesman in the press, J. A. Spender became the greatest single exponent of Free Trade doctrines among the imperial journalists. Nowhere more than in his *Westminster Gazette* can we find better evidence to support the contention that in denouncing Tariff Reform men of his persuasion were defending their own concept of imperial unity. At the time of the Canadian reciprocity debates in the British press, for example, the *Westminster* had this to say about that concept:

> The Free Trader, of course, denies the whole doctrine [i.e., Tariff Reform]. If he is an Englishman, he leaves Canada to decide for herself what her trade relations with the United States shall be, but, which ever way she decides, he believes her nationality and her attachment to the Empire to be based on stronger and deeper foundations than any arrangement in restraint of trade with another power . . . . For the same reason he

> thinks it even greater folly to rely on a trade preference with the United Kingdom to bind Canada to the United Kingdom. All this line of policy is, in his opinion, to substitute weak, temporary, and perilous ties of self-interest for the strong and deep attachment, based on permanent forces and tendencies, which alone can keep the Empire together.[60]

The most interesting accompanying circumstance to come out of the controversy over Tariff Reform in the second half of the Edwardian era was the way in which it revitalized discussion about imperial unity.

But that revival, which became so manifest in the commentary of the imperial journalists, was not the result of the Tariff Reform debate alone. It emerged from a cluster of events and episodes that occurred in these years. The sequence of imperial conferences held and the organizational and consultative outcomes they produced as well as the crisis in imperial defense and the new level of dominion cooperation it occasioned were subjects that commanded the attention of publicists and politicians. They were topics that also created a new and enlarged context for the public debate, one whose boundaries the imperial journalists helped to extend. At the end of the period we have studied, *The Times* commented on the important steps the Liberal government had taken "in the direction of Imperial unity." The failure of Tariff Reform notwithstanding, it found the Liberals' record remarkable. It constituted, *The Times* said, a real advancement toward the imperial idea.[61] So it seemed that the Empire, after all, had a future. The imperial lull of 1906 indeed had been overcome, and the journalists featured in the present study had played an instrumental role in the resurgence of interest in imperial unity that occurred in the following year. By 1913, however, the Irish problem grew to such proportions that it commanded the bulk of public attention. As it did, the dialogue about imperial unity receded.

10

Retrospect

We turn now from specific issues to an examination of general themes bearing upon the work of the imperial journalists. Three questions need to be considered for an understanding of their collective work in the context of their own time and also in the broader perspective of the twentieth century. First, what motivated their imperial advocacy? Second, was their work "good" journalism and does it deserve continued contemplation by practitioners of the craft? Third, what was the fate of the cause they espoused?

Regarding the question of motivation, the possibility that their advocacy had an economic foundation must be considered. There is, of course, an immense body of literature on economic imperialism, and as Robin W. Winks points out, "Economic questions remain fundamental to an understanding of any empire."[1] It is obvious that economic considerations were involved in the Tariff Reform and Free Trade controversies and that Free Traders as well as Tariff Reformers freely stated their beliefs about the advantages of imperial trade. But Free Traders like Spender and Strachey believed that a preferential system would be harmful to the Empire. To them Free Trade was an extension of individual liberty. It was a policy that favored consumers' interests over those of sellers and producers and one that favored natural rather than artificially supported industrial interests. They spoke of the Empire as a thing beyond imperial trade. That was important and men like Spender and Strachey were grateful for its existence, but to them the Empire was about the maintenance of the principles of liberty and self-government in all of its parts and the ties between them based on mutual appreciation and common culture. Were all of their pronouncements on that theme mere rhetoric? That seems unlikely. They were made too emphatically both in private and in public to represent sham. Their Empire was not to be based on commercial imperialism. That was the mistaken policy of the British Empire of a century or more ago, and they never tired of explaining that political expediency alone dictated that such mistakes should not be repeated. Tariff

Reformers, on the other hand, did speak more about the Empire as an economic advantage than did Spender and Strachey, and they saw it as conducive to Britain's industrial and commercial enterprise. But they valued the Empire for other reasons too. At the least, one can conclude that the imperial journalists were of divided opinion regarding the economic motive as justification for the Empire.

Consider the case of Chinese labor in the Transvaal. Was that an evidence of economic imperialism? Since the time of John Hobson's classic study, a number of theorists have viewed imperialism as an extension of capitalism.[2] The South African gold-mining industry has a prominent place in their studies, particularly as they pertained to pre–Anglo-Boer War years. Did the imperial journalists premise their arguments for or against the use of Chinese indentured laborers in the mines on economic considerations? In this instance the economic argument held only to a point. Other considerations about imperial principles and policies were more important in the long run. Even in the case of arguments advanced in favor of the experiment there were reservations and it was only viewed as a means to an end that had little to do with capitalistic investments. The present investigation of that subject tends to support conclusions recently reached by Robert V. Kubicek. "British strategists," he wrote, "wanted the industry's development to foster the imperial connection. . . . International capitalism, British imperialism, and Afrikaner nationalism did to some extent coexist. But these forces, all well entrenched in South Africa before 1914, were fundamentally at cross purposes." In his estimate, developments in South Africa "should be seen basically as a function of clashing priorities and the inability of any one or combination of these forces to achieve supremacy."[3]

It can also be demonstrated from the record of the imperial journalists that their support for the Empire was partly motivated by social concerns. The term "social" is used in this case in reference to theories of social imperialism. Proponents of those theories contend that imperial strategists used the lure of domestic social reform to gain the support of the industrial working classes for imperial policies. Indeed, in an age when mass democracy was rising, how to gain the backing of the masses for the existing political structure and for imperial programs was a serious problem.

Some of the imperial journalists used social imperialistic arguments to various extents in advancing the cause of Empire. Surely J. L. Garvin's arguments for Tariff Reform had a strong social imperialist thrust. So did those of other Unionist journalists. It was Garvin who told Northcliffe at one point that "even social reform, in which I most ardently believe, is to me chiefly a means of making a stronger and better organized people." But for what purpose? He wanted better social organization so the Empire could "more surely hold its own" against all pressures.[4] That is a clear enough statement of social imperialism, and it is consistent with Garvin's many other statements on the subject. *The Times*, however, while recognizing the need for some degree of social reform, was more interested in Tariff Reform for purposes of imperial organization, and as a sound fiscal policy as well as a remedy for the stationary or even declining status of British industry in its world setting. Strachey was consistently adamant about the need of citizens to assume imperial responsibilities as a mark of good character, but he was hardly an advanced social reformer. Spender, his Liberalism always intact, denounced Chamberlain's program as a reckless imperial policy and linked social reform to budget revision. Still the leaders at *The Times*, as well as Strachey and Spender, all portrayed the Empire as part of the nation's prosperity and as an object worthy of working class support. It can be argued, however, that they did so out of concern for the workingman and for national interests rather than in effort to manipulate the working-class voters to support narrow upper-class or capitalistic interests. Social imperialistic motives, even if allowance is made for differences between that force in Britain and its more aggressive continental counterparts, only partially explain the reasoning for the imperial journalists' attachment to Empire.

More than anything else, a strong imperial world-view lay at the bottom of their advocacy of Empire. To them the Empire was a force for good in the world. This view pulled together their knowledge of the past and their national hopes for the future, and it provided a framework for the major role Britain played, and through imperial unity would continue to play, in the world of grand politics. It was also an outlook that reflected the pride they took in Britain's imperial achievement.

The imperial journalists perceived the British empire as a unique power in a world dominated by great powers. Truly it was a *great* power, and they took pride in the way in which it reflected the achievements of British civilization and the manner in which those achievements had proven suitable for export. Despite the concentration on trade and power present in the nineteenth-century empire, a sense of mission lingered about it. This can be seen in the many Edwardian references to the effort Englishmen made everywhere they went to establish "law and order." That term implied none of the authoritarian connotation sometimes associated with it later in the twentieth century. "Security of life and person within the bounds of an organized imperial control," as A. P. Thornton observes, "was at once a symbol of a disciplined civilization and a hope of greater things to come."[5] Like justice, education, peace, prosperity, and good government, "law and order" was a commodity the British felt they could disseminate to the far corners of the empire. Likewise they took pride in the technical achievements, products of industrial civilization, that the empire spread far and wide. Such achievements were part of a legacy that the imperial journalists, like other Edwardians of their class, valued. "England without an Empire! England in that case would not be the England we love."[6] So spoke Joseph Chamberlain in 1906, and one did not have to be a disciple of his to agree with this sentiment. To men like the imperial journalists, the presence of the British empire was conducive to world peace and to international good will and prosperity. It held a unique place in the world.

This idea runs throughout the imperial journalists' commentary and at times received explicit expression. At one point *The Times* extolled the virtues of the empire in this way:

> We have done in the last three centuries what no nation has ever done or dreamed of doing before. Our just boast is not only that we have reared an Empire greater than mankind has ever seen, but that its rise has been for the good of all who dwell within its borders. We have made mistakes; we have been guilty of wrongdoing, but wisdom and justice have been its foundation. We set no vast conceptions of statesmanship and no lofty moral ideas before us in its beginning, or in the chief stages of its extension, but as it came to us our fathers instinctively applied to it the principles they brought with them from home. Those principles have been the root of our system of self-governing states and of our rule as the responsible trustees of subject people. They sprang from our national character. It is to that character that the Empire owes its distinctive features, and upon which its future mainly depends.[7]

Among the imperial journalists, this sentiment ran strong. Even Spender's *Westminster Gazette*, which was careful to show moderation in expressing such ideas, took pride in the belief that "freedom, justice, and peace" formed the broad basis of the empire, and in the case of India, it professed that "pride in the administration of India . . . is a common heritage of all Englishmen."[8]

The reference to the Indian Empire is important. British achievements there meant a great deal to the imperial journalists who felt that they added a special significance to Britain's world position. The *Westminster Gazette* can be cited again for a summary of this belief. "During the past half-century," it reflected, "we have bestowed unbroken peace; we have done justice impartially; we have made roads and railways, promoted works of public utility and improvement, and done all that skill and devotion are capable of doing to mitigate the calamities of plague and famine. The Indian Civil Service has been a model to the world for loyal and disinterested work for the public good." Prosperity had risen in the subcontinent but a mass amount of poverty still existed along with discontent made "by our own act." These things, the *Westminster* said, would continue until "civilization and education" raised the standard of Indian life. The British could only expect Indians to complain about the "paternal benevolent rule which assumes they are unable to govern themselves." The paper went on to claim that Britain's real reward was in knowing that it had refused to act as a despot, refused to deny Indians the "knowledge and mental development" that could be used in criticism of the British rule. In conclusion it said, "This is the moral basis of our rule and its justification as an effort towards civilization."[9]

In subsequent years, historians would take a harder look at the British record in India, but at this time the imperial journalists all agreed with the general theme of the *Westminster*'s statement. Their own versions of it contained several variations, and particularly in the hands of Strachey, they could convey strong overtones of cultural and racial superiority. Yet the fact remains that they all took pride in the British achievement in India and felt that the British rule there had a justifiable, even a moral, foundation. The imperial journalists made similar claims about the British administration of Egypt and occasionally about British contributions in various dependencies. Although a close examination of attitudes on the Indian Empire and the numerous British dependencies is beyond the scope of this study, the basic sense of achievement that is apparent in them is worthy of note. It is an indication of the positive qualities that the imperial journalists attached to the presence in the world of the entire British empire in all of its variety and vastness. Their pride in achievement was nowhere more noticeable than in their perception of the evolution of the self-governing dominions. To them that evolution proved the viability of British ideas and institutions and was proof of the peaceful goals of British power. So construed, the Empire was the centerpiece of the imperial journalists' view of Britain's world position.

It is difficult to overstate the importance they attached to the Empire of the self-governing dominions. The modern British empire began with settlement colonies, and by the beginning of the twentieth century they had come to hold a particular place in imperial perceptions of the nation and empire in the world. Repeated references by the imperial journalists to the development of colonial self-government and to the great accomplishment of consolidation of the colonies in Canada and Australia (and by 1910 in South Africa) underscore the sense of achievement they attached to the political development of the dominions. It proved what constructive imperial policy could produce and was evidence of the idea that the British were worthy of their imperial world position. To Edwardian imperial advocates, the dominions held a place of special importance. Their significance to Britain went far beyond the sense of achievement attached to the role Britain played in their development. Their growing significance in the British imperial outlook was due to the confluence of a number of circumstances in the imperial world order.

We have already seen how these circumstances made Britain's world position more insecure. Whether they involved new industrial powers, European rivalries, German naval building, or nationalist and revolutionary movements in the Middle East, India, and China, they represented serious shifts in the international order that pressured Britain's position in that order. Moreover, the mounting international tensions in Europe forced her to become more involved in Continental affairs. As A. J. P. Taylor observes, "The European Balance of Power, which had been ignored for forty years, again dominated British foreign policy; and henceforth every German move was interpreted as a bid for continental hegemony."[10] The new international circumstance increased the dominions' value to Britain. Without the dominions Britain could be outdistanced by her chief rivals in terms of population and resources. In a sense,

Britain needed the dominions at her side. Her future relations with India, despite all of India's economic and strategic value, were uncertain. The future of the dependent empire was at best vague. Consequently, the dominions became Britain's greatest resource in any effort to retain her position among the powers in what Eric Hobsbawn reminds us was still "the Age of Empire."[11] The Empire was crucial to Britain's prosperity, to its defense and foreign policies, and to its world position. It was a source of pride and believed to be a source of strength. Without the dominions the entire character of the British empire would be changed. Without the dominions Britain's ability to perform as a great power in a world of great powers would be impaired. Small wonder the Empire of the dominions held the place it did in the world perception of the imperial journalists, and small wonder, indeed, that they concentrated so much on the nature of the relationship between Britain and the dominions.

The imperial journalists grasped that relationship in the broad perspective of time. In his famous study, *The Expansion of England*, which Edwardians as well as their late Victorian predecessors knew so well, J. R. Seeley explored the connection between history and politics. "The ultimate object of all my teaching here," he wrote, "is to establish this fundamental connection, to show that politics and history are only different aspects of the same study." That was the approach he recommended for engaging the question of "whether Greater Britain [the Empire], now that it exists, may be expected to prosper and endure or to fall."[12] In this manner the imperial journalists integrated history and politics in their writings. Nothing is more certain than the fact that they wrote from wide knowledge of the past. They roamed over not only British history but also over that of past empires. In time most of them who lived on would turn to writing history in some form.[13] At this point their sense of history informed their political journalism, as did their political ideology. Both allowed a political-historical theme to pervade their arguments. The natural continuum of that theme was the projection of their imperial thought into speculation about the future of Empire.

All political planning, rooted in the past as it is, has a future orientation. The imperial journalists' vision extended in this direction too. "Who can tell," mused *The Times* at one point, "what the next forty years may accomplish not in Canada only, but in all British dominions beyond the seas? On that issue hang the fate of the Empire and the final judgment which generations to come will form of the wisdom or folly of our time."[14] Speculation upon the Empire's future was commonplace and it could vary. With his Conservative moorings holding firm, Garvin tended to be pessimistic (he would say realistic) about it, but Strachey, the Whig, and Spender, the Liberal, remained optimistic regarding the Imperial future.

The theme that best illustrates the integration of the historical and future dimensions in imperial journalistic thought is the constant reference to imperial unity that permeated it. In a typical statement we find *The Times* insisting, "No one to whom Imperial unity is anything more than a misty sentiment can dissent from the general position that if unity is to increase there must be increasing organization of some kind."[15] Garvin never tired of proclaiming Imperial unity the "greatest thing" to which Unionists were supposed to be committed. Strachey and Spender agreed with the idea of imperial unity but believed it would ensue as a result of maintaining liberal principles as the real "bond of unity for the British Empire."[16] In fact, the theme of imperial unity ran through the commentary of all the problems examined in this inquiry, regardless of the political preference of the commentators.

In one sense, all of the imperial journalists were of one mind when it came to the more neutral aspects of unity. On these points their differences, when they appeared, were minor. They all professed to see a common stock of British ideas and ideals in the Empire. They supported imperial education, a term by which they meant mutual understanding by the British and the people of the dominions of one another's history, politics, and common concerns. Improving imperial communications and, in large measure, imperial security received their broad endorsement. Moreover, they all agreed that imperial relations were evolving into a type of partnership. Beyond considerations such as these, sharp differences could occur, as we have seen. But when differences did occur, they were over the means to and the nature of imperial unity, not about the merits of the idea of unity itself. Of course, at this time *imperial unity* was an ill-defined term that meant something far different from a strong federal union. In general it meant stronger ties of inter-imperial cooperation, but as we have seen, there were different ideas about the form that cooperation should take.

How would the Empire hold together? Unionist imperial journalists believed better imperial organization was the answer, though they were not always in agreement about what form that organization should take. On the other hand, the liberally-minded Spender and Strachey believed it should result from informal ties of common culture and from mutual needs that occasioned mutual response. The establishment of an imperial secretariat (actually a department within the Colonial Office), the progress of the colonial and imperial conferences, the consultation of the dominions on matters of defense policy, and all the steps taken in the name of consultation and voluntary cooperation pleased imperial journalists like Spender and Strachey. The other imperial journalists also accepted them as encouraging signs, but they clearly wished for stronger imperial ties in matters of economics, political organization, and defense. Nevertheless, despite differences about how it should be achieved and the nature it should assume, all of the imperial journalists endorsed the idea of improving imperial unity. Anything less than that would have called their imperial credentials into question.

There were, however, other reasons that explained their support for better imperial unity. They were geopolitical ones. The imperial journalists were all men drawn to what might be called grand politics, the politics of major political party programs and of national and international issues. The Empire, particularly with stronger unity, was an essential element in their grand political schemes. Take the case of J. L. Garvin. Although it is true that he frequently linked together the Empire and social reform in his writing and that he was a foremost promoter of imperial preferences, it is important to understand that these were not his only political interests. Foreign affairs, he confided to Northcliffe, "were my first passion and deepest study for many years, and the tariff financial and Imperial theories are branched off from prolonged concern with foreign policy."[17] At other times, he spoke of his passion for the Empire. To what did he give priority of interest? The answer is to different things at different times. Garvin saw all the important political issues in national and international politics as part of an integrated whole. "As the power and union of the Empire have been the steady objects of my thought all my life, and *means* must necessarily alter if men through long periods of time keep *ends* in view."[18] To Garvin the Empire was, as he said, "the steady object" of his political outlook, for without it Britain's role as a great world power would be reduced.

The imperial journalists, in fact, shared the view of the Empire as part of a multi-dimensional world of grand politics. Strachey considered uniting the Empire "above all things" and gave his "cordial support" to "encouraging a closer connection between the colonies and the Empire."[19] To him membership in the Empire was "one of the highest and greatest privileges obtainable by any community," and he believed, furthermore, that it was a natural magnet that held together the union with Ireland.[20] While it is true that Strachey was more interested in national and imperial politics than in foreign affairs, it is also true that he had a great interest in sea power and in preserving Britain "against the blood and iron politics of the ruling caste in Germany."[21] Moreover, he stayed in close touch with Sir Edward Grey and other people in the Foreign Office and, beyond that, had an absorbing interest in the affairs of the Indian Empire. Since the Empire bore relation to all of these interests, it can be said that it was part of Strachey's wider perspective of world affairs. Like Strachey, Spender saw the Empire in relation to his wider interest in grand politics. In 1912 he explained Britain's new role in European diplomatic affairs (i.e., after the Anglo-French Entente of 1904 and the Anglo-Russian Entente of 1907) in these terms: "We have to ask what kind of naval and military policy will yield the best results, given that we are both an Island and an Empire, and involve us in the least conflict and competition with our neighbours; how far we can organize the Empire or rely on its assistance in time of war; what are the forces which tend to keep the Empire together; and what, if any, those which threaten its unity."[22] Spender believed that the unity of the Empire was practical rather than "a cast-iron contract," and his *Westminster Gazette* repeatedly proclaimed how the involvement of the dominions in matters of sea power and imperial defense increased that unity. But he also believed that the Empire was but one of the foundations of British policy, albeit an indispensable one, that also involved sea power, extensive strategic interests, and the abandonment of her previous "splendid isolation" from European alliances. Like that of the other imperial journalists, Spender's thinking on the Empire must be placed against the threatening international currents of the time.

No journalist in Britain combined interest in imperial and foreign affairs more than *The Times'* foreign editor, Valentine Chirol. His prominence in both areas was undisputed. It is interesting, therefore, to see how he positioned the Empire amid his ranging interests. On one occasion, he explained his perception of grand politics in this manner:

> The world [is] growing every day so much bigger or from another point of view so much smaller, our columns are invaded by questions which 10 or 15 years ago did not exist for us: [the] Far East, the internal situation in India, Labour questions in Australia and New Zealand, Preferential relations with our colonies, capital v. Labour in the U.S., the position of coloured labour in all our colonies, the new regime in S.A., etc. etc. Many of these are big questions affecting not only political interests but the whole future of our Empire, the whole structure of society.[23]

The Empire was part of his comprehensive view of world affairs. It did not exist in isolation. Even when considering Canada, which Chirol believed would become "the centre of stability" of the Empire, he was equally determined to see relations between Britain and the United States "grow every year more intimate."[24] That was a common hope of all the imperial journalists. Moreover, if the columns of *The Times* throughout the era indicate anything when considered collectively, it is that the paper assumed the importance of the Empire in the context of Britain's wider interest in world affairs, both at the present and in the future. All of the imperial journalists concurred in that assumption.

They also concurred in the belief that the type of political journalism they practiced contributed to the well-being of their craft. Therefore we are led to inquire into the proposition of whether or not theirs was "good" journalism in an age of expanding democracy. The criteria for good journalism vary according to time, type, and circumstance. In this case, the journalists studied were associated with the quality press at a precarious time in its evolution. It is interesting to see that, despite all the pressures that endangered both the quality and fact of their existence, all the publications featured in this study survived the era. In three cases (*The Times*, the *Observer*, and the *Spectator*) they survived with greater strength and have continued as major publications to the present day. What did the imperial journalists do that helped to give their papers longer life and what contribution did they make to the practice of political journalism? The answer to those questions involves matters of business acumen, the style and tone of their writing, indications of influence, and journalistic ethics.

First of all, it appears their work contributed to a more commercially sound enterprise than might be expected. With Northcliffe's help, *The Times* slowly began to raise its daily circulation to nearly 50,000 by the end of the period—not great compared to the leading paper of the popular press, the *Daily Mail*, that reached over 700,000, but a solid increase over the 38,000 of a few years before.[25] Garvin made the *Observer* a solid journalistic property with a circulation of 200,000 by 1915. Strachey, who made his presence felt in every department of the *Spectator*, turned that journal into a prosperous publication property. He more than doubled its revenue and circulation. In 1903 the latter reached a record high of 23,000.[26]

Spender, on the other hand, was unable to make the *Westminster* prosper. He failed to see how it could be made to pay, but that was not the purpose of the paper, as its slender news service indicated. Its influence far exceeded its small circulation of around 20,000. The paper was tied to the forces of parliamentary Liberalism; as Stephen Koss observed, "It was more or less an accredited organ."[27] At the end of the nineteenth century, there were nine evening newspapers in London. By 1921 three of the best publications in that category, the *Westminster Gazette*, the *Globe*, and the *Pall Mall Gazette*, were gone while more popular papers like the *Evening News* and the *Evening Standard*, which were published in conjunction with morning papers, flourished. The *Westminster* was an intellectual and political evening paper, and the British preferences for evening newspapers were shifting to mass circulation popular papers. Caught in that shift, Spender refused to alter the character of his paper to make it more popular. It is interesting to note in comparison that, for all of his drive and ability, Garvin failed to make the evening *Pall Mall Gazette* a paying property after he became its editor in 1912. All indications suggest that commercialization and popularization of evening papers combined with readers' preference to make it impossible for small circulation, serious evening papers to survive as paying publications. Even so, Lord Northcliffe, that acknowledged master of producing the mass circulating modern newspaper, said that Spender was "one of the few men who knew how to edit a daily political newspaper."[28]

Regardless of Spender's continuing need for a subsidy to sustain his paper, it can be concluded that the imperial journalists contributed to the prosperity of their publications where it was possible to do so. The success of a publication, of course, depends on many things that are beyond the scope of this study. In terms of content alone, news, entertainment, special reports, and advertisements all have a share in creating the appeal of a paper. The editorial page is also important in creating that appeal in terms of format, layout, and content. Since this study is about political commentary, it is only fair to ask if the appearance of that commentary helped or hindered the appeal of the publication in which it appeared.

The style and tone that marked the editorial writing of the imperial journalists were engaging for upper- and middle-class, informed readers. They were the ones the editors hoped to reach, and in most cases, did reach in increasing numbers. Their work had more variety and was more modern in appearance than generally supposed. *The Times* looked brighter in 1908 than in 1903, and brighter yet in 1913. Its magisterial leading articles became gradually more attractive to the modern reader. A "temperate and judicious" quality characterized Spender's writing. Indeed, John Burns, the labor leader, liked to chaff him about his "philandering with politics in an amiable and Marcus Aurelius style."[29] Burns had a point, for Spender's leading articles were polished daily essays, lucid and elegant in appearance and reasonable and generous in spirit. Strachey's *Spectator* compared well to other weekly journals of its class. Thought of by some contemporaries as *The Times* of weekly journalism, it was dignified, serious, and restrained in appearance and conveyed a high intellectual and critical quality. Strachey's writing gave it character. His style had moralistic, romantic, even *ex cathedra* strains, but it was full of candor, argumentation, and urbanity as it ranged across a remarkably wide field of interests. The remaining editor, Garvin, occupied a class by himself.

To say that Garvin's writing was forceful understates the truth. Despite the controversial nature of his advocacy, which could be impatient and urgent (his critics said nervous and hysterical), the engaging style of his leading articles, both in terms of format and language, gained him a reputation as a genius among journalists. Friend and foe granted him that. W. T. Stead called him "the New Disraeli" who, like Disraeli, "was hated and feared" by the party he chose to defend. Garvin combined, as Stead said, "splendid audacity" and "inexhaustible energy."[30] His rare combination of editorial brilliance and political passion resulted in leading articles of uncommon force. In the words of Sir Linton Andrews:

> His articles were not only important; they looked important, more important than any others elsewhere. They had the appearance and the weight of an institution. In larger type than their old-fashioned, closely set predecessors, they ran to several wide columns, led into action by a band of well-phrased headlines and marshaled into sections, each with a trenchant subheading. The articles moved forward with regimental splendor and a glittering array of weapons—steely phrases, poetical quotations, historical parallels, citations of heroism, analogies from science, experience of foreign lands—all the resources of an almost encyclopedically full mind.[31]

The style of which Andrews spoke was the one that characterized Garvin's editorship of the *Observer* until 1942, and he developed it during the Edwardian era.

The matter of political influence is more difficult to determine than style and appearance. There can be no doubt that the political elite thought the imperial journalists exerted influence. Why else was there such ado over what *The Times* said or such reaction to what Garvin wrote? Why else did the Liberals take such care to subsidize the *Westminster Gazette* and why did the Unionists think it so necessary to introduce the *Outlook* to counter the Free Trade influence of the *Spectator*? The imperial journalists were men whose views had impact among the politically informed. They were widely quoted at home and abroad, and their private correspondence with political leaders provides abundant evidence that the parties appreciated their support.

Garvin once said that influence would come as a result of "real earnestness, conviction, [and] steady hammering."[32] Those qualities appeared in the work of all the imperial journalists, and if contemporaneous opinion can be accepted as proof of influence, it can be concluded that they achieved an impressive degree of it. Although any effort to measure their influence would be a nebulous undertaking since they argued both sides of the major questions and since those questions never occurred as problems isolated from other issues, it is possible to generalize upon its impact. By their ongoing commentary on imperial issues from the beginning to the end of the era, they helped to make the Empire one of the two or three commanding subjects of the time and extended the parameters of discussion about it. Had the Empire failed to receive that type of attention, the Edwardian public debate would have been far different.

There remains the matter of their commitment to canons of high-level political journalism to consider. The record of their work on the Empire is proof of the fact that their writing was dignified, truthful, and informed. It embodied the will of men who wrote with the courage of their beliefs and who were willing to be relentless in their pursuit of cause when necessary. In an age during which the forces of popularization and commercialization were pressuring the citadel of quality journalism, the work of the imperial journalists remained resistant to trivialization, superficiality, brevity, and base sensationalism. They practiced a serious, but by no means dull, brand of journalism based on the belief that it served the public good. Their objective was influence, not financial profit.

These men believed that the modern newspaper combined news, advertisements, and opinion about things of public importance. Judging from the content of their papers, they even accepted the idea that entertainment had a place there too. But when they spoke of journalism as a profession, they had political journalism in mind. As Spender put it: "It is a great profession of constantly increasing importance in the modern world of propaganda and loud-speaking. That it should be efficiency manned by men of ability and sincerity who take their work seriously is of the highest national importance."[33] Spender wrote those lines many years after he left the *Westminster* in 1922 and after his old paper merged into oblivion with the *Daily News*. There may have been no place for a paper like the *Westminster* in the press as it developed in the twentieth century, but according to his latter-day writings he believed a place still remained for political journalism grounded in independent thought.

In fact, independence lay at the core of political journalism as the imperial journalists conceived it. Since they all defended their editorial independence by word and deed, the point deserves elaboration. Strachey, for instance, believed that an editor's independence was the finest asset a paper could have. An editor had to be free to interpret public issues according to his own convictions, even when his readers might disagree with them or even be angered by them.[34] That sentiment was in line with Moberly Bell's determination to have *The Times* express its own judgment "fearlessly without regard to either party or self interest." It can be found in Garvin's determination "to give the public what they don't want," by which he meant that he intended to explore issues in depth and according to his own independent thought—independent from political control.[35] The other imperial journalists adhered to a similar journalistic philosophy. It all was quite the opposite from the canons that guided Northcliffe in his popular journalism. As proprietor, he interfered in editorial policy; he was ever mindful of the commercial interests of a paper and expanded business staff at the expense of others; and he preferred to follow rather than lead public opinion in instances where the latter might reduce a paper's circulation. The imperial journalists, and other political publicists like them, held that it was their purpose to lead and influence public opinion and to do it they had to have the freedom to editorialize according to their own dictates of thought, knowledge, and responsibility.

To practice this freedom they had to resist a number of pressures. The correspondence of Buckle and others at Printing House Square is full of evidence of their struggle against Northcliffe's proprietary interference in editorial matters. For a number of years Strachey watched the *Spectator* become a "political outcast" due to Unionist party policies that he opposed and refused to stop opposing. Garvin was also deeply involved in Unionist party politics, but acted on the basis of his own opinion. Sometimes he led party opinion. Spender, who enjoyed such regular and close professional relations with Liberal leaders, told Strachey that in composing his editorials on controversial topics he "always found it best . . . to plunge in first" and consult others only after committing himself.[36] Years later he would return to the point of his editorial independence a number of times in his autobiographical writings.

While remaining editor of the *Spectator* until 1925, just two years before his death, Strachey also produced several books in his latter years including his autobiography. In them he too returned to the theme of editorial independence in journalism. It had long been one of his favorite topics to discuss in private and public. Strachey was fond of describing his brand of journalism as that of a "watch-dog" variety—a phrase he borrowed from W. T. Stead. He never relinquished that fondness. An editor who accepted "regular and specific" instructions from a proprietor, he wrote in his autobiography, was "not really the Editor but only the Proprietor's mouthpiece." And what of the journalist who knows little of his "watch-dog" role? He may fall into "a kind of intellectual prostitution," Strachey said.[37]

J. L. Garvin went on as editor of the *Observer* until 1942. In later years he also wrote three volumes of *The Life of Joseph Chamberlain*, thus contributing to the literary monument for the statesman he so admired, and became the editor of the *Encyclopaedia Britannica*, a great tribute to a man who entered the world of high culture with so few academic and social advantages. At one point during those years, late in 1929, the *Spectator* sponsored a luncheon on Garvin's behalf. G. E. Buckle was unable to attend. In his note of regret, he referred to the *Observer*'s editor as one "whose sturdy independence and brilliant workmanship command so general an admiration among his brother journalists."[38] In that casual comment, Buckle touched on a principle of editorship by which they both lived. Garvin maintained it throughout his professional life. In a sense, it was fitting that his departure from the editorship of the *Observer* after holding it for thirty-four years came over a difference of opinion with the paper's proprietor over its editorial policy.

The meaning of these many references to and defenses of editorial independence is clear enough. The journalists perceived that their opinions were worth having because they were those of thoughtful and well-informed observers of public affairs, and that type of opinion had to remain central to political journalism unless the press was willing to forsake its historic role and become an appendage of business enterprise.

As valuable as editorial independence was and remains to political journalism, it is no guarantee of wisdom. The imperial journalists were wise in many cases, and they wrote with depth and clarity of argument. But they were not seers, and in some cases, they failed to grasp the ramification, inconsistency, or even the deficiency of their line of argument.

Time and again they stressed their belief in the principle of dominion self-government, but they somehow failed to grasp the full force of dominion nationalism. Jealous of their own independence, the dominions were unlikely to accept any type of imperial economic union such as the Tariff Reformers desired. On the other hand, Spender and Strachey believed in Free Trade with a religious conviction that would have pleased Adam Smith and felt that ties of sentiment and necessity would hold together the Empire. They too overlooked the full force of dominion nationalism. That fact weakened their argument about imperial unity. Britain and the dominions did not necessarily share the same strategic priorities. The case of the Anglo-Japanese alliance of 1902, which the British negotiated out of necessity and the Australians opposed, should have made that point evident.

Or, take the case of their commentary on South Africa. They all were upholders of the tradition of imperial idealism, but the responses they made to the use of Chinese indentured laborers in the Transvaal ran counter to that tradition in several instances. It would have served the Unionists better had Garvin and the leaders at *The Times* balked at that proposition in the name of imperial idealism. On this same problem we have seen how all of the imperial journalists referred to South Africa as a "white man's country." Even with increased immigration from Britain, South Africa could only be a white man's country in the sense that it was a place where white men could dominate. That idea reflected the racial biases common among upper- and middle-class Englishmen at the time, but it did not manifest imperial idealism. Along these same lines, consider their response to the South Africa Act of Union in 1909, which established a color bar against the native franchise beyond the Cape in the new dominion. They all regretted the native franchise provisions in the constitution and said so, but they yielded to the forces of necessity and in the name of practicality approved the document without making the native franchise a major issue. In this instance, words probably would have failed to alter the deed. But it would seem, despite all the explanations that can be offered for accepting the act, that the dictates of imperial idealism would have demanded greater publicity of the native franchise provisions of the constitution than it received in the hands of the imperial journalist. Looking back on these years (he had the Irish Council's Bill of 1907 in mind), Spender spoke of "the occasions on which a journalist ought not to have busied himself with the doings of politicians behind the scenes or joined in their hunt for formulas, but to have taken a simple line on the merits of the question from the outside and pursued it unflinchingly."[39] In the debates about South African problems, there were several occasions when Spender's advice could have been applied to help the cause of Empire.

When viewed in retrospect, it also appears that the imperial journalists may have impaired the cause of Empire in one important way. Since the Empire was a vital national interest, and since the journalists were in agreement about a number of imperial concerns, they would have served the cause well if they had devoted greater effort to publicizing the areas in which consensus of opinion existed and perhaps searched for other such areas. The specter of their Tariff Reform and Free Trade convictions prevented them from being more effective in pursuing these ends. While it is refreshing to view the candor with which they defended those persuasions, it is also possible to detect rhetorical excesses in their charges and countercharges. Editors on both sides of the issue allowed their economic philosophy to become a panacea. They wrote, of course, without the benefit of retrospection that would allow them to see that Edwardian prosperity made it unlikely that the British would accept any Tariff Reform program while the Great Depression of the 1930s compelled them to abandon Free Trade and to introduce a system of tariffs and imperial preferences in 1932. They were writers who personified not only the political reasoning of their time but also the political emotions of their class. Their emotive attachment to their economic philosophies added a lively quality to their writing and helps us to grasp the temper of the times, but it also tended to polarize thinking about imperial concerns and to make the editors unappreciative of the contribution the opposite party made to the cause of Empire. There were some instances when they acknowledged the opposing party's contribution to the cause, but they were few.[40]

The work of the imperial journalists had its flaws, as the above cases show, as well as its strengths. Taken as a whole, however, their brand of journalism remains impressive. Their commitment to editorial independence, the depth and range of knowledge that stood behind their commentaries, their conviction to a cause they believed to be for national good, and their ability to provide dignified and prolonged expression to that cause combine to make their work a worthy contribution to the best tradition of political journalism.

It is, of course, necessary for political journalism to reach the masses, and Northcliffe was correct in perceiving that need. But there must also be room in it for depth of argument and the certainty that a subject will be examined and explained for however long it remains an important public interest. No doubt the practice of political journalism must take several forms, some more popular than others. Nevertheless, the form it took in the hands of the Edwardian imperial journalists is an important one to retain in its essence.

Their journalism merits continued attention by practitioners of the craft. Journalism has a number of unchanging qualities, some more to its credit than others. Sometimes the press has abused its position as a medium of public communication. Sometimes it has been threatened by outside controls and influence. In a sense, particularly in the case of the political press, it has always existed in a state of crisis. In the latter part of the twentieth century, it continues to face many serious problems. The forces of commercialization and popularization still impair the work of political journalists. Full, fair, and prolonged presentation of news and opinion is still a problem, even in the quality press. Tension still exists between editors and proprietors, and today proprietary influence has grown at the expense of that of the editors. Amid all of the modifications that characterize the evolution of the press in this century, the tradition the imperial journalists upheld remains important to the practice of political journalism. Even now when political journalism has become more complex and less partisan, and even if journalism has become a profession within an industry, that tradition is vital to retain. The contribution the imperial journalists made to it was one of their finest achievements.

Was their support for the cause of the Empire a comparable achievement? Since the Empire failed to survive the impact of twentieth-century forces and redefined national needs, was it all simply a futile effort in behalf of a losing cause? Quite the contrary is the case. For ten years the figures featured in this study helped to keep the problems and the image of the Empire in the public debate. They scrutinized the subject and gave it prominence. In doing that, they helped to explore a possible alternative to new international realities that challenged Britain's world position. The manner of their elaboration of ideas about the great imperial questions of the day and the way in which they linked that discussion to the theme of imperial unity demonstrated their recognition of the fact that the relationship between Britain and the dominions was changing. They wished to turn that change into constructive channels. In the process, they helped to create a momentum for greater dominion involvement in the affairs of the Empire and an acceptance of the fact that the relationship between Britain and the dominions was losing its imperial nature and acquiring one of partnership. The fact that the emerging partnership held together during World War I and World War II is a tribute to the statesmen and the publicists who grappled with its transition in the Edwardian era. In time the Empire was transformed into the British Commonwealth of Nations and later yet into the Commonwealth of Nations (though some still prefer to keep the designation "British" in the name).

The resulting Commonwealth is a far different polity than the Edwardians envisioned. But in the words of Nicholas Mansergh, "The commonwealth came into being in revulsion against Empire, but historically it could not escape being among other things, the heir to Empire."[41] In the long perspective, the Edwardians can be seen engaged in an open debate about the manner of this transformation. Some of the imperial ideas they advocated proved unworkable. Others had a better fate and merged with the idea of Commonwealth.

It is also possible to detect other long-run ramifications of the place the imperial journalists gave the Empire in the Edwardian public debate. Perhaps it contributed a momentum to the tendency to believe in the Empire as a source of Britain's prosperity and power long after it was in the nation's best interest to do so. Since the beginning of their overseas empire, Englishmen had assumed that colonial trade contributed to the nation's prosperity, and during the Edwardian era they attached great importance to trade with the dominions. Yet at that time, the bulk of British trade (a little over 70 percent) was with foreign countries, and in that trade Britain had become less competitive.[42] Some historians argue that the emphasis placed on economic links with the Empire encouraged rigidity in the British market. It would have been better to have placed that emphasis on modernizing British productivity and on technical education. According to this line of argument, making Britain an effective trading partner anywhere in the world was more important than fostering her economic relations with the Empire.[43] Since some authorities on the subject trace Britain's industrial decline to the years 1870 to 1914, this argument merits serious attention, but there are a number of realities to consider in any evaluation of it.[44] First of all, Britain remained prosperous during the Edwardian era despite the growth of larger competitive powers (e.g., Germany and the United States), with larger populations, and consequently, larger domestic markets. British trade with semi-industrialized countries, including those of the Empire, was rising. Moreover, British overseas investments experienced a tremendous growth during these years.[45] With investments abroad equaling 43 percent of all the world's foreign investments, Britain had obvious financial strength—regardless of her relative but, with the arrival of new industrial competitors several decades before, understandable industrial decline.[46] Then too, caution must be used when tracing the roots of economic decline in any case. The reasons are complex, resistant to monocausal explanation, and full of variables. For instance, who could expect the Edwardians to have been able to anticipate the long-range world market changes occasioned by World War I, the stock market crash of 1929, the Great Depression, and World War II? At any rate, when considering the roots of Britain's industrial decline whatever the period of their origin, the dominions are a major element on the larger imperial side of the economic balance sheet.

A similar argument can be made about the long-range effects of imperial power, which so captivated the imperial journalists. Were they mistaken in believing that the Empire magnified British strength? Was imperial power a reality or a delusion? Did it enhance British force, or spread it out too thin? Was the Empire an asset or a burden in World War I and again in World War II? Did the concern British leaders had for dominion opinion in responding to Nazi moves in central Europe in the mid-1930s, help or hinder efforts to stop Nazi aggression?[47] Such questions cannot be dismissed, but they usually involve compound answers. In some cases, they have no clear answer. The Empire, however, should not be undervalued in any estimate of Britain's twentieth-century strength.

In evaluating the place of the Empire-Commonwealth in the history of the first half of this century, it is fair to say that it extended British vulnerability as it extended British force. Dominion forces made significant contributions to the Allied victory in World War I and an even greater contribution to Allied victory in World War II. In the years between the two wars, when the Italian, German, and Japanese empires embarked upon paths of aggression, the dominions were part of the British Commonwealth and Empire, which was an international entity of peaceful purpose. Anthony Clayton did not exaggerate when he wrote that the "disintegration of the Empire in the 1930s would have had catastrophic results for the world as a whole."[48] Consequently, if the Edwardian emphasis on the Empire in the public debate contributed to a later blurring of Britain's international priorities, it also contributed to a belief in a world community of states and people that later helped to preserve Britain and other nations from the new expansionistic imperialisms of the post–World War I and World War II eras.

Notes

CHAPTER 1: THE EDWARDIAN PUBLIC DEBATE AND THE PRESS

1. W. T. Stead, "His Majesty's Public Councillors: To Wit, The Editors of the London Daily Papers," *Review of Reviews* (British) 30 (December 1904): 593.

2. Quoted in Donald Read, *Edwardian England, 1901-1915: Society and Politics* (London: Harrap, 1972), 14.

3. Nicholas Mansergh, *The Commonwealth Experience*, vol. 1, *The Durham Report to the Anglo-Irish Treaty*, 2d ed. (Toronto: University of Toronto Press, 1982), ix.

4. *Westminster Gazette*, 8 December 1911, 1.

5. *The Times*, 3 January 1903, 9. For an extended treatment of the idea, see L. S. Amery, *The Case Against Home Rule* (London: West Strand Publishing Co., 1912), 12 and 40-41.

6. For data about the papers included in this classification, see Viscount Cambrose, *British Newspapers and Their Controllers* (London: Cassell and Company, 1947), and Stanley Morison, *The English Newspaper, 1622-1932* (Cambridge: Cambridge University Press, 1932).

7. William Maxwell, "Old Lamps for New: Some Reflections on Recent Changes in Journalism," *Nineteenth Century and After* 75 (May 1914): 1095.

8. Alan J. Lee, *The Origins of the Popular Press in England, 1855-1914* (London: Croom Helm, 1976), 79 and 94.

9. Robert Donald, "New Forces in Journalism," in H. A. Taylor, *Robert Donald* (London: Stanley Paul and Co., c. 1934), 266.

10. Stephen Koss, *The Rise and Fall of the Political Press in Britain*, vol. 2, *The Twentieth Century* (Chapel Hill: University of North Carolina Press, 1984), 1.

11. Lee, *Origins of the Popular Press in England*, 213.

12. Quoted in ibid.

13. Francis Williams, *Dangerous Estate: The Anatomy of Newspapers* (London: Longmans, Green and Co., 1957), 172.

14. Koss, *Rise and Fall of the Political Press*, 2: 121-22.

15. A. J. P. Taylor, *Beaverbrook* (Harmondsworth, Middlesex, England: Penguin Books, 1974), 85, 110, 132, and 141.

16. For detailed description of the New Journalism and explanation of its origins see: J. O. Baylen, "The 'New Journalism' in late Victorian Britain," *Australian Journal of Politics and History* 17 (December 1972): 371; Lucy Brown, *Victorian News and Newspapers* (Oxford: Clarendon Press, 1985), 30-32; G. A. Cranfield, *The Press and Society from Caxton to Northcliffe* (London: Longman, 1978), chaps. 1 and 2; Lee, *Origins of the Popular Press in England*, 117-30; and "The Beginnings of the New Journalism," Part I of Joel H. Wiener, ed., *Papers for the Millions: The New Journalism in Britain, 1850s to 1914*, (New York: Greenwood Press, 1988), 1-87.

17. The *Daily Mail*'s circulation figures for 1896-1929 are listed in Hamilton Fyfe, *Northcliffe: An Intimate Biography* (1930; reprint, New York: AMS Press, 1969), 110.

18. An Old Journalist, "New Journalism," *Cornhill* 122 (1909), 443.

19. Tony Mason, "Sporting News, 1860-1914," in *The Press in English Society from the Seventeenth to the Nineteenth Centuries*, eds. Michael Harris and Alan Lee (Rutherford, N.J.: Fairleigh Dickinson Press, 1986), 175-76.

20. "New Journalism," 445.

21. The *Daily Telegraph* was London's first morning newspaper priced at one penny, and according to office records, by 1888 its daily circulation reached 300,000. Cambrose, *British Newspapers and Their Controllers*, 27.

22. See for instance, reference to it in Maxwell, "Old Lamps for New" and Kurt von Stutterheim, *The Press in England* (London: George Allen & Unwin, 1934), 187.

23. R. A. Scott-James, *The Influence of the Press* (London: S. W. Partridge & Co., c. 1913), 233.

24. Strachey to John Buchan, 19 June 1908, John St. Loe Strachey Papers, 3/2/35, House of Lords Record Office, London. Hereafter cited as Strachey Papers.

25. Edward Porritt, "The Value of Political Editorials," *Sell's Dictionary of the World's Press* (1910): 508.

26. Quoted in George Boyce, "The Fourth Estate: The Reappraisal of a Concept," in *Newspaper History from the Seventeenth Century to the Present Day*, ed. George Boyce, James Curran, and Pauline Wingate (London: Constable, 1978), 3.

27. "The World's Press," *Sell's Dictionary of the World's Press* (1901): 24.

28. Boyce, "The Fourth Estate," 6-40. Numerous reasons exist to question the proposition that the press was a Fourth Estate. It can be argued that the press was not and never has been free of government and commercial influences. Indeed, the Victorian press played a major role in what can broadly be called the political machine. There is good reason to doubt the wisdom of applying the general label "professional" to Victorian journalists, although there were men among them who would have dignified any profession at any time. Nor can one accept the idea that the

various organs of the press represented or appealed to public opinion as such. They all had their special audiences, and they quarreled among themselves regarding all the great controversies of the day. Was the press, moreover, capable of making its weight felt in matters of government policy? Could it initiate or produce changes in that policy? It would be more correct to say that the influence that any journal or alignment of journals exerted on government policy varied according to time, personalities, and circumstances. Considering abolition of the stamp duty on newspapers and the ending of other taxes on advertisement and paper that the press won in the mid-nineteenth century, the expansion it experienced in national life, the growth of democratic processes of government, and the increased political importance attached to public opinion, one can understand the appeal that the theory of the press as the Fourth Estate would have to the Victorians. That does not, however, make the myth any more real. Nevertheless, it is possible to go too far in discounting the theory, for the press was an important factor in the Victorian relationship between politicians, parties, and the public.

29. H. A. Gwynne to A. J. Balfour, 6 May 1911, A. J. Balfour Papers, Add. MS. 49797, British Library of the British Museum, London. Hereafter cited as Balfour Papers.

CHAPTER 2: THE IMPERIAL JOURNALISTS

1. Koss, *Rise and Fall of the Political Press*, 2: 7.
2. David Ayerst, *Garvin of the Observer* (London: Croom Helm, 1985), 7-8.
3. Ibid., 11.
4. Quoted in ibid., 17.
5. Quoted in ibid., 15.
6. Ursula Slaghek, J. L. Garvin's daughter, personal interview by author, 14 June 1977, London.
7. Ayerst, *Garvin of the Observer*, 11.
8. J. L. Garvin, "Parnell and His Power," *Fortnightly Review* 70 (December 1898): 873, 878, and 882.
9. J. L. Lockhart and Hon. C. M. Woodhouse, *Cecil Rhodes: The Colossus of Southern Africa* (New York: Macmillan Company, 1963), 162.
10. Garvin to St. Loe Strachey, 13 February 1909, Strachey Papers, S/7/1/1.
11. Ayerst, *Garvin of the Observer*, 18-19.
12. Garvin to the editor of the *Irish Weekly*, 26 September 1907, James Louis Garvin Papers, Harry Ransom Humanities Research Center, the University of Texas at Austin. Hereafter cited as Garvin Papers.
13. Garvin to Austen Chamberlain, 20 October 1910, Sir Austen Chamberlain Papers, AC 8/6/38, University of Birmingham, Birmingham, England. Hereafter cited as Austen Chamberlain Papers.

14. In one instance Lloyd George made the taunt. In Garvin's own words: "Mr. Lloyd George . . . at the National Liberal Club denounced Mr. Garvin as a Parnellite turned Imperialist. There was a sufficient amount of partial truth in the description to make it as misleading as possible." "Autobiographical Fragment," n.d., Garvin Papers, Works.

15. Alfred M. Gollin, *"The Observer" and J. L. Garvin, 1908-1914: A Study in Great Editorship* (London: Oxford University Press, 1960), 6.

16. Leo Maxse to Garvin, 8 November 1906, Garvin Papers.

17. Linton Andrews and H. A. Taylor, *Lords and Laborers of the Press: Men Who Fashioned the Modern British Newspaper* (Carbondale, Ill.: Southern Illinois Press, 1970), 83.

18. Garvin to Northcliffe, 1 December 1906, Northcliffe Papers, Box 84, British Library of the British Museum, London. Hereafter cited as Northcliffe Papers, BL.

19. Strachey to Lord Grey, 16 January 1904 and 11 June 1908, papers of Earl Grey, 4th Earl, University of Durham, Department of Paleography and Diplomatic, Durham, England. Hereafter cited as Earl Grey Papers.

20. John St. Loe Strachey, *The Adventure of Living* (New York: G. P. Putnam's Sons, 1922), 66-72 and 365. See also Strachey to Lord Grey, 16 January 1904, Lord Grey Papers, and Strachey to Lord Grey, 26 October 1907, Strachey Papers, S/7/7/11.

21. After rebellions in Upper and Lower Canada startled London in 1837, Lord Durham was dispatched to British North America as governor general and high commissioner. Two years later he submitted his famous report that is a landmark document in the development of self-government in the colonies and eventually in their transformation into commonwealth status.

22. Strachey, *Adventure of Living*, 36.

23. Strachey to President Theodore Roosevelt, 1 October 1904, Theodore Roosevelt papers, Microfilm Series 1, Reel 48, Manuscript Division, Library of Congress, Washington, D.C. Hereafter cited as Roosevelt Papers.

24. Strachey, *Adventure of Living*, 37.

25. Strachey to Lord Grey, 24 June 1907, Strachey Papers, S/7/7/10.

26. Strachey, *Adventure of Living*, 300-301.

27. Ibid., 4.

28. Ibid., 424.

29. J. St. Loe Strachey, "The Ethics of Journalism," Paper read before the Pan-Anglican Congress, 1908, and published in *Educational Review* 36 (September 1908), 127.

30. Strachey to Northcliffe, 20 September 1912, Strachey Papers, S/11/4.

31. J. A. Spender, *Life, Journalism and Politics,* 2 vols. (New York: Frederick A. Stokes Company, 1927), 1: 2.

32. Ibid., 8.

33. Quoted in Wilson Harris, *J. A. Spender* (London: Cassell and Company, 1946), 8.

34. J. A. Spender, *New Lamps and Ancient Lights* (London: Cassell and Company, 1940), 231.

35. W. T. Stead, "His Majesty's Public Councillors," 595.

36. Max Beloff, *Imperial Sunset*, vol. 1, *Britain's Liberal Empire, 1897-1921* (New York: Alfred A. Knopf, 1970), 141, n. 2.

37. Spender, *Life, Journalism and Politics,* 1: 91-94.

38. Spender to Lord Rosebery, 22 October 1904, John Alfred Spender Papers, Add. MS 46387, British Library of the British Museum, London. Hereafter cited as Spender Papers.

39. Alfred F. Havighurst, *Radical Journalist: H. W. Massingham (1860-1942)* (London: Cambridge University Press, 1974), 175.

40. See for instance, Koss, *Rise and Fall of the Political Press*, 2: 55 and 101.

41. Edward Grey to Spender, 27 August 1905, Spender Papers, Add. MS 46389.

42. J. A. Spender, *The Public Life*, 2 vols. (London: Cassell and Company, 1925), 2: 107-9.

43. Spender to Asquith, 7 October 1926, MS. Asquith 35, fol. 269, Bodleian Library, Oxford. Hereafter cited as Asquith Papers.

44. Spender, *The Public Life*, 2: 131.

45. Williams, *Dangerous Estate*, 91 and 93.

46. See for instance, Valentine Chirol to Cecil Spring Rice, n.d. October 1906, Sir Cecil Spring Rice Papers, 1/11/34, Churchill College Library, Cambridge; and G. E. Buckle to Geoffrey Robinson, 14 August 191, Geoffrey Dawson Papers, unclassified, Bodleian Library, Oxford. Hereafter cited as Dawson Papers, Bodleian.

47. *Nation*, 18 July 1908, 567.

48. Williams, *Dangerous Estate*, 100.

49. Ibid., 113.

50. The assassinations referred to occurred in Phoenix Park, Dublin. There on May 6, 1882, Lord Frederick Cavendish, the new chief secretary for Ireland, and Thomas Henry Burke, the under-secretary, were killed. A special commission appointed in 1888 to inquire into *The Times*' accusations against Parnell exonerated him of the most serious charges *The Times* had made. The commission made its final report on February 13, 1890.

51. T. H. Ward, "Mr. G. E. Buckle," MS, 1922, G. E. Buckle Papers, Archives of *The Times*, London. Hereafter cited as Buckle Papers.

52. Ibid.

53. Buckle to Geoffrey Dawson, 24 February 1919, quoted in John Evelyn Wrench, *Geoffrey Dawson and Our Times* (London: Hutchinson, 1955), 174.

54. J. B. Capper, "An Appreciation of an Old Colleague," MS, n.d., Buckle Papers.

55. Ward, "Mr. G. E. Buckle," Buckle Papers.

56. [Stanley Morison], *The History of The Times*, vol. 3, *The Twentieth Century Test, 1884-1912* (1947; reprint ed., Nendeln, Liechtenstein: Kraus Reprint, 1971), 114.

57. Reginald Pound and Geoffrey Harmsworth, *Northcliffe* (New York: Frederick A. Praeger, Publishers, 1960), 451.

58. [Morison], *The History of The Times*, 3: 128.

59. [Morison],*The History of The Times*, vol. 4, Part I, *The 150th Anniversary and Beyond, 1912-1948* (London, 1952; reprint ed., Nendeln, Liechtenstein, 1971), 2.

60. E. H. C. Moberly Bell, *The Life and Letters of C. F. Moberly Bell* (London: The Richards Press, 1927), 201.

61. Buckle to Geoffrey Robinson (Dawson), 23 December 1912, Buckle Papers.

62. Julian Amery, "Introduction," to *The Leo Amery Diaries*, vol. 1, ed. John Barnes and David Nicholson (London: Hutchinson, 1980), 11.

63. Joseph Chamberlain to the Hononable G. H. Reid, 13 June 1902, Joseph Chamberlain Papers, JC 17/2/5, University of Birmingham, Birmingham, England. Hereafter cited as Joseph Chamberlain Papers.

CHAPTER 3: THE CRUCIBLE OF TARIFF REFORM

1. Bernard Porter, *Critics of Empire: British Radical Attitudes to Colonialism in Africa, 1895-1914* (London: Macmillan, 1968), 63.

2. Ronald Hyam, *Britain's Imperial Century, 1815-1914: A Study of Empire and Expansion* (New York: Harper & Row Publishers, 1976), 98.

3. Mansergh, *The Commonwealth Experience*, 1: 159.

4. Ibid., 160.

5. R. C. K. Ensor, *England, 1870-1914* (1936; reprint ed., Oxford: Clarendon Press, 1952), 389.

6. Joseph Chamberlain to the Honorable G. H. Reed, 13 June 1902, Joseph Chamberlain Papers, JC 17/2/5.

7. Amy Strachey, *St. Loe Strachey: His Life and His Paper* (London: Victor Gollanez, 1930), 93.

8. Quoted in Richard A. Rempel, *Unionists Divided: Arthur Balfour, Joseph Chamberlain, and the Unionist Free Traders* (Newton Abbot, Devon, England: David & Charles Publishers, 1972), 18.

9. Quoted in Donald Read, *Edwardian England*, 125.

10. Churchill to Alfred Harmsworth, 1 September 1913, Northcliffe Papers, BL, vol. 4.

11. Buckle to Robinson, 23 December 1912, Buckle Papers.

12. Buckle to Robinson, 14 August 1912, quoted in Wrench, *Geoffrey Dawson and Our Times*, 83-84.

13. L. S. Amery, *My Political Life*, vol. 1, *England Before the Storm, 1896-1914* (London: Hutchinson, 1953), 238.

14. Bell, *Life and Letters of C. F. Moberly Bell*, 225.

15. *The History of The Times*, 4, Part I: 6-7.

16. Bell to A. Ireland, 5 August 1903, C. F. Moberly Bell Papers, Letter Books, Archives of *The Times*, London. Hereafter cited as Moberly Bell Papers.

17. Buckle to J. S. Sandars, 11 January 1915, J. S. Sandars Papers, MS. Eng. hist. C 776, fols. 31-35, Bodleian Library, Oxford. Hereafter cited as Sandars Papers.

18. Buckle, untitled biographical notes, MS, n.d., Buckle Papers, box 4.

19. W. A. S. Hewins, *The Apologia of an Imperialist: Forty Years of Empire Policy* (London: Constable & Co., 1929), 67.

20. *The Times*, 15 May 1903, 12.

21. Ibid., 15 June 1903, 11.

22. Ibid., 3 July 1903, 9.

23. Ibid., 11 July 1903, 11.

24. Ibid., 21 May 1903, 9.

25. Ibid., 29 May 1903, 7.

26. Ibid., 21 May 1903, 9.

27. Ibid., 14 August 1903, 7.

28. Ibid., 7 October 1903, 7.

29. Ibid., 14 August 1903, 7.

30. Beloff, *Imperial Sunset*, 1: 95.

31. *The Times*, 15 June 1903, 11.

32. Ibid., 25 June 1903, 9.

33. Ibid., 22 August 1903, 7.

34. Ibid.

35. Bell, *Life and Letters of C. F. Moberly Bell*, 226, and Bell to Strachey, 9 February 1905, Strachey Papers, S/2/9/11.

36. Hewins, *The Apologia of an Imperialist*, 66.

37. Ibid., 69.

38. Barnes and Nicholson, eds., *The Leo Amery Diaries*, 1: 47.

39. Amery, *My Political Life*, I, 255.

40. Julian Amery, *The Life of Joseph Chamberlain*, vol. 5, *Joseph Chamberlain and the Tariff Reform Campaign* (London: Macmillan, 1969), 295. For Amery's own pro-Tariff Reform views, see his *The Fundamentals of Free Trade* (London: The National Review Office, 1906).

41. Ibid., 294.

42. *The History of The Times*, 4, Part I: 10.

43. Bell to Strachey, 1 June 1904, Strachey Papers, S/2/9/10.

44. Bell to Strachey, 28 May 1904, Strachey Papers, S/2/9/9.

45. When Canada granted preference to Britain, Germany responded with extra duties against Canadian goods. See *The Times*, 21 May 1903, 9; and 28 May 1903, 7.

46. Bell to Strachey, 9 February 1905, Strachey Papers, S/2/9/11.

47. [J. L. Garvin], *Imperial Reciprocity: A Study of Fiscal Policy* (London: The Daily Telegraph, 1903), 1-2. This is a series of Garvin's articles, revised and reprinted from the *Daily Telegraph*.

48. Calchas [J. L. Garvin], "Cobdenism and Capital," *The Fortnightly Review* 80 (June and August 1903): 20.

49. [Garvin], *Imperial Reciprocity*, 35.

50. Ibid., 40-41.

51. Calchas [J. L. Garvin], "Cobdenism and the Colonies," 194.

52. [Garvin], *Imperial Reciprocity*, 5.

53. Ibid., 27.

54. Ibid., 15.

55. Ibid., 106.

56. Ibid., 110.

57. Calchas [J. L. Garvin], "Cobdenism and Capital," 33.

58. Calchas [J. L. Garvin], "Imperial Reciprocity," 16 and 22.

59. The Assistant-Editor [J. L. Garvin], "The Economics of Empire," *The National Review* 42, Special Supplement in two Parts (September and December 1903): I, 23-24.

60. [Garvin], *Imperial Reciprocity*, 28.

61. [Garvin], "The Economics of Empire," II, 11.

62. [Garvin], *Imperial Reciprocity*, 24.

63. Ibid., 6.

64. Ibid., 15.

65. Ibid., 17.

66. Ibid., 6.

67. Ibid., 78, 8, and 88-89.

68. Ibid., 91 and 98.

69. Ibid., 107.

70. Ibid., 67.

71. [Garvin], "The Economics of Empire," II, 35.

72. J. L. Garvin, "The Maintenance of Empire: A Study in the Economics of Power," Introduction to C. S. Goldman, *The Empire and the Century* (London: John Murray, 1905), 123.

73. Ibid., 120.

74. Ibid., 124.

75. Ibid., 140.

76. Ibid., 142.

77. [Garvin], "The Economics of Empire," II, 60.

78. Ibid., II, 61.

79. Ibid., II, 62.

80. The articles appeared in the *Daily Telegraph* between May and August 1903.

81. Joseph Chamberlain, MS of a preface for a second edition of Garvin's *Imperial Reciprocity*, 2 March 1905, Joseph Chamberlain Papers, JC 20/4/70.

82. Strachey, *Adventure of Living*, 380-83.

83. Ibid., 384-85. Strachey's wife, however, fixed the time of her husband's break with Chamberlain a few years before by claiming it ended with the Anglo-Boer

War. Amy Strachey, *St. Loe Strachey*, 93. St. Loe's own correspondence with Chamberlain confirms her interpretation.

84. Chamberlain to Strachey, 23 January 1899, Strachey Papers, S/4/6/10.

85. *Spectator*, 10 October 1903, 549.

86. Garvin, "The Maintenance of Empire," 139.

87. For an account of the rise and fall of the Unionist Free Traders, see Rempel, *Unionist Divided.*

88. Ibid., 91 and 149.

89. *Spectator*, 25 July 1903, 124-25.

90. Ibid., 10 October 1903, 548-49.

91. Ibid., 8 August 1903, 192-93.

92. Ibid., 23 January 1904, 116.

93. Ibid., 30 May 1903, 848.

94. Ibid., 20 June 1903, 964.

95. Ibid., 11 July 1903, 45-46.

96. Ibid., 11 June 1903, 908-9.

97. Ibid., 23 May 1903, 808-9.

98. Ibid., 7 November 1903, 752.

99. Ibid., 4 July 1903, 6.

100. J. St. Loe Strachey, "Free Trade and the Empire," in *The Empire and the Century*, 144, 156, and 158.

101. Chirol to Strachey, 30 June 1903, Strachey Papers, S/4/9/10.

102. Spender, *Life, Journalism and Politics*, 1: 118.

103. Strachey, *Adventure of Living*, 448.

104. Ibid., 440-41 and 451-53.

105. Spender, *Life, Journalism and Politics*, 109.

106. Ibid., 116-17.

107. Spender's articles were unsigned. But he was a writing editor, and it is probable that the bulk of these leaders were his own. The arguments in them correspond to those in a signed article he wrote for the *Fortnightly Review* (July–December 1903) and to those set forth in his *A Modern Journal: Being The Diary of Greville Minor for the Year of Agitation* (London: Methuen & Co., 1904).

108. *Westminster Gazette*, 3 December 1903, 1.

109. Spender, *Life, Journalism and Politics*, 111.

110. *Westminster Gazette*, 29 May 1903, 1.

111. Ibid., 18 May 1903, 1.

112. Ibid., 29 May 1903, 1.

113. Ibid., 19 June 1903, 1.

114. Ibid., 5 November 1903, 1.

115. Ibid., 7 October 1903, 1.

116. Ibid., 27 June 1903, 1.

117. Ibid., 16 May 1903, 1.

118. Ibid., 18 May 1903, 1.

119. Ibid., 22 June 1903, 1.

120. Ibid., 7 October 1903, 1.

121. Ibid., 26 June 1903, 1.

122. [Garvin], *Imperial Reciprocity*, 11.

123. *Westminster Gazette*, 14 July 1903, 1.

124. Ibid., 18 May 1903, 1.

125. Ibid., 14 December 1903, 1.

126. Spender, *Life, Journalism and Politics*, 1: 112.

127. The *Annual Register: A Review of Public Events at Home and Abroad for the Year 1903* (London: Longmans, Green, and Co., 1904), 235.

128. Chamberlain to Colonel Denison, 2 December 1903, Joseph Chamberlain Papers, JC 18/4/3.

CHAPTER 4: CHINESE LABOR IN SOUTH AFRICA: PART I, 1903-1904

1. The term "the Boers" refers to Afrikaners. Mainly of Dutch descent, these people, along with other emigrants from France, Germany, and Scandinavia who mixed with them, formed the original white population of South Africa. They settled there in the seventeenth century. Gradually they became known as "Africaander," which later became modified into "Afrikaner." During the time of the present study, they were known as "Boers" or "the Dutch." Sometimes the term "Boers," which literally means farmer, carried a harsh connotation, referring to those Afrikaners who opposed the British before and during the war (1899-1902).

2. When the Europeans first arrived at the Cape, they found the area thinly populated by a pigmy race of aboriginal Stone Age people, the Bushmen (today the preferred name for them is "San"), and a more advanced group of pastoral people, the Hottentots (today the preferred name is "Khoikhoi" or "Khoi"). The Bushmen clashed with the Europeans and gradually retreated to the fringes of the white settlement, and there they continued their nomadic existence. For a while after the arrival of the Europeans, the Hottentots traded with the new settlers. They served as middlemen between them and Xhosa, who were located farther to the east. However, defeat in battle in the seventeenth century and the ravages of two smallpox epidemics in 1713 and 1755 depleted their numbers, and the survivors lost their separate cultural identity. By the 1770s most had become laborers for the Europeans in one capacity or another and many had intermarried with slaves or other people to become part of the Cape Coloured, a group composed of a mixture of descendants of Bushmen, Hottentots, whites, and slaves that might be identified as neither white nor Bantu nor Asiatic.

The Bantu were far more formidable than any of the previously mentioned indigenous groups. As a term "Bantu" can refer to a family of languages spoken by millions of people in South Africa. It also came to denote the people who spoke those languages such as the Basuto, Bechuana, Mashona, Matabele, Swazi, Xosa, and Zulu. In time "Bantu" replaced "Kaffir," a term derived from the Arabic word for "non-believer" as a reference to the people of those nations because of the objectionable connotation of the latter term. Since World War II the appellations "Bantu" or "native" have come into common usage, although the Bantu themselves would prefer to be known as "Africans." In the decade before World War I, however, the terms "Kaffirs" and "natives" were normally used unless the comment referred to a particular Bantu nation such as the Zulu.

3. T. R. H. Davenport, *South Africa: A Modern History* (Toronto: University of Toronto Press, 1978), 7.

4. Ibid., 40.

5. Before 1882 the term of residency for acquiring the franchise in the Transvaal was one year. In that year the Republic raised it to five years. In 1890 it became fourteen years. See Eric A. Walker, *A History of Southern Africa*, 3d ed. (London: Longman's, 1968), 435-36.

6. Concise accounts of the coming of the war can be found in Davenport, *South Africa*, 121-39; G. H. L. LeMay, *British Supremacy in South Africa, 1899-1907* (Oxford: Clarendon Press, 1965), 1-37; and Bernard Porter, *The Lion's Share: A Short History of British Imperialism, 1850-1970* (London: Longman, 1975), 167-78.

7. James Morris, *Farewell the Trumpets: An Imperial Retreat* (London: Harcourt Brace Jovanovich, A Helen Kurt Wolff Book), 89.

8. Cecil Headlam, *The Milner Papers: South Africa, 1899-1905*, 2 vols. (London: Cassell & Company, 1931), I, 221.

9. Ibid., II, 501.

10. Ibid., 503.

11. Quoted in Donald Denoon, *A Grand Illusion: The Failure of Imperial Policy in the Transvaal Colony during the Period of Reconstruction, 1900-1905* (London: Longman, 1973), 105.

12. Milner's postwar policy and energetic administration produced a number of accomplishments. Boer fighting men and their families were rehabilitated, railroads repaired and extended, bridges built, drainage systems in cities and towns built or improved, telephone communications enlarged, agricultural experiment stations established, etc. See Vladimir Halperin, *Lord Milner and the Empire* (London: Odhams Press, 1952), 127-28 and 132-35.

13. The above discussion of the labor problem is based on Peter Richardson, "Chinese Indentured Labour in the Transvaal Gold Mining Industry, 1904-1910," in *Indentured Labour in the British Empire, 1834-1920*, ed. Kay Saunders (London: Croom Helm, 1984), 60-67, and Peter Richardson, *Chinese Mine Labour in the Transvaal* (London: Macmillan Press, 1982), 8-20. In addition, Donald Denoon points out that the search for labor extended all the way to Nigeria, Morocco, and Egypt. Still it failed to produce new recruits. Some laborers were found in Nyasaland, but there settler hostility developed to resist the exportation of their own labor supply. When the Foreign Office did agree to a recruitment of 1,000 laborers from

Nyasaland, the results were disastrous. The laborers intensely disliked the work and one in ten died as a result of new climate, diet, and disease. Denoon, *A Grand Illusion*, 131.

14. Ibid., 134.

15. Benjamin Sacks, *South Africa: An Imperial Dilemma* (Albuquerque: University of New Mexico Press, 1967), 53.

16. Amery, *My Political Life*, I, 175.

17. Buckle to Walter, 2 July 1902, Buckle Papers.

18. Buckle, untitled autobiographical notes, MS, n.d., Buckle Papers.

19. Chirol to Geoffrey Robinson (Dawson), 24 January 1908, Geoffrey Dawson Papers, box 1906-1918, Archives of *The Times*, London. Hereafter cited as Dawson Papers (TA).

20. *The Times*, 16 January 1903, 7.

21. *Spectator*, 17 January 1903, 77-78.

22. *Westminster Gazette*, 28 January 1903, 1, and 11 February 1903, 1.

23. Ibid., 2 March 1903, 1.

24. "Touts" were labor recruiters. The labor associations had been formed to control recruiting costs and unevenness of labor supply. The Rand Native Labour Association dated from 1896 and the Witwatersrand Native Labour Association from 1900.

25. *Westminster Gazette*, 30 January 1903, 1.

26. Headlam, *Milner Papers*, 2: 477.

27. Denoon, *A Grand Illusion*, 477, and Sacks, *South Africa: An Imperial Dilemma*, 32.

28. Ibid., 32-34.

29. Benjamin Sacks has indicated that the Colonial Office understood that Wybergh's resignation was due to his inefficient management of his department and that he had resigned under pressure but used the Asiatic question as an excuse to save face. With Monypenny the case leaves no room for doubt. As the former correspondent for *The Times* and as editor of the Johannesburg *Star*, the largest and most influential English-language paper in the Transvaal, he was a respected journalist and one who held firm convictions. A group of mineowners, however, owned the *Star*, and Monypenny opposed the introduction of Chinese labor. He resigned over the policy of Chinese immigration and said so with the bluntest of language when he announced his resignation in the paper. Sacks, *South Africa: An Imperial Dilemma*, 49-50.

30. Buckle, untitled autobiographical note, MS, n.d., Buckle Papers.

31. Chirol to Strachey, 30 June 1903, Strachey Papers, S/4/9/10.

32. *The Times*, 29 October 1903, 7.

33. Ibid., 23 November 1903, 9.

34. Ibid., 3 December 1903, 8.

35. *Spectator*, 24 October 1903, 640-41.

36. *Westminster Gazette*, 3 November 1903, 1.

37. Ibid., 24 November 1903, 1.

38. Ibid., 4 December 1903, 1.

39. L. S. Amery, ed., *The Times History of the War in South Africa*, 7 vols. (London: Sampson Low, Marston and Company, 1909), VI, 119, and Walker, *A History of South Africa*, 511. It appears that the critics' claims were valid to some extent. See Denoon, *A Grand Illusion*, 146-47.

40. *The Times*, 26 February 1904, 7.

41. Ibid., 5 February 1904, 7.

42. Denoon, *A Grand Illusion*, 137.

43. *The Times*, 7 January 1904, 7; 1 February 1904, 9; 17 February 1904, 9; and 2 April 1904, 7.

44. Ibid., 1 January 1904, 7.

45. Ibid., 5 February 1904, 7.

46. Ibid., 5 March 1904, 11.

47. *Spectator*, 13 February 1904, 247-48.

48. Ibid., 26 May 1904, 480-81.

49. Bell to Strachey, 1 June 1904, Strachey Papers, S/2/9/10.

50. *Westminster Gazette*, 25 January 1904, 1.

51. Ibid., 17 February 1904, 1.

52. Ibid., 17 February 1904, 1; 18 February 1904, 1; and 25 March 1904, 1.

53. Ibid., 18 February 1904, 1.

54. Ibid., 21 March 1904, 1.

55. John Wilson, *CB: A Life of Sir Henry Campbell-Bannerman* (London: Constable, 1973), 399.

56. *Westminster Gazette*, 18 April 1904, 1.

57. Ibid., 19 March 1904, 1.

58. *The Times*, 13 February 1904, 11.

59. Ibid., 26 February 1904, 7.

60. Ibid., 14 May 1904, 11.

61. Ibid., 13 February 1904, 11.

62. Ibid., 12 March 1904, 11.

63. Ibid., 5 March 1904, 11.

64. Ibid., 8 April 1904, 7.

65. Ibid., 14 May 1904, 11.

66. Ibid., 12 May 1904, 11.

67. Milner to Lyttelton, 30 November 1904, Alfred Lyttelton Papers, CHAN I, 2/23, Churchill Library, Cambridge. Hereafter cited as Lyttelton Papers.

CHAPTER 5: CHINESE LABOR IN SOUTH AFRICA: PART II, 1905-1906

1.*Outlook*, 7 January 1905, 35.

2. Ibid., 4 March 1905, 272.

3. *The Times*, 12 January 1905, 9.

4. *Westminster Gazette*, 14 January 1905, 1.

5. Ibid., 2 March 1905, 1.

6. *Spectator*, 21 January 1905, 74.

7. Sacks, *South Africa: An Imperial Dilemma*, 79.

8. Ibid., 67. Flogging was officially discontinued in June 1905 because of widespread protest against it. See Richardson, *Chinese Mine Labour in the Transvaal*, 174.

9. *The Times*, 5 September 1905, 10.

10. Ibid., 13 September 1905, 7.

11. *Westminster Gazette*, 5 September 1905, 1, and 13 September 1905, 1.

12. *Spectator*, 30 September 1905, 458.

13. *The Times*, 2 January 1906, 7.

14. Garvin to Amery, n.d., March 1905, Garvin Papers.

15. Garvin to Milner, 21 December 1905, MS. Milner Papers, box 217, fol. 62, Bodleian Library, Oxford.

16. *Outlook*, 6 January 1906, 11.

17. Ibid., 20 January 1906, 77. "Peak-cowled inquisitors" was a reference to the Education Act of 1902 by which the state assumed the expenses for church schools at the primary and secondary levels. The act aroused Nonconformist indignation. "Twopenny loaves" was a reference to the Free Traders argument that Tariff Reform would increase the price of bread. Augustine Birrell was president of the Board of Education from 1905 to 1907.

18. *Westminster Gazette*, 22 December 1905, 1; 23 December 1905, 1; 28 December 1905, 1; and 9 January 1906, 1.

19. Ibid., 10 January 1906, 1.

20. Ronald Hyam, *Elgin and Churchill at the Colonial Office* (London: Macmillan, 1968), 66.

21. There was some discrepancy regarding the number of licenses issued. Some sources placed the figure as low as 11,000.

22. Hyam, *Elgin and Churchill*, 76.

23. *The Times*, 17 January 1906, 9.

24. Ibid., 21 February 1906, 9.

25. Ibid., 24 February 1906, 11.

26. Hyam, *Elgin and Churchill*, 77.

27. *The Times*, 2 March 1906, 9.

28. *Outlook*, 3 March 1906, 290.

29. *Westminster Gazette*, 22 December 1905, 1.

30. Ibid., 9 January 1906, 1.

31. Ibid., 21 February 1906, 1.

32. Ibid., 28 February 1906, 1.

33. Ibid., 15 March 1906, 1.

34. A. M. Gollin, *Proconsul in Politics: A Study of Lord Milner in Opposition and in Power* (London: Anthony Blond, 1964), 77-80.

35. There is some reason to believe that Milner had not sanctioned the flogging at all, that Evans, in fact, had introduced the idea to cover himself. See Terence H. O'Brien, *Milner: Viscount Milner at St. James's and Cape Town* (London: Constable, 1979), 234.

36. Gollin, *Proconsul in Politics*, 84-85.

37. Ibid., 88-89.

38. *The Times*, 12 March 1906, 9.

39. *Outlook*, 24 March 1906, 398.

40. Strachey to Asquith, 17 March 1906, Strachey Papers, S/11/6/5.

41. Asquith to Strachey, 20 March 1906, ibid.

42. *Spectator*, 24 March 1906, 444.

43. *Westminster Gazette*, 22 March 1906, 1.

44. Ibid., 30 March 1906, 1.

45. *Annual Register: A Review of Public Events at Home and Abroad for the Year 1906* (London: Longmans, Green, and Co., 1907), 75.

46. Regarding the House of Lords' statement of appreciation, Gollin believes it was an action that placed the Lords on a road that "led them to reject a Budget in 1909 and to pass the Parliament Act in 1911." Gollin, *Proconsul in Politics*, 94. O'Brien, however, claims that contemporaries saw it more as "an assertion of Imperialist faith against 'Little England.'" O'Brien, *Milner*, 231. The comments of the pro-Milner press at the time substantiate O'Brien's claim.

47. Bell, *Life and Letters of C. F. Moberly Bell*, 218-19.

48. Chirol to Robinson, 24 January 1908, Dawson Papers (TA).

49. J. Amery, *Joseph Chamberlain*, 4: 334-35, and 5: 281. In fact, in 1908 Chamberlain confided to Lord Selborne that he "entirely disapproved of Chinese Labour & told Milner and Lyttelton of my settled opinion." Ibid., 6: 927.

50. Calchas [Garvin], "The Ebbing Tide of Liberalism," *Fortnightly Review*, new series, 82 (August 1907): 180. See also "X" [Garvin], "Mr. Balfour and the Unionist Party: A Study and a Postscript," *Fortnightly Review*, new series, 81 (March 1906): 42.

51. J. A. Spender, *Great Britain: Empire and Commonwealth* 1886-1935 (London: Cassell, 1936), 218.

52. Ibid., 254.

53. Sacks, *South Africa: An Imperial Dilemma*, 90, and G. B. Pyrah, *Imperial Policy and South Africa, 1902-1910* (London: Oxford University Press, 1955), 192. See also H. W. Massingham's "Persons and politics" and "Pictures in Parliament" columns in the *Daily News* from 1903 to 1906, and his special series of articles on South Africa in the *Daily News*, January 1906.

54. Charles Sydney Goldman, "South Africa and Her Labour Problem," *The Nineteenth Century* 55 (May 1904): 858.

55. Amery, *The Times History of the War*, 6: 124.

56. Quoted in Roderick Jones, "The Black Peril in South Africa," *The Nineteenth Century* 55 (May 1904): 712.

57. E. Edmund Garrett, "Lord Milner and the Struggle for South African Union: A Retrospect, 1897-1905," *The National Review* 46 (December-February, 1905-1906): 1116.

58. *Westminster Gazette*, 11 February 1903, 1, and *Spectator*, 17 January 1903, 78.

59. *Westminster Gazette*, 26 May 1904, 1, and *Spectator*, 15 October 1904, 546.

60. Garrett, "Lord Milner and the Struggle for South African Union," 1117.

61. Sacks, *South Africa: An Imperial Dilemma*, 338.

62. Pyral, *Imperial Policy and South Africa, 1902-1910*, 198.

63. *Westminster Gazette*, 24 November 1903, 1, and *Spectator*, 17 January 1903, 77.

64. Ibid., 3 March 1906, 324.

65. Supporters of the policy argued that Chinese labor saved the Transvaal from ruin. Critics noted that the departure of the Chinese failed to bring economic disaster to the area. Between 1904 and 1910 the native labor force in the Transvaal increased to 195,216 (more than double its 1904 status) while white labor increased from 12,414 to 21,305. Sacks, *South Africa: An Imperial Dilemma*, 104. Supporters said the Chinese stayed long enough to "materially affect the balance of population" (Amery, *The Times History of the War*, VI, 127) while critics argued that those two increases in labor proved that the need for Chinese labor had been contrived.

CHAPTER 6: THE POLITICAL RECONSTRUCTION OF SOUTH AFRICA: PART I, 1905-1906

1. Milner to Lyttelton, 6 February 1905, Lyttelton Papers, CHAN I, 2/23.

2. Milner to Lyttelton, 23 January 1905, ibid., 2/24.

3. Headlam, *Milner Papers*, 2: 522.

4. Ibid., 502.

5. Ibid., 523.

6. *The Times*, 18 November 1904, 6.

7. Headlam, *Milner Papers*, 2: 531.

8. Its counterpart in the Orange River Colony, the *Orangie Unie*, was founded in July 1905.

9. Headlam, *Milner Papers*, 2: 531.

10. Ibid., 2: 520-21.

11. Ibid., 522 and 526-27.

12. The normal monetary qualification was £100 earnings a year or property valued at £100 with an annual rental of £10.

13. Quoted in Amery, *The Times History of the War*, 6: 167.

14. LeMay, *British Supremacy in South Africa*, 178.

15. *The Times*, 11 January 1905, 7.

16. Ibid., 17 January 1905, 7.

17. Ibid., 31 January 1905, 9.

18. *Outlook*, 14 January 1905, 43 and 1 January 1905, 80-81.

19. *Spectator*, 7 January 1905, 5-6.

20. *The Times*, 26 April 1905, 7.

21. *Outlook*, 29 April 1905, 598-99.

22. *Spectator*, 29 April 1905, 630-31.

23. *Westminster Gazette*, 26 April 1905, 1.

24. Ibid., 27 April 1905, 1.

25. John Wilson, *CB: A Life of Sir Henry Campbell-Bannerman* (London: Constable, 1973), 476.

26. See for example, Ronald Hyam and Ged Martin, *Reappraisals in British Imperial History* (Toronto: Macmillan of Canada, 1975), 162-72; Randolph Churchill, *Winston S. Churchill*, vol. 2, *Young Statesman: 1901-1914* (Boston: Houghton Mifflin Company, 1967), 145-48; and Wilson, *CB*, 481-83.

27. Hyam and Martin, *Reappraisals*, 173 ff., and Wilson, CB, 484.

28. Hyam and Martin, *Reappraisals*, 179.

29. It had been decided to send a committee rather than the commission that Campbell-Bannerman originally proposed at the Cabinet meeting of February 8.

30. Robinson to Amery, 9 April 1906, Dawson Papers (TA).

31. Amery to Robinson, 21 May 1906, ibid.

32. *The Times*, 25 January 1906, 9.

33. Ibid., 11 April 1906, 9.

34. Ibid., 27 January 1906, 9.

35. Ibid., 25 January 1906, 9.

36. Ibid., 4 June 1906, 7.

37. Ibid., 24 July 1906, 9.

38. Ibid., 26 July 1906, 7.

39. Ibid., 30 July 1906, 9.

40. *Outlook*, 3 March 1906, 291.

41. Ibid., 23 June 1906, 835.

42. Ibid., 10 March 1906, 291.

43. Ibid., 3 March 1906, 291.

44. Ibid., 17 February 1906, 222-23.

45. Ibid., 21 July 1906, 78-79.

46. *Spectator*, 3 March 1906, 324.

47. Ibid., 21 July 1906, 81-82.

48. Ibid., 28 July 1906, 118-19.

49. *Westminster Gazette*, 25 January 1906, 1.

50. Ibid., 27 January 1906, 1.

51. Ibid., 12 February 1906, 1.

52. Ibid., 25 January 1906, 1.

53. Ibid., 27 February 1906, 1.

54. Ibid., 26 March 1906, 1.

55. Ibid., 17 July 1906, 1.

56. Ibid., 26 July 1906, 1.

CHAPTER 7: THE POLITICAL RECONSTRUCTION OF SOUTH AFRICA: PART II, 1906-1914

1. Quoted in *The Times*, 1 August 1906, 7-8.

2. Quoted in ibid., 7 and 10, and in H. W. Massingham, "Pictures in Parliament," *Daily News*, 1 August 1906, 7-8.

3. Quoted in *The Times*, 1 August 1906, 6.

4. Ibid., 9.

5. *Outlook*, 4 August 1906, 146-47.

6. *Spectator*, 4 August 1906, 153.

7. *Westminster Gazette*, 1 August 1906, 1.

8. *The Times*, 24 July 1906, 9. See also ibid., 4 June 1906, 7, and 17 July 1906, 9.

9. Amery to Robinson [Dawson], 21 May 1906, Dawson Papers (TA).

10. Amery, *The Times History of the War*, 6: 182-83.

11. Robinson to Amery, 7 January 1907, Dawson Papers (TA).

12. *Westminster Gazette*, 27 February 1906, 1.

13. Pyral, *Imperial Policy and South Africa, 1902-1910*, 87-93.

14. Milner to Lyttelton, 16 March 1906, Lyttelton Papers, CHAN I, 2/23.

15. J. A. Spender, *The Life of the Right Hon. Sir Henry Campbell-Bannerman*, 2 vols. (London: Hodder and Stoughton, 1923), 2: 244.

16. Amery to Robinson, 31 May 1907, Dawson Papers (TA).

17. *The Times*, 7 January 1908, 7.

18. Chirol to Robinson, 24 January 1908, Dawson Papers (TA).

19. Strachey to Lord Grey, 11 June 1908, Earl Grey Papers.

20. Robinson to Amery, 15 October 1906, Dawson Papers (TA).

21. Amery to Lord Grey, 15 July 1907, Earl Grey Papers.

22. Garvin, "Imperial and Foreign Affairs," *Fortnightly Review* 92 (2 August 1909): 194.

23. Robinson to W. C. Bridgeman, M. P., 24 February 1909, Dawson Papers, Bodleian.

24. Amery to Lord Grey, 3 April 1909, Earl Grey Papers.

25. *The Times*, 1 July 1909, 5.

26. *Westminster Gazette*, 11 February 1905, 1. See also ibid., 12 May 1905, 1, and 31 May 1910, 1.

27. *The Times*, 31 May 1910, 11.

28. *Observer*, 10 October 1909, 8.

29. *Spectator*, 15 May 1909, 764.

30. *Westminster Gazette*, 31 May 1910, 1.

31. Quoted in E. A. Benians, Sir James Butler, and C. E. Carrington, *The Cambridge History of the British Empire*, vol. 3, *The Empire-Commonwealth* (Cambridge: Cambridge University Press, 1959), 373.

32. *The Times*, 26 July 1909, 9, and 28 July 1909, 13.

33. Ibid., 20 August 1909, 9.

34. *Observer*, 1 August 1909, 6.

35. *Spectator*, 10 July 1909, 43-44.

36. *Westminster Gazette*, 4 August 1909, 1.

37. Churchill to Lord Crewe, 3 June 1909, Lord Crewe Papers, Box C/7, Cambridge University Library. Hereafter cited as Crewe Papers.

38. See for example, *The Times*, 1 October 1913, 7; 19 November 1913, 9; 8 November 1913, 9; 23 December 1913, 9; *Westminster Gazette*, 7 November 1913, 1; and 18 November 1913, 1; *Spectator*, 22 November 1913, 855-56. Garvin addressed the matter in the *Pall Mall Gazette* where he relegated it to a paragraph in "Notes of the Day," 18 November 1913, 6.

39. *Spectator*, 23 November 1913, 855-56.

40. *The Times*, 9 February 1914, 7.

41. *Westminster Gazette*, 3 February 1914, 1.

42. Robinson to Amery, 22 April 1907, Dawson Papers (TA).

43. *Westminster Gazette*, 7 November 1913, 1.

CHAPTER 8: THE QUEST FOR IMPERIAL PARTNERSHIP: PART I, 1907-1910

1. There had been some earlier unofficial meetings before the first official conference met. See W. David McIntyre, *The Commonwealth of Nations: Origins and Impact, 1869-1971* (Minneapolis: University of Minnesota Press, 1977), 30, 155, and 157.

2. Mansergh, *The Commonwealth Experience*, 1: 152.

3. Quoted in ibid., 155.

4. Originally scheduled for 1906, the conference was postponed late in 1905 owing to the difficulty the prime ministers of Australia and New Zealand said they would have in attending a conference the following spring. *The Times*, 2 June 1906, 11.

5. Regarding Balfour's conversion to Tariff Reform, see Alan Sykes, *Tariff Reform in British Politics, 1903-1913* (Oxford: Clarendon Press, 1979), chaps. 5 and 6.

6. *The Times*, 16 February 1907, 9.

7. Ibid., 14 March 1907, 9, and 19 March 1907, 9.

8. Garvin, "Time and the Contract: A Foreword to the Colonial Conference," *The National Review* 49 (April 1907): 207-18.

9. Ibid., 211.

10. Ibid., 216.

11. Garvin to Maxse, 6 March 1907, Leopold Maxse Papers, vol. 457/S 495, West Sussex Record Office, Chichester. Hereafter cited as Maxse Papers.

12. Garvin to Maxse, n.d., 1907, ibid., vol. 457/S 623.

13. *Westminster Gazette*, 16 February 1907, 1.

14. Ibid., 28 March 1907, 1.

15. Ibid., 4 April 1907, 1.

16. Ibid., 11 April 1907, 1.

17. Quoted in Rempel, *Unionist Divided*, 172.

18. *Spectator*, 6 April 1907, 521.

19. *Westminster Gazette*, 16 April 1907, 1.

20. *The Times*, 27 February 1907, 9.

21. The conference was held at the Colonial Office and presided over by Lord Elgin, assisted by Churchill and other members of the government as the discussion might merit. Seven self-governing colonies (i.e., Australia, Canada, Cape Colony, Natal, Newfoundland, New Zealand, and the Transvaal) sent representatives. The Orange River Colony sent no representative because its new constitution had not been in place in time to allow for it. Benians, Butler, and Carrington, *The Cambridge History of the British Empire*, 3: 422-23.

22. McIntyre, *The Commonwealth of Nations*, 164.

23. *The Times*, 15 April 1907, 9.

24. Ibid., 22 April 1907, 11.

25. Ibid., 3 May 1907, 9.

26. Ibid., 10 May 1907, 13.

27. *Westminster Gazette*, 15 April 1907, 1.

28. Ibid., 16 April 1907, 1.

29. Ibid., 27 April 1907, 1.

30. Ibid., 16 May 1907, 1.

31. McIntyre, *The Commonwealth of Nations*, 164.

32. *The Times*, 21 May 1907, 7.

33. The election returns for January 1910 were Liberals 275, Unionists 273, Irish nationalists 82, and Labour 40. The Unionists had hoped for a majority of about 100, based on a study of by-elections. The returns for December 1910 were Liberals 272, Unionists 272, Irish nationalists 84, and Labour 42. Ensor, *England, 1870-1914*, 418 and 427.

34. Harmsworth to Lord Rosebery, 1 September 1903, Northcliffe Papers, BL, vol. 2. See also A. M. Gollin, "Lord Northcliffe's Change of Course," *Journalism Quarterly* 39 (Winter 1962): 48.

35. Ibid., 49-50.

36. *Daily Mail*, 2 May 1907, 6.

37. Bell, *Life and Letters of C. F. Moberly Bell*, 225 and 232.

38. Bell to Garvin, 15 November 1907, Garvin Papers.

39. Buckle to Maxse, 6 July 1906, Maxse Papers, vol. 455/S 242.

40. *The Times*, 22 November 1907, 11, and 17 January 1908, 11.

41. Ibid., 2 April 1908, 9.

42. Ibid., 15 November 1907, 11.

43. Ibid., 29 June 1908, 11. See also ibid., 2 April 1908, 9; 12 January 1910, 11; and 9 July 1910, 13.

44. Ibid., 2 January 1909, 9.

45. Ibid., 2 May 1910, 11.

46. Garvin to Northcliffe, 1 December 1906, Northcliffe Papers, BL, vol. 84.

47. Quoted in Gollin, *"The Observer" and J. L. Garvin, 1908-1914*, 6.

48. Lord Grey to Henderson, 20 January 1908, Earl Grey Papers.

49. Ayerst, *Garvin of the Observer*, 73.

50. Gollin, *"The Observer" and J. L. Garvin, 1908-1914*, 93.

51. Ibid., 106.

52. Garvin to Northcliffe, 4 August 1909, Northcliffe Papers, BL, vol. 84.

53. Garvin to Northcliffe, 5 August 1909, ibid.

54. Gollin, *"The Observer" and J. L. Garvin 1908-1914*, 120.

55. Ibid., 117.

56. Ibid., 185 and 196.

57. Ibid., 201.

58. Ibid., 207.

59. *Observer*, 16 October 1910, 8.

60. Ibid., 23 October 1910, 11, and 30 October 1910, 8.

61. Garvin to Austen Chamberlain, 22 and 25 October 1910, Garvin Papers.

62. Garvin to Balfour, 17 October 1910 and Balfour to Garvin, 22 October 1910, Balfour Papers, Add. MS. 49795.

63. Lord Grey to Moreton Frewen, 1 November 1910, Morton Frewen Papers, box 22, Manuscript Division, Library of Congress, Washington, D.C. Lord Grey repeated that phrase in a number of letters he wrote at this time.

64. Gollin, *"The Observer" and J. L. Garvin, 1908-1914*, 266. The role of Garvin in the referendum tactic is fully recounted in ibid., 258-75.

65. Garvin to Strachey, n.d., February 1909, Strachey Papers, S/7/1/1.

66. Garvin to Strachey, 13 February 1909, ibid.

67. Garvin to Sandars, 29 January 1910, Sandars Papers, MS. Eng. hist. C 760, fols. 29-30.

68. *Observer*, 3 May 1908, 6.

69. Ibid., 13 September 1908, 6.

70. Ibid., 31 January 1909, 6.

71. Ibid., 16 May 1909, 8.

72. Ibid., 21 August 1910, 6.

73. Ibid., 16 October 1910, 9.

74. The "Valentine Letters" refers to an exchange of correspondence between Balfour and Joseph Chamberlain that was published on 14 February 1906. In his letter, Balfour agreed to support a tariff and colonial preference as party policy. Rempel, *Unionist Divided*, 169.

75. *Spectator*, 30 July 1907, 76.

76. Strachey to Lord Rosebery, 22 July 1907, Strachey Papers, S/12/7/2, and Strachey to Margot Asquith, 5 July 1907, Strachey Papers, S/11/7/16.

77. Strachey to Margot Asquith, 9 December 1908, ibid., S/11/7/20.

78. Margot Asquith to Strachey, 6 December 1908, ibid.

79. See pp. 157-58.

80. Strachey to Balfour, 30 November 1909, Balfour Papers, Add.MS. 49797.

81. Balfour to Strachey, 8 December 1909, ibid.

82. Strachey to Lord Grey, 24 March 1910, Strachey Papers, S/7/7/17.

83. Strachey to A. V. Dicey, 22 November 1910, ibid., S/5/5/20.

84. Quoted in Gollin, *"The Observer" and J. L. Garvin, 1908-1914*, 267.

85. Richard A. Cosgrove, *The Rule of Law: Albert Venn Dicey, Victorian Jurist* (Chapel Hill: University of North Carolina Press, 1980), 107 and 109. Strachey consulted A. V. Dicey frequently. The two men engaged in a regular and exacting correspondence from 1894 to 1922.

86. Strachey to Garvin, 16 February 1909, Strachey Papers, S/7/1/1.

87. Harris, *J. A. Spender*, 82, 88, and 94. Harris lists Spender's chief political friends as H. H. Asquith, James Bryce, Earl of Crewe, Lord Fitzmaurice, Herbert Gladstone, Sir Edward Grey, Richard Haldane, Reginald McKenna, and John Morley. Ibid., 85. All but Bryce, who was ambassador to the United States, were members of the Liberal Cabinet at some point during these years.

88. *Westminster Gazette*, 28 July 1909, 1.

89. Ibid., April 1909, 1.

90. Ibid., 7 December 1908, 1.

91. Ibid., 24 May 1910, 1.

92. Ibid., 26 July 1910, 1.

93. Ibid., 9 August 1910, 1, and 17 August 1910, 1.

94. Ibid., 14 November 1910, 1.

95. For example, see Arthur J. Marder, *From Dreadnought to Scapa Flow: The Royal Navy in the Fisher Era*, vol. 1, *The Road to War, 1904-1914* (London: Oxford University Press, 1961), 43-71 and 105-110; Jonathan Steinberg, *Yesterday's Deterrent: Tirpitz and the Birth of the German Battle Fleet* (New York: Macmillan Company, 1965); and E. L. Woodward, *Great Britain and the German Navy* (Oxford: Clarendon Press, 1935), 203-40. For a consideration of the broader context of the growing Anglo-German hostility see Paul Kennedy, *The Rise of Anglo-German Antagonism* (London: Allen and Unwin, 1980). A treatment of the naval crisis featuring the roles of various politicians and publicists from the national rather than imperial perspective can be found in A. J. A. Morris, *The Scaremongers: The Advocacy of War and Rearmament, 1896-1914* (London: Routledge and Kegan Paul,

1984). For a brief account of this large subject see Michael Howards, "The Edwardian Arms Race" in Donald Read, ed., *Edwardian England* (New Brunswick, N.J.: Rutgers University Press, 1982), 145-61.

96. The "Kruger telegram" refers to a message the kaiser sent to President Kruger of the Transvaal congratulating him on the successful repealing of Dr. Jameson's ill-fated and subsequently famous raid. The kaiser sent his message of 3 January 1896, the day after the raid collapsed. His telegram caused a serious crack in the already troubled Anglo-German relations.

97. When the "Young Turks" staged their successful rebellion against Abdul Hamid's government, Bulgaria seized the opportunity to declare its complete independence from the Ottoman Empire and Austria-Hungary annexed Bosnia and Herzegovina. The latter had repercussions on Russian foreign policy, which in the wake of defeat in the Russo-Japanese War had become more active in the Balkans. The fact that Austria-Hungary acted unilaterally in the annexation caused anxiety across Europe.

98. The naval estimates for 1906-1907 were down by £1,520,000 from the previous year, and the saving for 1907-1908 was £450,000. Original estimates for 1909-1910, although they reduced new construction, proposed an increase of £900,000. Peter Rowland, *The Last Liberal Governments: The Promised Land, 1905-1910* (London: Barrie & Rockliff, Cresset Press, 1968), 250.

99. Fisher to Spender, 6 February 1909, Spender Papers, Add. MS. 46390.

100. For a detailed account of the Fisher-Garvin correspondence, see Gollin, *"The Observer" and J. L. Garvin*, 64-92.

101. Garvin to Stead, 25 March 1909, Garvin Papers.

102. Garvin to Northcliffe, 6 April 1909, Northcliffe Papers, BL, vol. 84.

103. Criticism of the "scare" began almost immediately with Norman Angell's *The Great Illusion* (1909; 4th, rev. ed., New York: G. P. Putnam's Sons, 1913), 68-81. He contended that it was ridiculous to believe that Dreadnoughts could guarantee trade. Strangely enough Angell, a socialist and a critic of Northcliffe's big navy ideas, was also the manager of his Continental *Daily Mail*. Pound and Harmsworth, *Northcliffe*, 291. F. W. Hirst, a Gladstonian Radical who edited the weekly *Economist* starting in 1907, made the naval crisis of 1909 one of the panics covered in his *The Six Panics and Other Essays* (London: Methuen & Co., 1913), 59-102. He considered the excitement over Dreadnoughts absurd, and his book became a source used by later anti-war writers. See, for instance, G. Lowes Dickinson, *The International Anarchy, 1904-1914* (New York: Century Co., 1926), 377-78.

104. Quoted in Havighurst, *Radical Journalist*, 187.

105. Quoted in Trevor Wilson, ed., *The Political Diaries of C. P. Scott, 1911-1928* (Ithaca, N.Y.: Cornell University Press, 1970), 37. Churchill later wrote of his opposition to the increased expenditures at this time saying it was based on his belief that the figures on German construction were exaggerated. But he also reflected that although he and Lloyd George were right "in the narrow sense, we were absolutely

wrong in relation to the deep tides of destiny." Winston Churchill, *The World Crisis*, vol. 1 (1923; reprint ed., New York: Charles Scribner's Sons, 1951), 32 and 33.

106. Edward David, ed., *Inside Asquith's Cabinet: From the Diaries of Charles Hobhouse* (New York: St. Martin's Press, 1978), 77.

107. Most historians accept the idea that the German threat was real. See, for example, D. F. Fleming, *The Origins and Legacies of World War I* (Greenwich, Conn.: Fawcett Publications, 1968), 110-118; Paul Kennedy, *Strategy and Diplomacy, 1870-1945* (London: George Allen & Unwin, 1983), 109-126; and Zara Steiner, *Britain and the Origins of the First World War* (New York: St. Martin's Press, 1977), 48-59. Morris, however, while admitting that British official sources had reason to believe that the Germans had accelerated their naval building, contends that a "naval scare had been worked" on the British public. In his opinion the chief culprits were Admiral Fisher, who was always willing to exaggerate figures to get more Dreadnoughts, and Garvin, whose powerful editorials inspired the navalist press to greater adamancy as they stoked the fires of the panic. He believes that Garvin may have acted from patriotic motives or perhaps to embarrass the Liberals and thus gain a political edge for Unionists. But, while he acknowledges the editor's journalistic genius, he also claims he was "not a little mad and bad." *The Scaremongers*, 174, 175, 179, and 183. Concerning Germany's behavior, one might recall her actions regarding the First Moroccan Crisis (1905), the Second Hague Peace Conference (1907), and the Second Moroccan Crisis (1911), plus the pronouncements of the German Naval League that number around 900,000 and spoke with a swagger that hardly reassured the British as well as the brusqueness of German diplomacy in the years surrounding the crisis.

108. The colonial premiers who attended the conference were Joseph Ward (New Zealand), John Xavier Merriman (Cape Colony), and Abraham Fischer (Orange Free State). Ward was the only premier attending from a senior dominion. The others sent representatives of cabinet rank. They were joined in London by various British experts. Asquith opened the conference and claimed that it was a purely consultative one.

109. Morris, *The Scaremongers*, 203-17.

110. *Spectator*, 17 June 1911, 912.

111. *Westminster Gazette*, 5 November 1910, 1.

112. *Spectator*, 5 August 1910, 203.

113. Ibid., 17 June 1911, 2.

114. *Westminster Gazette*, 15 July 1910, 1.

115. *The Times*, 24 March 1909, 11.

116. Garvin, "Imperial and Foreign Affairs: A Review of Events," *Fortnightly Review* 93 (January 1910): 33.

117. A. J. A. Morris, *Edwardian Radicalism, 1900-1914: Some Aspects of British Radicalism* (London: Routledge & Kegan Paul, 1974), 163.

118. Austen Chamberlain to Michael Herbert, 17 December 1902, The Honorable Sir Michael Herbert Papers, Official Diplomatic Correspondence, box 51, Wilton House.

119. Two previous cable lines had been completed to South Africa by 1889. For a discussion of this subject see Benians, Butler, and Carrington, *The Cambridge History of the British Empire*, II, 473-74.

120. *Westminster Gazette*, 2 May 1907, 1. The "All Red Line" would have required the government's subsidizing the fast steamers between England and Canada. Sir Wilfred pointed out that five years before the government had subsidized steamer lines between Liverpool and New York, implying that Britain could do for the Empire what she had done already for trade between Britain and a foreign country. In response the *Westminster* noted that those subsidized ships were to be available for Admiralty use in time of war, but it admitted Laurier's basic point. The *Gazette* concluded that this case should be examined on its own merits and that its Free Trade principles would not rule out its support of using public funds for imperial purposes. *Westminster Gazette*, 2 July 1907, 1.

121. *The Times*, 15 May 1907, 9. See also ibid., 23 November 1908, 9.

122. Harry Brittain joined the staff of the *Standard* and the *Evening Standard* in 1902, but he is better remembered as a director of various other publications including the *Illustrated London News*. He was the founder of The Pilgrims and served for years as its secretary. In 1918 he was made a Knight Commander of the British Empire for his services in World War I, and he was made a Companion of the Order of St. Michael and St. George in 1924.

123. Sir Harry Brittain, *Pilgrims and Pioneers* (London: Hutchinson & Co., 1946), 181.

124. Buckle to Bell, 17 November 1908, Buckle Papers.

125. Northcliffe to Sir John Fisher, 13 March 1909, Northcliffe Papers, BL, vol. 7.

126. Brittain to Northcliffe, 26 June 1909 and 10 July 1912, ibid., vol. 14. It might be reasoned that Brittain would naturally be generous in his comments to Northcliffe in correspondence with him and that no doubt he hoped for the press baron's continued support for the Empire Press Union. But Sir Harry took the same line when writing his memoirs many years after Northcliffe died. Brittain, *Pilgrims and Pioneers*, 192-95. In fact, Brittain was even more generous to Northcliffe in his rough notes for those memoirs. See Sir Harry Brittain Papers, box 2, British Library of Political and Economic Science, London.

127. All of these addresses can be found in Thomas H. Hardman, *A Parliament of the Press: The First Imperial Press Conference* (London: Horace Marshall & Son, 1909).

128. Ibid., 2.

CHAPTER 9: THE QUEST FOR IMPERIAL PARTNERSHIP: PART II, 1911-1913

1. *Westminster Gazette*, 26 April 1909, 1.

2. Strachey to Lord Grey, 1 July 1908, Earl Grey Papers.

3. Strachey to Lord Grey, 23 February 1906, Strachey Papers, S/7/7/5.

4. Northcliffe to F. S. Oliver, 17 November 1910, Northcliffe Papers, BL, vol. 13.

5. Northcliffe to Evelyn Wrench, 19 August 1913, ibid., vol. 70.

6. Lord Grey to Northcliffe, 7 December 1908, Earl Grey Papers.

7. Lord Grey to Lord Milner, 4 December 1908, ibid.

8. Northcliffe to Buckle, 13 February 1909, Northcliffe Papers, BL, vol. 13.

9. *Westminster Gazette*, 15 February 1911, 1. See also *Spectator*, 11 February 1911, 206.

10. *Daily Mail*, 30 January 1911, 6.

11. William G. Tyrrell to Bryce, 8 February 1911, MS. Bryce USA, vol. 31, fol. 97, Bodleian Library, Oxford. Tyrrell reported to Bryce that Northcliffe made this statement to him ten days before.

12. *The Times*, 28 January 1911, 11.

13. Northcliffe to Garvin, 2 February 1911, quoted in Gollin, *"The Observer" and J. L. Garvin*, 289.

14. Garvin to Northcliffe, 2 February 1911, Northcliffe Papers, BL, vol. 85. The Aitken referred to in the letter was William Maxwell Aitken (later Lord Beaverbrook), a Canadian living in England and a Tariff Reformer recently elected to Parliament. He opposed the so-called food tax at this time. He impressed Northcliffe who was somewhat under his influence at this point as well as that of Andrew Bonar Law. Gollin, *"The Observer" and J. L. Garvin*, 291-95.

15. Quoted in ibid., 284.

16. Northcliffe to F. S. Oliver, 9 February 1911, Northcliffe Papers, BL, vol. 13. The Leo mentioned in the quote was probably Leopold Maxse rather than Leopold Amery, since his name was paired with Garvin's.

17. The Committee of Imperial Defence (CID) was first formed in 1902 and was formally created in 1904. Although it addressed matters of imperial defense, it was a solely British group. It was a consultative and advisory group with no fixed membership, and it could be summoned by the prime minister who was its sole permanent member. In August 1909, dominion delegates attended a meeting of the CID at which the resolutions of the special Imperial Defence Conference were approved. John Edward Kendle, *The Colonial and Imperial Conferences, 1887-1911: A Study in Imperial Organization* (London: Longmans, 1967), 186-91.

18. *Observer*, 18 June 1911, 8. For Liberal opinion see *Westminster Gazette*, 7, 8, and 14 June 1911, 1, and *Spectator*, 17 June 1911, 915-16.

19. Stead to Garvin, 15 June 1911, Garvin Papers.

20. Robert Blake, *The Unknown Prime Minister: The Life and Times of Andrew Bonar Law, 1858-1923* (London: Eyre & Spottiswood, 1955), 533.

21. [Morison], *The History of "The Times,"* 3: 743 and 769.

22. The correspondence regarding his retirement is lengthy, involving a number of letters between Buckle, Northcliffe, and John Walter. They can be found mainly in the Buckle and Northcliffe Papers in the archives of *The Times*. Regarding the reasons for Buckle's retirement, Valentine Chirol, who was close enough to know, explained it this way. "I am just now congratulating myself more than ever that I retired from *The Times* when and as I did. For poor old Buckle has just been told to go with an abruptness which is really quite brutal. This between you and me, for as far as the public is concerned he resigns in accordance with his own desire which is just technically accurate. . . . Nor is it on account of his shortcomings that he has been shelved but similarly because he was not pliant enough to meet Northcliffe's views of what the Editor of one of his papers should be." (Sir Valentine Chirol to Lord Hardinge, 8 August 1912, Lord Hardinge Papers, vol. 70, fols. 252-56, Cambridge University Library, Cambridge, England)

23. Buckle to Bonar Law, 13 November 1911, Andrew Bonar Law Papers, 24/3/29, House of Lords Record Office, London. Hereafter cited as Bonar Law Papers.

24. Buckle to Bonar Law, 30 July 1912, ibid., 26/5/52.

25. Buckle to Robinson, 14 August 1912, Dawson Papers, Bodleian.

26. Northcliffe to Robinson, 8 August 1912, Northcliffe Papers, BL, vol. 91.

27. Buckle to Northcliffe, 1 March 1911, Buckle Papers.

28. Northcliffe to Buckle, 3 March 1911, Northcliffe Papers, BL, vol. 91. See also Northcliffe to Moberly Bell, 3 March 1911, ibid., vol. 106.

29. *Observer*, 7 April 191, 26.

30. Lord Grey to Laurier, 2 April 1913, Earl Grey Papers.

31. Laurier to Lord Grey, 14 June 1913, ibid.

32. *Westminster Gazette*, 30 August 1912, 1.

33. See, for example, *The Times*, 23 May 1913, 9; *Spectator*, 7 September 1912, 324; *Observer*, 25 May 1913, 12; and *Westminster Gazette*, 6 December 1912, 1.

34. Ibid., 9 December 1912, 1.

35. Austen Chamberlain to Mary E. Chamberlain, 17 January 1912, quoted in Sir Austen Chamberlain, *Politics from Inside: An Epistolary Chronicle, 1906-1914* (New Haven: Yale University Press, 1937), 408.

36. Amery, *My Political Life*, 1: 413-14.

37. Blake, *The Unknown Prime Minister*, 108-12.

38. Barnes and Nicholson, *The Leo Amery Diaries*, 1: 87.

39. Quoted in Sykes, *Tariff Reform in British Politics*, 268.

40. Strachey to Bonar Law, 19 December 1912, Strachey Papers, S/28/1/63.

41. Strachey to Bonar Law, 12 December 1912, ibid., S/28/1/26.

42. Strachey to Bonar Law, 19 December 1912, ibid., S/28/1/63.

43. L. S. Amery to H. G. Gwynne, 3 January 1913, Howell Arthur Gwynne Papers, box 14, Bodleian Library, Oxford.

44. Robinson to Chirol, 9 January 1913, Dawson Papers (TA).

45. Robinson to F. S. Oliver, 3 January 1913, Dawson Papers, Bodleian, box 63, fol. 100.

46. *The Times*, 2 January 1913, 9, and 6 January 1913, 7.

47. Ibid., 8 January 1913, 7.

48. Robinson to Chirol, 9 January 1913, Dawson Papers (TA).

49. Garvin to Bonar Law, 27 December 1912, Bonar Law Papers, 28/1/95.

50. Garvin to Astor, 19 December 1913, quoted in Gollin, *"The Observer" and J. L. Garvin*, 374.

51. Garvin to Maxse, 8 January 1913, Maxse Papers, vol. 468/S256.

52. *Observer*, 12 January 1913, 8.

53. Bonar Law to Henry Chaplin, 10 January 1913, quoted in Blake, *The Unknown Prime Minister*, 116.

54. Gollin, *"The Observer" and J. L. Garvin*, 384.

55. Quoted in Ayerst, *Garvin and the Observer*, 132.

56. Strachey to Bonar Law, 11 January 1913, Bonar Law Papers, 28/2/54.

57. Bonar Law to Lansdowne, 25 December 1912, ibid., 33/4/83.

58. Quoted in Taylor, *Beaverbrook*, 115.

59. Churchill to Garvin, 27 January 1912, Garvin Papers.

60. *Westminster Gazette*, 6 May 1912, 1.

61. *The Times*, 15 May 1913, 7.

CHAPTER 10: RETROSPECT

1. Robin W. Winks, "Problem Child of British History: The Empire-Commonwealth," in *Recent Views on British History: Essays on Historical Writing since 1966*, ed. Richard Schlatter (New Brunswick, N.J.: Rutgers University Press, 1984), 466.

2. Robert V. Kubicek, *Economic Imperialism in Theory and Practice* (Durham, N.C.: Duke University Press, 1979), 4.

3. Ibid., 203-4.

4. Garvin to Northcliffe, 1 December 1906, Northcliffe Papers, BL, vol. 84. See also Garvin "Upon the Necessity, the Method, and the Limits of Social Reform Considered as a Part of Unionist Policy," MS statement, n.d. [c. 1907], Garvin Papers, Works; and Garvin to Northcliffe, 4 August 1909, Northcliffe Papers, BL, vol. 84.

5. A. P. Thornton, *Doctrines of Imperialism* (New York: John Wiley and Sons, 1965), 63.

6. C. C. Eldridge, *England's Mission: The Imperial Idea in the Age of Gladstone and Disraeli, 1868-1880* (Chapel Hill: University of North Carolina Press, 1973), 254.

7. *The Times*, 24 May 1911, 11.

8. *Westminster Gazette*, 24 May 1911, 1, and 9 July 1910, 1.

9. Ibid., 2 November 1908, 1.

10. A. J. P. Taylor, *The Struggle for Mastery in Europe*, 1848-1918 (1954; reprint ed., Oxford: Clarendon Press, 1965), 438.

11. Eric Hobsbawn, *The Age of Empire, 1875-1914* (New York: Pantheon Books, 1987), chap. 1.

12. J. R. Seeley, The Expansion of England (1884; reprint ed., Chicago: University of Chicago Press, 1971), 107 and 134.

13. Buckle completed the *Life of Benjamin Disraeli* begun by W. F. Monypenny; Garvin wrote three volumes of the *Life of Joseph Chamberlain*; Spender wrote *Great Britain: Empire and Commonwealth, 1886-1935*, a biography of Campbell-Bannerman, plus a number of autobiographical and reflective studies. Aside from his memoirs, *The Adventure of Living*, Strachey wrote *The River of Life*, a diary of his thoughts between 1922 and 1924 that roamed through time touching on topics of history, classical literature, philosophy, and religion.

14. *The Times*, 2 July 1907, 9.

15. Ibid., 15 June 1910, 11.

16. For example, see *Westminster Gazette*, 20 August 1909, 1, and *Spectator*, 22 April 1905, 580.

17. Garvin to Northcliffe, 1 December 1906, Northcliffe Papers, BL, vol. 84.

18. Garvin to Austen Chamberlain, 20 October 1910, Austen Chamberlain Papers, AC 12/18.

19. Strachey, *The Adventure of Living*, 448. See also Strachey to Lord Grey, 24 June 1907, Strachey Papers, S/7/7/10.

20. Strachey, *The Adventure of Living*, 447.

21. Strachey to Robert Blatchford, 8 March 1910, Strachey Papers, S/2/11/1.

22. J. A. Spender, *The Foundations of British Policy* (London: Westminster Gazette, 1912), 2-3.

23. Chirol to W. Stead, 4 December 1909, Chirol Papers, box 2, Archives of *The Times*, London.

24. Chirol to Northcliffe, 12 October 1909, Northcliffe Papers, BL, vol. 99.

25. [Morison], *The History of "The Times,"* 3: 768 and 770.

26. William Beach Thomas, *The Story of the "Spectator," 1828-1928* (1928; reprint ed., Freeport, N.Y.: Books for Libraries Press, 1971), 87 and 102.

27. Koss, *Rise and Fall of the Political Press*, 2: 10.

28. Quoted in Andrews and Taylor, *Lords and Laborers of the Press*, 79.

29. Diary of John Burns, 26 February 1903, John Burns Papers, British Library, British Museum, London. The term "temperate and judicious" is Bryce's. Bryce to Spender, 22 March 1901, Spender Papers, Add. MS 46391.

30. William T. Stead, "The Man Who Has Been Dominating British Politics," MS. copy in Stead to Garvin, 27 September 1910, Garvin Papers.

31. Andrews and Taylor, *Lords and Laborers of the Press*, 89.

32. Garvin to Northcliffe, 1 December 1906, Northcliffe Papers, BL, vol. 84.

33. Spender, *New Lamps and Ancient Lights*, 234.

34. Strachey to Northcliffe, 20 September 1912, Strachey Papers, S/11/4.

35. Bell to P. E. Doble, 25 May 1904, Moberly Bell Papers. Garvin's statement is quoted in Andrews and Taylor, *Lords and Laborers of the Press*, 83.

36. Spender to Strachey, 4 February 1910, Strachey Papers, S/13/13/9.

37. Strachey, *The Adventure of Living*, 26.

38. Buckle to E. Chaplin, 8 November 1929, Garvin Papers, Misc.

39. Spender, *Life, Journalism and Politics*, 3: 10.

40. For examples of such acknowledgement, see *Observer*, 8 December 1912, 10, and *Westminster Gazette*, 26 May 1913, 1.

41. Mansergh, *The Commonwealth Experience*, 1: 15.

42. G. P. Jones and A. G. Pool, *A Hundred Years of Economic Development in Great Britain (1840-1940)*, (1940; reprint ed., London: Gerald Duckworth & Co., 1971), 194, and Paul Kennedy, *The Rise and Fall of the Great Powers: Economic Change and Military Conflict from 1500-2000* (New York: Random House, 1987), 228.

43. Porter, *The Lion's Share*, 353.

44. For example, see E. J. Hobsbawn, *Industry and Empire: The Making of Modern English Society, Vol. II: 1750 to the Present Day* (New York: Pantheon Books, 1968), 161-62, and opinion cited in Alan Sked, *Britain's Decline: Problems and Perspectives* (Oxford: Basil Blackwell, 1987), 18.

45. Ibid.

46. Kennedy, *Rise and Fall of the Great Powers*, 230.

47. The appeasers of the 1930s frequently cited dominion opinion as a justification for their policy. Martin Gilbert and Richard Gott, *The Appeasers* (Boston: Houghton Mifflin Company, 1963), 115. For a frank account of Geoffrey Robinson's [Dawson] attachment to dominion opinion when he was again editor of *The Times* in the 1930s and an appeaser, see [Morison], *The History of "The Times,"* vol. 4, Part 2, 1020-21.

48. Anthony Clayton, *The British Empire as a Superpower, 1919-39* (Athens: University of Georgia Press, 1986), 517.

Bibliography

MANUSCRIPT SOURCES

Leopold Amery Papers, Archives of *The Times*, London.

H. H. Asquith Papers, Bodleian Library, Oxford.

A. J. Balfour Papers, British Library, London.

C. F. Moberly Bell Papers, Archives of *The Times*, London.

R. D. Blumenfeld Papers, House of Lords Record Office, London.

Andrew Bonar Law Papers, House of Lords Record Office, London.

Sir Harry Brittain Papers, British Library of Political and Economic Science, London (additional papers by courtesy of Lady Brittain).

James Bryce Papers, Bodleian Library, Oxford.

G. E. Buckle Papers, Archives of *The Times*, London.

John Burns Papers, British Library, London.

Sir Henry Campbell-Bannerman Papers, British Library, London.

Sir Austen Chamberlain Papers, University of Birmingham.

Joseph Chamberlain Papers, University of Birmingham.

Sir Valentine Chirol Papers, Archives of *The Times*, London.

Lord Crewe (R.O.A. Crewe-Milnes, 2d Baron Houghton) Papers, Cambridge University Library.

Lord Cromer (Evelyn Baring, 1st Earl of Cromer) Papers, Public Record Office, London.

Lord Curzon (George Nathaniel Curzon, 5th Baron Scarsdale, Marquess Curzon of Kedleston) Papers, India Office Library, London.

Geoffrey (Robinson) Dawson Papers, Archives of *The Times*, London (additional papers by courtesy of Mrs. William Bell, since transferred to Bodleian Library, Oxford).

Robert Donald Papers, House of Lords Record Office, London.

Moreton Frewen Papers, Manuscript Division, Library of Congress, Washington, D.C.

J. L. Garvin Papers, Harry Ransom Humanities Research Center, University of Texas at Austin.

Lord Grey (Albert Henry George Grey, 4th Earl Grey) Papers, Department of Paleography and Diplomatic, University of Durham.

Sir Edward Grey Papers, Public Record Office, London.

H. A. Gwynne Papers, Bodleian Library, Oxford.

Lewis Harcourt Papers, Bodleian Library, Oxford.

Lord Hardinge (Charles Hardinge, Baron Hardinge of Penhurst) Papers, Cambridge University Library.

The Honorable Sir Michael Herbert Papers, Wilton House, Salisbury.

Alfred Lyttelton Papers, Churchill College Library, Cambridge.

H. W. Massingham Papers, Norfolk Record Office, Norwich.

Leopold Maxse Papers, West Sussex Record Office, Chichester.

Lord Milner (Sir Alfred Milner) Papers, Bodleian Library, Oxford.

Lord Northcliffe (Alfred Harmsworth) Papers, British Library (additional papers at the Archives of *The Times*), London.

Theodore Roosevelt Papers, Manuscript Division, Library of Congress, microfilm, Washington, D.C.

J. S. Sandars Papers, Bodleian Library, Oxford.

Lord Selborne (2d Earl of Selborne) Papers, Bodleian Library, Oxford.

J. A. Spender Papers, British Library, London.

Sir Cecil Spring Rice Papers, Churchill College Library, Cambridge.

J. St. Loe Strachey Papers, House of Lords Record Office, London.

John Walter IV Papers, Archives of *The Times*, London.

NEWSPAPERS AND JOURNALS

The *Clarion*. 1905-1914.

The *Daily Express*. 1902-1903.

The *Daily Mail*. 1896 and 1902-1914.

The *Daily Mail Over-Seas Edition*. 1904-1914.

The *Daily News*. 1903-1909.

The *Daily Telegraph*. 1896 and 1903.

The *Evening News*. 1906-1914.

The *Nation*. 1907-1914.

The *Observer*. 1908-1914.

The *Outlook*. 1905-1906.

The *Pall Mall Gazette*. 1912-1914.

The *Round Table*. 1910-1914.

The *Speaker*. 1903-1906.

The *Spectator*. 1896-1914.
The Times. 1900-1914.
The *Westminster Gazette*. 1896 and 1902-1914.

PARLIAMENTARY PAPERS

South Africa: Further Correspondence Relating to the Affairs of the Transvaal and the Orange River Colony, February 1904 (Cd. 1895).

Transvaal: Further Correspondence Regarding the Transvaal Labour Question, February 1904 (Cd. 1899).

Transvaal: Further Correspondence Relating to Labour in the Transvaal Mines, April 1905 (Cd. 2401).

Transvaal: Further Correspondence Relating to Labour in the Transvaal Mines, December 1905 (Cd. 2786).

Transvaal: Further Correspondence Relating to Labour in the Transvaal Mines, February 1906 (Cd. 2819).

Transvaal: Further Correspondence Relating to Labour in the Transvaal Mines, July 1906 (Cd. 3025).

Transvaal: Telegraphic Correspondence Relating to the Transvaal Labour Importation Ordinance, February 1904 (Cd. 1898).

OTHER DOCUMENTARY SOURCES

Cabinet Letters, Photographic Copies of Cabinet Letters in the Royal Archives, 1886-1916, Public Record Office, London, CAB 41.

W. D. Handcock, ed. *English Historical Documents, 1874-1914*. Vol.12. New York: Oxford University Press, 1977.

Report of the Commission: South Africa Native Affairs Commission, 1903-1905. Cape Town: Cape Times, Government Printers, 1905.

CONTEMPORANEOUS ARTICLES AND BOOKS BY THE FEATURED JOURNALISTS

Amery, L. S. *The Case Against Home Rule*. London: West Strand Publishing Co., 1912.

________. *The Fundamental Fallacies of Free Trade*. London: National Review Office, 1906.

________, ed. *The Times History of the War in South Africa, 1899-1902*. Vol. 2. London: Sampson Law, Marsten, 1909.

Bell, C. F. Moberly. *From Pharaoh to Fellah.* London: Wells Gardner, Darton & Co., 1888.

Buckle, George Earle. *The Life of Benjamin Disraeli, Earl of Beaconsfield.* Vols. 4 and 6 [Vol. 4 with W. F. Monypenny]. London: J. Murray, 1910-1920.

Calchas [Garvin, J. L.]. "Cobdenism and Capital." *Fortnightly Review* 80 (June 1903): 19-34.

________. "Cobdenism and the Colonies." *Fortnightly Review* 80 (August 1903): 193-211.

________. "The Ebbing Tide of Liberalism." *Fortnightly Review* 82 (August 1907): 177-92.

________. "The Eve of the Campaign." *Fortnightly Review* 80 (September 1903): 412-27.

________. "First Principles in the Far East." *Fortnightly Review* 81 (February 1904): 194-210.

________. "The Man of Emergency." *Fortnightly Review* 77 (February 1902): 181-83.

________."Mr. Chamberlain: The Protagonist and the Future." *Fortnightly Review* 80 (November 1903): 734-46.

________. "The Test of Efficiency." *Fortnightly Review* 78 (September 1902): 403-18.

Garvin, J. L. "The Boom—And After: Some Confessions and a Moral." *National Review* 50 (January 1908): 710-21.

________. *The Economic Foundations of Peace: Or World-Partnership as the Truer Basin of the League of Nations.* London: Macmillan & Co., 1919.

________. "The Economics of Empire." Parts 1, 2. *National Review*, Special Supplement (September, December 1903): 1-106, 1-62.

________. "The Falsehood of Extremes." *National Review* 50 (September 1907): 553-66.

________. "Free Trade as a Socialist Policy." *National Review* 50 (September 1907): 47-60.

________. "Imperial and Foreign Affairs." *Fortnightly Review* 91-93 (February 1909-June 1910). Commentary in series.

________. *Imperial Reciprocity: A Study of Fiscal Policy.* London: Daily Telegraph, 1903.

________. "Imperial Union and American Reciprocity." *Fortnightly Review* 95 (March 1911): 388-404.

________. "Introduction." In *The Observer, 1791-1921.* London: Observer House, 1921.

________. *The Life of Joseph Chamberlain.* Vol. 1, *1836-1885, Chamberlain and Democracy*. Vol. 2, *1885-1895, Disruption and Combat.* Vol. 3, *1885-1900, Empire and World Policy.* London: Macmillan and Co., 1933-1935.

________. "Lord Cromer and Free Trade." *National Review* 50 (February 1908): 581-99.

________. "The Maintenance of Empire." In *The Empire and the Century*, ed. C. S. Goldman, 69-143. London: John Murray, 1905.

________. "The Ocean Trust and National Policy." *Fortnightly Review* 77 (June 1902): 942-56.

________. "Parnell and His Power." *Fortnightly Review* 70 (December 1899): 872-83.

________. "A Party with a Future." *Fortnightly Review* 64 (September 1895): 325-39.

________. "Preference or McKinleyism: The Truth about the Australian Tariff." *National Review* 50 (October 1907): 204-17.

________. *Tariff or Budget: The Nation and the Crisis*. London: n.p., 1909.

________. "Time and the Contract: A Foreword to the Colonial Conference." *National Review* 49 (April 1907): 207-18.

________. "Why is Unionism Unpopular?" *Fortnightly Review* 22 (August 1899); 282-90.

X [Garvin, J. L.]. "Mr. Balfour and the Unionist Party: A Study and a Postscript." *Fortnightly Review* 81 (May 1906): 409-26.

Spender, J. A. "The First Six Months." *Contemporary Review* 89 (August 1906): 153-163.

________. *The Foundations of British Policy*. London: Westminster Gazette, 1912.

________. "Free Trade and Its Fruits." *Fortnightly Review* 74 (July-December 1903): 391-411.

________. *The Government of Mankind*. 2d ed. London: Cassell and Company, 1940.

________. *Great Britain: Empire and Commonwealth, 1886-1935*. London: Methuen and Co., 1936.

________. *The Indian Scene*. London: Methuen and Co., 1912.

________. *Life, Journalism and Politics*. 2 vols. London: Cassell and Company, 1927.

________. *The Life of the Right Hon. Sir Henry Campbell-Bannerman, G.C.B.* 2 vols. London: Hodder and Stoughton, 1923.

________. *Men and Things*. London: Cassell and Company, 1937; reprint ed., Freeport, N.Y.: Books for Libraries Press, 1968.

________. "The New Government and Its Problems." *Contemporary Review* 89 (April 1906): 457-71.

________. *New Lamps and Ancient Lights*. London: Cassell and Company, 1940.

________. *The Public Life*. 2 vols. London: Cassell and Company, 1925.

________, ed. *A Modern Journal: Being the Diary of Greville Minor for the Year of Agitation, 1903-1904*. London: Methuen and Co., 1904.

Strachey, J. St. Loe. *The Adventure of Living*. New York: G. P. Putnam's Sons, 1922.

________. *The Citizen and the State: Industrial and Social Life and the Empire*. 4th ed. London: Macmillan and Co., 1913.

________. "The Ethics of Journalism." *Educational Review* 36 (September 1908): 121-31.

________. "Free Trade and the Empire." In *Empire and the Century*, ed. C. S. Goldman, 144-59. London: John Murray, 1905.

________. *The Problems and Perils of Socialism: Letters to a Working Man.* London: Macmillan and Co., 1908.

________. *The River of Life*. London: Hodder and Stoughton, c. 1924.

________. "Ulster and Home Rule." *Nineteenth Century* 31 (June 1892): 875-84.

OTHER CONTEMPORANEOUS ARTICLES AND BOOKS

Angell, Norman. *The Great Illusion*. New York: G. P. Putnam's Sons, 1913.

The *Annual Register: A Review of Public Events at Home and Abroad*. Vols. 1903-1910. London: Longmans, Green, and Co., 1904-1911.

Arnold, Matthew. "Up for Easter." *Nineteenth Century* 123 (May 1887): 629-43.

Birnbaum, Doris. "Chinese Labour in the Transvaal." *Independent Review* 6 (June 1905): 142-53.

Blatchford, Robert. *Germany and England*. London: Associated Newspapers, 1911.

Bretton, Monk. "South African Loyalty." *Nineteenth Century* 61 (May 1907): 727-35.

Brittain, Harry. *Canada: There and Back*. London: Privately printed, 1908.

Burnham, Viscount (Harry Lawson). "The Influence of the Press on the Development of the Empire." *United Empire: The Royal Colonial Institute Journal*, new series, 14 (December 1923): 700-712.

Burns, John. "Slavery in South Africa." *Independent Review* 2 (May 1904): 594-611.

Cave, Albert. "The Newest Journalism." *Contemporary Review* 91 (January 1907): 18-32

Chesterton, Cecil. "An Open Letter to Mr. A. G. Gardiner." *New Witness* (17 December 1914): 54-55.

Courtney, Leonard. "The Making and Reading of Newspapers." *Contemporary Review* 79 (March 1901): 365-76.

Creswell, F. H. P. "The Transvaal Labour Problem." *Independent Review* 2 (February 1904): 124-36.

Curzon, George Nathaniel (1st Marquess). "The True Imperialism." *Nineteenth Century and After* 63 (January-June 1908): 151-65.

Devonshire, 8th Duke of (Cavendish, Spencer Compton). "The British Empire." *The Empire Review* 1 (February 1901): 4-7.

Dibble, G. Binney. *The Newspaper*. London: Williams and Norgate, c. 1913.

Dicey, Edward. "Journalism Old and New." *Fortnightly Review* 83 (May 1905): 904-18.

Escott, T. H. S. *Master of English Journalism*. 1911. Reprint. Folcroft, Penn. Folcroft Library Edition, 1970.

Flower, B. O. "W. T. Stead: A Journalist with Twentieth Century Ideas." *Arena* 25 (June 1901): 613-33.

Garrett, Edmund F. "Lord Milner and the Struggle for South African Union: A Retrospect, 1897-1905." *National Review* 46 (December-February 1905-1906): 1103-25.

________."Sir Alfred Milner and His Work." *Contemporary Review* 58 (August 1900): 153-71.

Goldman, Charles Sydney, ed. *The Empire and the Century*. London: John Murray, 1905.

________. "South Africa and Her Labour Problem." *Nineteeth Century* 55 (May 1906): 848-62.

Hales, Frank. "The Transvaal Labour Difficulties." *Fortnightly Review* 82 (July 1904): 110-23.

Hardman, Thomas H. *A Parliament of the Press: The First Imperial Press Conference*. London: Horace Marshall and Son, 1909.

Harmsworth, Alfred. "The Making of the Modern Newspaper." *World Today* 9 (December 1905): 1279-82.

________. "The Making of a Newspaper." In *Journalism as a Profession*, ed. Arthur Lawrence, 167-89. London: Hodder and Stoughton, 1903.

________. "The Simultaneous Newspapers of the Twentieth Century." *North American Review* 172 (January 1901): 72-90.

Hirst, F. W. *The Six Panics and Other Essays*. London: Methuen and Co., 1913.

Hobhouse, L. T. *Democracy and Reaction*. London: T. Fisher Union, 1904.

Hobson, John. "Capitalism and Imperialism in South Africa." *Contemporary Review* 77 (January 1900): 1-18.

________. *Imperialism, A Study*. New York: J. Pott and Company, 1902.

Jones, Roderick. "The Black Peril in South Africa." *Nineteenth Century* 55 (May 1904): 712-23.

"Journalism and the South African War." *Sell's Dictionary of the World's Press* (1901): 45-65.

Kinlock-Cooke, Sir C. "The British Parliament and the Transvaal." *Empire Review* 9 (April 1906): 197-213.

________. "Chinese Labour: And after the Tr ansvaal Constitution." *Empire Review* 11 (March 1906): 103-11.

________. "Chinese Labour in the Transvaal." *Empire Review* 10 (January 1906): 517-52, and 11 (February 1906): 13-44.

________. "Introductory Note." *Empire Review* 1 (February 1901): 1-3.

"The Last Colonial Conference: Minister of Proceedings of the Colonial Conference, 1907." *Quarterly Review* 207 (Summer 1907): 273-95.

"Lord Grey in Canada." *The Round Table* 1 (May 1911): 315-17.

Lucas, Sir C. P. *Greater Rome and Greater Britain*. Oxford: Clarendon Press, 1912.

Massingham, H. W. "Diary of the Week." Weekly commentary in the *Nation* (March 1907–January 1912).

________. *The London Daily Press*. New York: Fleming H. Revell Company, 1892.

________. "Persons and Politics." Weekly commentary in the *Speaker* (June 1903–March 1906).

________. "Pictures in Parliament." Continuing columns of parliamentary correspondence in the *Daily News* (1903–1906).

________. "The Revival of Parliament." *Contemporary Review* 89 (March 1906): 305-12.

________. "The South African Constitution." *World's Work* 13 (November 1906): 8297-8300.

________. "The Success of the Government." *Contemporary Review* 89 (June 1906): 867-75.

________. "An Unconstitutional Minister." *Contemporary Review* 89 (July 1905): 111-19.

________. "Victory and What to Do with It." *Contemporary Review* 89 (February 1906): 267-73.

Maxwell, William. "Old Lamps for New: Some Reflections on Recent Changes in Journalism." *Nineteenth Century and After* 75 (May 1914): 1085-96.

Mills, J. Saxon. "Chinese Labour and the Government." *Fortnightly Review* 85 (April 1906): 648-59.

"New Journalism." *Cornhill* 99 (1909): 441-48.

"Newspapers of the New Century." *Sell's Dictionary of the World's Press* (1901): 17-27.

Palmer, H. A. "The Outlook for Liberal Journalism from a Conservative Point of View." *Sell's Dictionary of the World's Press* (1902): 32-36.

Phillips, Evelyn March. "The New Journalism." *New Review* 13 (August 1895): 182-89.

Porritt, Edward. "The Value of Political Editorials." *Sell's Dictionary of the World's Press* (1910): 508-92.

Powell, Ellis T. "The Faith of an Imperialist." *United Empire* 3 (June 1912): 475-92.

Rea, Russell. "The Liberal Government and the Colonial Conference." *Nineteenth Century and After* 69 (May 1906): 801-10.

Russell, Sir Edward. "The Outlook for Liberal Journalism: From a Liberal Point of View." *Sell's Dictionary of the World's Press* (1902): 27-31.

Samuel, Herbert. "The Chinese Labour Question." *The Contemporary Review* 85 (April 1904): 457-67.

Scott-James, R. A. *The Influence of the Press*. London: S. W. Partridge and Co., c. 1913.

Seeley, J. R. *The Expansion of England*. 1884. Reprint. Chicago: University of Chicago Press, 1971.

Sheldrake, T. Swinborne. "The Building of the British Empire." *Sell's Dictionary of the World's Press* (1903): 17-40.

Stead, W. T. "His Majesty's Public Councillors: To Wit, the Editors of the London Daily Papers." *Review of Reviews* (British) 30 (December 1904): 593-606.

Stephen, Leslie. "Journalism." *Atlantic Monthly* 92 (November 1903): 611-22.

Thomson, H. C. "Chinese Labour and Imperial Responsibility." *Contemporary Review* 89 (January–June 1906): 430-70.

"The World's Press." *Sell's Dictionary of the World's Press* (1902): 2-26.

BIOGRAPHICAL LITERATURE, DIARIES, AND MEMOIRS

Amery, Julian. *The Life of Joseph Chamberlain.* Vols. 4, 5, and 6. London: Macmillan and Co., 1951-1969.

Amery, L. S. *My Political Life.* Vol. 1, *England before the Storm.* London: Hutchinson, 1953.

Andrews, Linton, and H. A. Taylor. *The Lords and Laborers of the Press: Men Who Fashioned the Modern British Newspaper.* Carbondale: Southern Illinois University Press, 1970.

Ayerst, David. "'Garve': The Emergence of an Editor." *Library Chronicle* 9 (1978): 13-27.

________. *Garvin of the Observer.* London: Croom Helm, 1985.

Barnes, John, and David Nicholson. *The Leo Amery Diaries.* Vol. 1. London: Hutchinson, 1980.

Bell, E. H. C. Moberly. *The Life and Letters of C. F. Moberly Bell.* London: Richards Press, 1927.

Begbie, Harold. *Albert Fourth Earl Grey: A Last Word.* London: Hodder and Stoughton, 1918.

Birrell, Augustine. *Things Past Redress.* London: Faber and Faber, 1937.

Blake, Robert. *The Unknown Prime Minister: The Life and Times of Andrew Bonar Law, 1858-1923.* London: Eyre & Spottiswoode, 1955.

Blatchford, Robert. *My Eighty Years.* London: Cassell and Company, 1931.

Blumenfeld, R. D. *All in a Lifetime.* London: Ernest Benn, 1931.

________. *R. D. B.'s Diary, 1887-1914.* London: William Heinemann, 1930.

Brendon, Piers. *Eminent Edwardians.* London: Secker & Warburg, 1979.

Brett, Maurice V. *Journals and Letters of Reginald Viscount Esher.* Vol. 2, *1903-1910.* London: Ivor Nicholson & Watson, 1934.

Brittain, Sir Harry. *Happy Pilgrimage.* London: Hutchinson & Co., 1949.

________. *Pilgrims and Pioneers.* London: Hutchinson & Co., 1946.

Carter, Mark Bonham. *The Autobiography of Margot Asquith.* Boston: Houghton Mifflin Company, 1963.

Chamberlain, Sir Austen. *Politics from Inside: An Epistolary Chronicle, 1906-1914.* New York: Yale University Press, 1937.

Chirol, Sir Valentine. *Fifty Years in a Changing World.* London: Jonathan Cape, 1927.

Churchill, Randolph. *Winston S. Churchill.* Vol. 2, *Young Statesman.* Boston: Houghton Mifflin Company, 1967.

Cook, E. T. *Edmund Garrett: A Memoir*. London: Edward Arnold, 1909.

Cosgrove, Richard A. *The Rule of Law: Albert Venn Dicey, Victorian Jurist*. Chapel Hill: University of North Carolina Press, 1980.

Cross, Brigadier Lionel. "Sir Harry Brittain." *CPU Quarterly* (August 1974): 9-12, 31.

David, Edward, ed. *Inside Asquith's Cabinet: From the Diaries ofCharles Hobhouse*. New York: St. Martin's Press, 1977.

Ferris, Paul. *House of Northcliffe: Biography of an Empire*. New York: World Publishing, 1972.

Francke, Warren T. "W. T. Stead: The First New Journalist?" *Journalism History* 1 (Summer 1974): 36, 63-66.

Fyfe, Hamilton. *Northcliffe: An Intimate Biography*. 1930. Reprint. New York: AMS Press, 1969.

Garvin, Katherine. *J. L. Garvin: A Memoir*. London: William Heinemann, 1948.

Gibbs, Philip. *The Journalist's London*. London: Allan Wingate, 1952.

Gollin, Alfred. *Balfour's Burden: Arthur Balfour and Imperial Preference*. London: Anthony Blond, 1965.

________. "Lord Northcliffe's Changes of Course." *Journalism Quarterly* 39 (Winter 1962): 46-52.

________. *"The Observer" and J. L. Garvin: 1908-1914, A Study in a Great Editorship*. London: Oxford University Press, 1960.

________. *Proconsul in Politics: A Study of Lord Milner in Opposition and in Power*. London: Anthony Blond, 1964.

Grey, Edward, Viscount. *Twenty-Five Years, 1892-1916*. Vol. 1. New York: Frederick A. Stokes Company, 1925.

Grigg, John. *Lloyd George: The People's Champion, 1902-1911*. Berkeley: University of California Press, 1978.

Halperin, Vladimir. *Lord Milner and the Empire*. London: Odhams Press, 1952.

Hammerton, J. A. *Books and Myself*. London: MacDonald & Co., 1944.

Harris, Wilson. *J. A. Spender*. London: Cassell and Company, 1946.

Harrison, Henry. *Parnell, Joseph Chamberlain, and Mr. Garvin*. London: Robert Hale, 1938.

Havighurst, Alfred F. *Radical Journalist: H. W. Massingham*. London: Cambridge University Press, 1974.

Headlam, Cecil. *The Milner Papers*. Vol. 2, *South Africa, 1899-1905*. London: Cassell and Company, 1931.

Hewins, W. A. S. *The Apologia of an Imperialist*. London: Constable & Co., 1929.

Higgenbottom, F. G. *The Vivid Life: A Journalist's Career*. London: Simpkin Marshall, 1934.

Hutcheson, John A. *Leopold Maxse and the "National Review," 1893-1914: Right Wing Politics and Journalism in the Edwardian Era*. New York: Garland, 1989.

Hyam, Ronald. *Elgin and Churchill at the Colonial Office, 1905-1908*. London: Macmillan and Co., 1968.

James, Robert Rhodes. *Memorial of a Conservative: J. C. C. Davidson's Memoirs and Papers*. New York: The Macmillan Company, 1970.

Jenkins, Roy. *Asquith: Portrait of a Man and an Era*. New York: Chilmark Press, 1964.

Jones, Kennedy. *Fleet Street and Downing Street*. London: Hutchinson & Co., 1919.

Judd, Denis. *Balfour and the British Empire: A Study in Imperial Evolution, 1874-1932*. London: Macmillan and Co., 1968.

Kitchen, Harcourt. *Moberly Bell and His Times*. London: Philip Allan & Co., 1925.

Koss, Stephen. *Asquith*. New York: St. Martin's Press, 1976.

________. *Fleet Street Radical: A. G. Gardiner and the Daily News*. Hamden, Conn.: Shoe String Press, 1973.

________. *John Morley at the India Office, 1905-1910*. New Haven: Yale University Press, 1969.

Lockhart, J. L., and C. M. Woodhouse. *Cecil Rhodes: The Colossus of Southern Africa*. New York: Macmillan Company, 1963.

Mackay, Ruddock F. *Balfour: Intellectual Statesman*. New York: Oxford University Press, 1985.

Massingham, H. J., ed. *H. W. M.: A Selection from the Writings of H. W. Massingham*. London: Jonathan Cape, 1925.

Mills, J. Saxon. *Sir Edward Cook*. London: Constable & Co., 1921.

O'Brien, Terence H. *Milner: Viscount Milner of St. James's and Cape Town*. London: Constable, 1979.

Pemberton, Max. *Lord Northcliffe: A Memoir*. London: Hodder and Stoughton, 1922.

Petrie, Sir Charles. *The Life and Letters of the Right Honorable Sir Austen Chamberlain*. Vol. 1. London: Cassell and Company, 1929.

Pound, Reginald, and Geoffrey Harmsworth. *Northcliffe*. New York: Frederick A. Praeger, 1960.

Robbins, Keith. *Sir Edward Grey: A Biography of Lord Grey of Falladon*. London: Cassell and Company, 1971.

Schultz, Raymond L. *Crusader in Babylon: W. T. Stead and the Pall Mall Gazette*. Lincoln: University of Nebraska Press, 1972.

Strachey, Amy. *St. Loe Strachey: His Life and His Papers*. London: Victor Gollanez, 1930.

Taylor, A. J. P. *Beaverbrook*. Harmondsworth: Penguin Books, 1974.

Taylor, H. A. *Robert Donald*. London: Stanley Paul and Co., c.1934.

Whyte, Frederic. *The Life of W. T. Stead*. 2 vols. London: Jonathan Cape, 1925.

Wilson, John. *CB: A Life of Sir Henry Campbell-Bannerman*. London: Constable and Co., 1973.

Wilson, Trevor, ed. *The Political Diaries of C. P. Scott, 1911-1928*. Ithaca: Cornell University Press, 1970.

Wrench, John Evelyn. *Alfred Lord Milner: The Man of no Illusion, 1854-1925*. London: Eyre & Spottiswoode, 1958.

________. *Geoffrey Dawson and Our Times*. London: Hutchinson & Co., 1955.

________. *Uphill: The First Stage in a Strenuous Life*. London: Ivor Nicholson & Watson, 1934.

Zebel, Sydney. *Balfour: A Political Biography*. London: Cambridge University Press, 1973.

LATER LITERATURE: BOOKS AND ARTICLES

Books

Altick, Richard. *Victorian People and Ideas*. New York: Norton and Company, 1973.

Ayerst, David. *The Manchester Guardian: Biography of a Newspaper*. Ithaca: Cornell University Press, 1971.

Barker, Sir Ernest. *The Ideas and Ideals of the British Empire*. 2d ed. New York: Greenwood Press, 1971.

Barnett, Correlli. *The Collapse of British Power*. New York: William Morrow & Company, 1972.

Beloff, Max. *Imperial Sunset*. Vol. 1, *Britain's Liberal Empire, 1897–1921*. New York: Alfred A. Knopf, 1970.

Benians, E. A., Sir James Butler, and C. E. Carrington, eds. *The Cambridge History of the British Empire*. Vol. 3, *The Empire-Commonwealth, 1870-1919*. Cambridge, England: The University Press, 1959.

Blake, Robert. *The Conservative Party from Peel to Churchill*. London: Eyre & Spottiswoode, 1970.

Blewett, Neal. *The Press, the Parties, and the People: The British General Election of 1910*. Toronto: University of Toronto Press, 1972.

Blumenfeld, R. D. *The Press in My Time*. London: Rich and Cowan, 1933.

Bodelsen, C. A. *Studies in Mid-Victorian Imperialism*. New York: Alfred A. Knopf, 1925.

Boyce, George, James Curran, and Pauline Wingate, eds. *Newspaper History: From the Seventeenth Century to the Present Day*. Beverly Hills, Calif.: Sage Publications, 1978.

Briggs, Asa. *A Social History of England*. New York: Viking Press, 1983.

Brown, Lucy. *Victorian News and Newspapers*. Oxford: Clarendon Press, 1985.

Brown, Michael Barratt. *The Economics of Imperialism*. 1974. Reprint. New York: Penguin Books, 1978.

Cambrose, Viscount (William Berry). *British Newspapers and Their Controllers*. London: Cassell and Company, 1947.

Campbell, Persia Crawford. *Chinese Coolie Emigration to Countries within the British Empire*. 1923. Reprint. London: Frank Case & Co., 1971.

Churchill, Winston S. *The World Crisis*. Vol. 1, 1923. Reprint. New York: Charles Scribner's Sons, 1951.

Clayton, Anthony. *The British Empire as a Superpower, 1919-1939*. Athens: University of Georgia Press, 1986.

Cook, Chris. *A Short History of the Liberal Party, 1900-1976*. New York: St. Martin's Press, 1976.

Cranfield, G. A. *The Press and Society: From Caxton to Northcliffe*. London: Longman, 1978.

Creighton, Donald. *Canada's First Century, 1867-1967*. Toronto: Macmillan of Canada, 1970.

Cross, Colin. *The Liberals in Power*. London: Barrie and Rockcliffe with Pall Mall Press, 1963.

Dangerfield, George. *The Strange Death of Liberal England*. 1935. Reprint. New York: Capricorn Books, 1961.

Davenport, T. R. H. *South Africa: A Modern History*. London: Macmillan and Co., 1977.

Denoon, Donald. *A Grand Illusion: The Failure of Imperial Policy in the Transvaal Colony during the Period of Reconstruction, 1900-1905*. London: Longman, 1973.

Diamond, B. I. "A Precursor of the New Journalism: Frederick Greenwood of the *Pall Mall Gazette*." In *Papers for the Millions: The New Journalism in Britain, 1850s to 1914*, ed. Joel H. Wiener, 25-45. New York: Greenwood Press, 1988.

Dickinson, G. Lowes. *The International Anarchy, 1904-1914*. New York: Century Co., 1926.

Eldridge, C. C. *British Imperialism in the Nineteenth Century*. New York: St. Martin's Press, 1984.

________. *England's Mission: The Imperial Idea in the Age of Gladstone and Disraeli, 1868-1880*. Chapel Hill: University of North Carolina Press, 1973.

Ensor, R. C. K. *England, 1870-1914*. 1936. Reprint. Oxford: Clarendon Press, 1963.

Faber, Richard. *The Vision and the Need: Late Victorian Imperialist Aims*. London: Faber and Faber, 1966.

Farwell, Byron. *The Great Anglo-Boer War*. New York: Harper & Row, 1976.

Field, H. John. *Toward a Programme of Imperial Life: The British Empire at the Turn of the Century*. Westport, Conn.: Greenwood Press, 1982.

Fieldhouse, D. K. *The Colonial Empires: A Comparative Survey from the Eighteenth Century*. New York: Dell Publishing House, 1966.

Fischer, Fritz. *Germany's Aims in the First World War*. New York: W. W. Norton & Company, 1967.

Fisher, John. *The Afrikaners*. London: Cassell and Company, 1969.

Fleming, D. F. *The Origins and Legacies of World War I*. Greenwich, Conn.: Fawcett Publications, 1968.

Gilbert, Martin, and Richard Gott. *The Appeasers*. Boston: Houghton Mifflin Company, 1963.

Gordon, Donald. *The Dominion Partnership in Imperial Defense, 1870- 1914*. Baltimore: Johns Hopkins Press, 1965.

Grierson, Edward. *The Imperial Dream: British Commonwealth and Empire, 1775-1969*. Newton Abbot, Devon, England: Readers Union, 1972.

Harlow, Alvin F. *Old Wires and New Waves*. New York: D. Appleton-Century Company, 1936.

Harris, Michael, and Alan Lee, eds. *The Press in English Society from the Seventeenth to the Nineteenth Centuries*. Rutherford, N.J.: Fairleigh Dickinson University Press, 1986.

Headrick, Daniel R. *The Tools of Empire: Technology and European Imperialism in the Nineteenth Century*. New York: Oxford University Press, 1981.

Hearnshaw, F. J. C., ed. *Edwardian England: 1901-1910*. Freeport, N.Y.: Books for Libraries Press, 1968.

Hobsbawm, E. J. *The Age of Empire, 1875-1914*. New York: Pantheon Books, 1987.

________. *Industry and Empire: The Making of Modern English Society*. Vol. 1, *1750 to the Present*. New York: Random House, 1968.

Hyam, Ronald. *Britain's Imperial Century, 1815-1914: A Study of Empire and Expansion*. New York: Harper & Row, 1976.

Hyam, Ronald, and Ged Martin. *Reappraisals in British Imperial History*. Toronto: Macmillan of Canada, 1975.

Jones, G. P., and A. G. Pool. *A Hundred Years of Economic Development in Great Britain (1840-1940)*. 1940. Reprint. London: Gerald Duckworth & Co., 1971.

Judd, Denis, and Peter Slim. *The Evolution of the Modern Commonwealth, 1902-1980*. London: Macmillan and Co., 1982.

Kendle, John Edward. *The Colonial and Imperial Conferences, 1887-1911: A Study in Imperial Organization*. London: Longmans, 1967.

________. *The Round Table Movement and Imperial Union*. Toronto: University of Toronto Press, 1975.

Kennedy, Paul. *The Rise and Fall of the Great Powers: Economic Change and Military Conflict from 1500 to 2000*. New York: Random House, 1987.

________. *The Rise of the Anglo-German Antagonism*. London: George Allen and Unwin, 1980.

________. *Strategy and Diplomacy, 1870-1945: Eight Studies*. London: George Allen and Unwin, 1983.

Koebner, Richard, and Helmut Dan Schmidt. *Imperialism: The Study and Significance of a Political Word, 1840-1960*. Cambridge: Cambridge University Press, 1965.

Koss, Stephen. *The Rise and Fall of the Political Press in Britain*. 2 vols. Chapel Hill: University of North Carolina Press, 1981 and 1984.

Kubicek, Robert V. *Economic Imperialism in Theory and Practice: The Case of South African Gold Mining Finance, 1886-1914*. Durham: Duke University Press, 1965.

Lee, Alan J. *The Origins of the Popular Press in England, 1855-1914*. London: Croom Helm, 1976.

LeMay, G. H. L. *British Supremacy in South Africa, 1899-1907*. London: Clarendon Press, 1965.

McInnis, Edgar. *Canada: A Political and Social History*. 1947. Rev. ed., New York: Holt Rinehart and Winston, 1967.

McIntyre, W. David. *Commonwealth of Nations: Origin and Impact, 1969-1971*. Minneapolis: University of Minnesota Press, 1972.

MacKenzie, John M. *Propaganda and Empire: The Manipulation of British Public Opinion, 1880-1960*. Manchester: Manchester University Press, 1984.

McNaught, Kenneth. *The Pelican History of Canada*. 1969. Reprint. Harmondsworth, Middlesex, England: Penguin Books, 1978.

Mansergh, Nicholas. *The Commonwealth Experience*. Vol. 1, *The Durham Report to the Anglo-Irish Treaty*. 2d ed. Toronto: University of Toronto Press, 1982.

________. *South Africa, 1906-1961: The Price of Magnanimity*. New York: Frederick A. Praeger, 1962.

Marder, Arthur. *From the Dreadnought to Scapa Flow: The Royal Navy in the Fisher Era, 1904-1919*. Vol. 1, *The Road to War, 1904-1914*. London: Oxford University Press, 1961.

Maurois, Andre. *The Edwardian Era*. Translated by Hamish Miles. New York: D. Appleton-Century Company, 1933.

Miller, J. D. B. *Britain and the Old Dominions*. Baltimore: Johns Hopkins Press, 1966.

Mills, J. Saxon. *The Press and Communications of the Empire*. London: W. Collins and Co., 1914.

Mommsen, Wolfgang J. *Theories of Imperialism*. Translated by P. S. Falla. New York: Random House, 1980.

Morison, Stanley. *The English Newspaper, 1622–1932*. Cambridge: Cambridge University Press, 1932.

[Morison, Stanley]. *History of The Times*. Vol. 3, *Twentieth Century Test, 1884-1912*; Vol. 4, *The 150th Anniversary and Beyond, 1912-1948*. 1947. Reprint. Nendeln, Liechtenstein: Kraus Reprint, 1971.

Morris, A. J. A. *Edwardian Radicalism, 1900-1914: Some Aspects of British Radicalism*. London: Routledge and Kegan Paul, 1974.

________. *The Scaremongers: The Advocacy of War and Rearmament, 1896-1914*. London: Routledge and Kegan Paul, 1984.

Morris, James. *Farewell the Trumpets: An Imperial Retreat*. London: Harcourt Brace Jovanovich, A Helen Kurt Wolff Book, 1978.

________. *Pax Britannica: The Climax of an Empire*. London: Faber and Faber, 1968.

Mullett, Charles. *The British Empire-Commonwealth*. Washington, D.C.: American Historical Association, 1961.

Nimocks, Walter. *Milner's Young Men: The Kindergarten in Edwardian Imperial Affairs*. Durham: Duke University Press, 1968.

O'Day, Alan, ed. *The Edwardian Age: Conflict and Stability, 1900-1914*. London: Macmillan and Co., 1979.

Pachai, B. *The International Aspects of the South African Indian Question, 1860-1971*. Cape Town: C. Struik, 1971.

Petrie, Sir Charles. *The Carleton Club*. London: Eyre and Spottiswoode, 1955.

________. *The Edwardians*. New York: W. W. Norton and Company, 1965.

________. *The Victorians*. New York: David McKay Co., 1962.

Phillips, Gregory D. *The Diehards: Aristocratic Society and Politics in Edwardian England*. Cambridge: Harvard University Press, 1979.

Pillay, Bala. *British Indians in the Transvaal: Trade, Politics, and Imperial Relations*. London: Longman, 1976.

Porter, Bernard. *Critics of Empire: British Radical Attitudes to Colonialism in Africa, 1895-1914*. London: Macmillan and Co., 1968.

________. *The Lion's Share: A Short History of British Imperialism, 1850-1970*. London: Longman, 1975.

Priestley, J. B. *The Edwardians*. New York: Harper & Row, 1970.

Pyrah, G. B. *Imperial Policy and South Africa, 1902-1910*. London: Oxford University Press, 1955.

Read, Donald. *Edwardian England, 1901-15: Society and Politics*. London: Harrap, 1972.

________, ed. *Edwardian England*. New Brunswick, N.J.: Rutgers University Press. 1982.

Rempel, Richard A. *Unionist Divided: Arthur Balfour, Joseph Chamberlain, and the Unionist Free Traders*. Hamden, Conn.: Archon Books, 1972.

Rich, Paul. *Race and Empire in British Politics*. Cambridge: Cambridge University Press, 1986.

Richardson, Peter. *Chinese Mine Labour in the Transvaal*. London: Macmillan and Co., 1982.

Robinson, Ronald, and John Gallagher with Alice Denny. *Africa and the Victorians: The Climax of Imperialism*. Garden City, N.J.: Doubleday and Company, 1968.

Rose, Jonathan. *The Edwardian Temperament, 1895-1919*. Athens, Ohio: Ohio University Press, 1986.

Rowland, Peter. *The Last Liberal Governments: The Promised Land, 1905-1910*. London: Cresset Press, 1968.

Russell, A. K. *Liberal Landslide: The General Election of 1906*. Hamden, Conn.: Archon Books, 1973.

Sacks, Benjamin. *South Africa: An Imperial Dilemma*. Albuquerque: University of New Mexico Press, 1967.

Saunders, Kay, ed. *Indentured Labour in the British Empire, 1834-1920*. London: Croom Helm, 1984.

Schlatter, Richard, ed. *Recent Views on British History: Essays on Historical Writing since 1966*. New Brunswick, N.J.: Rutgers University Press, 1984.

Searle, G. R. *The Quest for National Efficiency: A Study in British Politics and Political Thought, 1899-1914*. Berkeley: University of California Press, 1971.

Semmel, Bernard. *Imperialism and Social Reform: English Social-Imperial Thought, 1895-1914*. Garden City, N.J.: Doubleday and Company, Anchor Books, 1968.

Shannon, Richard. *The Crisis of Imperialism, 1865-1915*. London: Granada Publishing, 1979.

Shattock, Joanne, and Michael Wolff, eds. *The Victorian Periodical Press: Samplings and Soundings*. Toronto: University of Toronto Press, 1982.

Sked, Alan. *Britain's Decline: Problems and Perspectives*. Oxford: Basil Blackwell, 1987.

Steinberg, Jonathan. *Yesterday's Deterrent: Tirpitz and the Birth of the German Battle Fleet*. New York: Macmillan Company, 1965.

Steinberg, S. H. *Five Hundred Years of Printing*. 3d rev. ed. New York: Penguin Books, 1974.

Steiner, Zara S. *Britain and the Origins of the First World War*. New York: St. Martin's Press, 1977.

Stutterheim, Kurt von. *The Press in England*. Translated by W. H. Johnston. London: George Allen and Unwin, 1934.

Sykes, Alan. *Tariff Reform in British Politics, 1903-1913*. Oxford: Clarendon Press, 1979.

Taylor, A. J. P. *The Struggle for Mastery in Europe, 1848-1918*. 1954. Reprint. Oxford: Clarendon Press, 1965.

Thomas, William Beach. *The Story of the "Spectator," 1828-1928*. 1928. Reprint. Freeport, N.Y.: Books for Libraries Press, 1971.

Thompson, L. M. *The Unification of South Africa, 1902-1910*. London: Oxford University Press, 1960.

Thornton, A. P. *Doctrines of Imperialism*. New York: John Wiley and Sons, 1965.

________. *For the File on Empire: Essays and Reviews*. London: Macmillan and Co., 1968.

________. *The Imperial Idea and Its Enemies: A Study in British Power*. Garden City, N.J.: Doubleday and Company, Anchor Books, 1968.

________. *Imperialism in the Twentieth Century*. Minneapolis: University of Minnesota Press, 1977.

Van Jaarsveld, F. A. *The Awakening of Afrikaner Nationalism, 1868-1881*. Cape Town: Haman and Rousseau, 1961.

Walker, Eric A. *A History of Southern Africa*. 3d ed. London: Longmans, Green and Co., 1968.

Weiner, Joel, ed. *Innovators and Preachers: The Role of the Editor in Victorian England*. Westport, Conn.: Greenwood Press, 1985.

Williams, Francis. *Dangerous Estate: The Anatomy of Newspapers*. London: Longmans, Green and Co., 1957.

Wilson, Monica, and Leonard Thompson, eds. *The Oxford History of South Africa*. Vol. 2, *South Africa, 1870-1966*. New York: Oxford University Press, 1971.

Winks, Robin W., ed. *The Historiography of the British Empire-Commonwealth: Trends, Interpretations, and Resources*. Durham, N.C.: Duke University Press, 1966.

Wood, John Cunningham. *British Economists and the Empire*. London: Croom Helm, 1983.

Woodward, E. L. *Great Britain and the German Navy*. Oxford: Clarendon Press, 1935.

Articles

Baylen, J. O. "The 'New Journalism' in Late Victorian Britain." *Australian Journal of Politics* 17 (December 1972): 367-85.

Betts, Raymond F. "The Allusion to Rome in British Imperial Thought of the Late Nineteenth and Early Twentieth Centuries." *Victorian Studies* 15 (December 1971): 149-59.

Birley, Sir Robert. "The Imperial Idea in South Africa: Briton, Boer and Bantu." *Round Table* 60 (November 1970): 603-11.

Blewett, Neal. "Free Fooders, Balfourites, Whole Hoggers. Factionalism within the Unionist Party, 1906-1910." *Historical Journal* 2 (1968): 95-124.

Carrington, C. E. "The Historians and the Empire-Commonwealth: A Personal Viewpoint." *Journal of Imperial and Commonwealth History* 3 (May 1925): 408-18.

Curtin, Philip D. "The British Empire and Commonwealth in Recent Historiography." *American Historical Review* 55 (October 1959): 72-91.

Eley, Geoff. "Defining Social Imperialism: Use and Abuse of an Idea." *Social History* No. 3 (October 1976): 265-90.

Fair, John D. "From Liberal to Conservative: The Flight of the Liberal Unionists after 1886." *Victorian Studies* 29 (Winter 1968): 291-314.

Fraser, P. "The Liberal Unionist Alliance: Chamberlain, Hartington, and the Conservatives, 1886-1904." *English Historical Review* 77 (January 1962): 53-78.

Galbraith, John S. "Myths of the 'Little England' Era." *American Historical Review* 67 (October 1961): 34-48.

Green, William A. "The Crest of Empire." *Victorian Studies* 18 (March 1975): 345-54.

Hodson, H. V. "The Round Table's Early Life." *Round Table* No. 264 (October 1976): 415-20.

Kennedy, P. M. "Imperial Cable Communications and Strategy, 1870-1914." *English Historical Review* 86 (October 1971): 728-53.

Kunze, Neil. "Late Victorian Periodical Editors and Politicians." *Victorian Periodicals Review* 20 (Summer 1987): 57-61.

Langer, William L. "A Critique of Imperialism." *Foreign Affairs* 14 (October 1935): 102-19.

Lichtheim, George. "Imperialism: I." *Commentary* 49 (April 1970): 42-76.

McCreedy, H. W. "The Revolt of the Unionist Free Traders." *Parliamentary Affairs* 16 (1962-1963): 188-206.

Mackintosh, John. "The Role of the Committee of Imperial Defence before 1914." *American Historical Review* 77 (July 1962): 490-503.

Marks, Shula. "Africa and Afrikaner History." *Journal of African History* 2 (1970): 435-47.

Millar, T. B. "Empire into Commonwealth into History." *International Organization* 24 (Winter 1970): 93-99.

Porter, A. N. "Sir Alfred Milner and the Press, 1897-1899." *Historical Journal* 16 (1973): 323-39.

Robbins, Keith. "Sir Edward Grey and the British Empire." *Journal of Imperial and Commonwealth History* 16 (May 1988): 213-21.

Sykes, Alan. "The Confederacy and the Purge of the Unionist Free Traders, 1906-1910." *Historical Journal* 18 (1975): 349-66.

Tulloch, Gordon. "Hobson's Imperialism." *Modern Age* 7 (Spring 1963): 157-61.

Tweton, D. Jerome. "The Border Farmer and the Canadian Reciprocity Issue, 1911-1912." *Agricultural History* 37 (1963): 235-41.

Wells, Ronald A. "The Voice of Empire: The Daily Mail and British Emigration to North America." *Historian* 43 (February 1981): 240-57.

MISCELLANEOUS SOURCES

Goodman, Gordon L. "The Liberal Unionist Party, 1886-1895." Ph.D. diss., University of Chicago, 1956.

Mitchell, B. R. *European Historical Statistics, 1750-1970*. New York: Columbia University Press, 1975.

Slaghek, Ursula (J. L. Garvin's daughter). Interview by author, 14 June 1977, London.

Index

About the Author

JAMES D. STARTT is Professor of History at Valparaiso University in Indiana. He has authored a wide variety of articles on British history and journalism, as well as two books.